PELIC

A HISTO

VOLUM

Romila Thapar was born in India in 1931 of a well-known
Punjabi family and spent her childhood in various parts of
India, as her father was then in the army. She took her
first degree in India – from the Punjab University – and her
doctorate at London University in 1958. During the following year she was a Lecturer in the Ancient History of South
Asia at the School of Oriental and African Studies, University of London. Now Professor of Ancient Indian History
at the Jawaharlal Nehru University, New Delhi, she spent
a sabbatical year at Lady Margaret Hall, Oxford, in 1968.

She has travelled extensively in Europe and Asia. In 1957
she did a study tour of Buddhist cave-sites in China, including that of Tun-Huang in the Gobi Desert. When in
London, Romila Thapar broadcast frequently from the
B.B.C., both for 'English Talks for Asia' and for the Home
and Third programmes. Among her other publications are
a study of the Emperor Aśoka, *Aśoka and the Decline of
the Mauryas*, and a children's book, *Indian Tales*.

ROMILA THAPAR

A HISTORY OF INDIA

VOLUME ONE

PENGUIN BOOKS

Penguin Books Ltd, Harmondsworth, Middlesex, England
Viking Penguin Inc., 40 West 23rd Street, New York, New York 10010, U.S.A.
Penguin Books Australia Ltd, Ringwood, Victoria, Australia
Penguin Books Canada Limited, 2801 John Street, Markham, Ontario, Canada L3R 1B4
Penguin Books (N.Z.) Ltd, 182–190 Wairau Road, Auckland 10, New Zealand

—

First published 1966
Reprinted 1968, 1969, 1972, 1974, 1975, 1976, 1977, 1979,
1981, 1982, 1983, 1984, 1985, 1986

—

—

Made and printed in Great Britain by
Hazell Watson & Viney Limited,
Member of the BPCC Group,
Aylesbury, Bucks
Set in Linotype Granjon

For Sergei

CONTENTS

Contents

Contents

MAPS

LINE DRAWINGS

ACKNOWLEDGEMENTS

I am grateful to the following for permission to print quotations: the Archaeological Survey of India, for quotations from *Epigraphia Indica, South Indian Inscriptions*, and *Archaeological Survey of India Report*; Kitab Mahal (Wholesale Division) Private Ltd, for quotations from *History of India as Told by its own Historians* – Eliot and Dowson; Allen & Unwin Ltd, for quotation from *A Forgotten Empire* – Sewell.

PREFACE

THIS book is not intended for the specialist in Indian history. It is intended for those who have a general interest in India and might wish to acquaint themselves with the major developments in India's early history.

The history of India in the first volume begins with the culture of the Indo-Aryans and not with the prehistoric cultures of India. There is already a useful study of Indian prehistory and proto-history in the Pelican series (Stuart Piggott, *Prehistoric India*), and there is no point in repeating the same material. The present volume covers the history of the sub-continent until the arrival of the Europeans in the sixteenth century. Hence the choice of the date 1526 as the terminal. From the perspective of historical evolution within the sub-continent, this is perhaps an awkward date at which to stop, since the momentum of the preceding period was continued into subsequent centuries. But 1526 marks the arrival of the Mughuls in northern India and they were (amongst other things) actively involved in the future of Europe in India.

To those who took the trouble to read the manuscript and offer their comments I am most grateful. I would like particularly to thank Professor A. L. Basham, Mr A. Ghosh, Mr S. Mahdi, and my father. I would also like to thank the Archaeological Survey of India for the maps.

ROMILA THAPAR

THE ANTECEDENTS

FOR many Europeans, India evoked a picture of Maharajas, snake-charmers, and the rope-trick. This has lent both allure and romanticism to things Indian. But in the last couple of decades, with the increasing reference to India as an economically under-developed country, the image of India as a vital, pulsating land has begun to emerge from the fog of Maharajas, snake-charmers, and the rope-trick. The Maharajas are now fast disappearing and the rope-trick was at best a hallucination. Only the snake-charmer remains : generally an ill-fed man who risks his life to catch a snake, remove its poisonous fangs, and make it sway to the movement of the gourd pipe; and all this in the hope of the occasional coin to feed him, his family, and the snake.

In the imagination of Europe, India had always been the fabulous land of untold wealth and mystical happenings, with more than just a normal share of wise men. From the gold-digging ants to the philosophers who lived naked in the forests, these were all part of the picture which the ancient Greeks had of the Indians and this image persisted throughout many centuries. It might be more charitable not to destroy it, but to preserve it would mean the perpetuation of a myth.

Wealth in India, as in every other ancient culture, was limited to the few. Mystical activities were also the preoccupation of but a handful of people. It is true, however, that acceptance of such activities was characteristic of the majority. Whereas in some other cultures the rope-trick would have been ascribed to the promptings of the devil and all reference to it suppressed, in India it was regarded with amused benevolence. The funda-mental sanity of Indian civilization has been due to an absence of Satan.

The association of India with wealth, magic, and wisdom re-mained current for many centuries. But this attitude began to change in the nineteenth century when Europe entered the modern age, and the lack of enthusiasm for Indian culture in certain circles became almost proportionate to the earlier over-enthusiasm. It was now discovered that India had none of the qualities which the new Europe admired. There was apparently no stress on the values of rational thought and individualism. India's culture was a stagnant culture and was regarded with supreme disdain, an attitude perhaps best typified in Macaulay's contempt for things Indian. The political institutions of India, visualized largely as the rule of the Maharajas and Sultans, were dismissed as despotic and totally unrepresentative of public opinion. And this, in an age of democratic revolutions, was about the worst of sins.

Yet, a contrary attitude emerged from amongst a small section of European scholars who had discovered India largely through its ancient philosophy and its literature in Sanskrit. This attitude deliberately stressed the non-modern, non-utilitarian aspects of Indian culture, where the existence of a continuity of religion of over three thousand years was acclaimed; and where it was believed that the Indian pattern of life was so concerned with metaphysics and the subtleties of religious belief that there was no time for the mundane things of life. German romanticism was the most vehement in its support of this image of India : a vehemence which was to do as much damage to India as Macaulay's rejection of Indian culture. India now became the mystic land for many Europeans, where even the most ordinary actions were imbued with symbolism. India was the genesis of the spiritual East, and also, incidentally, the refuge of European intellectuals seeking escape from their own pattern of life. A dichotomy in values was maintained, Indian values being described as 'spiritual' and European values as 'materialistic', with little attempt at placing these supposedly spiritual values in the context of Indian society (which might have led to some rather disturbing results). This theme was taken up by a section of Indian thinkers during the last hundred years and became a consolation to the Indian intelligentsia for its inability to compete with the technical superiority of Britain.

The discovery of the Indian past, and its revelation to Europe in the eighteenth century, was largely the work of Jesuits in India and of Europeans employed by the East India Company, such as Sir William Jones and Charles Wilkins. Soon the numbers of those interested in studying the classical languages and literatures of India grew, and the early nineteenth century saw considerable achievements in linguistics, ethnography, and other fields of Indology. Scholars in Europe expressed a keen interest in this new field of inquiry as is evident from the number of persons who took to Indology and of one of whom at least mention must be made – F. Max Muller.

Those who were most directly concerned with India in the nineteenth century were the British administrators, and the early non-Indian historians of India came largely from this group. Consequently, the early histories were 'administrator's histories', concerned mainly with the rise and fall of dynasties and empires. The protagonists of Indian history were the kings and the narration of events revolved around them. The autocratic king, oppressive and unconcerned with the welfare of his subjects, was the standard image of the Indian ruler, but for exceptions such as Ashoka, Chandragupta II, or Akbar. As for actual governing, the underlying assumption was that British administration was in fact superior to any other known to the history of the subcontinent.

This interpretation of Indian history made its impact on Indian historians writing in the late nineteenth and early twentieth centuries. Dynastic histories with a high-lighting of the lives of rulers were the main content of standard works. But the second aspect of the interpretation produced a different reaction. Most of the Indian historians had either participated in the national movement for independence or had been influenced by it. Their contention was that the Golden Age in India had existed prior to the coming of the British and that the ancient past of India was a particularly glorious period of her history. This view was a natural and inevitable adjunct to the national aspirations of the Indian people in the early twentieth century.

In this connexion there was another *bête noire* which cast its shadow on much of the early writing on ancient India. European historians working on this period had been brought up on the classical tradition of Europe, where it was firmly believed that the greatest human achievement was the civilization of the ancient Greeks – *le miracle Grec*. Consequently, every newly discovered culture was measured against ancient Greece and invariably found to be lacking. Or, if there were individual features worth admiring, the instinct was to try and connect them with

Greek culture. Vincent Smith, for some decades regarded as the pre-eminent historian of early India, was prone to this tendency. When writing of the murals at the famous Buddhist site at Ajanta, and particularly of a painting supposedly depicting the arrival of an embassy from a Sassanian king of Persia in the seventh century A.D., totally unconnected with Greece both artistically and historically, he states :

. . . The picture, in addition to its interest as a contemporary record of unusual political relations between India and Persia, is one of the highest value as a landmark in the history of art. It not only fixes the date of some of the most important paintings at Ajanta and so establishes a standard by which the date of others can be judged, but also suggests the possibility that the Ajanta school of pictorial art may have been derived from Persia and ultimately from Greece.[1]

Not surprisingly Indian historians reacted sharply to such statements. Attempts were made to prove either that India had not derived any part of its culture from Greece or else that the culture of India was a close parallel to that of Greece, manifesting all the qualities which were present in the latter. That every civilization is its own miracle was not as yet recognized either by European or by Indian historians. The idea of assessing a civilization on its own merits was to come at a later stage.

When European scholars first established a relationship with India in the eighteenth century and became curious about its past, their sources of information were the brahman priests – the acknowledged guardians of the ancient tradition, who maintained that this tradition was preserved in the Sanskrit sources with which only they were familiar. Thus, much of the early history of India was reconstructed almost entirely from Sanskrit sources, i.e., from material preserved in the ancient classical language. Many of these works were religious in nature and this naturally coloured the interpretation of the past. Even somewhat more secular literature such as the *Dharmashastras* (Law Books) had brahman authors and commentators and was therefore biased in favour of those in authority and generally adhered to the brahmanical interpretation of the past, irrespective of its historical validity. For example, the caste system as described in these sources appears to have been a rigid stratification of society, apparently imposed from an early period and thereafter preserved almost intact for many centuries. Yet the actual working of caste in Indian society permitted of much variation, which naturally the authors of the Law Books did not wish to admit.

The use of evidence from a variety of different sources at a later period was both a challenge to certain aspects of brahmanical evidence and a corroboration of others, thus providing a more accurate picture of the past. Evidence from contemporary inscriptions and coins became increasingly important. The descriptions left by foreign travellers and recorded in non-Indian sources – Greek, Latin, Chinese, and Arabic – allowed of new perspectives, as also did the more tangible remains of the past made available through excavations. The corpus of evidence on Buddhism, for instance, was increased with the availability of the Pali Canon as recorded in Ceylon and from Chinese sources. Sources in Arabic and Persian relating to the history of India in the post-thirteenth centuries began to be studied in their own right and ceased being regarded as supplements to Islamic culture in western Asia.

The concentration on dynastic histories in the early studies was also due to the assumption that in 'Oriental' societies the power of the ruler was supreme even in the day-to-day functioning of the government. Yet authority for routine functions was rarely concentrated at the centre in the Indian political systems. The unique feature of Indian society – the caste system – integrated as it was to both politics and professional activity, localized many of the functions which would normally be associated with a truly 'oriental despotism'. The understanding of the functioning of power in India lies in analyses of the caste and sub-caste relationships and of institutions such as the guilds and village councils, and not merely in the survey of dynastic power. Unfortunately, the significance of such studies has only recently been recognized, and it will probably take another decade or two of intensive scholarship before historically valid generalizations can be made. For the present, one can at best indicate the possible generators of power.

That the study of institutions did not receive much emphasis was in part due to the belief that they did not undergo much change : an idea which also fostered the theory that Indian culture has been a static, unchanging culture for many centuries, largely owing to the lethargy of the Indian and his gloomy, fatalistic attitude to life. This of course is an exaggeration. Even a superficial analysis of the changing social relationships within the caste structure, or the agrarian systems, or the vigorous mercantile activities of Indians throughout the centuries, points to anything but a static socio-economic pattern. It is true that at certain levels there is in India a continuous cultural tradition extending over three thousand years, but this continuity should not be confused with stagnation. The chanting of the *gayatri** verse by a Hindu has a history of three millenia, but the context in which it is chanted today can hardly be said to have remained unchanged. It is surprising that, whilst work on Europe during the nineteenth century laid tremendous stress on discovering patterns of evolution in the history of Europe, the same approach was never applied to the study of Asian history. Indian history was treated as a series of islands in time each named after a particular dynasty, and the same format was followed in most standard works by Indian historians. This is not to suggest that studies on other aspects were ignored. Some very interesting information was collected throughout the nineteenth century on various aspects of Indian society and religion. But somehow this information was rarely integrated into standard historical works.

Emphasis on dynasties led to the division of Indian history into three major periods, Ancient, Medieval, and Modern. The Ancient period frequently begins with the coming of Aryan culture (and in later publications with the Indus Valley Civilization) and concludes with the Turkish raids in northern India in *c.* A.D. 1000, which in turn inaugurate the Medieval period, lasting until the coming of the British in the mid-eighteenth century. This division was buttressed by the inappropriate equation of Ancient with Hindu and Medieval with Muslim, since most of the dynasties of the first period were Hindu in origin and those of the second Muslim. The Muslim period was imbued with a distinctive character to distinguish it from the earlier period by stressing the separateness of Muslim culture at all levels. Justification for this thesis was sought in the writings of the theologians and court chroniclers of the Muslim rulers. In any case, political trends being what they were in twentieth-century India, the

---

*A hymn from the *Rig-Veda* dedicated to the solar god Savitri and regarded as the most holy verse in Hindu scripture.

Hindu and Muslim periodization was accepted by both Indian and non-Indian historians of India. But such a periodization of Indian history is misleading in its emphasis apart from being questionable in its assumptions. Religion was by no means the pre-eminent motivating factor of change in Indian history, as these titles would imply : it was one among a number of forces. Recently, attempts have been made at redefining the major periods of Indian history on the basis of changes of a less arbitrary kind than the above. (In order to prevent confusion the use of terms of division has been avoided in the chapters which follow.)

There was yet another factor which up to a point conditioned the emphasis of historical interpretation : the geographical structure of the sub-continent. The vast northern Indo-Gangetic plain lent itself more easily to the emergence of large unitary kingdoms. The southern half of the sub-continent, the peninsula, was cut up into smaller regions by mountains, plateaux, and river valleys – the changing topography permitting of less political uniformity than the northern plain. In an age of empires as was the nineteenth and early twentieth century, the larger kingdoms of the north attracted the attention of historians. Periods when large kingdoms flourished became the 'Golden Ages' and those which saw the growth of smaller regional states became the 'Dark Ages'. The history of the peninsula received far less attention, except during those periods when it too could boast of empires. It suffered further from the fact that political strategy in the peninsula and its economic potential was not identical with that of the north. The northern kingdoms based their strength primarily on acquiring large areas of territory, and their revenue came mainly from the land. This was a simple and easily recognizable pattern for any historian. The structure of the southern kingdoms had also to take into account the more than marginal effects of sea power and the economics of maritime activities, which produced a more complicated pattern than that of the north.

The purpose of indicating the changing outlook of historical writing on India is not to dismiss the work of the early historians as being without value or to denigrate the importance of their scholarship. The inadequacies of their interpretation were often the inadequacies of their times, for a historian is frequently far more representative of his age than he is aware. Despite their shortcomings these studies laid the foundations of the history of India and gave a firm chronological framework, around which fresh interpretations can be constructed which will place the ideas and institutions of Indian civilization in their correct perspective.

The historian of India has in the past been regarded primarily as an Orientalist in the days when Orientalists were those who studied the languages and cultures of Asia and whose studies, in the popular mind at any rate, were fragrant with exotica. The nineteenth-century concept of Oriental studies has changed in the present century both in Europe and in India. In the contemporary world history is being increasingly regarded as part of the social sciences and less as the study of classical cultures *per se*. This newly developing interest seeks to ask a different set of questions from the Indian past : different from those asked by the Orientalist. The difference is largely one of changing historical emphases. Political histories and dynastic studies remain an important aspect of historical interpretation but these are viewed in the light of other features which go into the making of a people and a culture. Changes in the political pattern are inextricably entwined in changes in the economic structure and these in turn have a bearing on social relationships. If a religious movement finds a large following then its attraction must have some relevance to the kind of people who support it. A new language and a new literature can only emerge if they fulfil a need for the society in which they are rooted. It is not enough for the historian of India to present or to analyse the ideas of those who attempted to create the forms and contours of the history of India. It is essential to know why the people of India through the centuries have either accepted or rejected or modified these ideas.

An attempt has been made in this book to anticipate a few of these questions. The purpose of the book has been to indicate the institutions and the events which have contributed to the evolution of Indian culture. But the tendency to evaluate Indian culture and to make categorical value judgements has been avoided, since such an evaluation within the space of a brief history such as this would merely result in meaningless platitudes. This is not primarily a political history. Dynastic chronology has been treated largely as a framework in time. In the course of tracing the evolution of certain aspects of Indian life – the economic structure, changing social relationships, the historical context of religious movements, the emergence and growth of languages, to mention but a few – certain patterns have emerged. It is intended in this book to describe these patterns and interpret the facts along lines which appear to be the most convincing.

In recent years the early history of India has been enriched by the incorporation of evidence provided by two new techniques – the systematic study of society in its various facets, and the extensive use of contemporary evidence from archaeology. The importance of the former lies in the fact that it indicates the possibilities of new ways of approaching the Indian past; and of posing questions, in the answers to which may lie a more real comprehension of the history of India. Such an approach has already been used effectively in certain types of research. The study of society has also stimulated an interest in comparative studies, not along the old lines of declaring one culture to be the norm and judging others by its standards, but rather in terms of a comparative analysis of many cultures. It is this approach which has made historical studies such as Marc Bloch's work on European feudalism relevant to the intellectual equipment of the historian of India.

Archaeology has provided tangible, three-dimensional facts, in the material remains discovered through survey and excavation. These facts not only corroborate literary evidence and provide statistical data but they also help to fill in the gaps, particularly in the earliest period of Indian history. Evidence on Indian pre-history obtained in the last fifteen years has been of considerable value in suggesting the origins of later patterns of culture. Even a superficial familiarity with the archaeological picture of the sub-continent in the centuries preceding the historical period is helpful in understanding the early history of India.

The earliest traces of human activity in India, so far discovered, go back to the Second Inter-Glacial period between 400,000 and 200,000 B.C. and these show evidence of the use of stone implements. There followed a long period of slow evolution, which gathered momentum towards the end and resulted in the spectacular Indus Valley Civilization (or the Harappa Culture as it has been more recently named) in *c.* 2300 B.C. The antecedents of the Harappa Culture are the village sites of the Baluchistan hills – the Nal Culture, and of the Makran coast to the west of the Indus delta – the Kulli Culture, and certain of the village communities along the rivers in Rajasthan and Punjab.

The Harappa Culture was the most extensive of the ancient civilizations in area, including not only the Indus plain (the Punjab and Sind), but also northern Rajasthan and the region of Kathiawar in western India. It was essentially a city culture and among the centres of authority were the two cities of Mohenjo-daro and Harappa.* These were maintained from the surplus produce of the country, judging by the elaborately constructed granaries found in both cities. Another source of income was the profit from a flourishing trade both within the northern and western areas of the sub-continent and between the people of this culture and those of the Persian Gulf and Mesopotamia.

The cities show evidence of an advanced sense of civic planning and organization. Each city was divided into the citadel area, where the essential institutions of civic and religious life were located, and the residential area where the urban population lived.

Amongst the many remains of the Harappa culture perhaps the most puzzling are the seals – small, flat, square, or rectangular objects with a pictorial motif, human or animal, and an inscription. The latter remains undeciphered and holds promise of interesting information when it can be finally read. These seals, numbering about two thousand, appear to have been the tokens of the merchants, or possibly they were connected with the produce of the countryside which was brought into the cities.

Political continuity between the Harappa culture and the later Aryan culture was prevented by the intrusion of less civilized peoples who occupied the sites of the Indus valley in the first half of the second millenium B.C. By 1700 B.C. the Harappa culture had declined and the migration of the Indo-Aryans from Iran in about 1500 B.C. introduced new features into the cul-

---

* Recent excavations have revealed a series of cities – Kot Diji (in Sind), Kalibangan (in Rajasthan), Rupar (in Punjab), and the port-town of Lothal (in Gujarat). But the two earlier cities appear to have been the most important.

tural background of north-western India. This region of the sub-continent was always to remain in communication with areas to the north and the west of the Indus river and the Hindu Kush mountains. Sometimes it was absorbed into the politics of these regions and became a part of their cultural complex. Similarly, western India retained contact with the maritime areas to the west, those of the Persian Gulf and the Red Sea. This tended to emphasize the separateness of the developments in the Indus and the Ganges plains.

Further east in the Ganges valley there is evidence of small settlements of people in the transition stage between hunting and agriculture, using a variety of stone and copper implements and an inferior type of ochre-coloured pottery. These were presumably the people whom the Indo-Aryans met when they moved into the Ganges valley, since the Painted-Grey Ware associated (tentatively) with the Indo-Aryans has been found at some sites superimposed on levels containing the earlier ochre-coloured ware.

Painted-Grey Ware sites have been found in the western half of the Ganges valley and range in date from 1100–500 B.C. More recently iron has also been found at some of the earlier sites, which may lead to an earlier date for the use of iron in India than the generally accepted one of *c*. 800 B.C. The Painted-Grey Ware sites indicate argicultural communities where the breeding of cattle and horses were also known. They were generally familiar with the use of copper. The horse is conspicuously absent at Harappan sites and this evidence is used as one of the bases for tentatively suggesting that the Painted-Grey Ware sites may have been those of the Aryan culture. The evidence so far available from these sites is in broad agreement with the description of Aryan culture in the Vedic sources.

The Deccan shows evidence of a microlithic industry – the making of tiny flint tools – in association later with a chalcolithic culture where bronze and copper were used together with stone. This gave way in the first half of the first millenium B.C. to the superior technology of the Ganges valley, as is apparent from the introduction of iron and subsequently of a special type of pottery – the northern black polished ware – both of which are associated with the Aryan culture of the Ganges valley. Evidently, the

Aryans had by now begun to move southwards into the Deccan and communication had been established between the Ganges valley and the Deccan. The Deccan was being prepared for the role it was to play for many centuries in the history of the sub-continent, that of being a bridge between the north and the south. Not only did it receive elements of Aryan culture from the north, but by about 300 B.C. the sites of the lower Deccan were in contact with the Megalithic culture of the extreme south of India.

The Megalithic culture of south India (Madras, Kerala, and Mysore) has close similarities with the Megalithic cultures of the Mediterranean and may have arrived in south India from western Asia, the earliest contact in what was to become a close relationship between the two areas which lasted till well into recent times.

The south Indian megaliths or burial monuments were either rock-cut cave sepulchres or else circular enclosures in the midst of which were rectangular stone cists or pottery sarcophagi containing bones and such grave furnishings as were customary (e.g. a special black-and-red ware). These monuments are generally found in the vicinity of fertile land irrigated from tanks specially built for storing water, which suggests a remarkable degree of cooperative effort on the part of the builders. The Megalithic culture which dates to *c.* 500 B.C. and A.D. 100 brings us to the historical period in south India.

The ethnic composition of the people involved in these various cultures was not identical. Ethnological studies have revealed six main races in the Indian sub-continent. The earliest was apparently the Negrito and this was followed by the Proto-Australoid, the Mongoloid, the Mediterranean, and later those associated with Aryan culture. There is evidence of the Proto-Australoid, the Mediterranean, Alpine, and Mongoloid in the skeletal remains at Harappan sites. Presumably by this time the first five of the races mentioned above were well settled in India. The Proto-Australoid were the basic element in the Indian population and their speech was of the Austric linguistic group, a specimen of which survives in the Munda speech of certain primitive tribes. The Mediterranean race is generally associated with Dravidian culture. The concentration of the Mongoloid people was in the north-eastern and northern fringes of the sub-continent, and their speech conforms to the Sino-Tibetan group. The last to come were the people commonly referred to as the Aryans. Aryan is in fact a linguistic term indicating a speech-group of Indo-European origin, and is *not* an ethnic term. To refer to the coming of the Aryans is therefore inaccurate. However, this inaccuracy has become so current in historical studies of early India that it would sound unduly pedantic to refer to the Aryans as 'the Aryan-speaking peoples'. Their ethnic identity is not known on the basis of the Indian evidence.

Tentative calculations have been made of the population of the sub-continent during various periods, but these remain largely conjectural. An estimate suggested for the sub-continent at the end of the fourth century B.C. is 181 million.* This estimate is based partly on the size of the Indian army as described in Greek sources when referring to the campaign of Alexander of Macedon in northern India. It is possible of course that Greek writers were exaggerating the figures in order to demonstrate to their readers the formidable military strength which Alexander would have had to face had he pursued his campaign into the Ganges valley. The estimate of 181 million appears to be rather high: a figure of about 100 million or less for the early period might be more credible. An estimate for the early seventeenth century is 100 million.† The first census of the British Indian administration covering the entire sub-continent carried out in 1881 put the population at a little over 253 million.

It was against this background of peoples and cultures of Indian prehistory that the Aryan-speaking tribes arrived in the north and made their contribution to Indian civilization.

* J. M. Datta, 'Population of India about 320 B.C.', *Man in India*, Vol. 42, No. 4, Oct.–Dec. 1962.

† W. H. Moreland, *India at the Death of Akbar*, (Delhi, 1962) p. 21.

THE IMPACT OF ARYAN CULTURE

It was once the tradition that the first king of India was Manu Svayambhu (the Self-born Manu). Manu was born directly of the god Brahma, and was a hermaphrodite. From the female half of his body he bore two sons and three daughters, from whom descended a series of Manus. One of them, called Prithu, became the first consecrated king of the earth, and gave to the earth her name, Prithvi. He cleared the forests, cultivated the land, and introduced cattle-breeding, commerce, and other activities associated with a settled life. But the tenth Manu was the most famous of them all. It was when he ruled over the earth that the great flood occurred, when everything was submerged and only Manu survived. The god Vishnu warned Manu of the flood, and Manu built a boat to carry his family and the seven sages of antiquity. Vishnu took the form of a large fish, to which the boat was fastened, swam through the flood, and lodged the boat on a mountain peak. Here Manu, his family, and the seven sages remained, until the water had subsided and they could safely return. The human race sprang from Manu and his family, the survivors of the great flood. Manu had nine sons, the eldest of whom was a hermaphrodite – hence known by a dual name Ila and Ilā. From this son arose the two main lines of royal descent, the Solar dynasty (*Suryavamsha*) from Ila and the Lunar dynasty (*Chandravamsha*) from Ilā.

This is the traditional history as recorded in the *Puranas* and the *Brahmanas*. The flood supposedly occurred many thousand years ago. The *Puranas* trace the descent of Manu's progeny to the kings of the epic period – the royal heroes of the two epics, the *Ramayana* and the *Mahabharata* – and then continue to chronicle the dynasties of the historical period (3102 B.C. is the traditional date for the war described in the *Mahabharata*). The sequence of kings is unbroken and follows a pattern which is indicative of much care and thought. Had this literary source been the only one available the basis for discussion of the beginnings of Indian history would have been limited, but in the late eighteenth and early nineteenth century another type of evidence provided historical material which conflicted with the traditional story, the evidence provided by philology, the study of which in the nineteenth century developed importantly both in Europe and elsewhere. In India, European scholars of Sanskrit realized with some surprise that Sanskrit was related in structure and possibly in sound to Greek and Latin, and that the relationship was a close one. This led to the theory of a common language originally spoken by the Indo-European people, the ancestors of the Aryan-speaking tribes. The Indo-Europeans emerged from the region of the Caspian Sea and the southern Russian steppes, and gradually divided into a number of tribes which spread far afield in search of pasture, to Greece and Asia Minor, to Iran, and to India, by which time they were called 'Aryans'. Vedic literature (that associated with the Aryans in India) came in for intensive study, and it appeared to be proved that the beginning of Indian history was to be the coming of the 'Aryans', some time in the second millennium B.C.

But this carefully constructed picture of the past was again to be disturbed in the twentieth century. In 1921–2 archaeology revealed the existence of a pre-Aryan civilization in the north-west of India, the Indus Valley civilization, with its two urban centres at Mohenjodaro and Harappa. This discovery consigns the early part of the traditional account very firmly to the realms of mythology. The Harappa culture dates from *c.* 3000 B.C. to *c.* 1500 B.C. so that the physical coexistence of the Harappa culture with the family of Manus is difficult to imagine, since the cultural patterns of the two were totally different.

There are thus two separate sources of information on the past; the historical, which consists of the archaeological evidence and that derived from Vedic literature, and the traditional, consisting of the stories in the *Puranas*, the latter being composed at a later date than the Vedic. The historical sequence of events seemed to have been as follows. The Indus Valley civilization declined in the second millennium B.C. and had almost completely disintegrated when (by 1500 B.C.) the Aryans entered the north-west of India. The Aryans or Indo-Aryans – descendants of the Indo-Europeans – had remained for some time in Bactria and the northern Iranian plateau, but by about 1500 B.C. they migrated into northern India through the passes in the Hindu Kush mountains. At first they wandered across the plains of the Punjab, searching for pastures, as they were mainly a cattle-breeding people. Finally they settled in small village communities in forest clearings and gradually took to agriculture, which had been the main economy of the earlier Indus valley people.* It was during this period that the hymns of the *Rig-Veda*† (the earliest examples of Vedic literature) were memorized and collected.

The traditional accounts in the *Puranas* were collected many centuries later (between *c.* 500 B.C. and A.D. 500), hence the discrepancy in the events described. They are not entirely mythical, since they contain references to historical events. The name Manu provided the generic base for *manava* meaning 'mankind'. The description of king Prithu clearing the forests and introducing cultivation has echoes of the early Aryan settlements in the Ganges–Yamuna region. The story of the flood immediately brings to mind the Babylonian legend, also borrowed by the Hebrews in the story of Noah's Ark. In the Indian sources it may have been a memory from the time when the Aryans were still on the Iranian plateau and in contact with the Babylonians, from whom they may have heard of the flood : or else it was the same legend derived from the Indus valley people, who in turn had heard of it from the Babylonians. A further possibility may be a vague memory of the Mesopotamian flood confused with the frequent flooding of the Indus river, and thus the adaptation of the Babylonian story to the Indian scene. At the time when the *Puranas* were finally revised and edited, royalty in India began

---

* Archaeological evidence to corroborate Aryan culture has not yet been conclusively indicated. A possible identification with the Painted-Grey Ware culture has been suggested. Sites of the Painted-Grey Ware culture have been found in the western half of the Ganges valley and range in date from 1100–500 B.C., the earliest date being 1025±110 B.C. based on Carbon 14 tests of material from Atranji Khera (in the vicinity of Aligarh). The Painted-Grey Ware people were agriculturists who bred animals including the horse. They lived in wattle and daub houses and were familiar with the use of copper, and at some sites with the use of iron as well. This description tallies broadly with the type of culture described in Vedic sources.

† The *Rig-Veda* consists of 1028 hymns dedicated to the gods of the Aryans and was composed by various families of priests. They are not narrations of events, but provide incidental evidence on the life of the Aryans. They can be treated as being historically fairly authentic, since their composition was contemporary with the period described.

tracing its origin to the Solar and Lunar lines, and there would naturally be an attempt to connect these with the earliest known king.

Our earliest literary source is the *Rig-Veda*, parts of which were originally composed prior to 1000 B.C. The remaining Vedic literature – the *Sama, Yajur,* and *Atharva Vedas* – is of later date. The historical reconstruction of Aryan life and institutions is based on this literature. The two epics, the *Ramayana* and the *Mahabharata* are concerned with events which took place between *c.* 1000 and 700 B.C., but as the versions which survive date from the first half of the first millennium A.D. they too can hardly be regarded as authentic sources for the study of the period to which they pertain. Incidents from the Epics can be accepted as historically valid if supporting evidence can be found to bear them out.*

The *Mahabharata* as it survives today is the longest single poem in the world. The main action of the epic revolves around the famous struggle at Kurukshetra between the Kauravas and the Pandavas over land-rights, and is set in the fertile and strategic region north of Delhi. The Kauravas, with their capital at Hastinapur, were the hundred sons of Dhritrashtra, and the Pandavas (the five sons of Pandu) were their cousins. The Pandavas became the heirs to the Kuru throne, since Dhritrashtra was blind and therefore not eligible to rule. The five brothers were resented by the Kauravas, who plotted against them and finally forced them to leave the country. Dhritrashtra, in the hope of avoiding a conflict, divided the kingdom and gave half to the Pandavas, who ruled from Indraprastha (in the vicinity of Delhi). But this arrangement did not satisfy the Kauravas, who then challenged the Pandavas to a gambling match. The latter

* This is happening through some of the excavations relating to this period. For instance the site at Hastinapur, the capital of one of the families involved in the *Mahabharata* war, was recently excavated, and a part of it was found to have been washed away in about 800 B.C. by the flooding of the river Ganges, on the banks of which it was situated. This incident is referred to in the *Puranas* as having occurred in the reign of the seventh successor to the king ruling at Hastinapur immediately after the war, which would suggest *c.* 900 B.C. as the approximate date for the war. Incidentally, the evidence of the flood is also the level at which the Painted-Grey Ware culture ends at Hastinapur.

lost their half of the kingdom, but as a compromise were permitted to retain the kingdom provided they first went into exile for thirteen years. At the end of this period the Pandavas claimed their kingdom, but the Kauravas were unwilling to allow them to rule, so the Pandavas declared war on the Kauravas. The battle between the two, fought on the plain at Kurukshetra, lasted eighteen days and resulted in the annihilation of the Kauravas. The Pandavas ruled long and peacefully. They finally renounced the kingdom, installed the grandson of one of the original Pandava brothers, and went to the City of the Gods in the Himalayas.

Originally the *Mahabharata* may have been the description of a local feud, but it caught the imagination of the bards and in its final form we find all the tribes and peoples of the sub-continent participating in the battle. Its composition is traditionally ascribed to a brahman poet, Vyasa, but it is not the work of a single person, since it is no longer the story of the war, but has acquired a number of episodes (some of which are unrelated to the main story) and a variety of interpolations, many of which are important in themselves.

The *Ramayana* is shorter than the *Mahabharata* and with fewer interpolations. The original version is attributed to the poet Valmiki. The events described in the *Ramayana* probably occurred somewhat later, since the scene is set further east than that of the *Mahabharata*, in eastern Uttar Pradesh.

Rama, the heir of the king of Kosala, married Sita, the princess of Videha. Rama's stepmother wanted her own son to succeed to the throne of Kosala and contrived successfully to have Rama, Sita, and Lakshmana (one of Rama's younger brothers) banished for fourteen years. This exile took the three of them into the forests of the peninsula where they lived as hermits. But Ravana – the demon king of Lanka (Ceylon) – kidnapped Sita. Rama organized an army, taking the assistance of Hanuman, the leader of the monkeys. A fierce battle was fought against Ravana, in which the demon king and his army were destroyed and Sita was rescued. Sita had to prove her innocence by undergoing the fire ordeal, and was eventually reunited with Rama. The fourteen years having ended, Rama, Sita, and Lakshmana returned to Kosala and were warmly welcomed. Rama was installed as king, and his reign is associated with prosperity and justice. To this day the term *Ramarajya* (the reign of Rama) is used to describe a utopian state. The description of Rama crossing the peninsula and conquering Ceylon is clearly a representation of Aryan penetration into the peninsula. As the southward movement of the Aryans is generally dated to about 800 B.C. the original Ramayana must have been composed at least fifty or a hundred years later. An earlier date for the original Ramayana is possible if it is conceded that the conflict between Rama and Ravana is a description of local conflicts between the agriculturists of the Ganges valley and the more primitive hunting and food-gathering societies of the Vindhyan region. The transference of these events to a more southerly location and the reference to Ceylon may have been the work of an editor of a later period.

The extent of the geographical knowledge of the Aryans at the time of the *Rig-Veda* can be ascertained by reference in the hymns to various rivers. It would appear that in the Rig-Vedic period they had spread to the Punjab and Delhi regions but that the tribes had not yet begun to move eastwards. The later Vedic sources, which could well have been contemporary with events described in the two epics, show a wider knowledge of Indian geography; they mention 'the two seas', the Himalaya and Vindhya mountains, and generally the entire Indo-Gangetic plain.

Climatically the region was far wetter than it is today, and forests covered what are now vast plains and deserts. In the first few hundred years Aryan expansion was slow; stone, bronze, and copper axes were used for clearing the forests, iron not being introduced until about 800 B.C. Excavations at Hastinapur show familiarity with the use of iron objects by about 700 B.C. Improved iron implements accelerated the process of expansion. This relieved the pressure of work on the land and provided leisure for religious and philosophical speculation, as is evident from the *Brahmanas* and the *Upanishads*, composed from about 700 B.C. onwards.

Many of the Rig-Vedic tribes are mentioned in the hymns, especially where there are references to inter-tribal conflicts such as the Battle of the Ten Kings. Sudas, we are told, was the king of the Bharat tribe settled in western Punjab, and Vishvamitra was his chief priest, who had conducted successful campaigns for the king. But Sudas wished to dismiss Vishvamitra and appoint another chief priest in his place, Vasishtha, since the latter was supposed to have greater priestly knowledge. This infuriated Vishvamitra, who formed a confederacy of ten tribes and attacked Sudas, but Sudas was victorious. Cattle-stealing and land disputes were probably a frequent cause of inter-tribal wars.

Wars were not confined to inter-tribal fighting alone. The Aryans had still to contend with the indigenous people of northern India, who were of non-Aryan origin, and of whom the Aryans were contemptuous. The enemies are described as Panis and Dasas. The Panis were troublesome, as they were cattle-thieves and cattle were the main wealth of the Aryans. In addition, the Panis worshipped strange gods. The fight with the Dasas was more protracted, as they were well settled on the land. That the Aryans were finally victorious is clear from the fact that the word *dasa* later came to mean a slave. The Dasas were held to be inferior because of their darker colour and flat features, so unlike the Aryans who had fair skins and clear-cut features. In addition, the Dasas spoke a totally different language (some words of which inevitably crept into the Vedic Sanskrit spoken by the Aryans), and their living habits were also foreign to the newcomers. From some points of view the coming of the Aryans was a backward step, since the Harappan culture had been far more advanced than that of the Aryans who were as yet pre-urban. Northern India had to re-experience the process of evolving urban cultures from agrarian and nomadic systems.

The Aryans came as semi-nomadic pastoralists living chiefly on the produce of cattle, and for some time cattle-rearing remained their main occupation. The cow was the measure of value and was a very precious commodity. Many early linguistic expressions were associated with cattle. Thus *gavishti*, literally 'to search for cows', came to mean 'to fight' – the obvious implication being that cattle raids and lost cattle frequently led to tribal fights. Perhaps the cow was regarded as a totem animal by these tribes and an object of veneration. Its meat was taboo except on specific occasions when beef-eating was regarded as particularly auspicious. The economic value of the cow enhanced the usual veneration given to it. This may have been the origin of the later irrational attitude of regarding the cow as sacred. Of the other animals reared by the Aryans, the horse held pride of place. The horse was essential to movement, to speed in war, and it drew the chariots both of men and of gods. Of the wild animals the lion was known earlier than the tiger. The elephant was looked upon as a curiosity and was described as the beast with a hand, *mrigahastin*, a reference to the trunk. The snake was associated with evil, a common enough association among most primitive peoples. It was also invested with power, perhaps as a result of the conflict with the powerful Naga tribes, who worshipped snakes.

The more permanent settling-down of the tribes led to a change of occupation. From tending herds of cattle they took to agriculture, particularly when, with the use of iron, the clearing of land became a less arduous task. Fire played its part in this process, and no doubt some of the forests were burnt. However, wood being a material basic to Aryan life, cutting rather than burning forests was probably a more usual means of clearing the land. To begin with, land was owned in common by the village, but with the decline of tribal units land was divided between the families in the village and thus private property came into being, bringing with it related problems of ownership, land disputes, and inheritance. The change to agriculture led to a wider range of occupations. The carpenter remained a highly honoured member of the community, for not only was he the maker of the chariot but he was now also the maker of the plough; and the increasing availability of wood from the forests made carpentry a lucrative profession, which must have given it additional status. Other essential members of the village community were the metal-workers, using copper, bronze, and iron, the potter, the tanner, the reed-worker, and the weaver.

Agriculture led to trade. With the clearing of the land eastwards along the Ganges valley, the river became a natural highway of trade, the numerous settlements on its banks acting as markets. The more wealthy landowners, who could afford to employ others to cultivate their land, were the potential traders, since they had both leisure and capital. Thus the trading community arose from an originally landowning section of society. To start with, trade was restricted to local areas, and the Aryans probably did not venture very far afield; yet there are references in the *Rig-Veda* to ships and sea voyages, which could not have been entirely imaginary. The west-Asian maritime centres along the Persian Gulf may have attempted to retain as much of the Indian trade from the time of the Harappa people as was possible, although more than likely this trade was restricted to the coastal areas and probably did not make a significant impact on the Aryan economy. The less advanced technology of the Aryans had a restrictive influence and tended to confine the possibilities of trade to local areas. Barter was the common practice in trade, the cow being the unit of value in large-scale transactions, which further limited the geographical reach of a particular trader. The *nishka* is also mentioned as a measure of value. Later it came to be the name of a gold coin, but at this stage it may have been merely a measure of gold.

The emerging political organization of the Aryans can be traced in some of their legends on the origin of government. The gods and the demons were at war, and the gods appeared to be losing, so they gathered together and elected a king amongst themselves to lead them, and eventually they won the war. This and similar legends reflect the coming of the idea of kingship. The tribes were organized as patriarchal groups, and in the early stages the chief of the tribe was merely the tribal leader. As the need for protection grew, the most capable protector was elected chief, and he gradually began to assume privileges generally associated with kingship. The rapid development of monarchies was kept in check, however, by the two tribal assemblies, the *sabha* and the *samiti*, the precise functions of which are not definitely known. The *sabha* may have been the council of the tribal elders and therefore more exclusive, whereas the *samiti* may have been a general assembly of the entire tribe. Among tribes which had no elected monarch, these assemblies exercised the functions of government and authority, and such tribes were by no means rare. Political units tended to be small, particularly if they were kingdoms, since the king was still largely a tribal chief with special powers.

To begin with, the Vedic king was primarily a military leader, whose skill in war and the defence of the tribe were essential to his remaining king. He received voluntary gifts in kind; there was no regular tax which he could claim, nor had he any rights over the land. He was entitled to a portion of the booty from successful cattle-raids or battles. In the religious sphere his role was at first negligible, the functions of the priest being quite distinct, but gradually there was a change in the position of the king, due mainly to the emergence of the idea of divinity in kingship. A later legend tells us that, not only did the gods elect a king to lead them to victory, but that this king was endowed with certain distinctive attributes. Similarly, mortal kings were invested with attributes of divinity. Special sacrifices were evolved to bestow divinity on the king through the intermediaries between men and gods, the priests. The priest had come into his own with the acceptance of the idea of the divine king, and this was the beginning of the mutual interdependence of the king and the priest. Not surprisingly there was now a tendency for kingship to become hereditary. The status of the *sabha* and *samiti* also underwent a consequential change; they could act as checks on the king, but the king was the final authority.

A rudimentary administrative system was introduced, with the king as the pivot. The tribal kingdom (*rashtra*) contained tribes (*jana*), tribal units (*vish*), and villages (*grama*). The nucleus was the family (*kula*), with the eldest male member as its head (*kulapa*). The king was assisted by a court of the elders of the tribe and by the village headmen. Even closer to him were two officers : the *purohita* or chief priest, who combined the function of priest, astrologer, and adviser; and the *senani* or military commander. Spies and messengers completed his entourage. Later sources mention a more elaborate group surrounding the king : the charioteer, the treasurer, the steward, and the superintendent of dicing. The latter is not surprising, considering the love of gambling among both royalty and commoners.

When the Aryans first came to India they were divided into three social classes, the warriors or aristocracy, the priests, and the common people. There was no consciousness of caste, as is clear from remarks such as 'a bard am I, my father is a leech and my mother grinds corn'. Professions were not hereditary, nor were there any rules limiting marriages within these classes, or taboos on whom one could eat with. The three divisions merely facilitated social and economic organization. The first step in the direction of caste (as distinct from class) was taken when the Aryans treated the Dasas as beyond the social pale, probably owing to a fear of the Dasas and the even greater fear that assimilation with them would lead to a loss of Aryan identity. Ostensibly the distinction was largely that of colour, the Dasas being darker and of an alien culture. The Sanskrit word for caste, *varna*, actually means colour. The colour element of caste was emphasized, throughout this period, and was eventually to become deep-rooted in north-Indian Aryan culture. Initially, therefore, the division was between the Aryans and the non-Aryans. The Aryans were the *dvija* or twice-born castes (the first being physical birth and the second the initiation into caste status), consisting of the *kshatriyas** (warriors and aristocracy), the *brahmans* (priests), and the *vaishyas* (cultivators); the fourth caste, the *shudras*, were the Dasas and those of mixed Aryan-Dasa origin.

The actual mechanism of caste was not a formal division of society into four broad groups. The first three castes were probably a theoretical framework evolved by the brahmans, into which they systematically arranged various professions. Combinations and permutations within the latter were inevitable and were explained as originating in the inter-mixing of castes. The fourth caste, however, appears to have been based both on race as well as occupation (as was also the case later with the emergence of the out-castes, whose position was so low that in later centuries even their touch was held to be polluting). The caste status of an occupation could change over a long period. Gradually the Aryan *vaishyas* became traders and landowners and the *shudras* moved up the scale to become the cultivators (though not in the condition of serfs). Aryan ascendancy over the Dasas was now complete. But although the *shudras* were permitted to cultivate the land, they were still excluded from *dvija* status, and were to remain so, an exclusion which prevented them from participating in Vedic ritual and led them to worship their own gods. This vertical division of society made it easier in later centuries to accept new ethnic groups. Each new group to arrive in

---

* In the early sources the warriors and the aristocracy are referred to as *rajanya*. The use of the term *kshatriya* is of a later period. To avoid confusion only the term *kshatriya* has been used here.

India took on the characteristics of a separate sub-caste and was thereby assimilated into the larger caste structure. The position of the new sub-caste in the hierarchy was dependent on its occupation and, on occasion, on its social origins.

The establishment of caste was no doubt promoted by other factors as well, and the process by which the *shudras* became cultivators is inherent in these factors. With the transition from nomadic pastoralism to a settled agrarian economy, specialization of labour gradually became a marked feature of Aryan society. The clearing of the forests and the existence of new settlements led to the emergence of a trading community engaged in the supply and exchange of goods. There was thus a natural separation between the agriculturists, those who cleared and colonized the land, and the traders, those who established the economic links between the settlements, the latter coming from the class of wealthier landowners who could afford economic speculation. The priests were in any case a group by themselves. The warriors, led by the king, believed their function to be solely that of protection, on which function the entire well-being of each community depended. The king emerged as the dominant power, and the warriors (*kshatriyas*) were therefore of the first rank in caste. The priests (brahmans) came next, followed by the more prosperous landowners and traders (*vaishyas*), and finally the cultivators (*shudras*).

The priests were not slow to realize the significance of such a division of society and the supreme authority which could be invested in the highest caste. They not only managed to usurp the first position by claiming that they alone could bestow divinity on the king (which was by now essential to kingship) but they also gave religious sanction to caste divisions. A late hymn of the *Rig-Veda* provides a mythical origin of the castes:

> When the gods made a sacrifice with the Man as their victim. . . .
> When they divided the Man, into how many parts did they divide him?
> What was his mouth, what were his arms, what were his thighs and his feet called?
> The brahman was his mouth, of his arms were made the warrior.

His thighs became the vaishya, of his feet the shudra was born.
With Sacrifice the gods sacrificed to Sacrifice, these were the
    first of the sacred laws.
These mighty beings reached the sky, where are the eternal
    spirits, the gods.[1]

The continuance of caste was secured by its being made hereditary : the primitive taboo on commensality (eating together) became a caste law, and this in turn made it necessary to define
marriage limits, leading to elaborate rules of endogamy and
exogamy. The basis and continuance of the caste system depended not on the four-fold division but on the vast network of
sub-castes, which was intimately connected with occupation.
Eventually, the sub-caste (*jati*, literally 'birth') came to have more
relevance for the day-to-day working of Hindu society than the
main caste (*varna*), since the functioning of society was dependent on sub-caste relationships and adjustments, the *varna*
remaining an over-all theoretical framework. Sub-caste relationships were based on specialization of work and economic interdependence. With caste becoming hereditary, and the close
connexion between occupation and sub-caste, there was an automatic check on individuals moving up in the hierarchy of castes.
Vertical mobility was possible to the sub-caste as a whole and
depended upon the entire group acting as one and changing both
its location and its work. An individual could express his protest
only by joining a sect which disavowed caste, such as were to
evolve from the sixth century B.C. onwards.*

The unit of society was the family, which was patriarchal. A
number of families constituted a sept, *grama*, which word was
later used for village, suggesting that the families in the early
settlements were related. The family unit was a large one,
generally extending over three generations and with the male
offspring living together. Very early marriages were not customary, and there was a fair amount of choice in the selection of
a mate. Both dowry and bride-price were recognized. The birth
of a son was especially welcome in an Aryan family for the son's
presence was essential at important ceremonies. The position of

* The evolution of a caste society was naturally a slow process. In order
to avoid confusion, the process has been somewhat telescoped in the above
description.

women was on the whole free, but it is curious that, unlike the Greeks, the Indo-Aryans did not attribute much power to their goddesses, who remained gentle figures in the background. A widow had to perform a symbolic self-immolation at the death of her husband. It is not clear whether the rite was restricted to the aristocracy alone. It may have been the origin of the practice of *sati* (suttee) when in later centuries a widow actually burnt herself on her husband's funeral pyre. That '*sati*' was merely symbolic during the Vedic period seems evident from the fact that later Vedic literature refers to the remarriage of widows, generally to the husband's brother. Monogamy appears to have been the accepted pattern, although polygamy was known and polyandry is mentioned in later writings. Marriage within re-lated groups was strictly regulated. The Aryans had a terror of incestuous relationships (although it seemed permissible in some cases amongst the gods). Mankind is said to have descended from primeval twins, yet when Yami, the sister of Yama, the god of Death, declares her love for her brother, Yama rejects her. It is curious that the god of Death is associated with the incest theme, suggesting that abhorrence of incest was equated with the fear of death.

The house was a large all-inclusive structure with family and animals living under the same roof. The family hearth was particularly venerated and the fire was kept burning continu-ously. Houses were built round a wooden framework. The room was held by a pillar at each of the four corners and by cross-beams around which were constructed walls of reed stuffed with straw. The roof was made of bamboo ribs supporting thatch. This continued to be the method of construction in villages until the change to mud walls in later centuries, when the climate became dry. The staple diet was milk and *ghi* (clarified butter), vegetables, fruit, and barley in various forms. On ceremonial occasions – as a religious feast or the arrival of a guest – a more elaborate meal was customary, including the flesh of ox, goat, and sheep, washed down with *sura* or *madhu*, both highly in-toxicating, the latter being a type of mead.

Clothes were simple, most people wearing only a lower gar-ment or a cloak, but ornaments were more elaborate and clearly a source of pleasure to their owners. Leisure hours were spent mainly in playing music, singing, dancing, and gambling, and chariot-racing for the more energetic. The Aryan interest in music can be seen not only from the variety of instruments mentioned – the drum, lute, and flute being the normal accompanying instruments, with cymbals and the harp as later additions – but also from the highly developed knowledge of sound, tone, and pitch which was used in the system of chanting the *Sama-Veda*. The Aryans were familiar with a heptatonic scale. Gambling was a favourite pastime. The gamblers lamented and bemoaned their luck, but played on, and many details regarding the dice and the rules of the game can be gathered from the hymns. Chariot-racing was a prestige sport and was included as part of the ritual at certain royal ceremonies. The chariots were drawn by two horses, had spoked wheels, and were lightly built to carry two persons.

Despite the fact that the Harappan people had used a script, the Aryans themselves had no writing until much later. It is possible that a script came to be used by about 700 B.C. since there are references to writing as a normal activity by 500 B.C. Judging from the earliest specimens found in India (the stone inscriptions of the emperor Ashoka, of the third century B.C.) the early script may have been influenced by a Semitic system of writing. During the earlier Vedic period instruction remained entirely oral. There is a delightful description of frogs gathering and croaking during the rainy season, echoing each other's voices, a description which is compared with that of pupils repeating lessons after the teacher. However, the method of memorizing was highly systematic. In the later Vedic period, the institution of the *brahmacharin* had become regularized – the student who lived with a teacher for a number of years away from urban life. Education was restricted to the upper castes, and the teaching of the Vedas generally to the brahmans, although in theory it was open to all *dvija* castes. Arithmetic, grammar, and prosody were included as subjects of study. Some of the Rig-Vedic hymns incorporated ritual dancing and the recitation of dialogues, thus constituting the rudiments of a dramatic form. The stories of the bards, from which the epic compositions originated, also lent themselves to dramatic presentations.

There were no regular legal institutions at this stage. Custom was law and the arbiters were the king and his chief priest, perhaps advised by certain elders of the community. Varieties of theft, particularly cattle-stealing, were the commonest crimes. Punishment for homicide was based on *wergeld*, and the usual payment for killing a man was a hundred cows. Capital punishment was a later idea. Trial by ordeal was practised, the culprit having to prove his innocence by placing his tongue on a heated axe-head. In later Vedic sources there are references to problems relating to land disputes and inheritance. A tendency towards primogeniture can be noticed, but it did not survive. It was also at this stage that caste considerations entered into legal practice, the higher castes being more lightly punished.

As in the case of caste, religious worship to begin with also followed Aryan and non-Aryan forms. Facets of both have survived in present-day Hinduism, in some cases separate but coexisting, in others subtly mingled. The Harappa people worshipped the symbols of fertility – the Mother Goddess, the Bull, the Horned Deity, and sacred trees – and these have continued in Hindu worship. The more abstract brahman systems of belief, founded on the Vedas, appealed to a limited few, and, whereas their impact can be seen in the philosophical aspects of Indian culture, the majority preferred more earthly forms of religion and worship. The hymns of the *Rig-Veda* reflect the archetypal religion of the Aryans. The religion of the *Rig-Veda*, although it contributed to certain facets of latter-day Hinduism, is nevertheless distinct from it.

The earliest religious ideas of the Aryans were those of a primitive animism where the forces around them, which they could not control or understand, were invested with divinity and were personified as male or female gods. Indra was the Aryan super-man, the god of strength, foremost in battle, always ready to smite dragons and demons and to destroy cities. He was the god of thunder, the rainmaker, and the victor over the forces which the Aryans could not vanquish. Agni,* the god of Fire, received many beautiful tributes; he dominated the domestic hearth, and marriages were solemnized in the presence of fire, as they are to this day in Hindu rites. Fire was the purest of

* This name carries a resemblance to *igneus*, the Latin for 'fire'.

the five elements and was held in particular esteem. It was also the intermediary between gods and men. The older gods can be traced back to the Indo-European past, and amongst them Dyaus (Zeus) was the father-god, but had lost his position of prominence in the Vedic pantheon. Other gods were Surya (Sun), Savitri (a solar deity to whom the famous *gayatri mantra* is dedicated), Soma (god of the intoxicating juice *soma*), and Varuna, a patriarchal god (cf Uranus) who sat in splendid dignity in the Heavens. Yama, the god of Death, had a prominent place. For the rest, the cosmos was peopled by a large variety of celestial beings of every shape and description – Gandharvas, Apsaras, Maruts, Vishvedevas – and the numbers of these could be multiplied as and when desired. The worship of man-made objects was a subsidiary part of the religious ritual. Hymns were dedicated to the power residing in the sacrificial implements, especially the sacrificial altar, to the stones used for pressing the *soma* plant, to the plough, weapons of war, drum, and mortar and pestle.

The central feature of Aryan religious life was, however, sacrifice. Small oblations were restricted to the domestic sacrifice, but from time to time larger sacrifices were organized in which not only the entire village but perhaps the entire tribe participated. The goodwill of the gods was necessary to the continually warring tribes, and the Aryans felt that the sacrifice persuaded the gods into granting them boons. The gods were believed to participate, unseen by the humans. The sacrifice was certainly a solemn institution, but it also served the purpose of releasing energies and inhibitions, through the general conviviality which followed at the end of the sacrifice and particularly after the liberal drinking of *soma*.

The ritual of the Aryan sacrifice evolved from early primitive procedures involved in ceremonies of sacrifice. One aspect was the important role of the priests, hence the description *brahman*, applied to him who possessed the mysterious and magical power *brahma* (equated by some writers with the primitive idea of *mana*); another was the gradual acceptance that the god, the priests, and the offering passed through a moment of complete identity. Naturally, sacrificial rites tended to increase the power of the priest, without whom the sacrifice itself could not take place, and the king, who possessed the wealth required for it. The ritual of sacrifice resulted in some interesting by-products. Mathematical knowledge grew, since elementary mathematics was necessary for the elaborate calculations required to establish the positions of the various objects in the sacrificial arena. The frequent sacrifice of animals led to some knowledge of animal anatomy, and for a long time anatomy was more advanced than physiology or pathology.

The Aryan conception of the universe was a limited one. The world grew out of a vast cosmic sacrifice and was maintained by the proper performing of sacrifices. Yet this idea was not entirely accepted, as is evident from the later Creation Hymn composed towards the end of the Vedic period, which doubts the birth of the universe and postulates creation emerging from Nothing :

> Then even nothingness was not, nor existence.
> There was no air then, nor the heavens beyond it.
> Who covered it? Where was it? In whose keeping?
> Was there then cosmic water, in depths unfathomed? . . .
> But, after all, who knows, and who can say,
> Whence it all came, and how creation happened?
> The gods themselves are later than creation,
> So who knows truly whence it has arisen?[2]

The dead were either buried or cremated, the former being the earlier custom. The erection of a standing post or barrier suggests burial in a mound surrounded by post-circles, reminiscent of Bronze-Age Europe. The association of fire with purification may have led to cremation becoming more popular than burial* which it later totally superseded.

Life after death was envisaged in terms of punishment for sin and reward for virtue. Sinners went to the House of Clay, the equivalent of Hades, over which the god Varuna held sway. Those to be rewarded went to the World of the Fathers, the Aryan equivalent of the Elysian fields. In some of the later hymns there is a hint of metempsychosis, of souls being reborn

* Although a practical and hygienic method of disposal of the dead, for the historian this was an unhappy choice, since graves together with grave furnishings provide excellent historical evidence. Had the Indians buried their dead as did the Egyptians and Chinese our knowledge of the Indian past would have been far more complete and vivid.

in plants, but the idea of the transmigration of souls was as yet vague. When it did finally gain currency, a logical outcome was the theory that souls were born to happiness or to sorrow according to their conduct in their previous life. This was to evolve into the doctrine of *Karma* (action), which has ever since dominated Hindu thought. The doctrine of *Karma* also provided a philosophical justification for caste. One's birth into a high or low caste was also dependent on one's actions in a previous life, and this led to the hope of social improvement in one's next incarnation. The doctrine of *Karma* came to be systematized in the broader concept of *Dharma* : the word defies translation into English, but in this context can perhaps be best described as the natural law. The natural law of society was the maintaining of the social order, in fact the caste laws.

The doubts expressed in the Creation Hymn were symptomatic of a wider spirit of inquiry which prevailed at this time. Some of this led to asceticism, people withdrawing from the community and living either as hermits or in small groups away from centres of habitation. Asceticism might have had either of two purposes – to acquire mysterious and magical powers by practising physical austerities and meditation, or to seek freedom from having to adjust to society by physically withdrawing from it, as is evident from the denial of Vedic ritual and the unconventional customs of some groups of ascetics, e.g. nudism.

There was a further reason for this desire to remove oneself from the community. The old traditions and structures of early Aryan society had changed by the seventh century B.C. The tribal communities were giving way to more stable republics and monarchies with strong political ambitions. This was the atmosphere that was to produce the political doctrine of *matsyanyaya*, unbridled competition in which the powerful preyed upon the weak without restraint, or, to use the language of the texts – 'where the big fish swallowed the little fish in a condition of anarchy'. Village lands were split into private holdings or owned by the local ruler, the communal ownership of land being on the decline. Competition in trade had intensified with the development of river traffic on the Ganges. There was an element of insecurity and uncertainty, from which more sensitive persons sought escape.

However, the ascetics did not spend all their time isolated in forests or on mountain tops. Some of them returned to their communities and challenged the existing social and religious norms. The brahmans may have seen this as a danger to their position and they advocated a sequence in which the life of a man was divided into four stages, called *ashramas*, refuges. He was first to be a student, then a family-man or householder, then a hermit withdrawn from social life, and finally a wandering ascetic. Asceticism was placed at the end of a man's life because of his social obligation to his community. Needless to say this pattern applied only to the upper castes, who could afford to follow it, and even so it remained largely a theoretical arrangement. Another compromise on the part of the brahmans was that the teachings of some of the ascetics were incorporated in the *Aranyakas* and the *Upanishads*, the mystical section of the *Vedas*.

But asceticism was not always escapism. Many ascetics were genuinely concerned with seeking answers to certain fundamental questions, as is clear from the *Upanishads*. How did creation come about? Through a cosmic sexual act? Through heat? Through asceticism? Is there a soul? What is the soul? What is the relation between the human soul and the universal soul?

> 'Fetch me a fruit of the Banyan tree.'
> 'Here is one, sir.'
> 'Break it.'
> 'I have broken it, sir.'
> 'What do you see?'
> 'Very tiny seeds, sir.'
> 'Break one.'
> 'I have broken it, sir.'
> 'What do you see now?'
> 'Nothing, sir.'
> 'My son,' the father said, 'what you do not perceive is the essence, and in that essence the mighty banyan tree exists. Believe me, my son, in that essence is the self of all that is. That is the True, That is the Self. . . . '[3]

The Vedic period is popularly thought of as a glorious age of the distant past: the age when gods mingled with men and when men were heroes and defenders of righteousness. The historical reconstruction of these centuries is full of uncertainties and lacunae, and further light on this can only be thrown by the evidence of archaeology. But it is in the sphere of social institutions and religion that Vedic culture made its most significant contribution. Many of the institutions of Indian life – especially the Hindu – trace their origin to an Aryan beginning.* The Aryans not only contributed the Sanskrit language, the idea of caste society and of religious sacrifice, and the philosophy of the *Upanishads*, but played a physical part in the clearing of land for large-scale agriculture. What was more important was that these contributions generated further ideas and institutions, either through their acceptance or by arousing opposition to them.

Sanskrit soon became the language of the educated upper castes, amongst whom it remained a unifying factor throughout the sub-continent for many centuries. But, as it tended to isolate these castes from other articulate and significant sections of society who used other languages, it later became obscured.

The caste system has survived in India for two thousand years despite frequent efforts to break its grip. Its role in determining political institutions, for instance, has been considerable. At the basic level of everyday life interrelationships between the sub-castes within the community were the most influential factor in village life, and this tended to divert attention from political relationships and loyalties to local caste relationships and loyalties. Central political authority became more and more remote.

At a different level, the opposition to caste and Vedic sacrifices were prominent features of later social movements. From the metaphysical subtleties of the *Upanishads* sprang many of the later systems of thought. The clearing of the forests in the Ganges valley, and the establishing of an agrarian system, led to the creation of powerful kingdoms in this area, deriving revenue from agriculture; and these were to dominate the history of northern India for many centuries.

Underlying these developments was the continuous but veiled

* Insistence on and faith in these origins has been such that socio-religious reformers, even of the last century, have sought the sanction of Vedic texts to give authority to their ideas.

conflict between pre-Aryan and Aryan culture; although the former never triumphed over the latter, it did modify and change the pattern of Aryan culture. The development of India as we know it stems from the impetus of the coming of the Aryans and the culture they brought, but there were to be many other and often divergent forces which affected the course of Indian history.

REPUBLICS AND KINGDOMS
c. 600–321 B.C.

WITH the establishment of republics and kingdoms in northern India by about 600 B.C. the details of Indian history begin to emerge with greater certainty. The preceding century had been an age of political contradiction as tribal organization came into conflict with a new political phenomenon, the monarchy. Permanent settlement in a particular area gave a geographical identity to a tribe or a group of tribes and subsequently this identity was given concrete shape in the possession of the area, which was generally named after the tribe. To maintain this possession required political organization, either as a republic or a monarchy.

Whereas the monarchies were concentrated in the Ganges plain, the republics were ranged round the northern periphery of these kingdoms – in the foothills of the Himalayas and just south of these, and in north-western India in modern Punjab. Except for those in the Punjab, the republics tended to occupy the less fertile, hilly areas, which may suggest that the establishment of the republics pre-dated the monarchies, since the wooded low-lying hills would probably have been easier to clear than the marshy jungles of the plain. What is equally plausible, however, is that the more independent-minded Aryan settlers of the plains, rebelling against the increasing strength of orthodoxy in the monarchies, moved up towards the hills and established communities which were more in keeping with tribal traditions, such as the early settlements in the Punjab. The nature of the republican reaction to Vedic orthodoxy indicates that the people of the republics were maintaining an older and continuous tradition.

The republics consisted of either a single tribe such as the Shakyas, Koliyas, and Mallas, or a confederacy of tribes such as the Vrijis and Yadavas. The republics had emerged from the Vedic tribes and retained much more tribal tradition than did the monarchies. In the transition from tribe to republic they lost the essential democratic pattern of the tribe but retained the idea of government through an assembly representing the tribe.

Legends relating to their origin generally refer to two curious features – that they were frequently founded by persons of royal lineage who, for a variety of reasons, had left their homeland, and that often the founding family resulted from an incestuous union between brother and sister. This would indicate that either the legends went back to a very early period of Aryan life when there was no conscious taboo on incest or, as is more likely, the republics were parting company with Vedic orthodoxy; this trend is also apparent from at least one brahman source, which describes certain republican tribes as degenerate *kshatriyas* and even *shudras*, because they have ceased to honour the brahmans and to observe Vedic ritual. This is also evident from the worship of popular cult objects – the *chaityas* and sacred enclosures round trees, etc. – which was common in the republics.

In the monarchies tribal loyalty weakened and gave way to caste loyalties. The political expansion of the kingdoms over large areas also weakened the popular assemblies, since the great distances prevented frequent meetings. Tribal organization was based on a smaller geographical area and permitted the functioning of a popular government more effectively. It is significant that the Vriji confederacy was a confederacy of independent tribes with equal status, and that the identity of each was maintained despite their having joined the confederacy. In the monarchical system, the divinity of the king with its corollary of the power of the priests and of Vedic ritual further reduced the status of the popular assemblies of early Vedic times.

The corporate aspect of government was held to be the major strength of the republics. The actual procedure of government involved the meeting of the representatives of the tribes or the heads of families in the Public Assembly or *Moot Hall* of the capital city. The assembly was presided over by one of the representatives who took the title of *raja*. This office was not hereditary and he was regarded as a chief rather than a king. The matter for discussion was placed before the assembly and debated and if a unanimous decision could not be reached it was put to the vote.* The administration was in the hands of officials such as the assistants to the chief, the treasurer, the commander of the forces.

---

* This procedure, incidentally, impressed the Buddha who used it as a prototype of the meetings of monks organized in Buddhist monasteries.

Judicial procedure was extremely elaborate : the suspected criminal had to face in turn a hierarchy of seven officials.

Social and political power lay with the *rajas* and the representatives at the assembly, generally of *kshatriya* origin. This may account for Buddhist sources often placing the *kshatriyas* first and the brahmans second in the caste hierarchy, since the Buddhists were more familiar with the republican background. Cattle-rearing was no longer the primary occupation, agriculture having taken its place in many areas. Land was either owned in common by the village or by a tribal chief who hired labourers to work it. Doubtless much of the income of the chiefs came from the land.

But land was not the only source of income. During these centuries a new factor had entered the economic life of northern India. Towns had come into existence as centres of industry and trade. Some, such as Shravasti, Champa, Rajagriha, Ayodhya, Kaushambi, and Kashi were of substantial importance to the economy of the Ganges plain. Others such as Vaishali, Ujjain, Taxila, or the port of Bharukachchha (Broach) had a wider economic reach. Towns grew around what had been villages – those which had specialized in particular crafts such as pottery, carpentry, cloth weaving – and trading centres. Specialized craftsmen tended to congregate, because this facilitated carriage of raw materials and the distribution of the finished article. In the case of pottery, for instance, the availability of the right type of clay led to potters working in large numbers in a particular area. The concentration of artisans in a town brought them within easier reach of the traders and of the markets.

Judging by descriptions of the republics, the urban centres appear to have played an important part in their life. The land-owning *kshatriyas* lived in the towns and they probably encouraged the activities of the artisans. We are told of a young man of Vaishali who travelled to Taxila, a long and difficult journey, to obtain training and then returned to his home town to become a craftsman. Had it not been worth his while it is unlikely that he would have made this journey.

The republics were less opposed to individualistic and independent opinion than the monarchies and were readier to tolerate unorthodox views. It was the republics that produced the two leaders of what were to become the important heterodox sects: Buddha belonged to the Shakya tribe and Mahavira, the founder of Jainism, to the Jñatrika tribe.

Not having a monarchical system, they could also afford not to accept fully the brahman political theories. Perhaps the most striking of the non-brahman theories was the Buddhist account of the origin of the state, possibly the earliest expression of the theory of social contract : there was a time in the early days of the universe when there was complete harmony among all created beings and men and women had no desires, everything being provided for. Gradually a process of decay began, when needs, wants, and desires became manifest. The concept of family led to private property which in turn led to disputes and struggles which necessitated law and a controlling authority. Thus it was decided that one person be elected to rule and maintain justice. He was to be the Great Elect (*Mahasammata*) and was given a fixed share in the produce of the land as salary. Such a theory suited the political systems of the republics.

The republican areas, by and large, remained less orthodox than the Ganges plain. Despite repeated attacks, isolated tribal republics continued to survive until the fourth century A.D. These were the areas in which Buddhism found considerable support, and where the foreign invaders – the Greeks, Shakas, Kushanas, and Huns – were successfully assimilated.

The two systems, republican and monarchical, were not mutually exclusive and a change from one to the other was not unheard of. Kamboja, for instance, changed from a monarchy to a republic. But this was less common in the Ganges plain where monarchy was the predominant pattern. The decline of tribal culture, in combination with a growing dependence on an agrarian economy, stimulated the growth of monarchies.

A number of kingdoms are mentioned in the literature of the period, and among these Kashi (the region of Banaras) was at first the most important, but its pre-eminence did not last for long. Kosala and later Magadha were rivals for the control of the plain, a control which had both strategic and economic advantages, since a large part of the Ganges valley trade was carried by the river and was centred on the river ports. Finally, there remained only four rival states; the three kingdoms of Kashi, Kosala (adjoining Kashi on the east), Magadha (modern southern Bihar), and the republic of the Vrijis (Janakpur in Nepal and the Muzaffarpur district of Bihar).

Kingship had by now become hereditary with a preference for rulers of the *kshatriya* caste, although this preference remained theoretical, since kings of all four castes are known to have ruled, according to political expediency. The divine nature of kingship was an established idea. It was reinforced from time to time by means of elaborate ritual sacrifices which the king initiated. After the coronation, when his legal status as king had been established, he began the year-long royal consecration (*rajasuya*) which invested him with divinity brought from the gods by the magic power of the priests. The ritual was highly symbolic, the king undergoing purification and mystical rebirth as a divine king. Towards the end of the year, the king was required to make an offering to the twelve 'jewels' (*ratnins*), i.e. his ministers, members of his household, and certain sections of the population – in return for their loyalty. The consecration was followed after some years by sacrifices intended to rejuvenate the king.

Perhaps the most popular of the major sacrifices was the *Ashvamedha* or horse-sacrifice, where a special horse was permitted to wander at will, the king claiming all the territory over which it wandered. This was theoretically permitted only to kings who were very powerful and could support such a claim. But many minor kings performed the sacrifice and doubtless some manipulating of the wandering of the horse must have saved their self-respect. The sacrifices were conducted on a vast scale, involving many hundreds of priests and large herds of animals, not to mention the various objects used in the ceremony. For the population they were vast spectacles to be talked of for generations. No doubt they kept the more critical minds diverted, and depicted the king as an exceptional person in communicating with the gods, even if only through the priests. The priests too were not ordinary mortals, since they were in effect the transmitters of divinity. Thus the throne and the priesthood worked hand in hand.

The battle for political pre-eminence in the region among the four states of Kashi, Kosala, Magadha, and the Vrijis lasted for about a hundred years. Magadha emerged victorious and established itself as the centre of political activity in northern India, a position which it maintained for some centuries. The first important king of Magadha was Bimbisara : a man of determination and political foresight. He realized the potentialities of a large state controlling the river and decided that it should be Magadha. Bimbisara became king some time in the second half of the sixth century B.C. Dynastic relations based on marriage both with the royal house of Kosala and with a princess from Vaishali assisted him in his expansionist policy. Having thus secured his western and northern frontiers he went on to conquer Anga to the south-east, which controlled the trade and the routes to the sea ports in the Ganges delta, which in turn had commercial contacts with the coast of Burma and the east coast of India and was thus economically a valuable support to the kingdom of Magadha.

Bimbisara was the earliest of Indian kings to stress the need for efficient administration. His ministers were hand-picked and he was reputed never to ignore their advice. Officers were divided into various categories according to their work, and the beginnings of an administrative system took root. The building of roads was recognized as essential to good administration. The basic unit of social and economic organization in general remained the village. Officials were appointed to measure the land under cultivation and evaluate the crop. Each village was under the jurisdiction of a headman who was responsible for collecting taxes, which were brought to the royal treasury by the other officials.

Surrounding the stockaded village were fields and pasture, beyond which lay the waste land and the jungles. The latter were crown property and the king alone could sanction their clearance for cultivation; as theoretically the land was owned by the king this justified his taking a certain percentage, generally one sixth of the produce, as tax. Land was worked by the *shudra* cultivators, except in the case of privately owned land where hired labour was used. But private ownership was not widespread. When the king came to be regarded as the symbol of the state it was probable that he was similarly regarded as owner of the land. Gradually, as the distinction between king and state became less clear, the king's claim to ownership was not seriously challenged.

Agricultural development was largely dependent on the *shudra* cultivators who cleared the forests. The fact that many were landless labourers weakened their status. A category lower than that of the *shudras* came to be recognized during this period. These were the untouchables. They may well have been an aboriginal tribe, gradually edged away to the frontiers of areas of Aryan control, where they lived by hunting and food-gathering. They are described as having their own language distinct from Aryan speech. Their occupations such as rush-weaving and hunting came to be looked upon as extremely low.

Ajatashatru, the son of Bimbisara, impatient to rule Magadha, murdered his father in about 493 B.C. and became king. He was determined to continue his father's policy of expansion through military conquest. The capital of Magadha was at Rajagriha, a beautiful city surrounded by five hills forming a natural defence. Ajatashatru strengthened Rajagriha, and built a small fort, Pataligrama, in the vicinity of the Ganges. This was later to become the famous Mauryan metropolis of Pataliputra. His father having conquered the eastern state, Anga, Ajatashatru turned his attention to the north and the west. The king of Kosala was his maternal uncle, but this did not prevent Ajatashatru from annexing Kosala and continuing the advance west until he had included Kashi in his dominion. The war with the Vriji confederacy was a more lengthy affair and lasted for sixteen years, with Ajatashatru's minister trying to produce a rift in the confederacy.* Finally, Magadha was victorious and was recognized as the most powerful force in eastern India. Bimbisara's ambition had been fulfilled. The victory of Magadha was a victory for the monarchical system, which was now firmly established in the Ganges plain.

The rise of Magadha was not merely due to the political

* A description of this war mentions the use of two weapons which appear to have been new to Magadhan military technology. These were the *mahashilakantaka*, a large-sized catapult used for hurling heavy pieces of stone, and the *rathamushala*, a chariot with knives and cutting edges fixed on to it and a place under cover for the charioteer for driving through the opposing ranks and literally mowing them down.

ambitions of Bimbisara and Ajatashatru, for, although the latter was succeeded by a series of unsatisfactory rulers, Magadha remained powerful. Magadha was fortunate in that its geographical position gave it control over the lower Ganges plain, including the river, with its revenue from river trade. The conquest of Anga linked this internal trade with foreign trade, which was even more lucrative. Natural resources were also favourable to Magadha; the soil was rich for cultivation, the neighbouring forests provided both timber for building and elephants for the army, and local iron deposits made possible better implements and weapons and a profitable trade in iron.

Ajatashatru died in 461 B.C. He was succeeded by five kings all said to have been parricides. The people of Magadha, finally outraged by this, deposed the last of the five in 413 B.C. and appointed a viceroy, Shishunaga, as king. The Shishunaga dynasty lasted barely half a century and gave way to the usurper Mahapadma Nanda, who inaugurated a short-lived dynasty which ended in 321 B.C. Despite these rapid dynastic changes and the handicap of weak rulers, Magadha nevertheless continued to withstand all attacks (such as those from Avanti), and remained the foremost of the kingdoms in the Ganges plain.

The Nandas who usurped the throne of the Shishunaga dynasty were of low origin. Some sources state that the founder, Mahapadma, was the son of a *shudra* mother, others that he was born of the union of a barber with a courtesan. Curiously enough, the Nandas were the first of a number of non-*kshatriya* dynasties. Most of the leading dynasties of northern India from now on belonged to castes other than *kshatriya*, until the coming of the Rajput dynasties a thousand years later. There also appears to have been a strange reversal of roles as the religious teachers of this period were of *kshatriya* origin and some of the kings were brahmans.

The Nandas are sometimes described as the first empire builders of India. They inherited the large kingdom of Magadha and wished to extend it to yet more distant frontiers. To this purpose they built up a vast army – the estimates by Greek writers are almost certainly exaggerated – 20,000 cavalry, 200,000 infantry, 2,000 chariots, and 3,000 elephants being the least of the figures quoted. But the Nandas never had the opportunity to use this army against the Greeks, since Alexander's campaign terminated in the Punjab.

Another factor which assisted in the consolidation of the kingdom was that land taxes had become a substantial source of revenue for the treasury. The land was fertile, yielding rich harvests, and the tax could therefore be high. The Nandas made the methodical collection of taxes by regularly appointed officials a part of their administrative system. The treasury was continually replenished, the wealth of the Nandas being proverbial. The Nandas also built canals and carried out irrigation projects. The possibility of an imperial structure based on an essentially agrarian economy began to germinate in the Indian mind. But further development by the Nandas was cut short by Chandragupta Maurya, the young adventurer who usurped the Nanda throne in 321 B.C. It was under the Mauryas, therefore, that the imperial idea found expression.

Meanwhile the scene shifts back to north-western India, which during the sixth century B.C. had been isolated from developments in the rest of India and had closer connexions with Persian civilization, being politically a part of the Achaemenid empire. A little before 530 B.C., Cyrus, the Achaemenid emperor of Persia, crossed the Hindu Kush mountains and received tribute from the tribes of Kamboja, Gandhara, and the trans-Indus region.

Herodotus mentions Gandhara as the twentieth satrapy or province, counted amongst the most populous and wealthy in the Achaemenid empire. The Indian provinces provided mercenaries for the Persian armies fighting against the Greeks in the years 486–465 B.C. Herodotus describes them as dressed in cotton clothes and armed with reed bows, spears, and iron-tipped arrows of cane. Ktesias, a Greek physician, living at the court of the Persian emperor in the early half of the fifth century B.C., left a description of north-western India, some of which is useful but much of it is fanciful writing, as for instance his description of the tiger:

In each jaw it has three rows of teeth and at the tip of its tail it is armed with stings by which it defends itself in close fight and which it discharges against distant foes, just like an arrow shot by an archer.[1]

The capital of Gandhara was the famous city of Takshashila, or Taxila as the Greeks called it. It rapidly became a centre where both Vedic and Iranian learning mingled. The more orthodox brahmans treated this region as impure since it had come under Persian domination. The impact of Persian ideas was felt in various spheres of Indian life : Persian sigloi-type coins were copied in India; perhaps the idea of rock inscriptions used so effectively by the emperor Ashoka in the third century B.C. was inspired by the rock inscriptions of the Persian emperor Darius; the script used widely in north-western India, Kharoshthi, was derived from Aramaic, which was much used in Persia. The most interesting Indo-Iranian exchange was to occur some centuries later in the development of Buddhism – where early Buddhist thought influenced philosophic and religious movements in Persia further west, as in aspects of Manichaeism, and later, Zoroastrianism from Persia made its impact on the *Mahayana* type of Buddhism. Persian ascendency in north-western India ended with the conquest of Persia by Alexander of Macedon in *c*. 330 B.C. Soon after this north-west India was also to succumb to Alexander's armies.

In 327 B.C. Alexander of Macedon, continuing his march across the empire of Darius, entered the Indian provinces of the Achaemenid empire. The Greek campaign in north-western India lasted for about two years. It made no impression historically or politically on India, and not even a mention of Alexander is to be found in any older Indian sources. It seems that the Greeks departed as fast as they came. Alexander came to India in order to reach the easternmost parts of Darius's empire, to solve the 'problem of Ocean', the limits of which were a puzzle to Greek geographers, and, not unnaturally, to add the fabulous country of India to his list of conquests. The campaigns took him across the five rivers of the Punjab, at the last of which his soldiers laid down their arms and refused to go further. He then decided to follow the Indus as far as the sea, and from there return to Babylon, sending a part of his army by sea via the Persian Gulf and the remainder by land along the coast. The campaign involved some hard-fought battles, such as the now famous Battle of the Hydaspes against Poros (Puru), the king of the Jhelum region; the subduing of innumerable tribes, both republican and monarchical; the wounding of Alexander by the Malloi and the vengeance of the Greek on their tribe; and the extreme hardships of the army which made the journey along the Indus. Alexander left governors to rule his Indian conquests, but his death, following so close on his departure, caused a state of confusion in which his governors soon left India and sought their fortunes in the west.

The most significant outcome of Alexander's campaign was neither political nor military : it lay in the fact that he had with him a number of Greeks who recorded their impressions of India, and these are valuable for throwing light upon this period. It would appear that a number of non-Aryan practices were still prevalent in north-western India. Orthodox Aryanism had spread eastwards, leaving the north-west open to contact with the foreigners who were regarded as impure (*mlechchha*). Frequent reference to republics suggests that this system still survived to some extent despite the imperialism of Magadha.

The Greek accounts often stray into the realms of fantasy. Greater familiarity with India in the ensuing centuries corrected some of their more fantastic stories. These accounts are a curious mixture of fact and fable.

Nearchus, Alexander's admiral, describes the clothes worn by Indians :

The dress worn by the Indians is made of cotton produced on trees. But this cotton is either of a brighter white colour than any found anywhere else, or the darkness of the Indian complexion makes their apparel look so much whiter. They wear an undergarment of cotton which reaches below the knee halfway down to the ankles and an upper garment which they throw partly over their shoulders and partly twist in folds round their head. The Indians also wear earrings of ivory, but only the very wealthy do this. They use parasols as a screen from the heat. They wear shoes made of white leather and these are elaborately trimmed, while the soles are variegated, and made of great thickness, to make the wearer seem so much taller.[2]

But the fantastic was always present :

. . . they speak of people ten feet long and six feet wide, some without nostrils having instead merely two breathing holes above their mouths. There are stories of people who sleep in their ears. There are also certain mouthless people who are gentle by nature and live

round the sources of the Ganges and they sustain themselves by
means of vapours. . . .

There are places where brass rains from the sky in brazen
drops. . . .[3]

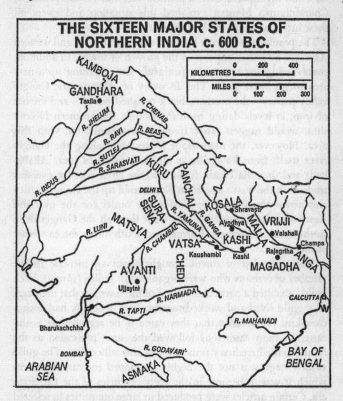

THE SIXTEEN MAJOR STATES OF NORTHERN INDIA c. 600 B.C.

KILOMETRES 0 200 400

MILES 0 100 200 300

KAMBOJA
GANDHARA
Taxila
R. JHELUM
R. CHENAB
R. RAVI
R. BEAS
R. SUTLEJ
R. SARASVATI
R. INDUS
KURU
DELHI
PANCHALA
SURA-SENA
R. YAMUNA
R. GANGA
KOSALA
Shravasti
Ayodhya
MALLA
VRIJJI
Vaishali
MATSYA
R. LUNI
R. CHAMBAL
VATSA
CHEDI
Kaushambi
KASHI
Kashi
Rajagriha
MAGADHA
ANGA
Champa
AVANTI
Ujjayini
R. NARMADA
R. TAPTI
CALCUTTA
R. MAHANADI
Bharukachchha
BOMBAY
R. GODAVARI
ARABIAN SEA
ASMAKA
BAY OF BENGAL

Alexander established a number of Greek settlements in the
Punjab, none of which however survived as towns. Probably the
Greek settlers moved into neighbouring towns and became part
of a floating Greek population in the north-west. The movement
of the Greek army starting from mainland Greece, across western Asia and Iran to India, opened up and reinforced a number
of trade routes between north-western India via Afghanistan and
Iran to Asia Minor and to the ports along the eastern Mediter-

ranean. This accelerated east–west trade and no doubt the Greek population in India must have had a large part in it. Alexander had overthrown the small kingdoms and republics of the north-west and his departure left a political vacuum. Not surprisingly, Chandragupta Maurya exploited this situation and swept all these little states into the Mauryan empire.

The possibilities of trade between north-west India and western Asia was a further impetus to the growth of towns. In addition, routes going south into the peninsula were opening up a new area to northern trade. The discovery of characteristic Ganges valley pottery – the northern black polished ware* – and the use of iron, at levels dating to this period in the northern Deccan sites, would suggest fairly frequent communication with this area. However, the main trade routes were along the Ganges river itself, from Rajagriha as far as Kaushambi (near Allaha-bad) and then via Ujjain to Broach, the chief port for overseas trade with the west : and from Kaushambi up the Ganges valley and across the Punjab to Taxila, the outlet for the overland western trade. Eastwards, trade went through the Ganges delta to the coast of northern Burma, and south along the east coast of India.

The expansion of towns brought about an increase in the number of artisans who were organized in guilds (*shreni*). Each guild inhabited a particular section of the town, so that members of a guild lived and worked together and generally had such a close-knit relationship that they came to be regarded as a sub-caste. In most cases sons followed the same profession as the father so the hereditary principle was also adhered to. The guild at this stage was not the highly developed mercantile system which it was to become in the early centuries of the Christian era. Certain articles were produced in large quantities in selected areas and then distributed throughout the country, as in the case of the northern black polished ware. The introduction of a monetary system considerably facilitated trade. Coins were of

---

* N.B.P. ware as it is often called was technically the finest pottery at this time. It has a brilliantly burnished dressing almost of the quality of a glaze, which ranges in colour from a jet black to a deep grey or a metallic steel blue, and which gives to the pottery a special lustre and brilliance. This was clearly a luxury ware used for dishes and small bowls.

silver and copper and were punch-marked. Copper cast coins have also been found. Usury was practised but the rate of interest is not known. Much of the long-distance trade was restricted to luxury articles, the more commonly produced goods finding local markets.

The use of a script, perhaps spread by expanding trade, was by now common. Examples of writing from the sixth century have not survived, but there are normal and frequent references in the literary sources of this period to the use of an alphabet. It was about this time that variant languages began to develop from Sanskrit. Classical Sanskrit became gradually and increasingly the language of brahmans and the learned few, or had a restricted use on certain occasions such as the issuing of proclamations and official documents, and during Vedic ceremonies. In the towns and the villages, a popular form of Sanskrit was spoken – Prakrit. This had local variations; the chief western variety was called Shauraseni and the eastern variety Magadhi, after the regions where they were spoken. Pali was another popular language based on Sanskrit and commonly used in these regions. The Buddha wishing to reach a wider audience taught in Magadhi.

The changing features of social and economic life, such as the growth of towns, expansion of the artisan class, and the rapid development of trade and commerce were closely linked with changes in another sphere; that of religion and philosophical speculation. The conflict between the established orthodoxy and the aspirations of newly rising groups in the urban centres must have intensified the process, which resulted in a remarkable richness and vigour in thought which was rarely surpassed in the centuries to come. The ascetics and the wandering sophists of the earlier age maintained a tradition of unorthodox thinking, and, in general, philosophical speculation ranged from determinism to materialism. Thinkers such as the *Ajivikas* were followers of a philosophy of complete predetermination – destiny controlled even the most insignificant action of each human being and nothing could change this. The *Ajivikas* had a body of monks – those becoming monks believing that this was predetermined – and their occupation was asceticism. There was a wide variety of atheistical sects, many of which, such as the *Charvakas*, preached total materialism. Man was made of dust and returned to dust. Ajita Keshakambalin thus described man :

Man is formed of the four elements. When he dies, earth returns to the aggregate of earth, water to water, fire to fire, and air to air, while his senses vanish into space. Four men with the bier take up the corpse : they gossip as far as the burning-ground, where his bones turn the colour of a dove's wing and his sacrifices end in ashes. They are fools who preach almsgiving, and those who maintain the existence [of immaterial categories] speak vain and lying nonsense. When the body dies both fool and wise alike are cut off and perish. They do not survive after death.[4]

These sects were regarded with scorn and were accused of immoral practices by the orthodox. The brahmans were particularly harsh, since the materialists objected to the senseless ritual and ceremonial on which the priests insisted, and which was their livelihood. In fact, references to materialist schools of thought were blurred in the priestly writings that have survived, and until recently it was generally thought that Indian philosophy had more or less by-passed materialism.

But, of all these sects, the two which came to stay were the puritanical sects of Jainism and Buddhism, both of which were to become independent religions. Jaina ideas were in circulation in the seventh century, but it was the teacher Mahavira who gave shape to them in the sixth century, and his teaching led to the rapid spread and organization of the Jaina sect. (Jaina is a secondary formation from *Jina* 'the Conqueror' which refers to Mahavira.) At the age of thirty (i.e. in *c.* 510 B.C.) he renounced his family and became an ascetic. For twelve years he wandered seeking the truth and eventually gained enlightenment. Mahavira's teaching was confined to the Ganges valley, though in later centuries Jainism moved to western India (where there are to this day some two million practising Jainas), parts of northern India, and to the south in the region of Mysore.

Jaina teaching was at first preserved in an oral tradition, but in the third century B.C. it was collated and recorded, the final version being edited in the fifth century A.D. Jainism was atheistic in nature, the existence of God being irrelevant to its doctrine.

The universe functions according to an eternal law and is continually passing through a series of cosmic waves of progress and decline. Everything in the universe, material or otherwise, has a soul. The purification of the soul is the purpose of living, for the pure soul is released from the body and then resides in bliss. Purification is not achieved through knowledge, as some of the Upanishadic teachers taught, knowledge being a relative quality. This is explained by the famous story of the six blind men, each touching a different part of an elephant and insisting that what they touched was not an elephant but a rope, a snake, a tree trunk, and so on. Each man sees only a fraction of true knowledge, which makes knowledge unreliable for salvation. The purification of the soul required living what the Jainas regard as a balanced life, but which, as described by Mahavira, was only possible for a monk. The vow of non-violence was impressed to such an extreme that even the unconscious killing of an ant whilst walking was regarded as a sin : non-violence was an obsession with the Jainas, and they wore a muslin mask covering the mouth and nose to prevent the involuntary inhalation of even the tiniest of insects.

Jainism spread rapidly amongst the trading community. The emphasis on non-violence (*ahimsa*) prevented agriculturalists from being Jainas, since cultivation involved killing insects and pests; it also excluded crafts endangering the life of other creatures. Trade and commerce were possible occupations and the encouragement of frugality in Jainism coincided with a similar sentiment in commercial activity. The strict limitation of private property enforced by the Jainas was interpreted to mean landed property. The Jainas specialized in conducting the exchange of manufactured goods and acting as middle-men, confining themselves to financial transactions. Thus Jainism came to be associated with the spread of urban culture. The west coast provided maritime commerce, where the Jainas became the money-lenders whilst others voyaged overseas with the merchandise.

Of the two contemporaries, Mahavira and Gautama Buddha, the latter is the more famous, since he founded a religion, Buddhism, which was to be the prevalent religion in Asia. The Buddha (or the Enlightened One), as he was called, came from the republican tribe of the Shakyas, and his father was the *kshatriya* chief of this tribe. The legend of his life has curious similarities with the legendary episodes in Christ's life, such as the idea of the immaculate conception, and temptation by the Devil. He was born in about 566 B.C. and lived the life of a young prince but with increasing dissatisfaction, until he left his family and disappeared one night to become an ascetic. After an austere six years he decided that asceticism was not the path to salvation and discarded it. He then resolved to discover the means of salvation through meditation, and eventually on the forty-ninth day of his meditation he received enlightenment and understood the cause of suffering in this world. He preached his first sermon at the Deer Park at Sarnath (four miles from Banaras) and gathered his first five disciples.

This sermon was called the Turning of the Wheel of Law, and was the nucleus of Buddhist teaching. It incorporated the Four Noble Truths (that is, the world is full of suffering, suffering is caused by human desires, the renunciation of desire is the path to salvation, and this salvation is possible through the Eight-Fold Path), and the Eight-Fold Path which consisted of eight principles of action, leading to a balanced, moderate life (right views, resolves, speech, conduct, livelihood, effort, recollection, and meditation, the combination of which was described as the Middle Way). To understand this sermon did not call for complicated metaphysical thinking, and the rational undertone of the argument was characteristic of the Buddhist emphasis on causality as the basis of analysis, particularly in a system where nothing is left to divine intervention. Salvation lay in achieving *nirvana*, or extinction, freedom from the wheel of rebirth. Thus the doctrine of *karma* was essential to the Buddhist system of salvation. Unlike the brahmanical idea, *karma* was not used to explain away caste status, since the Buddha rejected caste. Buddhism was also atheistic, in as much as God was not essential to the Universe, there being a natural cosmic rise and decline. The universe had originally been a place of bliss but man's capitulation to desire has reduced it to a place of suffering. Brahmanical ritual was almost entirely eliminated and was disapproved of in the early pure form of Buddhism : popular cults such as the worship of trees and funerary tumuli were accepted and Buddhists were thus able to associate themselves with popular worship.

The religion was essentially a congregational one. Monastic orders were introduced. Monks wandered from place to place, preaching and seeking alms, and this gave the religion a missionary flavour. Later, monasteries and nunneries were built near towns, thereby facilitating begging for alms. The establishment of Buddhist monasteries accelerated education, since they became a source of teaching, additional to the brahmans; even more important was the fact that, as they accepted as monks and nuns men and women of all strata of society, education was therefore not restricted only to the top few. The acceptance of nuns was a revolutionary step from the point of view of the status of women, considering that brahman orthodoxy was gradually trying to place limitations on their activities.* The organization of the monasteries was democratic and clearly based on that of the republican assemblies. Regular fortnightly meetings were held and public confessions were heard.

The Buddhist canon was collected some five hundred years after the Buddha's death, which makes it extremely difficult to define the chronological sequence of the canon or to indicate with certainty the interpolations of his followers. Buddhism was to undergo many changes both in the country of its origin and in the course of its spread to other parts of Asia. The earliest surviving form, called Theravada, is still predominant in Ceylon and the South-East Asian countries. When Buddhism had to contend with Brahmanism, it introduced philosophical speculation, and the original, simple exposition became much more involved.

There was much in common between Buddhism and Jainism. Both were started by members of the *kshatriya* caste and were opposed to brahmanical orthodoxy, denying the authority of the Vedas, and antagonistic to the practice of animal sacrifices,

* The participation of women in a wider area of social activity than laid down by brahmanical sources was encouraged by all the socio-religious reform movements in India, such as the Tamil devotional cult, the *Bhakti* movement, and the nineteenth-century Brahmo-samaj and Arya-samaj.

which had by now become a keystone of brahmanical power. Both appealed to the socially down-trodden, the *vaishyas* who were economically powerful, but were not granted corresponding social status, and the *shudras* who were obviously oppressed. Buddhism and Jainism, though they did not directly attack the caste system, were nevertheless opposed to it and can, to that extent, be described as non-caste movements. This provided an opportunity for those of low caste to opt out of their caste by joining a non-caste sect.* The lack of expenses involved in worship, as contrasted with brahmanical worship, also attracted the same stratum in society.

Although not averse to royal disciples, the Buddha intended his teaching to reach the lower strata of society, hence his use of the popular language Magadhi in preference to Sanskrit. Buddhist following was drawn mainly from the mercantile community, the artisans, and the cultivators. Brahman Buddhists were not unknown, but they were looked upon as renegades by their caste fellows. *Kshatriya* adherents to Buddhism and Jainism were theoretically something of an anomaly since warriors can hardly be supporters of non-violence; but the *kshatriya* tribes in the republics which supported Buddhism were not merely professional warriors.

The pattern of association of these two heterodox sects – Buddhism and Jainism – with urban centres and largely with the lower castes was repeated in later centuries with the various phases of what came to be called the *Bhakti* movement. The formulators and leaders of reformist religious sects often drew their strength from lower caste urban groups. The social content of their teaching was an essential part of their religious doctrine. During this period from the sixth to the fourth century B.C., there was considerable economic prosperity, particularly with the expansion of trade. Although political control still lay largely with the *kshatriyas* and brahmans, the mercantile classes were

* This pattern has been repeated in India in the last decade, with a large-scale conversion to Buddhism of a socially downtrodden section of Maharashtrian society. In 1951, there was a total of 2,487 Buddhists in India. The 1961 census reports a total of 3,250,227. Rural Maharashtra claims over two million of these Buddhists who are largely converts from the untouchable castes, or Scheduled Castes as they have been called in recent years.

economically in the ascendant. Buddhism and Jainism were their answers to Brahmanism.

4

THE EMERGENCE OF EMPIRE
321–185 B.C.

WITH the coming of the Mauryas at the end of the fourth century B.C. the historical scene is illuminated by an abundance of evidence from many sources. The political picture is simplified by the fact that the empire of the Mauryas established a large area controlled by a single power. The political system acquired greater uniformity and it becomes possible to put forward more positive generalizations than were possible in respect of earlier centuries.

Chandragupta Maurya succeeded to the Nanda throne in 321 B.C. He was then a young man of about twenty-five and was the protégé of the brahman Kautalya, who was his guide and mentor both in acquiring a throne and in keeping it. The acquisition of Magadha was the first step in establishing the new dynasty. Chandragupta belonged to the Moriya tribe, but his caste was low, the family apparently being *vaishyas*. The young Maurya and his supporters were inferior in armed strength to the Nandas, and it was here that Kautalya's strategy came in useful. They began by harassing the outlying areas of the Nanda kingdom, gradually moving towards the centre: this strategy being based, we are told, on the moral drawn from the fact that the young emperor-to-be saw a woman scolding her child for eating from the centre of a dish, since the centre was bound to be much hotter than the sides. Once the Ganges valley was under his control, Chandragupta moved to the north-west to exploit the power vacuum created by Alexander's departure. The areas of the north-west fell to him rapidly until he reached the Indus. Here he paused for the moment, as the Greek Seleucid dynasty had fortified itself in Persia and was determined to hold the Trans-Indus region. Chandragupta moved to central India for a while and occupied the region north of the Narmada river. But 305 B.C. saw him back in the north-west involved in a campaign against Seleucus Nikator, which Chandragupta finally won in 303 B.C. The Seleucid provinces of the Trans-Indus, which today would cover part of Afghanistan, were ceded to the Maurya. The territorial foundation of the Mauryan empire had been laid, with Chandragupta controlling the Indus and Ganges plains and the far north-west – a formidable empire by any standards.

Despite the campaign against the Seleucids there was considerable contact of a friendly and inquisitive nature between the two people. Sandrocottos (Chandragupta) is frequently referred to in the Greek accounts. The treaty of 303 included a marriage alliance, of which unfortunately no details are given. It is possible that one of the daughters of Seleucus came to the Mauryan court at Pataliputra, in which case a number of Greek women would have accompanied her. Seleucus's ambassador Megasthenes lived for many years at Pataliputra and travelled extensively in India. There was a regular exchange of envoys between the Mauryas and the Seleucids, accompanied by an exchange of gifts (which included many potent aphrodisiacs!). That foreigners were welcome at Pataliputra seems evident from the statement that the municipality in the city had a special committee to look after the welfare of foreigners.

The Jainas claim that, towards the end of his life, Chandragupta was converted to Jainism and that he abdicated in favour of his son and became an ascetic. Together with one of the Jaina saints and many other monks he went to south India, and there he ended his life by deliberate slow starvation in the orthodox Jaina manner.

Chandragupta was succeeded by his son Bindusara in 297 B.C. To the Greeks Bindusara was known as Amitrochates, perhaps a Greek transcription of the Sanskrit *amitraghata*, the destroyer of foes. Apparently he was a man of wide interests and tastes, since tradition has it that he asked Antiochus I to send him some sweet wine, dried figs, and a sophist. Bindusara campaigned in the Deccan, extending Mauryan control in the peninsula as far south as Mysore. He is said to have conquered 'the land between the two seas', presumably the Arabian Sea and the Bay of Bengal. Early Tamil poets of the south speak of Mauryan chariots thundering across the land, their white pennants brilliant in the sunshine. At the time of Bindusara's death in 272 B.C., practically the entire sub-continent had come under Mauryan suzerainty. The extreme south was ready to submit, thus eliminating the need for military conquest. One area alone remained hostile and unconquered, Kalinga, on the east coast (modern Orissa). This was left to Bindusara's son Ashoka, who campaigned successfully against Kalinga.

Until about a hundred years ago, Ashoka was merely one of the many kings mentioned in the Mauryan dynastic list included in the *Puranas*. But in 1837, James Prinsep deciphered an inscription written in the earliest known Indian script, *Brahmi*. The inscription referred to a king called Devanamapiya Piyadassi (the beloved of gods, Piyadassi). The mysterious king Piyadassi remained a puzzle, since the name did not tally with any mentioned in the sources. Some years later the Buddhist chronicles of Ceylon were examined and were found to refer to a great and benevolent Mauryan king as Piyadassi. Slowly the clues were put together and seemed to make sense, but the final confirmation came in 1915 with the discovery of another inscription in which the author calls himself King Ashoka, Piyadassi. It was evident that Piyadassi was a second name used by Ashoka.

The edicts and inscriptions of Ashoka located in various parts of his empire acquaint us not only with the personality of the king but also with the events of his reign. Perhaps the best known of these was his conversion to Buddhism. This took place after the famous campaign in Kalinga. Kalinga controlled the routes to south India both by land and sea, and it was therefore necessary that it should become a part of the Mauryan empire. In 260 B.C. Ashoka campaigned against the Kalingans and utterly routed them. In the words of the Mauryan emperor, 'A hundred and fifty thousand people were deported, a hundred thousand were killed, and many times that number perished. . . .' The destruction caused by the war filled the king with remorse. In an effort to seek expiation he found himself attracted to Buddhist thinking. It has been stated in the past that he was dramatically converted to Buddhism immediately after the battle, with its attendant horrors. But his was not an overnight conversion; he states in one of his inscriptions that only after a period of two and a half years did he become a zealous devotee of Buddhism. It led him eventually to support the cause of non-violence and consequently to forswear war as a means of conquest.

It was during Ashoka's reign that the Buddhist church underwent reorganization, with the meeting of the Third Buddhist

Council at Pataliputra in *c.* 250 B.C. Buddhist sources have naturally tried to associate Ashoka with this important event, but Ashoka does not refer to it in any way in his inscriptions, not even in those relating specifically to the Buddhist Order (*Sangha*). Ashoka was careful to make a distinction between his personal belief in and support for Buddhism, and his duty as emperor to remain unattached and unbiased in favour of any religion. The Third Council of Buddhists is significant because it was the final attempt of the more sectarian Buddhists, the Theravada school, to exclude both dissidents and innovators from the Buddhist Order. In a sense this attitude led to the later schism of Buddhism into the Little Vehicle, the more orthodox branch, and the Greater Vehicle, the more expansive, heterogeneous type of Buddhism. Furthermore, it was at this Council that it was decided to send missionaries to various parts of the sub-continent and to make Buddhism an actively proselytizing religion – which in later centuries led to the propagation of Buddhism in south and east Asia.

Ashoka mentions various of his contemporaries in the Hellenic world with whom he exchanged missions, diplomatic and otherwise. A passage in one of his inscriptions dated 256–255 B.C. reads :

. . . . where reigns the Greek King named Amtiyoga and beyond the realm of that Amtiyoga in the lands of the four kings Tulamaya, Antekina, Maka, and Alikyashudala. . . .[1]

These have been identified as Antiochus II Theos of Syria (260–246 B.C.), the grandson of Selecus Nikator : Ptolemy III Philadelphus of Egypt (285–247 B.C.); Antigonus Gonatus of Macedonia (276–239 B.C.); Magas of Cyrene, and Alexander of Epirus.

Communications with the outside world were by now well developed. Most of the contacts were with countries to the south and to the west. The east was comparatively unexplored. Ashoka's missions to the Greek kingdoms familiarized the Hellenic world with Indian life and provoked an interest in things Indian. The closest of the Greek kingdoms was the Seleucid empire, whose border was contiguous with the Mauryan. There was a continual interchange of envoys between the two empires through three generations of kings. The north-western provinces, having once been part of the Achaemenid empire, retained many Persian features. It is not surprising that the capitals of the Ashokan pillars bear a remarkable similarity to those at Persepolis and may have been sculpted by craftsmen from the northwest province. The idea of making rock-inscriptions may have come to Ashoka after hearing about those of Darius. The occasional phrase reflects this, such as the opening form of address: Darius uses the expression :

Thus saith the king Darius. . . .[2]

and Ashoka writes;

The king, the Beloved of the Gods, Piyadassi, speaks thus. . . .[3]

The Ashokan inscriptions were in the local script. Thus, those found in the north-west, in the region near Peshawar, are in the *Kharoshthi* script, which is derived from the Aramaic script used in Iran. At the extreme west of the empire, near modern Kandahar, the inscriptions are in Greek and Aramaic; elsewhere in India they are in the *Brahmi* script.

Tradition asserts that Kashmir was included in the Mauryan empire, and that Ashoka built the city of Shrinagar. Khotan in Central Asia was also supposed to have come under Mauryan sway. Tibetan sources maintain that the kingdom of Khotan was jointly founded by Indian and Chinese political exiles, and that Ashoka actually visited Khotan. The latter statement sounds improbable in view of the difficult terrain which such a journey would have involved. Contacts with China are difficult to determine with any precision at this date. It was still too early for the Central Asian route to have been used. Whatever contact existed must have been via the eastern mountains in the direction of Assam and Burma. But the alignment of these mountains in a north–south direction and their height may have made them an effective barrier to communications. The Mauryans had close connexions with the area of modern Nepal, since the foothills were within the empire. One of Ashoka's daughters is said to have married a nobleman from the mountains of Nepal. On the east was the province of Vanga (part of modern Bengal), the Ganges delta region. The main port on the delta, Tamralipti, gave Vanga its importance, since ships heading for the Burma coast and south India began the voyage at Tamralipti.

The extent and influence of Mauryan power in south India can be gauged from the location of Ashoka's inscriptions in the south, which are not found beyond southern Mysore. Ashoka mentions the people of the south with whom he was on friendly terms – the Cholas, Pandyas, Satiyaputras, and Keralaputras. There is a tradition that poetry in Tamil (the earliest literary language of the extreme south) was first committed to writing in the third or second century B.C. by foreign immigrants, who are also associated with setting up stone inscriptions. This may be a vague reference to the Mauryans, though they did not actually rule in the Tamil country. It is possible that Tamil may have been a spoken language without a script, until contact with the Mauryans introduced the *Brahmi* script to the speakers of Tamil. Ashoka's contact with the southern kingdoms seems to have been of a friendly nature, otherwise he would have doubtless tried to conquer them. They in turn, having had experience of Mauryan arms from the campaigns of Bindusara, probably preferred to give pledges of friendship, and remain in peace.

Mauryan relations with Ceylon were extremely close and the Chronicles of Ceylon have much to say about the Mauryas. Not only did Ashoka's son Mahinda go as a Buddhist missionary to Ceylon, but the then king of Ceylon, Tissa, appears to have modelled himself on Ashoka. There were frequent exchanges of gifts and envoys. The Indian emperor sent a branch of the original *pipal* tree under which the Buddha had received enlightenment, which it is claimed still survives in Ceylon, although the parent tree in India was cut down in later centuries by an anti-Buddhist fanatic.

The reigns of the first three Mauryas – the first ninety years of the dynasty – were the most significant. The significance lay not merely in the conquest of the rulers but in the fact that they were able to weld the largely diverse elements of the sub-continent into an empire, and they gave expression to an imperial vision which was to dominate succeeding centuries of Indian political life. How and why this imperial idea was possible in the third century B.C. was determined by a variety of factors.

By the third century B.C. the economy of northern India was predominantly agrarian. Land revenue had become the accepted source of income for the government, and it was realized that regular assessments assured increased revenues as the agrarian economy expanded. The predictability of revenue from these taxes created a feeling of fiscal security. The administrative system was largely concerned with the efficient collection of taxes. Not surprisingly, Kautalya, who may be regarded as the theorist of this system, refers at length to methods of tax collection and related problems. Economic activities other than agrarian were not unknown or discouraged. Villages still maintained herds of animals which were also assessed and taxed. Commercial enterprises, particularly in the coastal regions, came under government supervision, and taxes were collected wherever and whenever possible, the techniques of taxation having developed from the original land tax system.

The majority of the population were agriculturists and lived in villages. The distinction between king and state becoming increasingly blurred, the idea that the land was owned by the king was not seriously challenged. This is evident from both the *Arthashastra** and instances where modifications in land tax appear to be the direct concern of the king and the cultivator without any indication of an intermediary. The clearing and settlement of new areas was organized by the government, large bodies of *shudras* being deported from over-populated areas. The whole procedure is well described in the *Arthashastra*. Doubtless the hundred and fifty thousand people deported from Kalinga were sent to clear waste land and establish new settlements. These settlers were denied arms, their sole work being cultivation, and the government took their surplus crops. The *shudra* helot had come into being under state control, to make large-scale slavery unnecessary for food production. But in fact there was little to choose between the status of the *shudra* and that of the slave, though legally the *shudra* was not a slave. Members of other castes and occupations moved into the settlement voluntarily, once it became economically worthwhile to do so.

Megasthenes, the Seleucid ambassador at the Mauryan court, has commented on the absence of slaves in India, but this is contradicted by Indian sources. Domestic slaves were a regular feature in prosperous households, where the slaves were of low

* The *Arthashastra*, a treatise on government and economics ascribed to Kautalya, the chief advisor of Chandragupta.

caste status but not outcastes. Slave labour was also used in the mines and by the guilds. The *Arthashastra* states that a man could be a slave either by birth, by voluntarily selling himself, by being captured in war, or as a result of a judicial punishment. Slavery was a recognized institution and the legal relationship between master and slave was clearly defined, e.g., if a female slave bore her master a son, not only was she legally free but the child was entitled to the legal status of the master's son. Megasthenes may have been confused by the caste status cutting across the economic stratification. Technically, there was no large-scale slavery for production. Greek society made a sharp distinction between the freeman and the slave, which distinction was not apparent in Indian society. A slave in India could buy back his freedom or be voluntarily released by his master : and, if he was an Aryan, he could return to his Aryan status, a system which would not prevail in Greece. What was immutable in Indian society was not freedom or slavery, but caste.

The fact of the king owning land did not exclude individuals from small-scale ownership. Such ownership extended to land that could be personally cultivated or required hired labour. The use of the latter both by the state and by individuals was a common feature, since it is referred to in the Ashokan inscriptions. Land revenue was of two kinds, rent for the use of the land and assessment on the produce, and the two were quite distinct. The assessment varied from region to region and ranged from one sixth to a quarter of the produce of the land. It was based on the land worked by each individual cultivator, not on the village as a whole, and also in accordance with the quality of the land. The treasury was entitled to tax the shepherds and livestock breeders on the number and the produce of the animals.

The importance of irrigation to Indian agricultural conditions was fully recognized. In certain areas water for irrigation was distributed and measured. The *Arthashastra* refers to a water tax which was regularly collected wherever the state assisted in providing irrigation. One of Chandragupta's governors was responsible for building a dam across a river near Girnar in western India, resulting in a large lake to supply water for the region. An inscription in the neighbourhood mentions the continuous maintenance of this dam for eight hundred years after it was built.

Although the construction and maintenance of reservoirs, tanks, canals, and wells were regarded as part of the functions of the government, there is no ground for holding that the control of irrigation was the key to the political control of the country.

If the agrarian economy helped to build a political empire, the latter in turn furthered another form of economic activity. One of the more notable results of the political unification of the sub-continent, and the security provided by a stable, centralized government, was the possibility of expansion in the various craft guilds and consequently in trade.* Efficiency in administration rendered the organization of trade easier, and crafts were gradually converted into small-scale industries. The state directly employed some of the artisans such as armourers, shipbuilders, etc., who were exempt from tax, but others who worked in state workshops, as for example the spinning and weaving shops and the state mines, were liable to tax. The rest worked either individually or, as was most often the case, as members of a guild. The guilds were large and complex in structure, and artisans found it advantageous to join them, since this eliminated the expense of working alone and having to compete with the guilds. From the point of view of the state, guilds facilitated the collection of taxes and the general running of the industry. Localization of occupation and the hereditary nature of occupations strengthened the guilds.

A tax was levied on all manufactured articles and the date was stamped on them so that consumers could distinguish between old goods and new. The sale of merchandise was strictly supervised. Various factors such as the current price, supply and demand, and the expenses of production were considered by the superintendent of commerce, before assessing the goods. A toll was fixed at one fifth of the value of the commodity and in addition there was a trade tax of one fifth of the toll. Tax evasion was known but was heavily punished. Prices were controlled to prevent too great a profit on the part of the merchant, the percentage of profit generally being fixed. There was no banking system but usury was customary. Fifteen per cent per annum

* The distribution of northern black polished ware in third century B.C. levels at sites in the peninsula is one indication of the expansion of trade during the Mauryan period.

was the recognized rate of interest on borrowed money. However, in less secure transactions involving long sea voyages, the rate could be as high as sixty per cent.

Megasthenes in his *Indika* speaks of Mauryan society as being divided into seven castes – philosophers, farmers, soldiers, herdsmen, artisans, magistrates, and councillors. Clearly he was confusing caste with occupation. Commenting on caste he says, 'No one is allowed to marry outside his own caste or exercise any calling or art except his own.'[4] The category of philosophers included brahmans, Buddhist monks, and followers of any of the other religious sects. The philosophers were exempt from taxation, as is corroborated by Indian sources. The farmers were mainly the *shudra* cultivators and the labourers working on the land. The soldiers were certainly an 'economic' class even if they did not all belong to the *kshatriya* caste. The Mauryan standing army was larger than that of the Nandas. Pliny quotes the figures at 9,000 elephants, 30,000 cavalry, and 600,000 infantry, and in peace time the army must have been an economic liability. Megasthenes writes, 'when they are not in service they spend their time in idleness and drinking bouts, being maintained at the expense of the royal treasury.' In the circumstances it is not surprising that the treasury had to be kept replenished at any cost, whether it meant taxing every possible taxable commodity or deporting whole communities to establish new settlements. The herdsmen were either of *shudra* origin or else outcastes. The caste of the artisan would depend on his particular craft. Metal-workers, for instance, were accorded a higher status than weavers and potters. The more wealthy were probably of the upper castes, whereas those working for them may again have been *shudras*. Magistrates and councillors were obviously part of the administrative system and would tend to be either brahmans or *kshatriyas*, although exceptions are on record.

The caste system did not work in the smooth manner envisaged by the brahman theoreticians. The first three castes, *dvija* or twice-born, were theoretically more privileged than the *shudras* and the outcastes. But *vaishyas*, though technically *dvijas*, did not benefit recognizably from their privileged position, since they were socially excluded by the first two castes. Yet the *vaishyas* by now were economically powerful, since

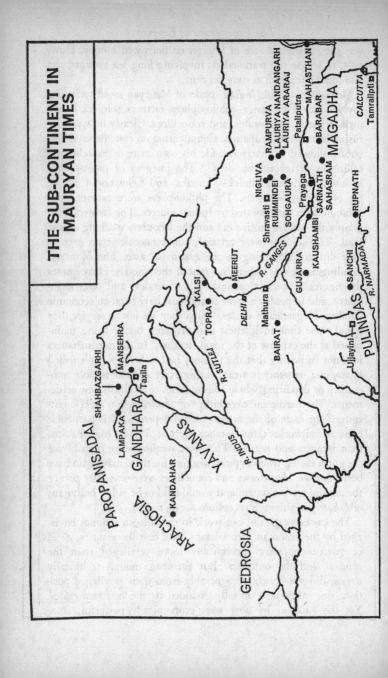

THE SUB-CONTINENT IN
MAURYAN TIMES

PAROPANISADAI

SHAHBAZGARHI

LAMPAKA

GANDHARA

MANSEHRA

Taxila

R. INDUS

YAVANAS

R. SUTLEJ

TOPRA

KALSI

MEERUT

DELHI

Mathura

BAIRAT

R. GANGES

Shravasti

NIGLIVA

RUMMINDEI

SOHGAURA

RAMPURVA

LAURIYA NANDANGARH

LAURIYA ARARAJ

Pataliputra

MAHASTHAN

Prayaga

KAUSHAMBI

GUJARRA

SARNATH

BARABAR

MAGADHA

SAHASRAM

RUPNATH

Ujjayini

SANCHI

R. NARMADA

PULINDAS

ARACHOSIA

KANDAHAR

GEDROSIA

CALCUTTA

Tamralipti

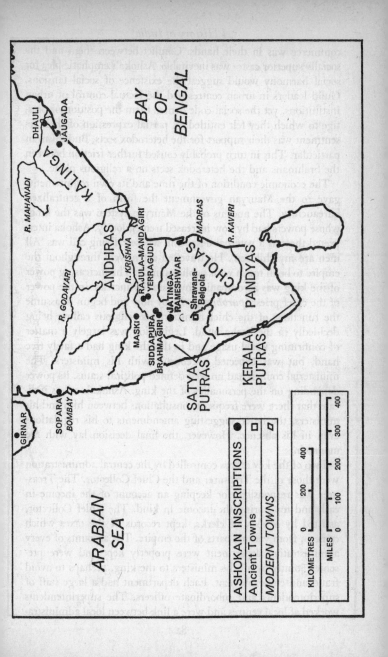

commerce was in their hands. Conflict between them and the socially superior castes was inevitable. Ashoka's emphatic plea for social harmony would suggest the existence of social tensions. Guild leaders in urban centres had the factual control of urban institutions, yet the social code denied them the position of prestige to which they felt entitled. A partial expression of their resentment was their support for the heterodox sects, Buddhism in particular. This in turn probably caused further friction between the brahmans and the heterodox sects on a religious plane.

The economic condition of the time and its own requirements gave to the Mauryan government the form of a centralized bureaucracy. The nucleus of the Mauryan system was the king, whose powers had by now increased tremendously. Ashoka interpreted these as a paternal despotism whose rallying call was 'All men are my children'. He travelled extensively throughout the empire to be in touch with public opinion. The increasing power of the king was accompanied by a similar increase in the power of the chief priest (*purohita*), who by now had begun to assume the functions of the chief minister, his religious calling being decidedly in the background. Legislation was largely a matter of confirming social usage and in this the king had a fairly free hand, but was expected to consult with his ministers. The ministerial council had no well-defined political status, its power depending on the personality of the king. Ashoka's edicts indicate that there were frequent consultations between him and his ministers, the latter suggesting amendments to his regulations even in his absence. However, the final decision lay with the monarch.

Two of the key offices controlled by the central administration were those of the Treasurer and the Chief Collector. The Treasurer was responsible for keeping an account of the income in cash and for storing the income in kind. The Chief Collector, assisted by a body of clerks, kept records of the taxes which came in from various parts of the empire. The accounts of every administrative department were properly kept and were presented jointly by all the ministers to the king, perhaps to avoid fraud and embezzlement. Each department had a large staff of superintendents and subordinate officers. The superintendents worked at local centres and were a link between local administration and the central government. Those specifically listed in the *Arthashastra* are the superintendents of gold and goldsmiths, and of the storehouse, commerce, forest produce, the armoury, weights and measures, tolls, weaving, agriculture, liquor, slaughterhouses, prostitutes, ships, cows, horses, elephants, chariots, infantry, passports, and the city.

Salaries of officials and expenditure on public works constituted a sizeable portion of the national expenses, one quarter of the total revenue being reserved for these. The higher officials were extremely well paid and this must have been a drain on the treasury. The chief minister, the *purohita*, and the army commander received 48,000 *panas*, the treasurer and the chief collector 24,000 *panas*; the accountants and clerks received 500 *panas*, whereas the ministers were paid 12,000 *panas*; and artisans received 120 *panas*. The value of the *pana* is not indicated, nor the interval at which salaries were paid, but the ratio of the clerk's salary to that of the most senior official works out at 1:96, and the ratio of the artisan's to that of the minister at 1:100. Public works covered a wide range of activity: building and maintaining roads, wells, and rest-houses; irrigation projects; maintaining the army; running the mines and state manufacturers; and the grants of the king to religious institutions and individuals, there being no privy purse for the king.

Apart from the metropolitan area, which was directly governed, the empire was divided into four provinces each under a prince or member of the royal family whose official status was that of a viceroy. Governors administering smaller units were selected from amongst the local people. The provincial ministers were powerful and could act as a check on the viceroy, and were on occasion the effective rulers. Ashoka sent inspectors on tour every five years for an additional audit and check on provincial administration. There were specially appointed judicial officers both in the cities and in the rural areas. In the latter regions (where they were known as *rajukas*), they combined their judicial functions with assessment duties, perhaps because rural disputes were mainly over land and related questions. Fines served as punishments in most cases. But certain crimes were considered too serious to be punished by fines alone, and capital punishment was inflicted even by Ashoka, although he was a supporter of non-violence.

Each province was sub-divided into districts, each of these into groups of villages, and the final unit of administration was the village: a system which has remained substantially unchanged through the centuries. The group of villages was staffed with an accountant, who maintained boundaries, registered land and deeds, kept a census of the population and a record of the livestock; and the tax-collector, who was concerned with the various types of revenue. Each village had its own officials, such as the headman, who was responsible to the accountant and the tax-collector. Officers at this level in rural administration were paid either by a remission of tax or by land grants.

Urban administration had its own hierarchy of officers. The city superintendent maintained law and order and the general cleanliness of the city. Cities were generally built of wood, necessitating the maintaining of fire precautions. The city superintendent was assisted by an accountant and a tax-collector, whose functions were similar to those of their village counterparts. Megasthenes has described the administration of Pataliputra in detail. The city was administered by thirty officials, divided into six committees of five. Each committee supervised one of the following functions: questions relating to industrial arts, the welfare of foreigners, the registering of births and deaths, matters relating to trade and commerce, supervision of the public sale of manufactured goods, and, finally, collection of the tax on articles sold (this being one tenth of the purchase price).

A fundamental aspect of Mauryan administration was the espionage system. The *Arthashastra* advocates the frequent use of spies, and recommends that they should work in the guise of recluses, householders, merchants, ascetics, students, mendicant women, and prostitutes. Policy was dictated at the centre although the initiative was left to local interest. Ashoka also refers to agents who bring him news and generally keep him informed on public opinion. This was one of the means through which the king kept a watch on even the more remote parts of the empire, which was necessary to Mauryan government.

It was against this background that Ashoka expounded an idea which was new to Indian political and social theory: and which has also received much attention in recent years in India resulting in Ashoka becoming extremely popular.* It is based on his interpretation of the 'philosophy' or idea of *Dhamma*, as he called it. (*Dhamma* is the Prakrit form of the Sanskrit word *Dharma*, meaning, according to the context, the Universal Law or Righteousness or, by extension, the Social and Religious Order as found in Hindu society. However, the word had a much more general connotation at the time and Ashoka used it in a very wide sense as is evident from his edicts.)

Early studies on Ashoka used the evidence of the Buddhist chronicles of Ceylon in conjunction with the king's own edicts, and this naturally gave a Buddhist bias to the interpretation of the edicts. His supposedly sudden conversion to Buddhism after the battle of Kalinga was dramatized and he was depicted as a paragon of Buddhist piety following his conversion – one historian actually maintaining that he was both a monk and a monarch at the same time. Ashoka was certainly attracted to Buddhism and became a practising Buddhist. But the Buddhism of his age was not merely a religious belief; it was in addition a social and intellectual movement at many levels, influencing many aspects of society. Obviously, any statesman worth the name would have had to come to terms with it.

The inscriptions of Ashoka are of two kinds. The smaller group consists of declarations of the king as a lay Buddhist, to his church, the Buddhist *Sangha*. These describe his own acceptance of Buddhism and his relationship with the *Sangha*. Here the voice is that of someone intolerant of differing opinion and the wholly confirmed believer, as for instance in a passage where he proclaims in no uncertain terms that dissident monks and nuns should be expelled from the Order. Another inscription mentions the various scriptures with which all good Buddhists should be familiar. Far more important, however, is the larger group of inscriptions known as the Major and Minor Rock Edicts inscribed on rock surfaces, and the Pillar Edicts inscribed on specially erected pillars, all of which were located in places where crowds were likely to gather. These may be described as proclamations to the public at large. They explain the idea of

* The emblem of the present Indian Republic has been adopted from the four-lion capital of one of Ashokas pillars.

Dhamma. It was in this concept in the context of Mauryan India that the true achievement of Ashoka lay. He did not see *Dhamma* as piety resulting from good deeds inspired by formal religious beliefs, but as an attitude of social responsibility. In the past, historians have generally interpreted Ashoka's *Dhamma* almost as a synonym for Buddhism, suggesting thereby that Ashoka was concerned with making Buddhism the state religion. It is doubtful if this was his intention. *Dhamma* was aimed at building up an attitude of mind in which social responsibility, the behaviour of one person towards another, was considered of great relevance. It was a plea for the recognition of the dignity of man, and for a humanistic spirit in the activities of society.

In examining this idea it is necessary to analyse the conditions which gave rise to it. It was in part a policy which was nurtured in the mind of Ashoka, but, since he saw it largely as a solution to existing problems, it is in the light of these problems that its true nature can be assessed. Ashoka's private beliefs and his immediate environment of course had their share in moulding this policy. As a family the Mauryas tended to favour the heterodox sects, although they never attacked Brahmanism. The impact of these sects and dissidents created conflicts in the social fabric, as we have seen. In addition there were the other tensions, created by the status of the mercantile community, the power of the guilds in urban centres, the strain of a highly centralized political system, and the sheer size of the empire. It would seem that the people of the Mauryan empire required a focus or common perspective to face all these divergent forces, something that would draw them together and give them a feeling of unity. Owing to the structure of Mauryan India, such a focus, in order to be successful, had to derive from the king. In seeking a group of unifying principles Ashoka concentrated on the fundamental aspects of each issue, and the result was his policy of *Dhamma*.

The principles of *Dhamma* were acceptable to people belonging to any religious sect. *Dhamma* was not defined in terms of rules and regulations. It seems to have been deliberately left vague in details, only the broad policy being indicated, which was required to mould general behaviour. Of the basic principles, Ashoka laid most stress on toleration. Toleration, accord-

ing to him, was of two kinds: toleration of people themselves
and also of their beliefs and ideas. He defined it as:

. . . consideration towards slaves and servants, obedience to mother
and father, generosity towards friends, acquaintances, and relatives,
and towards priests and monks. . . .
  But the Beloved of the Gods does not consider gifts of honour to be
as important as the essential advancement of all sects. Its basis is the
control of one's speech, so as not to extol one's own sect or disparage
that of another on unsuitable occasions. . . . On each occasion one
should honour another man's sect, for by doing so one increases the
influence of one's own sect and benefits that of the other man, while,
by doing otherwise, one diminishes the influence of one's own sect
and harms the other man's . . . therefore concord is to be commended
so that men may hear one another's principles. . . .[5]

This was a plea to suppress differences of opinion in the interests of general harmony. Yet it might be argued that tolerance
is best achieved by expressing differences of opinion openly and
admitting these differences, while, at the same time, tolerating
them. To suppress differences merely aggravates the concealed
tensions. One suspects that the emperor almost had a fear of
people becoming impassioned over differences of opinion. He
placed a ban on festive gatherings and meetings, which ban may
have had a political motive, since such gatherings could become
the starting-point for opposition.

Non-violence was another fundamental principle of *Dhamma*.
Non-violence implied both a renunciation of war and conquest
by violence and a restraint on the killing of animals. But he was
not adamant about wanting complete non-violence. He recognized that there were occasions when violence might be unavoidable, as for instance when the more primitive forest tribes were
troublesome. In a very moving passage on the general suffering,
physical and mental, caused by war, he declares that by adhering
to *Dhamma* he will refrain from using force in the future. He
also states that he would prefer his descendants not to conquer
by force, but should they have to do so he hopes that this conquest will be conducted with a maximum of mercy and
clemency.

The policy of *Dhamma* included measures which today are
associated with the welfare of citizens. The emperor claims that:

On the roads I have had banyan trees planted, which will give shade to beasts and men. I have had mango groves planted and I have had wells dug and rest houses built every nine miles. . . . And I have had many watering places made everywhere for the use of beasts and men. But this benefit is important, and indeed the world has enjoyed attention in many ways from former kings as well from me. But I have done these things in order that my people might conform to *Dhamma*.[6]

He attacked in no uncertain terms what he describes as 'useless ceremonies and sacrifices', held as a result of superstitious beliefs, as for example those meant to ensure a safe journey or a quick recovery from an illness. These were the stock-in-trade of the lower order of priests, who depended on these ceremonies for their livelihood. To implement the policy of *Dhamma*, Ashoka instituted his officers of *Dhamma*. They were responsible for publicizing it. They seem gradually to have developed into a type of priesthood of *Dhamma* with extensive powers of interference in the lives of the people, thus to some extent nullifying their very purpose.

Yet the policy of *Dhamma* did not succeed. It may have been because of Ashoka's over-anxiety that it be accepted, or his own weakness when in the latter part of his reign he became obsessed with *Dhamma*. Basically, it failed to provide a solution to the problems which it set out to solve. The social tensions remained, the sectarian conflicts continued. In a sense *Dhamma* was too vague a solution, because the problems lay at the very roots of the system. Nevertheless, Ashoka deserves admiration for recognizing the need for a guiding principle and trying to provide one.

Ashoka ruled for thirty-seven years and died in 232 B.C. With his death a political decline set in, and soon after the empire broke up. The Ganges valley remained under the Mauryas for another fifty years. The north-western areas were lost to the Bactrian Greeks by about 180 B.C. The reasons for this political decline are, up to a point, similar in the disintegration of most empires on the Indian sub-continent, until recent years. It has been asserted in the past that the decline of the Mauryan empire can be attributed largely to the policies of Ashoka. He has been accused of having caused a revolt of the brahmans because of his pro-Buddhist policy. But his general policy was neither specifically pro-Buddhist nor anti-brahman. It was open to acceptance or rejection by all or any. It has been said that his obsession with non-violence led to the emasculation of the army, thus laying the country open to invasion. Yet his non-violence was not of such an unrealistic nature, nor do the edicts imply that he weakened the army.

More probable reasons are to be found elsewhere. The suggestion that the Mauryan economy was under considerable pressure seems more likely. The need for vast revenues to maintain the army, and to finance the salaries of officials and settlements on newly cleared land must have strained the treasury. Although the excavation of the Mauryan urban sites points to an expanding economy in the early stages, the debasement of coins in the later Mauryan period suggests a different picture. The decreasing silver content of coins attributed to the later Mauryan kings has been interpreted as a severe pressure on the economy where the normal channels of revenue were not sufficient for the Mauryan state. However, this alone is not conclusive proof. Other economic factors had a more direct bearing on the question. Although an agrarian economy predominated in the Ganges valley, there was, all the same, great variation in economic patterns and revenue throughout the empire. This may well have disturbed the economic equilibrium, with the revenue from agrarian areas not being sufficient to maintain the entire empire.

An imperial structure requires two essentials – a well-organized administration and the political loyalty of the subjects. The administration of the Mauryas, although well-organized on the practical side, contained a fundamental weakness which was inevitably to prove it unsuccessful. The bureaucracy was highly centralized, with the ruler as the key figure, and all loyalty was directed to the person of the king. A change of king meant a re-alignment of loyalty, or, worse, a change of officials, the system of recruitment being arbitrary, where local governors appointed by the viceroys chose their officers; and the same pattern repeated itself throughout the hierarchy of office. Recruitment and administrative power remained within the same social group and was localized, which also meant that local cliques could dominate local administration. This might have been avoided if some form of recruitment had been adopted to eliminate the possibility of certain social groups and local cliques becoming predominant. The possibility of something like the Chinese examination system comes to mind. If the Mauryans had adopted a similar system their administrative structure might have enabled them to survive longer. The lack of any representative institutions to stabilize public opinion added to the problem. The system used by the Mauryas, espionage, must have created manifold tensions in both political and administrative activity.

The factor of political loyalty implies amongst its essentials loyalty to the state, the state being a concept which is over and above that of the king and the government. With the decline of the republics in India, the concept of the state receded into the background. The monarchical system, which leant heavily on religious orthodoxy, tended slowly to blur the concept of the state, and instead loyalty was directed to the social order.

The interdependence of caste and politics had gradually led to caste being accorded higher status than any political institution. This is seen in part in the changing attitude towards kingship and the functions of the king. To begin with, the divinity of the king had been emphasized in brahmanical sources, but the Buddhists and Jainas had introduced a contractual concept for the origin of the state. In order to lay stress on the necessity for a controlling authority, brahmanical sources also introduced the idea of a contract. Not only was the king invested with divinity but his status and power resulted from a contract between the people and the gods. The earlier theory of *matsyanyaya* had reflected a fear of anarchy, which was believed to be inevitable in a society without law. Two factors were gradually being emphasized as essential to the existence of the state. One was *danda* (punishment), which invests the state with the power to coerce and to enforce laws; the other, which became far more important, was *Dharma* (social order). Gradually *Dharma* replaced the idea of a state. Even a divine king was no longer infallible, because an unrighteous king could be removed.

In texts of political theory the highest authority on the empirical plane was the king and the government, and, on the abstract plane, *Dharma*. The function of the king was to protect and maintain the Social Order. The latter changed by slow degrees and the change was consequently hardly noticed, which ensured continued and unabated loyalty. The Social Order obtained its sanction from divine sources, which made it all the more imperative to defend it as a sacred duty. Loyalty to the Social Order was actuated at a local level, largely through the institution of caste, and this in turn contributed to an absence of a wider unity.

By 180 B.C. the first experiment in imperial government in India had ended. Other experiments were to be made in later centuries but the conditions were never quite the same. There was not the same degree of central control and direction, because later periods saw the intrusion between king and subject of intermediaries, both officials and landowners, to whom the king delegated much of his power. The uncultivated areas decreased with the steady development of waste land. There was less certainty of a sufficient revenue to support a vast army and to subsidize imperial enterprises. The desire for empire did not disappear but there was no longer the same compulsion and intensity with which the first of the empires had been built.

THE DISINTEGRATION OF EMPIRE

c. 200 B.C.–A.D. 300

POLITICAL events in India after the close of the Mauryan period became diffuse, involving a variety of kings, eras, and people. Evidence is gleaned from wherever possible, even as far afield as Ssu-ma-chien's history of China. Whereas the people of the peninsula and south India were seeking to define their personality, northern India found itself caught up in the turmoil of happenings in central Asia. The second century B.C. saw the sub-continent divided into a number of political regions, each with its own ambition. On a superficial view there appears to have been no connecting theme. Yet there was a theme, even though it was not apparent in political events.

The immediate heirs of what remained of the Mauryan empire in 180 B.C. were the Shungas, a brahman family of obscure origin. The Shungas came from the region of Ujjain in western India, where they were officials under the Mauryas. The founder of the dynasty, Pushyamitra, assassinated the last of the Mauryas and usurped the throne. Buddhist sources claim that he persecuted the Buddhists and destroyed their monasteries and places of worship, especially those which had been built by Ashoka. This was clearly an exaggeration, since archaeological evidence reveals that Buddhist monuments at this time were being renewed. However, Pushyamitra was a keen supporter of brahman orthodoxy (which is not surprising, since he was a brahman himself), and is known to have performed two horse-sacrifices.

The Shungas were constantly occupied with wars: they campaigned against their southern neighbours in the northern Deccan, against the Greek inroad in the north-west, and against the king of Kalinga to the south-east. The Shunga kingdom originally comprised almost the entire Ganges valley and parts of northern India, although some of the regions were not under their direct control and merely owed them political allegiance. Within a hundred years, however, the kingdom had dwindled to Magadha alone, and even here the Shunga hold was precarious: a situation which was to continue for another half-century under the Kanvas, who succeeded the Shungas and reigned until 28 B.C.

Kalinga remained a source of anxiety to the Magadhans. It rose to power in the middle of the first century B.C. under the king Kharavela. A long inscription which he caused to be made and which includes a biographical sketch survives at Hathi-gumpha – the Elephant's Cave – in Orissa. The inscription is tantalizing as it is badly damaged, and in such a way as to permit of alternative readings in names. Kharavela was a Jaina but despite his fervour for Jainism he was addicted to military conquests and conducted a number of successful campaigns in various directions. He claims to have defeated the king of the western Deccan, occupied Rajagriha to the north and conquered Magadha, attacked the Greeks in the north-west, and finally overrun parts of the Pandyan kingdom in the south of the peninsula, which he then had ploughed with an ass as a mark of utter contempt for the Pandyan rulers. Kharavela refers to irrigation canals built by the Nandas and takes a pride in his own efforts in this direction. There is no reference to the Mauryas, unless it was included in the sections of the inscription which are now illegible. Perhaps the memory of Ashoka's campaign was still bitter to the Kalingans. Besides references to conquests, he lays claim to spending vast sums on the welfare of his subjects. The inscription is in a rather flowery and pompous style and doubt-less much of it was royal panegyric. On Kharavela's death, Kalinga relapsed into quiescence.

Alexander's campaign in north-western India failed to bring Greece and India together in any essential way. The mingling of Greek and Indian came later, in the second century B.C., through the Greek kings who ruled in the north-west and who came to be called Indo-Greeks. The end of Achaemenid rule in Iran and the death of Alexander gave rise in Iran and neighbour-ing areas to kingdoms ruled by Alexander's erstwhile generals. In the process of creating kingdoms, the Greek rulers of Bactria and the Iranian rulers of Parthia made the most of this oppor-tunity. They broke away from Seleucid control in the mid third century B.C. and were for all practical purposes independent.

At first Bactria was the more forceful of the two. It lay in the region between the Hindu Kush and the Oxus, a fertile region well provided with natural resources. In addition, the main northern route from Gandhara to Persia, and from there to the Black Sea and Greece, ran through Bactria. The Greek settlements in Bactria traced their origin to the Achaemenid period (c. fifth century B.C.) when Persian emperors settled Greek exiles in the region. It is evident from the coinage of Bactria that it maintained close ties with Greece (the coins of Sophytes, for instance, are based on the Athenian 'owl' coins). The fertility of the region and its trading facilities resulted in cities of considerable size and prosperity.

Diodotus, the governor of Bactria, revolted against Antiochus, the Seleucid king. Antiochus was unable to suppress the revolt, chiefly because he was involved in the eastern Mediterranean where his primary interest lay, and consequently Diodotus became independent. This was eventually recognized by the Seleucids when, after a final and unsuccessful attempt by the Seleucids to destroy the independence of Bactria, the great-grandson of Diodotus was given a Seleucid bride in c. 200 B.C. The only positive gain for the Seleucid king was a subsidiary campaign in which he defeated an obscure Indian king Subhagasena after crossing the Hindu Kush mountains, and acquired from him many elephants and much booty.

The defeat of Subhagasena in 206 B.C. revealed that the north-west of India was unguarded. Demetrius, the son of Euthydemus (who had defeated the Seleucid king), marched in a south-easterly direction. He conquered Arachosia and eastern Gedrosia (modern southern Afghanistan and the Makran areas). Demetrius II was more ambitious and crossed into the Punjab, gradually working his way down the Indus valley to the delta and to Cutch, thus establishing Indo-Greek power in north-western India.

The best remembered of the Indo-Greek kings was undoubtedly Menander, who, as Milinda, attained fame in the Buddhist text *Milinda-panho* – the Questions of King Milinda – a catechismal discussion on Buddhism, supposedly conducted by Menander and the Buddhist philosopher Nagasena, resulting in Menander's conversion to Buddhism. Menander stabilised Indo-Greek power, in addition to extending its frontiers in India. During the years that he ruled, 155–130 B.C., he is known to have held the Swat valley, and the Hazara district and the Punjab as far as the Ravi river. His coins have been found as far as Kabul in the north and Mathura near Delhi. There is little doubt that he attempted to conquer territory in the Ganges valley, but he failed to retain it. He may well have attacked the Shungas in the Yamuna region, if not at Pataliputra itself. On his death his body was cremated and his popularity was such that the various cities of the north-west vied with each other for the ashes. But perhaps the Greeks were here confusing the legend of Buddha's death with that of Menander.

The history of the Indo-Greeks has been reconstructed mainly on the evidence of their coins bearing legends in Greek and later in *Brahmi* as well. The evidence is therefore often confusing, since many kings bore identical names and the coins did not always distinguish one from the other. Following Menander there appears to have been a regency, after which came the reign of Strato. Meanwhile the line of Eucratides, which had broken away from that of Euthydemus and from which the first Demetrius seems to have split off, was ruling in Bactria, and cast longing eyes at Gandhara, gradually advancing beyond Kabul and annexing the kingdom of Taxila. There is mention of Parthia taking an interest in the land across the Hindu Kush and it has been suggested that Mithridates I (*c.* 171–136 B.C.) annexed the region of Taxila, but the evidence for this is dubious. It is more likely that the Greeks continued to control Taxila.

There is an interesting inscription at Besnagar in western India on a pillar erected by a certain Heliodorus, who was the envoy of king Antialkidas of Taxila to the king of Besnagar, perhaps one of the later Shungas, in which he (Heliodorus) professes to be a follower of Vasudeva, associated with the god Vishnu, and obviously, though Greek, he had become a convert to Hinduism. But the Bactrian kings did not hold Taxila for very long.

The decline of the Greek kingdoms in the north-west coincided with an attack on Bactria itself by nomadic tribes from central Asia. These tribes included the Scythians, who were primarily responsible for destroying Bactrian power. The movement of these tribes westwards originated with the activities of the Chinese emperor Shi Huang Ti, who built the Great Wall in the last half of the third century B.C. to defend China's frontiers against the nomadic tribes of the Hiung-nu, Wu-sun, and Yueh-chi. The nomads kept herds of animals and pastured them in the plains to the west of China. Gradually, as their pasture lands began to dry up, they made intermittent raids into the Chinese empire in search not only of new pastures, but also the wealth of the more civilized Chinese. But with the construction of the Wall, China was closed to them, particularly as the Han dynasty, which succeeded Shi Huang Ti, took special care to maintain the defences at the Wall. The tribes were therefore forced to migrate south and west. Of the three main tribes the Yueh-chi were driven from the best lands and had to flee far across the continent. They split into two hordes – the Little Yueh-chi settled in northern Tibet and the Great Yueh-chi wandered further west to the shores of the Aral Sea, where they stopped for a while, displacing the inhabitants of the region, the Scythians, or the Shakas as they were called in Indian sources. The Shakas poured into Bactria and Parthia. A Chinese visitor records that by about 128 B.C. the land surrounding the Aral Sea had been cleared of the Scythians, and instead he had found the Yueh-chi settled there. The Parthians failed to hold back the Shakas except for a brief period during the reign of Mithridates II. On his death in 88 B.C. Parthia was overrun by the Shakas, who however did not pause there, but, using the Bolan Pass (near Quetta), swept down into the Indus valley, and settled in western India, their power eventually reaching as far as Mathura (in the neighbourhood of Delhi) and Gandhara in the north.

With the entry of the Shakas on the Indian historical scene, Chinese texts referring to events in central Asia become relevant to Indian history as well, together with the coins and inscriptions of the Shakas and references to them in Indian literary sources. The first Shaka king in India was Maues or Moga (*c.* 80 B.C.), who established Shaka power in Gandhara. His successor, Azes, successfully attacked the last of the Greek kings in northern India, Hippostratos. A later king, Gondophernes, achieved fame through the association of his name with that of St Thomas, it being held by tradition that St Thomas travelled from Israel to the court of Gondophernes. This would place Gondophernes in the first half of the first century A.D.

Shaka administration was broadly similar to that of the Achaemenid and Seleucid systems in Iran. The kingdom was divided into provinces each under a military governor called *mahakshatrapa* (great Satrap). Each of these provinces was further subdivided into units under the control of lesser governors or satraps, who not only issued their own inscriptions in whatever era they wished to observe, but also minted their own coins, thereby indicating a more independent status than was normal to an administrative governor. The Shaka kings took exalted titles such as 'great king' or 'king of kings', deriving from Greek and Achaemenid usage. This attempt to revive an imperial structure must have been bewildering to the recently nomadic Shakas.

The Shakas were destined once more to be driven out by the Yueh-chi. The Chinese historian Ssu-ma-chien records that a Yueh-chi chief, Kujula Khadphises, united the five tribes of the Yueh-chi and led them over the northern mountains into the Indian sub-continent, establishing himself in Kabul and Kashmir by defeating Hermaeus. Soon after the middle of the first century A.D. Kujula died at the age of eighty and was succeeded by his son, Vima Khadphises. Vima issued gold coins, which show a considerable Indian influence, unlike those of his father which included imitations of Roman *denarii* which were then circulating in central Asia following in the wake of Roman trade.

The relationship between the first two kings and Kanishka, who succeeded Vima, is uncertain. There is no doubt that he was of central Asian origin since he is depicted as such in one of the portraits of the Kushana kings discovered near Mathura, but he may not have been directly related to the first two kings. It was under him that the Kushana dynasty flourished, and the Kushana period (as it is often called) ranks as one of the significant phases in the cultural development of northern India. The accession of Kanishka has been dated anywhere between A.D. 78–144. An era based on A.D. 78 has come to be called the Shaka Era,* supposedly started by the Shakas. The Kushana kingdom extended southwards as far as Sanchi, and to the east as far as Banaras, with Mathura having the status almost of a second

---

* Used in addition to the Gregorian calendar by the present Indian government.

capital. The actual capital was at Purushapura near modern Peshawar.

The history of northern India under the Kushanas was closely associated with events in central Asia. The Buddhists claimed Kanishka as a royal patron, and during his reign the Fourth Buddhist Council was held to discuss matters pertaining to Buddhist theology and doctrine. The most significant result of this was that missionary activity was accelerated and Buddhist missions were sent to central Asia and China. Kanishka himself is believed to have died fighting in central Asia. Chinese annals refer to one of the Kushana kings who had asked for a Han princess in marriage and who was defeated by General Pan Ch'ao, campaigning in central Asia at the end of the first century A.D. If the story is true, then the king can only have been either Vima or Kanishka. The successors of Kanishka ruled for a hundred and fifty years, but Kushana power gradually diminished. Events in Persia were once again to intervene in the history of north-western India. In A.D. 226 Ardashir overthrew the Parthians and established Sassanian ascendancy. His successor conquered Peshawar and Taxila in the mid third century and the Kushana kings were reduced to vassals of the Sassanians.

The coming of the Kushanas had pushed the Shakas south into the region of Cutch, Kathiawar, and Malwa in western India. Here they were to remain until the early fifth century A.D., on the whole quiescent, but for one dramatic outburst in the mid second century under Rudradaman. With the weakening of Kushana power after the death of Kanishka, the Shakas once more asserted themselves. Rudradaman came from the region of Cutch, and at Junagarh a lengthy inscription (the earliest of any importance in Sanskrit) provides evidence of his deeds. The inscription dated in A.D. 150 records the repairing of the Mauryan dam (still in use) and refers in eulogistic terms to Rudradaman's conquest in the Narmada valley, his campaigns against the Sata-vahana king (south of the Narmada), and his victory over the Yaudheya tribes in Rajasthan. Rudradaman is described thus in the inscription :

(He) who by the right raising of his hand has caused the strong attachment of *Dharma*, who has attained wide fame by studying and remembering, by the knowledge and practice of grammar, music, logic, and other great sciences, who (is proficient in) the management of horses, elephants, and chariots, the wielding of sword and shield, pugilistic combat, and other . . . in acts of quickness and skill in opposing forces, who day by day is in the habit of bestowing presents and honours and eschewing disrespectful treatment, who is bountiful, whose treasury by the tribute, tolls, and shares rightfully obtained overflows with an accumulation of gold, silver, diamonds, beryl stones, and precious things; who (composes) prose and verse which are clear, agreeable, sweet, charming, beautiful, excelling by the proper use of words, and adorned; whose beautiful frame owns the most excellent marks and signs, such as auspicious height and dimension, voice, gait, colour, vigour, and strength, who himself has acquired the name of *mahakshatrapa*, who has been wreathed with many garlands at the *svayamvara** of the daughters of kings.[1]

After the death of Rudradaman, the Shakas lapsed into political quietude until the closing years of the fourth century A.D.

In the first century B.C. the northern Deccan contributed more fully to the history of the sub-continent on the rise of the Satavahana dynasty which established itself in the north-western part of the Deccan centred on modern Nasik. The Satavahanas were also called the Andhra dynasty, which has led to the assumption that they originated in the Andhra region, the delta of the Krishna and Godavari rivers on the east coast, from where they moved westwards up the Godavari river, finally establishing their power in the west during the general political confusion on the breaking up of the Mauryan empire. A contrary opinion has also been put forward that the family originated in the west and extended its control to the east coast, finally giving its name, Andhra, to this region. The Andhras held a position of importance as early as the Mauryan period, since they are specifically mentioned by Ashoka amongst the tribal peoples in his empire.

It is likely that the Satavahanas held administrative positions under the Mauryas. The *Puranas* refer to the Satavahanas destroying what remained of the Shunga strength in the Deccan, by then considerably diminished.

The earliest of the Satavahana kings to receive wide recognition was Satakarni, and this was due to his policy of military expansion in all directions. He is the 'Lord of the West' who

---

*A ceremony at which a princess chose her husband from amongst a number of eligible suitors invited to her father's court.

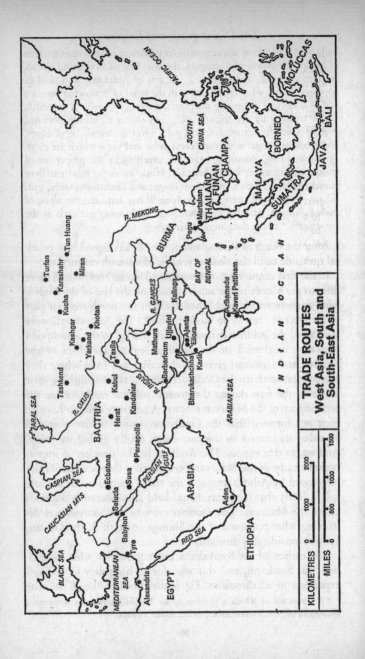

TRADE ROUTES
West Asia, South and
South-East Asia

KILOMETRES
0   1000   2000

MILES
0   500   1000   1500

defied Kharavela of Kalinga and against whom the latter campaigned. He is the 'Lord of Pratishthana', Pratishthana being the
modern Paithan (in the north-western Deccan), the capital of the
Satavahanas. His conquests took him north of the Narmada into
eastern Malva, which at the time was being threatened by the
Shakas and the Greeks. Satakarni gained control of the region of
Sanchi, and an inscription there refers to him as *Rajan Shri Satakarni*. His next move was in the southerly direction and on
conquering the Godavari valley he felt entitled to call himself
'Lord of the Southern Regions' (*Dakshina-pathapati*). Satakarni
supported the brahman orthodoxy and performed a horse-sacrifice to establish his claim to an empire.

The Satavahanas did not hold the western Deccan for long.
After the reign of Satakarni they suffered their biggest defeat, as
they were gradually pushed out of the west and had to flee to the
east coast. This was perhaps a blessing in disguise, since they were
able to establish themselves in the Andhra region, and when they
finally returned to the west coast they controlled the entire half
of the Deccan from coast to coast. Their western possessions had
been annexed by the very people whom Satakarni had feared, the
Shakas, who were by now powerful in western India north of
the Narmada. A number of coins struck by the Shaka satrap
Nahapana have been found in the Nasik area, indicating that by
the first century A.D. the Shakas controlled this region. But it
must have been soon after this that the Satavahanas regained
their western possessions, for the coins of Nahapana are often
found overstruck by the name Gautamiputra Satakarni, the king
who was responsible for re-establishing Satavahana power in this
region by driving out the Shakas.

Gautamiputra and his son Vasishthiputra, ruling in the first
half of the second century A.D., raised Satavahana power to a
position of eminence. Vasishthiputra had the additional name
of Shri Pulumavi, which led to his being identified with the Siro
Polemaios ruling at Baithana (Paithan), mentioned by Ptolemy
in his geography of India. The Deccan now became the connecting link between the north and the south, not only in terms of
politics, but more significantly in trade and in the exchange of
ideas. Vasishthiputra states that Gautamiputra had uprooted the
Shakas and destroyed the pride of the *kshatriyas* : that he had

stopped the contamination of the four *varnas*, and had furthered the interests of the twice-born. The Shakas were classed as being of mixed caste, something truly abhorrent, and the Greeks as degenerate *kshatriyas* by Hindu legal minds. Gautamiputra's mother refers in an inscription to her son rooting out 'The Shakas, Yavanas, and Pahlavas'.* This is perhaps the last occasion when the Greeks are referred to as being of some importance.

In an effort to compose the conflict between the Satavahanas and the Shakas a matrimonial alliance was concluded and the daughter of Rudradaman was married to the Satavahana king.† That this effort was not entirely successful is clear from Rudradaman's statement that he twice defeated the Satavahana king in battle, but refrained from annihilating him because of a close relationship. After the death of Rudradaman, the Satavahanas were more successful in their attacks on Shaka territory. Towards the end of the second century the Satavahanas held Kathiawar on the west coast, and the Krishna delta and northern Madras to the south-east. But this extensive domain was not to survive for long. The next century saw the weakening of the Satavahanas, with a corresponding increase in the power of local governors claiming independent status.

The Indo-Greek kings and the Kushanas maintained the myth of empire by taking exalted imperial titles borrowed from both Persians and the Chinese, such as *Maharajatiraja* (king of kings) and *Daivaputra* (Son of Heaven): and by raising past kings to the status of gods and dedicating temples to them. The Satavahanas, however, refrained from taking imperial titles, perhaps because their control over local chiefs and kings was not of a nature to justify such titles. This fact was conceded even in their administrative system, where power was distributed throughout the hierarchy of officials and not concentrated at the centre. Satavahana territory was divided into small provinces, each

* *Yavana* and *Yona* in Indian sources referred to the Greeks and, by extension, to foreigners from western Asia. The word was derived from Ionia. The *Pahlavas* were the Parthians.

† It is interesting that the Satavahanas, who boasted of having stopped the contamination of the four *varnas*, were agreeable to marrying into a Shaka family. This would again point to the discrepancy between the theory and practice of the caste system.

under a civil governor (*amatya*) and a military governor (*maha-senapati*). The latter were permitted to marry into the royal family, presumably in the hope that this would fortify their loyalty to the dynasty. Some were even allowed to mint their own coins. When the Satavahana power collapsed these governors set themselves up as independent rulers. Administration was left largely in local hands, though subject to the general control of royal officers. The village remained the administrative unit both in the north and in the Deccan. This was to remain unchanged so long as the village was the chief source of both taxes and soldiers. Changes in political relationships tended to be restricted to the higher level amongst provincial governors and their officers.

At the turn of the last century B.C. south India moved from pre-history into history, and literary records reflecting contemporary events are available. Ashoka in his inscriptions refers to the kingdoms of south India (the region comprising modern Andhra Pradesh, Madras, Mysore, and Kerala) as those of the Cholas, Pandyas, Satiyaputras, and Keralaputras. The first two of these came to dominate the east coast and were associated with the emergence of Tamil culture, called after Tamil, the predominant language of the Dravidian group. The nucleus of Tamil culture was the region just south of Madras city, which even today is called *Tamil-nad*, the Land of the Tamils. Kharavela the king of Kalinga speaks of defeating the Tamil confederacy, which was doubtless that of the 'three crowned kings', the Cholas, Pandyas, and Cheras (also known as Keralas) and their feudatories. Khara-vela established a trading relationship with the Pandya kingdom. Megasthenes mentions that the Pandya kingdom was founded by the daughter of Herakles. Perhaps this reflects the matrilineal society of early south India, which survived on the west coast in Kerala until half a century ago. The queen of the Pandyas is credited by Megasthenes with an army of 500 elephants, 4,000 cavalry, and 13,000 infantry.

The historical records of the time are contained in the *Shangam* literature – anthologies of poetry in some ways similar to the Vedic sources, but not directly religious in origin. Tradition has it that many centuries ago three successive assemblies (*Shang-ams*) were held at the town of Madurai, the capital of Tamil-nad.

All the poets and bards of the south gathered at these assemblies and their combined compositions constitute the *Shangam* literature. The first assembly, we are told, was attended by the gods, but the poetry composed at this session has not survived. At the second assembly, the *Tolkappiyam*, the earliest Tamil grammar, was supposedly written, though in fact it was written much later. At the third assembly the Eight Anthologies were compiled, consisting of over 2,000 poems composed mainly by bards and these have survived.

The Cheras, the Cholas, and Pandyas appear to have been continually at war with each other, which gave ample scope to the poets for heroic ballads and verses. The three kingdoms are said to have participated in the battle at Kurukshetra described in the *Mahabharata*. This was clearly an attempt to give them antiquity. Eventually the Tamils built a navy and attacked Ceylon in the second century B.C., and finally managed to occupy northern Ceylon, but only for a short while, as they were expelled by the Singhalese king Dutthagamini in the latter half of the second century B.C. A number of Chera kings are mentioned, but there is little information about them. One of them, however, stands out as something of a hero, Nedun Jeral Adan, who, it is claimed, conquered all the land as far as the Himalayas – clearly a poetic conceit. He is also said to have defeated a Roman fleet, which may have been an attack on Roman trading ships.

The early Chola kings (first to fourth century A.D.) figure prominently in the literature. Karikala, the 'man with the charred leg', fought and won the battle of Venni against the combined forces of the Pandyas, the Cheras, and eleven minor chieftains. The Cholas gained supremacy over the others and this in turn gave them access to both the east and the west coasts of the southern tip of the peninsula. This proved to be remarkably useful, for ports could be built on both coasts and the overland route as well as the sea route from the west coast to the east could be used, as was the case with the Roman trade. Another hero king of the Cholas was Nalangilli, who was remembered for the Vedic sacrifices which he frequently performed. Vedic ritual must have seemed strangely fascinating to the Tamils, used as they were to far more earthy cults such as the worship of Murugan, the god of war and fertility to whom offerings of rice and

blood were made accompanied by orgiastic ritual dancing, led
by the chief priests; or the simple worship of 'hero stones' commemorating those who had performed great feats in battle.

For the Tamils this was the period of evolution from tribal
chieftainships to kingdoms. The king remained primarily a war
leader whose function was to protect his kingdom or tribe.*
Village councils and local assemblies are mentioned but not
adequately defined. These were to develop into a powerful force
in later Tamil culture, as also the temple, which became the
centre of activity in each village.

Yet the Tamils did not remain at a pastoral–agrarian stage for
long. They rapidly moved towards a more complex politico-
economic structure; this was in part due to the increasing impact
of Aryan culture which brought with it the familiar pattern of
hereditary kings, taxation systems, etc., but much more significant was the fact that south India was absorbed into the commercial development of the sub-continent which was taking place at
the time. The emergence of Satavahana power, straddling across
the northern Deccan, provided lines of communication between
the north and the south, and trade within the sub-continent
increased. Roman trade with the east and west coasts and its
concentration in the south helped in ending the isolation of the
southern kingdoms. The word used in the Tamil records for a
citizen of the Roman empire is *yavana*, the identical word which
early Sanskrit sources use for the Greeks.

The whole of India was by now crossed by trade routes, some
of which continued further into central Asia and western Asia.
They tended to follow the highways and the river valleys. Rivers
were not bridged but ferries were common. Travel was restricted
to the dry summers and winters, the rainy season being a period
of rest. Caravans were large and often several would band together for greater safety. Oxen, mules, and asses were the cara-
van animals, though in the desert only camels were used. Coastal
shipping was common, water routes being cheaper than land
routes. There is an interesting passage in the *Arthashastra* com-

---

* It may be suggested that the reference in the *Ramayana* to Rama preparing for the attack against Ceylon assisted by a number and variety of
animals, including Hanuman, the leader of the monkeys, is in part a
memory of the totem symbols of tribes in the peninsula.

paring the advantages of land and water routes. Although sea travel is cheaper, the danger of pirates and the cost of losing ships to them makes it expensive. A coastal route is obviously safer than a mid-ocean route and it also affords greater opportunities for trade. Kautalya advises that in the south roads running through the mining areas should be taken, as these traversed the heavily populated regions and were therefore safer. This would suggest that mining, chiefly of precious metals and stones, was by now extensive. Buddhist sources refer to the more frequented routes, the north to south-west route from Shravasti to Pratish-thana, the north to south-east route from Shravasti to Rajagriha, and the east to west route which followed the river valleys of the north. The desert of Rajasthan was generally avoided. The port of Bharukachchha (modern Broach) continued to be the main port for the western sea trade as it had been in earlier centuries when it was in communication with Baveru (Babylon).

Overland trade with western Asia and the Hellenic world went through the cities of the north-west, primarily Taxila. The Mauryans had built a Royal Highway from Taxila to Patali-putra, a road which was rebuilt (approximating fairly closely to the original) throughout the centuries and which today sur-vives as the Grand Trunk Road. Pataliputra was connected by road with Tamluk in the Ganges delta, the chief port for Burma, the east coast of India, and Ceylon. Land routes to the south developed after the Mauryan period when trade de-mands were intensified. They continued to follow the river valleys and the coast, since the mountainous nature of the Dec-can plateau did not encourage east–west communication, except along rivers such as the Godavari and the Krishna. The plateau was still thickly wooded and therefore unsafe as compared with the clearings and settlements along the river valleys. Gaps and breaks in the mountains were of course utilized, as in the case of the route from the Malabar coast on the west, through the Coimbatore gap, across the Kaveri plain to the east-coast trading station at Arikamedu near Pondicherry.

The most widely-used highway westwards was from Taxila to Kabul, from where roads branched off in various directions. The northern route was via Bactria, the Oxus, the Caspian Sea, and the Caucasus to the Black Sea. A more southerly route went from Kandahar and Herat to Ecbatana (later Hamadan) and from there it was linked to the ports on the eastern Mediterranean. Another important highway connected Kandahar with Persepolis and Susa. Even further to the south was the road via the Persian Gulf and the Tigris to Seleucia. Ships travelling to western ports either followed the coast up the Persian Gulf to Babylon, or travelled across the Arabian Sea to Aden or Socotra, both of which had port facilities, and from there the voyage was continued up the Red Sea. Goods were landed at Suez or a point close to modern Suez and were sent overland to Alexandria, which was an entrepôt of the Mediterranean world. There appears to have been a more frequently used route overland to the Nile from Berenice and Myos Hormus (on the Red Sea), whence goods were taken downstream to Alexandria.

The coastal route from India to western Asia was both tedious and costly. The Arabs were the first to make use of the monsoon* winds which blew in a north-eastward direction across the Arabian Sea in summer. These winds made mid-ocean travelling speedier than the coastal route. In the mid-first century B.C. other traders from the Mediterranean world became aware of these winds and realized their usefulness. Classical tradition has it that the use of these winds for navigation was 'discovered' by Hippalus. But there was little to discover, since the Arabs knew of it earlier. Ships sailing from the Red Sea ports would wait for the south-west monsoon to start and would then set sail. The returning monsoon from across India in the winter would bring the ships back.

Owing to the trade between India and western Asia, there was much cultural contact with Afghanistan at this time. Eastern Afghanistan was regarded politically and culturally as a part of north-western India. Central Asia had also been opened to trade with routes traversing the oases and valleys of central Asia; one of these routes was later to become famous as the Old Silk Route. Indian traders were establishing trading stations and merchant colonies in places such as Kashgar, Yarkand, Khotan, Miran, Kuchi, Qara-shahr, and Turfan, remote regions which were soon to become opened up not only by Indian merchants but also by Buddhist missionaries. As a result of this activity in cen-

*Monsoon – Arab. *mauzim* = season.

tral Asia, communication with China improved. The Kushana
kings were in a sense a link between India and China, and Buddhist missionary activities made the connexions even closer. Trade
had already laid a foundation for this closeness with the import
of Chinese silk into India. Traders from Roman territories ventured occasionally as far as the Gobi desert, but Indian traders
were quick to see the advantage of being middlemen in a Sino-
Roman luxury trade. Trade with Rome was also partly responsible for spurring Indian interest in trade with south-east Asia.
Land routes via Burma and Assam were attempted but the sea
route was found more convenient. The risks were great, as is
evident from the stories which found their way into anthologies
of tales relating to the adventures of merchants in the Golden
Isles (Java, Sumatra, and Bali). But the great profits on the spices
sold to the Romans compensated for the hazards. Not surprisingly, therefore, it was the mercantile community of the west and
the south coasts of India who first ventured eastwards.

THE RISE OF THE MERCANTILE COMMUNITY

c. 200 B.C.–A.D. 300

THE political events described in the previous chapter were bewildering, yet beneath this apparent confusion there was one factor which gave continuity and consistency to this period – and that was trade. Through all the political vicissitudes of the Shungas, Satavahanas, Indo-Greeks, Shakas, Kushanas, Cheras, and Cholas, the merchant continued to grow from strength to strength. The Mauryan empire had opened up the sub-continent by building roads and attempting to develop a uniform system of administration. The occupation of north-western India by non-Indian peoples was advantageous to the merchant, since it led to trade with regions which had as yet been untapped. The Indo-Greek kings encouraged contact with western Asia and the Mediterranean world. The Shakas, Parthians, and Kushanas brought central Asia into the orbit of the Indian merchant and this in turn led to trade with China. The Roman demand for spices and similar luxuries took Indian traders to south-east Asia and brought Roman traders to southern and western India. Through all India the merchant community prospered, as is evident from inscriptions, from their donations to charities, and from the literature of the time. Not surprisingly, the religions supported by the merchants, Buddhism and Jainism, saw their heyday during these centuries. However, this is not to suggest that economic activity was limited to trade, or that agriculture had decreased; the latter continued to yield revenue. But the boom in mercantile activity had brought those associated with commerce to the fore.

In this connexion, the guilds, continuing from the Mauryan period, became an even more important factor in urban life, both in organizing production and in shaping public opinion. The vast majority of artisans joined the guilds, since it was difficult for them to compete as individuals against the guilds, which in addition offered social status and a degree of general security. With the increasing demand for particular commodities and the consequent necessity to raise their output, some guilds began to employ hired labour and slaves. The guilds had to be registered in the locality where they functioned and had to obtain permission from the local authorities to change their location. Artisans of no matter what craft could constitute a guild, and most crafts had their guilds, since these offered great advantages. Leading guilds were those of the potters, metal-workers, and carpenters. Their size can be gauged from the fact that even at an earlier period one wealthy potter named Saddalaputta had owned five hundred potter's workshops. In addition, he had organized his own distribution and owned a large number of boats which took the pottery from the workshops to the various ports on the Ganges. With an increase in commerce, the major guilds were even larger.

The guilds fixed rules of work and the quality of the finished product and its price to safeguard both the artisan and the customer. The guild also controlled the prices of manufactured articles, and these either depended on the quality of the work or were calculated according to a fixed scale. The behaviour of guild members was controlled through a guild court. Customary usage of the guild (*shreni-dharma*) had the force of law. That the guild also intervened in the private lives of its members is clear from the regulation that, if a married woman wished to join the Buddhist Order as a nun, she had to obtain not only permission from her husband but also from the guild to which he belonged.

The guild was kept well supplied in numbers by its association with caste : the children of a particular caste or sub-caste followed the same trade, and, since their father's trade was often the only one open to them, the guild could always depend on a regular number through the generations. The threat to the guild came in periods of transition when the occupation followed by a sub-caste underwent a change.

Apart from the guild there were other workers' bodies, such as workers' co-operatives. These generally included artisans and various crafts associated with a particular enterprise. Thus architecture – city building or temple building – was entrusted to co-operatives which had as their members specialized workers such as architects, engineers, brick-layers, and the like.

Excavations have led to the discovery of a number of seals

stamped with the emblems of guilds and corporations. The banners and insignia of the guilds were carried in procession on festive occasions. Insignia were also a means of advertising the guild: as in part were the munificent donations which many of the guilds made to religious institutions and charitable causes during this period. A guild of corn dealers donated a beautifully sculpted cave to the Buddhists; the ivory-workers' guild at Vidisa carved the stone sculpture on the gateways and railings surrounding the *stupa* at Sanchi; guilds of gold- and silversmiths were prolific in their gifts. One of the cave inscriptions at Nasik, inscribed at the order of a Shaka ruler, records the endowment to a temple for which a large sum of money was invested with a guild of weavers, the interest from which sum provided the endowment.

In the year 42, in the month Vesakha, Ushavadatta son of Dinika and son-in-law of king Nahapana, the Kshaharata Kshatrapa, has bestowed this cave on the Sangha generally; he has also given a perpetual endowment, three thousand – 3,000 *kahapanas* which, for the members of the Sangha of any sect and any origin dwelling in this cave, will serve as cloth money and money for outside life; and those *kahapanas* have been invested in guilds dwelling in Govardhana – 2,000 in a weavers guild, interest one *pratika* (monthly) for the hundred and 1,000 in another weavers guild, interest ¾ of a *padika* (monthly) for the hundred, and those *kahapanas* are not to be repaid, their interest only to be enjoyed. Out of them, the two thousand, 2,000 at one *pratika* per cent are the cloth money; out of them to every one of the twenty monks who keep the *vassa* (the rainy season when monks remained at the monastery) in my cave, a cloth money of twelve *kahapanas*. As to the thousand which has been invested at an interest of ¾ of a *pratika* per cent, out of them the money for Kushana. And at the village of Chinkalapandra in the Kapura district have been given eight thousand – 8,000 – stems of coconut trees, and all this has been proclaimed and registered at the town hall, at the record office, according to custom. . . .[1]

Two interesting points emerge from the cave inscription at Nasik quoted above. The first concerns the political importance of guilds. Although guild leaders were powerful figures in urban life, there is little sign of a desire to obtain political influence, politics being regarded as the prerogative of the king. A possible explanation for this is that the king appears to have had financial interests in the guilds. Investments in a commercial enterprise brought large returns, larger perhaps than the revenue from a piece of land of comparable value. Royalty invested its money in commercial activities and therefore had an interest in ensuring the well-being of the guild. Royal support in a tangible form and the lack of opposition from the king may have dulled the edge of political ambition amongst the guild leaders. Furthermore, the seizing of political power on the part of a given guild would require that it first ally itself with other guilds in order to obtain their loyalty, without which no political ambitions were likely to be achieved. Such cooperation may have been effectively prevented by caste rules, such as that forbidding eating together, which was an effective barrier between guilds of different caste.

Another fact which emerges from the inscription is that the guild could act as a banker, financier, and trustee as well. Generally, however, these functions were carried out by a different category of merchants, known as the *sreshthins* or financiers, the descendants of whom are the present day *seths* of north India and the *chettis* or *chettiyars* of south India. Banking was not a full time occupation and the *sreshthin* often had other interests as well. As a profession banking became more widespread with the establishment of a money economy, cowri-shells or the barter system being hardly conducive to investment. The post-Mauryan centuries saw a great spurt in the minting of coins. The kings of the north-west imitated Greek and Iranian coin-types, others issued local coins which were vastly superior to the punch-marked coins of the Mauryas. Foreign currencies such as the *denarii* of the Romans circulated freely. The Roman gold coins found in south India are believed to have been used as bullion. Usury was an accepted part of banking and the general rate of interest continued to be fifteen per cent. Money lent for sea trade often called for a higher rate of interest. One of the more authoritative writers of the time suggests that the rate of interest should vary according to the caste of the man to whom money is lent, i.e. the upper castes paying a smaller rate than the lower castes. The obvious reasoning behind this was that it was more difficult for the lower and economically poorer class to pay off debts. Indebtedness led to a lack of mobility and an attitude of submission.

The increasing use of money did not however drive out the

barter systems, which continued in use particularly in rural areas. In the Chola kingdom, for instance, despite the circulation of Roman gold coins and other smaller coinage in copper, paddy remained the unit of exchange for many centuries. In other parts of the country a large variety of coins were used in towns; these were of gold (*nishka, suvarna,* and *pala*), silver (*shatamana*), copper (*kakini*), and lead. The most commonly used coin was the *karshapana*, in all four metals. With expansion of commercial enterprise, weights and measures became increasingly detailed and complex.

In the main, industry was organized in areas where raw materials were readily found; or where a tradition of a particular craft existed, and artisans would gather there from surrounding areas. This was specially so with the spinning and weaving of cotton and silk. Women were frequently employed in the preparation of cotton textiles, where the aim was to produce cotton 'as fine as the slough of a snake and in which the yarn cannot be seen'. Textiles of various kinds were locally produced in every region and found a ready market throughout the country. Magadha continued to supply large quantities of iron, though other metals were more widely distributed. Copper was mined in Rajasthan, the Deccan, and the foothills of the Himalayas. The Himalayan slopes also supplied the much-used musk and saffron. The Salt Range of the Punjab was the main source of salt. South India provided spices, gold, precious stones, and sandalwood.

The southern kingdoms were familiar with large-scale maritime trade and their literature refers to harbours, docks, lighthouses, custom offices, and all the usual buildings associated with ports. Whereas, on the whole, Indians preferred to allow sailors of other nations to transport their goods, the Cholas retained a large share in the carrying trade of the Indian Ocean. They built a variety of ships, including light coastal vessels, large ships built of single logs tied together, and yet larger ones for long distance voyages to Malaya and to south-east Asia. According to Pliny the largest Indian ship was seventy-five tons, but other sources give bigger estimates. Ships depicted in paintings and sculpture do not suggest very large vessels, but these may represent only the coastal ships. Ships holding three, five, or even seven hundred passengers are frequently mentioned in literary sources. Ships arriving at Broach were received by pilot boats and conducted each into a separate berth at the docks.

The most profitable of the overseas trade was the Roman trade with south India. Yavana merchants (i.e. merchants from western Asia and the Mediterranean) had trading establishments both in the Satavahana kingdoms and in those of the far south. Another group of affluent merchants were the descendants of the Indo-Greeks and Shakas of the north and west whose presence is known from the donative inscriptions carved at various places on the west coast. Early Tamil literature describes Yavana ships arriving with their cargoes at the city of Kaveripattinam, the Yavana section of which city overflows with prosperity. Some of the Tamil kings kept Yavana bodyguards, which would suggest that the latter were regarded as both strange and special.

The *Periplus Maris Erythreae*, a maritime geography of the east–west trade, written in about the first century A.D., gives details of the commodities carried and the routes taken by traders and ships. The hinterland of Ethiopia provided African ivory and gold and was also a market for Indian muslin. The inland town of Petra in what is now Jordan linked the Red Sea routes with west Asian routes, as indeed did many of the coastal towns of Arabia. Dioscorides was the island of Socotra, an important port of exchange where Indian vessels brought rice, wheat, textiles, and female slaves, and took away tortoise-shell. Towns on the southern shores of the Persian Gulf received Indian copper, sandalwood, teak, and ebony, and sent to India pearls, purple dye, textiles, wine, dates, gold, and slaves. Some of these ports may well have been used long before by the Indus valley people in their trade with Sumer. Barbaricum on the Indus delta was another much frequented port, importing linen, topaz, coral, storax (a resin used for incense), frankincense, glass, silver, gold-plate, and wine; exporting a great variety of spices, turquoise, lapis-lazuli, muslin, silk yarn, and indigo. Barygaza (modern Broach), known as Bharukachchha in Indian sources, was the oldest and largest entrepôt on the west coast of India, and handled the bulk of the trade with western Asia. It imported an assortment of cargo including wine (Italian, Greek, and Arab) copper, tin, lead, coral, topaz, guaze, storax, sweet clover, glass, realgar (a species of resin), antimony, gold and silver coin, and various medicinal ointments. Presents were also sent to the local rulers, such as gold and silver trinkets, singing boys, maidens, and wines and textiles of a superior quality. Exports from Barygaza consisted of the usual variety of spices, spikenard, malabathrum (used in preparing ointments), diamonds, sapphires, and precious stones and tortoise-shell. Some of these ports have been located through archaeological surveys. The route for trade then proceeds round the tip of the peninsula and up the coast, where of all the ports mentioned there we have now fairly detailed knowledge of one – Arikamedu (known to the *Periplus* as Padouke), where extensive excavations in 1945 uncovered a sizeable Roman settlement which was a trading station, adjoining which was a port.

Arikamedu was therefore more than just a port of call on the route to Malaya and China; for, not only were Indian goods bought and shipped from here, but certain commodities such as muslin were manufactured at Arikamedu, presumably to Roman taste and specifications, and then shipped back to Rome. Judging from the type of Roman pottery, beads, glass, and terracotta finds it would seem that the Romans were using Arikamedu from the first century B.C. to the early second century A.D. The Romans paid for the goods mainly in gold currency. The frequency of hoards of Roman coins found in the Deccan and south India indicate the volume of this trade. Most of the coins are of Augustus and Tiberius, the debased coins of Nero not being thought worth hoarding. Many of the coins are marked with a bar, which perhaps prevented their being put into circulation and indicating that they were used as bullion. It is not surprising that Pliny complained of the Indian trade being a serious drain on the national income of Rome, when 550 million sesterces went to India each year. Imports from India were largely luxury articles – spices, jewels, textiles, and amusing animals (apes, parrots, and peacocks) – for the wealthy Roman and his family. In mercantilist terms this could hardly be described as a favourable trade for Rome.

Most of the urban centres of the south were ports which prospered on this trade, such as Kaverippattinam. An early Tamil poem describes the town as being divided into two sections by a

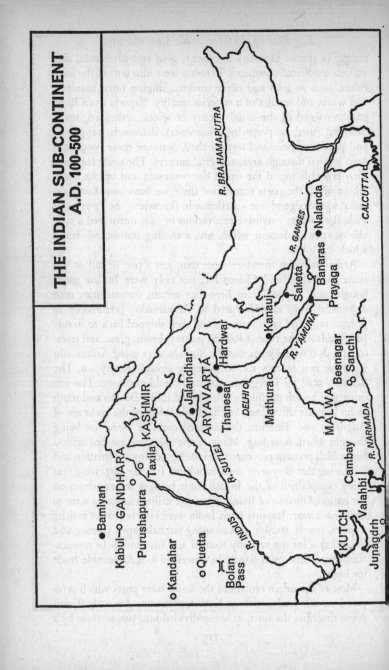

THE INDIAN SUB-CONTINENT
A.D. 100–500

R. BRAHAMAPUTRA

R. GANGES

R. YAMUNA

R. NARMADA

R. SUTLEJ

R. INDUS

Bamiyan
Kabul GANDHARA
Purushapura
Taxila
KASHMIR
Kandahar
Quetta
Bolan
Pass
Jalandhar
Thanesar
ARYAVARTA
DELHI
Hardwar
Kanauj
Saketa
Nalanda
Banaras
Prayaga
Mathura
Besnagar
Sanchi
MALWA
Cambay
KUTCH
Valabhi
Junagdrh
CALCUTTA

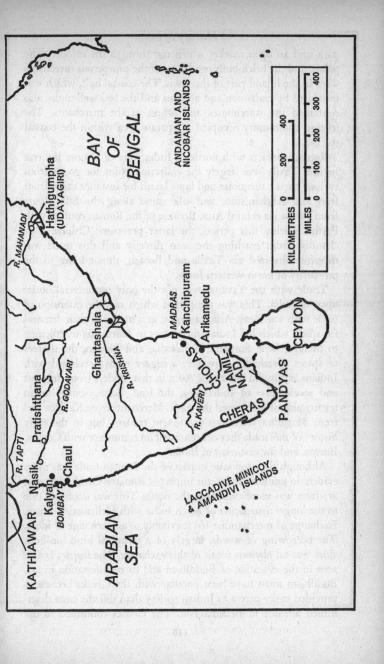

park and an open market which ran through the middle. The palace and the brick-built residences of the prosperous merchants were in the inland part of the town. The coastal half, which was inhabited by craftsmen and artisans and the less well-to-do, also contained the warehouses and offices of the merchants. The foreign community occupied a separate area within the coastal section.

Roman contacts with northern India were of a more indirect nature. Taxila was largely the collection point for goods from various parts : turquoise and lapis lazuli for instance came from Iran and Afghanistan, and silk came along the Silk Route from China via central Asia. Because of the Roman conflict with Parthia during this period, the latter prevented Chinese merchandise from reaching the west directly and this trade was therefore diverted via Taxila and Broach, thus adding to the prosperity of north-western India.

Trade with the Yavanas was not the only commercial outlet open to India. This was the period which saw the extension of trade with south-east Asia, caused at first by the Roman demand for spices which led Indian merchants to venture as middlemen to Malaya, Java, Sumatra, Cambodia, and Borneo, the sources of spices. Gradually, however, a bigger trade developed with Indians settling in south-east Asia; in this, traders from the west and south coast of India took the lead. Later, south Indian traders almost dominated the trade. Merchants from Kalinga and from Magadha were also prominent traders, but in the early history of this trade they concentrated on commerce with Ceylon, Burma, and the east coast of India.

Although the economic impact of the Roman trade was more evident in southern India, the impact of Romano-Greek ideas and artefacts was more evident in the north. This was doubtless due to the longer association of north India with Hellenistic culture. Exchange of merchandise led inevitably to an exchange of ideas. The borrowing of words, largely of a technical kind, on both sides was an obvious result of this exchange. The impact is also seen in the evolution of Buddhism and its manifestation in art. Buddhism must have been popular with the Greeks because it provided easier access to Indian society than did the caste-determined attitude of Brahmanism. The Greeks continued to use

Greek in addition to the local Indian language, since inscriptions in Greek occur on coins in the north-west. It has been suggested in the past that Greek drama led to the rise of classical drama in India, but this theory has now been rejected both by the discovery of early Indian plays which provide the clue to the origin of Indian drama and by the fact that plays in Sanskrit are totally different in sentiment from those in Greek. Indian folk-tales and fables travelled westwards and appeared in European literature under various guises. *Chaturanga*, chess named after the four traditional wings of the Indian army and played by four players, began to interest the Persians towards the end of this period.

One of the enduring results of this contact was the fairly detailed reference to India in the various works of the Mediterranean world, such as Strabo's *Geography*, Arrian's *Indika*, Pliny the Elder's *Natural History*, the *Periplus Maris Erythreae*, and Ptolemy's *Geography*. India had come to occupy an important position in the world as known to the Greco-Romans. The most direct and visible influence, however, was in the realm of art, with the emergence of the hybrid Indian–Greek style of Gandhara art, which during these centuries was the major artistic expression in Afghanistan and the north-west of India. Gandhara art originated from the Greco-Roman style of Alexandria, from where sculpture in bronze and stucco travelled along the west Asian trade routes. The arrival of Alexandrine art in north India coincided with the introduction of the multiplicity of saints and heavens in Buddhist theology, which lent themselves ideally to sculpture and painting.

The impact of Indian ideas in western Asia can also be traced to this period. In particular the doctrines of the Manichaeans, Gnostics, and Neo-Platonists constitute an interesting study from this point of view. Certain aspects of the life of Christ (the supernatural birth and the temptation by the Devil) are so closely parallel to events in the legends of the life of the Buddha that it is difficult to avoid suspecting some indirect borrowing. The observances of the Essenes (to which sect Christ is said to have originally belonged according to some theories), also indicate a knowledge of Indian religious belief and practice in the Mediterranean world. The interaction was of course two sided, as is clear for instance from the influence of Zoroastrianism on Buddhism.

Other aspects of Indian religion became fashionable in the west, among them asceticism (Paul of Alexandria and St Anthony), relic-worship, and the use of the rosary.

A number of Indian kingdoms sent embassies to Rome. Perhaps the best known was the one which sailed from Broach in about 25 B.C. and included a strange assortment of men and animals – tigers, pheasants, snakes, tortoises, a monk, and an armless boy who could shoot arrows with his toes – which were all regarded as appropriate for the Roman emperor. It took the mission four years to reach Rome and the animals were presented to Augustus about 21 B.C.

Communication with the west was not by any means the only one which held exciting possibilities, for these were the centuries which saw a growth in Sino-Indian relations and the introduction of Indian culture to south-east Asia : all of which began through trade. During the second and third centuries B.C. some goods of Chinese origin were in use in India whose names clearly derive from Chinese : e.g., Chinese cloth, *china patta*, and bamboo, *kichaka*, which is related to the Chinese *ki-chok*. Contact of a more sustained nature began in A.D. 65 with the first Buddhist missionaries who arrived in China and established themselves at the famous White Horse Monastery at Lo-Yang. In the process the inhabitants of the central Asian oases at which the missionaries halted were converted to Buddhism and monasteries grew up at places such as Yarkand, Khotan, Kashgar, Tashkend, Turfan, Miran, Kuchi, Qara-shahr and Tun-Huang. Manuscripts, paintings, and ritual objects were brought from India and for many centuries these monasteries maintained a close and lively interest in the development of Buddhism both in China and in India. In fact, much of the more significant knowledge of later Buddhist history has come from excavations at these sites. By the third century A.D. Chinese Buddhists were travelling to central Asia to study Buddhism.

Voyages to south-east Asian ports became more regular with the increasing contact with China, since the sea route to China touched these ports. Legends about the origin of kingdoms in south-east Asia often trace the story back to Indian princes and merchants. The Kalingans are said to have colonized the Irrawady delta in Burma, and various parts of Java. An Indian brahman, Kaundinya, who married a Cambodian princess, is remembered for having introduced Indian culture to Cambodia. Indian literature is replete with the adventures, both weird and fantastic, of Indian travellers in these parts.

There were by now quite considerable numbers of strangers in the port towns and trade centres of the sub-continent, though many of these people had become Indianized in habits and behaviour. The assimilation of these into a caste-based society was a problem for the social theorists. Social laws were becoming rigid and the theories of Manu, the patriarch who is the traditional author of the *Manava Dharmashastra* or Law Code, written sometime during the first two centuries A.D., were now quoted as the authority on social laws. Theoretically, the four castes were precisely and clearly defined and rules pertaining to their lawful activities and functions dominated all social activity. Yet in practice there were many discrepancies.

Conversion to Hinduism was technically difficult because of the interconnexion of caste and Hinduism. A large non-Hindu group could be gradually assimilated through its becoming a sub-caste, but the conversion of a single individual would create the problem of providing him with an appropriate caste and caste depended on birth. It was therefore easier for the Greeks, Kushanas, and Shakas to become Buddhists, as many did. As Buddhism at that time was in the ascendant its prestige made the adjustment of the newly converted much easier. Brahman orthodoxy had also to come to terms with people of non-Indo-Aryan origin, such as the Greeks and the Shakas, who had political power and could not therefore be treated as outcastes. The 'fallen *kshatriya*' status conferred on them was a shrewd manoeuvre. The presence in India of foreigners who achieved positions of political and economic importance created considerable social problems and must have further challenged the theoretical structure of caste. Doubtless the opportunity was not missed by those in an inferior caste to try and move up the scale by associating with the foreigners. Expansion in trade and commerce also meant an increase in guilds and the employment of many more artisans. The latter were largely drawn from the *shudra* caste, some of whom in changing their occupation and location probably improved their caste status.

These problems were more prevalent in the north, which was still the stronghold of Aryan culture. Elsewhere the process of Aryanization – the imposing of Sanskrit and the Aryan cultural pattern – had to be consciously fostered, as in the case of the Satavahana kings who pursued an Aryanizing policy through the use of Sanskrit and Prakrit rather than the local dialect (which was contemptuously described as 'goblin language'), and by instituting Vedic ceremonial. Still further south it was the proselytizing missions of Jainism and Buddhism which brought Aryanization with them.

Apart from their role in the economy, the guilds provided education as well, though not 'formal' education, which remained in the hands of the brahmans and the monks. The guilds, by restricting membership to artisans of a particular craft, were centres for technical education. Knowledge of mining, metallurgy, weaving, dyeing, carpentry, etc., was maintained and improved upon by the relevant guild. The spectacular progress achieved in this way is visible in the coins which have survived, in the pillars of the Mauryan and later periods when stone cutting and polishing reached a state of perfection, and even in something as simple as the northern black polished ware, which defies reproduction. Engineering skill in the building of dams and irrigation tanks is evident from the remains of these and from the inscriptions relating to them. Geometry began as a practical aid in the building of altars and sacrificial structures but slowly came to be applied to more complex architecture. The true arch, although it was known, was not commonly used in building, most of which continued to follow the constructional methods of wooden buildings. Nor did religious edifices at this stage provide much scope for constructional skill, since the Buddhists contented themselves with tumuli surrounded by gateways and railings, or else caves of a simple kind cut into hillsides.

Two of the sciences which benefited directly from familiarity with other parts of the world were astronomy and medicine. Deep-sea navigation required a reliable study of the stars, and no doubt mercantile patronage in the form of finance was forthcoming for this study, and communication with western Asia led to a fruitful exchange of knowledge in this field. The Indian medical system was based on the theory of the three humours – air, bile, and phlegm – the correct balance of these resulting in a healthy body. Medical encyclopedias and pharmacopeas were composed at this time, the most famous being that of Charaka, a contemporary of the king Kanishka, and another of a slightly later date, that of Sushruta. Evidently, Indian herbal knowledge had reached the western world, since the Greek botanist Theophrastus gives details of the medicinal use of various plants and herbs from India in his *History of Plants*. The systematic analysis of language had had a large and devoted following culminating in the great work of Panini on Sanskrit. Patanjali was the grammarian of this period whose commentary, *Mahabhashya*, is not only an impressive study of syntax and the evolution of words, but also provides, incidentally, useful material on the history of the time. Works on drama and versification written during these centuries have survived and are consulted to this day.

Formal education reflected these interests with considerable emphasis on grammar and study of the Vedic texts. Education was treated as the prerogative of the upper castes; the brahmans had access to all knowledge, the *kshatriyas* and *vaishyas* were expected to reconcile themselves to limited knowledge. The possibility of education for the *shudra* existed, but reference to it is extremely infrequent, as is reference to the education of women. Gradually, the educational system split into theoretical knowledge confined to the brahmans (and those whom they wished to teach), and practical and technical knowledge, which remained the preserve of the professionals. Buddhist monasteries managed to steer a middle course, their definition of formal education comprising both grammar and medicine, and their approach being generally less orthodox than that of the brahmans.

During this period there was much activity in the writing of Law Books (*Dharmashastras*). The rising importance of the *vaishyas* and the creation of new sub-castes, owing to the more liberal atmosphere of urban life, must doubtless have caused concern to the upholders of traditional social law and usage, and the time had come when social relationships had to be precisely defined. Not surprisingly the most important of Law Books reiterate at every step that the brahman is inherently superior in every way to other members of society and is to be shown the utmost respect, even by the wealthy *vaishyas*.

Literary output was not restricted to Law Books and Grammars, poetry and drama being extremely popular. Contemporary *kavya* (poetry) has survived in Tamil, the outstanding poem being *Shilappadigaram* (The Jewelled Anklet). It is set in the city of Kaverippattinam. Kovalan, a young, wealthy merchant falls in love with a royal courtesan and neglects his wife, who is devoted to him. The poem ends tragically with the death of all three, but husband and wife are reunited in heaven. A second poem, *Manimegalai*, was written as a continuation of the first, the heroine being the daughter of Kovalan and the courtesan, and an ardent Buddhist. Drama (*nataka*) has survived in the Sanskrit plays of Ashvaghosha and Bhasa. No two playwrights could have been more different. Manuscripts of Ashvaghosha's plays originally written in the first century A.D. were found in a monastery in Turfan (central Asia). Both plays deal with Buddhist themes, one of them being a dramatized version of the life of the Buddha. Ashvaghosha faithfully followed the rules laid down by Bharata in his 'Study of Dramatic Arts', *Natyashastra* (the *Natyashastra* having a position in Sanskrit literature similar to Aristotle's *Poetics*). But Bhasa writing a couple of centuries later has little use for these rules. Bhasa's plays are either based on incidents from the epics, the *Mahabharata* and the *Ramayana*, or are historical romances most of which depict the amorous exploits of king Udayin of Avanti. Bhasa wrote for the limited audience of the court circle, whereas Ashvaghosha's plays could well have been performed at religious assemblies, before a wider audience.

Almost the entire artistic expression of this age, whether architecture or sculpture, centred on Buddhism, and most of it was made possible through the patronage of wealthy merchants, guilds, and royal donations. Remains of religious architecture are the Buddhist *stupas* and the Buddhist cave-temples. The *stupa*, which traces its origin to pre-Buddhist burial mounds, was a hemispherical dome or mound built over a sacred relic either of the Buddha himself or of a sanctified monk or saint or a sacred text. The relic was generally kept in a casket in a smaller chamber in the centre of the base of the *stupa*. Encircling the *stupa* was a fenced path. At the four points of the compass there was a break in the railing with a gateway which gave the sculptor scope to show his skill. Of the *stupa* railings which have survived the earliest is the one at Bharhut (now dismantled and lodged in a museum at Calcutta), which dates to the second century B.C. The better known *stupa* at Sanchi was renovated and enlarged during this period.

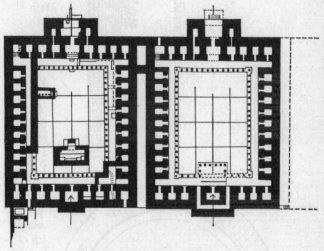

1. Plan of a Buddhist Monastery

The *stupa* itself did not offer much scope for an architect. The gateways were based on wooden prototypes used in villages and towns, and the adherence to the themes of wooden architecture was carried through into cave-temples as well. Caves were dug in hill-sides and were used as shrines or temples by monks. Where the excavation of a cave was accompanied by a generous donation from a patron ambitious attempts were made to simulate in a series of caves the entire complex of *stupa* – worshipping-hall (*chaitya*)* – monastery (*vihara*) as it had been established in

---

* The use of the word *chaitya* would associate this with the pre-Buddhist sacred enclosures, which were a regular part of the ritual of worship in the early republics.

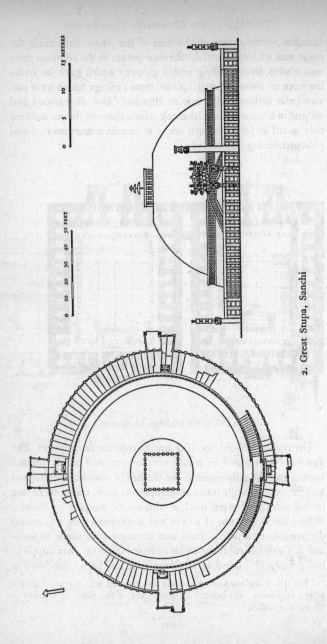

2. Great Stupa, Sanchi

structural, free-standing buildings. Thus the more elaborate caves, such as those in the western Deccan, especially at Karle, consist of a fairly complicated structure all cut into the rock. The cave is entered through a rectangular entrance, which leads into the hall of worship, again rectangular but with an apse at one end which contains a *stupa* in miniature. There are a series of cells cut into the hill-side on both sides of the cave, which were occupied by the monks. The ceiling of the Karle hall is in imitation of a barrel vault with wooden ribs, the representation of ribs here being totally irrelevant and a waste of effort. Buddhist cave-temples more elaborate in plan and richer in sculpture

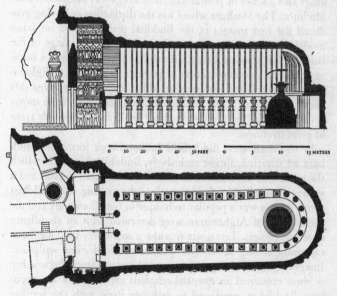

3. Chaitya hall at Karle: plan and elevation

than the early ones were also cut at the now famous sites at Ellora and Ajanta, and at the former site the tradition extended in later centuries to the Hindus as well. The Jainas also had cave-temples, but theirs were not nearly as elaborate as those of the Buddhists. Cave-temples were complete structures in themselves and did not permit of much evolution in architectural style.

Sculpture during this period was chiefly an adjunct of architecture, being essentially ornamental on the gateways and railings of the *stupas* and entrances to *chaityas*. The earlier sculptors were not familiar with working in stone and were more at home in the softer media of wood and ivory. But by the second century A.D. the sculptures at Amaravati and the Deccan caves show a mastery of stone sculpture. Devotees of Jainism patronized a school of free-standing sculpture centred on Mathura, which used the beautiful red sandstone found locally. The Mathura school, as it came to be called, also received the patronage of the Kushana kings and a series of portraits of these kings was discovered near Mathura. The Mathura school has the distinction of having produced the first images of the Buddha, perhaps based on Jaina models. In the earlier *stupa* sculptures there is no image of the Buddha, his presence being indicated by symbols such as a horse to represent the renunciation of princely life, a tree (enlightenment), a wheel (the first sermon which he preached), *stupa* (his death and *nirvana*). The Mathura sculpture and that of the *stupas* is distinguished by a full and earthly quality with a *joie de vivre* of great liveliness.

In the north-west the hybrid Indian–Greek forms of Gandhara art depicted, almost exclusively, Buddhist themes, in which the mother of the Buddha resembled an Athenian matron and a variety of Apollo-like faces went into the making of a Buddhist scene. Stucco was a popular technique in Gandharan art and the monasteries of Afghanistan were decorated with an abundance of stucco images. Terracotta was also a commonly used medium, especially among those who could not afford stone sculpture. Images of the mother goddess were abundant, since the worship of these remained an essential religious expression of the populace. Buddhism continued to associate itself with the fertility cult and other popular religious cults, as is evident from the symbolic importance of the *stupa* and the brackets with female figures sculpted on the gateways at Sanchi, which are in fact sophisticated mother goddess images.* Terracotta figures were also used as decoration in homes and as toys. They provide a fascinating glimpse of the dress and fashions of the time.

* The importance given to the goddess Hariti is another example.

Buddhism hovers in the background of most activities in this period, and it enjoined the support of the rich and powerful elements. It is not to be wondered at, therefore, that monasteries were richly endowed, that huge *stupas* were built, and that the Buddhist Order became affluent and respected. Some of the monasteries had such large endowments that they had to employ slaves and hired labour, the monks alone not being able to cope with the work. Gone were the days when the Buddhist monks lived entirely on the alms which they collected in the morning hours, for now they ate regular meals in vast monastic refectories. Monasteries were built either adjoining a town or else on some beautiful and secluded hill-side far removed from the clamour of cities. Secluded monasteries were sufficiently well endowed to enable the monks to live comfortably. The Buddhist Order thus tended to move away from the common people and isolate itself, which in turn diminished much of its religious strength, a development which one suspects the Buddha would not have found acceptable. Improvement in communications led to an increase in pilgrimages which in turn led to the spread of new ideas. Buddhism had become very active in sending missions to various parts of the sub-continent and outside, and, in the process of proselytizing, Buddhism also began to receive new ideas. This inevitably led to re-interpretations of the original doctrine, until finally there were major differences of opinion and the religion was split into two main sects. This schism, as well as the growing tendency of the Buddhist clergy to live off the affluent section of society, bred the seeds of decay in Buddhism.

Arguments over the real meaning of the original teaching of the Buddha began, as is generally the case, soon after the death of the founder. Attempts were made to eliminate or at least modify these differences by a series of Councils discussing the various points of view, similar to the Councils of the Catholic Church held for much the same reason. The Theravada sect which had its centre at Kaushambi and which collected the teachings of the Buddha into the Pali Canon (as it came to be called since it was written in Pali) was the oldest and most orthodox. The Sarvastivada sect, which originated at Mathura, spread northwards and finally established itself in central Asia collating material in Sanskrit. A number of changes had been introduced by all these sects, which would have been rejected by the founder. For instance, the Buddha had always opposed any tendency among his followers to deify him, yet, by the first century A.D., his image was carved in stone and worshipped as that of a god; the concept of the *bodhisattva*, also current by this time, was based on the idea that the *bodhisattva* is one who works for the good of humankind in an utterly unselfish manner and is willing to forego *nirvana* until such time as his work is completed. Another group of Buddhists interpreted the *bodhisattva* as being a previous incarnation of the Buddha, thus emphasizing the belief that one could accumulate merit through successive births. Furthermore, merit could also be transferred from one person to another by a pious act in the name of the person to whom this transference was made. Thus, wealthy merchants could acquire their credit of merit by donating caves to the Buddhist Order. (The analogy with the accumulation and transference of capital can hardly be overlooked.) The later *bodhisattva* doctrine was a significant departure from the original doctrine of Buddhism and it sharpened the cleavage amongst the Buddhists. At the Fourth Buddhist Council held in Kashmir in the early second century A.D., the schism was recognized. The more orthodox Buddhists maintained that theirs was the original teaching of the Buddha and they were called the *Hinayana* sect or the followers of the Lesser Vehicle. Those that accepted the new ideas were called the *Mahayana* sect or the followers of the Greater Vehicle. Eventually, *Hinayana* Buddhism found its stronghold in Ceylon, Burma, and the countries of south-east Asia, whereas *Mahayana* Buddhism became the dominant sect in India, central Asia, Tibet, China, and Japan.

The *Mahayana* doctrine is believed to have originated in about the first century B.C. in Andhra, and was later expounded by a group of Buddhist philosophers. Among these the most outstanding was Nagarjuna, a convert to Buddhism from a northern Deccan brahman family. To describe him as the St Paul of Buddhism would not be inappropriate. He taught the doctrine of the Void (*Shunyata*), stating that everything which surrounds us is empty and that whatever we see is an illusion. The Void was in fact the *Nirvana* or end to the cycle of rebirth which every Buddhist was seeking. These ideas were further developed into a variety of schools of idealistic philosophy and logic. The Buddhists now intensified their studies in the field of philosophical speculation to grapple with brahmanical theories. *Mahayana* Buddhism lent itself to this activity admirably and for many centuries the debate was to continue between the *Mahayanist* and brahman philosophers.

There were other aspects of *Mahayana* Buddhism which appear to have had their origin outside India. Among these is the idea of the coming of the Maitreya Buddha to save the world, with which was connected the concept of 'the suffering saviour' – the *bodhisattva* who redeems humanity through his own suffering : evidently the new beliefs current in Palestine were known to the Buddhists by this time. *Mahayana* Buddhism also introduced into its concepts a complicated system of heavens superimposed one upon the other in which dwelt innumerable *bodhisattvas*.

Jainism was not without support during these centuries. The teaching of Mahavira also suffered a schism, the Jainas being divided into the Sky-clad (*Digambara*, i.e. naked) or orthodox sect and the White-clad (*Shvetambara*) or more liberal sect. They moved from Magadha westwards, settling first at Mathura and Ujjain and finally in Saurashtra on the west coast, where they have remained prosperous and eminent members of society. Another group moved southwards to Kalinga where they enjoyed, but only for a short time, royal patronage under Kharavela. In southern India their main concentration was in Mysore and the Tamil country. By and large Jainism, supported as it was by a similar section of society as Buddhism, underwent crises much the same as those of Buddhism, but nevertheless it remained more faithful to its original teachings. Jainism maintained itself as a 'parish religion' with more determination than Buddhism : and hence the number of its adherents has remained fairly constant.

Brahmanism did not remain unchanged through all these centuries, nor was it impervious to the effects of Buddhism and Jainism. Some of the Vedic gods had quietly passed into oblivion and some were being reborn as new gods with additional attributes. This was the time when the brahmanical religion assumed features which today are recognized as Hinduism. To call it Hinduism at this stage is perhaps an anachronism, since the term was given currency by the Arabs in the eighth century A.D. when referring to those who followed the prevailing religion of India, the worship of Shiva and Vishnu. But for the sake of convenience the religion may be described as Hinduism from this point onwards. Hinduism was not founded by a historical personage as a result of a revelation : it is not a revealed religion but grew and evolved from a variety of cults and beliefs, of which some had their foundations in Vedic religion, and others were popular cults which became associated with the more sophisticated religion, a concession which the priests had to make to popular worship.

The successful attack of the 'heretical sects' on Vedic sacrifices and gods strengthened the trend of monotheistic thinking in brahmanical teaching, which trend had originated in the philosophy of the *Upanishads* with its concept of the Absolute or the Universal Soul. This concept also resulted in the idea of the trinity of gods at this time, with Brahma as the Creator, Vishnu as the Preserver, and Shiva as the god who eventually destroys the universe when it is evil-ridden. This concept was associated with the cyclical conception of nature where creation, preservation, and destruction were seen as the natural order of things. Of the three gods, Vishnu and Shiva gained a vast following and through ensuing centuries the *Vaishnavas* and the *Shaivas* remained the two main sects of Hindu belief, each believing that its god represented the Absolute. Brahma receded into the background.

Brahma created the world, upon which Vishnu, who had been sleeping in the primeval ocean on the coils of the thousand-headed snake, awoke. Vishnu took up residence in the highest of heavens from where he observes the universe, and at times, when evil is rampant, he assumes various forms or incarnations and enters the world of men in order to save them from evil. He is believed to have manifested himself in nine incarnations so far, the most recent being that of the Buddha, who was included when Buddhism ceased being a formidable rival to Hinduism. The tenth and final incarnation has yet to come, and on this occasion he will come in the form of Kalkin riding a white horse, which suggests a connexion with the idea of the Messiah and the coming of the Maitreya Buddha in *Mahayana* Buddhism.

Shiva evolved from the Vedic god Rudra and the Tamil god Murugan. The worship of Shiva incorporated a number of fertility cults, such as those of the phallic emblem (*lingam*), the bull (*nandi*), etc., and was also associated with a number of fertility goddesses. The most important form of Shaivite worship, the worship of the *lingam*, became current about the beginning of the Christian era. The belief in a variety of cults at the popular level continued simultaneously with the emergence of these gods. Animals, trees, mountains, and rivers were held sacred. The cow was regularly worshipped. The bull and the snake were centres of fertility rites, as were a number of commonly found trees. The two mountains, Vaikuntha and Kailasha, were sacred to Vishnu and Shiva respectively. The waters of the Ganges, having descended from heaven, were believed to have a purifying effect. Together with these cults were included myriads of demi-gods and celestial beings of various ranks.

Another characteristic of Hinduism was a gradual shift in emphasis from ritual alone to the view that a completely personal relationship between God and the devotee was possible. The monotheistic concept of God, with either Vishnu or Shiva as its manifestation, was gaining strength. The relationship was one where God could bestow his grace (*prasada*) on the devotee, and the degree of devotion (*bhakti*) varied from person to person. This idea of personal devotion or *bhakti*, as it was commonly called, was to become the dynamic force of later Hinduism.

Vedic sacrifices were not entirely rejected : they still provided the ceremonial content of occasions such as the coronation of kings, but people lost touch with Vedic tradition, which increasingly had become the preserve of the brahmans. The brahmans appropriated the Vedic texts and in their place people accepted the Epics, the *Dharmashastras*, and the *Puranas* as their religious literature. The Epic heroes, Rama, Krishna, etc., became incarnations of the god Vishnu, and the Epics, which had been essentially bardic poetry, were now given the sanctity of divine revelation. The Epics had originally been secular and therefore had now to be revised by the brahmans with a view to using them as religious literature; thus, many interpolations were made, the most famous being the addition of the *Bhagavad Gita* to the *Mahabharata*.

The change in the theological attitude is perhaps best expressed in the philosophy of the *Gita*. The doctrine of *karma*, transmigration, was central to Hindu belief at this time. Actions in the present life condition the next birth. This is not fatalism, since one can modify one's destiny by consciously performing good actions. The morality of an action depends on whether or not it is in conformity with *Dharma* (the sacred Law); the arbiters of *Dharma* were of course the brahmans. The *Gita* proclaims that each man must do his duty and act according to the sacred Law without questioning the results of his action : the example taken being Arjuna's disinclination to kill his kinsmen in war, upon which Krishna explains that Arjuna is exempt from the sin of killing since this is the demand of war and Arjuna is fighting for the righteous cause.* A concession to the personal factor in religious belief had been made, but the final judgement on the morality of an action was still in the hands of the brahmans. The *Gita* is from many points of view a remarkable document. Not only does it combine philosophical subtlety with a precise and lucid literary style, but even on a purely human plane it is a work of considerable quality. Not surprisingly it has come to be regarded as the sacred book, *par excellence*, of the Hindus.

It was during the first century A.D. that another religion – Christianity – entered India by way of the trading ships from the West. The coming of Christianity is associated with the legend of St Thomas, who, according to the Catholic Church of Edessa, came twice on missions to India. The first took him to the north-west to the Parthian king Gondophernes, but this tradition is open to doubt. The story of the second mission appears to be more credible. St Thomas is said to have arrived in Malabar in about A.D. 52. After establishing a number of Syrian churches along this coast, he travelled overland to the east coast to a place near Madras city, subsequently called Beth Thuma,† where he

---

* Arjuna was one of the five Pandava brothers, and the kinsmen in question were his cousins the Kauravas against whom the battle at Kurukshetra was being fought. Krishna acted as his charioteer, and was believed to be an incarnation of Vishnu.

† Beth Thuma='House of Thomas' in Hebrew.

began to preach. But here his preaching of a new religion was strongly opposed and he was killed in A.D. 68 at Mylapore in the vicinity of Madras. The Syrian church survives in strength in the region of Malabar and may well have been founded in the first century A.D. Considering the frequent communication between the Mediterranean world and south India during this century, it is not beyond belief that one of the disciples of Christ came to India to preach Christianity.

THE EVOLUTION OF THE 'CLASSICAL' PATTERN

c. A.D. 300–700

DESPITE the rise and fall of many kingdoms in the centuries following the Mauryan period, the imperial ambition did not die and there were frequent attempts to emulate the Mauryas, but none of these met with the same success. The rule of the Gupta dynasty in northern India (from the fourth to the sixth century A.D.) is often described as an imperial government, but this description is not entirely accurate. Centralized control, an essential of an imperial structure, was not as fully realized in the Gupta government or in its successors as it had been under the Mauryas. Had geographical extent been the only criterion, some came close to being empires.

The Gupta period is also referred to as the Classical Age of ancient India. The description is true in so far as we speak of the upper classes, amongst whom living standards reached a peak never before attained, and this was largely true for northern India. For historians writing in the early twentieth century, the 'golden age' had to be a utopia set in the distant past, and the period chosen by those working on the early history of India was one in which Hindu culture came to be firmly established. However, the classicism of the Gupta period was restricted to northern India alone, since in the Deccan and south India it was the post-Gupta period that saw the evolution of a high level of civilization.

The origin of the Guptas is somewhat obscure. It is possible that the family was one of wealthy landowners who gradually gained political control in the region of Magadha. The dynasty came into its own with the accession of Chandra Gupta I, who made his kingdom more than a mere principality. Chandra Gupta married a Lichchhavi princess. The Lichchhavis were an old established tribe and marrying into their royal family doubtless set a seal of acceptability to the Gupta dynasty. This was obviously a political advance for the Guptas, since Chandra Gupta I made much of it in his coins, a point which adds to the suspicion that the Guptas were not of royal origin. Chandra Gupta I ruled over Magadha and parts of eastern Uttar Pradesh (Saketa and Prayaga). He took the title of *maharajadhiraja* (great king of kings), though this did not have much significance since the title had been regularly used by the Kushanas. The Gupta era is taken as dating from his accession in about A.D. 319-20.

Chandra Gupta I appointed his son Samudra Gupta to succeed him in about A.D. 335. Fortunately, a lengthy eulogy to him was inscribed on an Ashokan pillar at Allahabad, which provides the basic information on his reign. It would seem that there was some trouble over the successor to Chandra Gupta I, and the coins of an obscure prince Kacha suggest that Samudra Gupta had a rival whom he finally overcame. Samudra Gupta's ambition was to establish an empire controlled from the Gupta capital at Pataliputra and including the entire sub-continent. The shades of the Mauryas were re-emerging on the scene. The eulogy gives an impressive list of kings and regions which succumbed to Samudra Gupta's triumphal march across the country. Four northern kings were conquered mainly in the area around Delhi and western Uttar Pradesh. Kings of the south and the east were forced to pay homage, and from the places mentioned it appears that Samudra Gupta campaigned down the east coast as far as Kanchipuram (near modern Madras). Nine kings of Aryavarta (the western half of the Ganges plain) were 'violently uprooted'. The forest kings (tribal chiefs of central India and the Deccan) were forced to pay tribute, as were the kings in eastern India – of Assam and Bengal, and those with small kingdoms in Nepal and the Punjab. Nine republics in Rajasthan, including the age-old Malavas and Yaudheyas, were forced to accept Gupta suzerainty. In addition, foreign kings, such as the *Daivaputra Shahanushahi* ('Descendant of the Son of Heaven, King of Kings', clearly a Kushana title), the Shakas, and the king of Ceylon also paid tribute, as did the inhabitants of all the islands.

Coming as it does from a eulogy this information must be treated with caution, but nevertheless the list of conquests is impressive. The kings of the south and of the Deccan were not under the suzerainty of Samudra Gupta but merely paid him homage, as did a number of the northern rulers. In the end his conquests resulted in the annexation of territory in northern India as he originally intended, and also the exaction of tribute from defeated rulers whose territory he could not annex. He probably met with a stronger opposition than he had bargained for. His direct political control was confined to the Ganges valley, since the Shakas remained unconquered in western India; the tribes of Rajasthan merely paid tribute, and the Punjab was also outside the limits of his direct authority.

His campaign certainly broke the power of the tribal republics in that region, which was to have disastrous consequences for the later Guptas when the Huns invaded north-western India and the Punjab and Rajasthan could no longer act as buffers for the Ganges valley. The relationship between the Guptas and the tribal republics was a curious one. The Guptas were proud of their connexion with the Lichchhavis, but they attacked the western republics. It is interesting that the republican tradition should have survived for so many centuries in the west, despite the repeated invasions of this area. Samudra Gupta's campaign was the final blow to the declining tribal system. The old conflict of caste versus tribe had resulted in a victory for caste.

The validity of the wider claims is questionable. Samudra Gupta's relationship with the Kushanas remains uncertain, though they had been considerably weakened by now. As regards Ceylon, there is evidence from a later Chinese source that a Ceylonese king sent presents and requested permission from the Gupta king to build a Buddhist monastery at Gaya : such a request can hardly be termed tribute and it is probable that his relationship with the other foreign kings was on a similar basis. Who the 'inhabitants of the islands' were remains dubious; the phrase may refer to the islands close to India, the Maldives and Andamans, or it may be a reference to south-east Asia, which by now boasted of large Indian colonies and increased contacts. Samudra Gupta's reign, lasting for about forty years, must have given him ample time to plan and organize these campaigns. He performed the horse-sacrifice to proclaim his conquests, and he certainly had more cause to do so than many another king. The character of Samudra Gupta was not however one entirely thirsting for conquest and battle. He appears to have had a gentler and more civilized side, being described in the eulogy as a lover of poetry and music. That this was not merely a poetic flight is borne out by the fact that many of his coins show him playing the *vina* (lute).

Of all the Gupta kings, Chandra Gupta II, named after his grandfather, Samudra Gupta's father, is reputed to have shown the most chivalrous and heroic qualities. He reigned for about forty years from A.D. 375 to 415. His reign had a rather mysterious beginning, as in the case of his father. A play written some two centuries later (*Devi-chandra-guptam*), supposedly dealing with events on the death of Samudra Gupta, suggests that Rama Gupta succeeded Samudra Gupta. The story goes that the reigning king was Rama Gupta and he was defeated in battle by the Shakas, to whom he agreed to surrender his wife, Dhruvadevi. His younger brother Chandra was disgusted at this, and disguising himself as the queen he gained access to the Shaka king's apartments and killed the king. This action gained him the affection of the people but created enmity between him and his brother Rama. Chandra finally killed Rama and married Dhruvadevi. The discovery of the coins of Rama Gupta and of inscriptions proving that Chandra Gupta's wife was called Dhruvadevi lend some colour to this story. Furthermore, Chandra Gupta's major campaign was fought against the Shakas.

This campaign took place between A.D. 388–409, after which the Shakas were finally defeated and western India was annexed by the Guptas, an event commemorated by the issuing of special silver coins by Chandra Gupta II. This was a significant conquest because not only was the western border of India now no longer a source of anxiety but also the Guptas thus gained control over northern India: in addition to which it gave them access to some of the Indian trade with the Mediterranean, since the western Indian ports were now in Gupta hands. During the reign of Chandra Gupta II an alliance was made to strengthen the position of the Guptas in the Deccan. Samudra Gupta had campaigned in the eastern Deccan and had left the west comparatively untouched. The western Deccan, the old Satavahana stronghold, was now in the hands of the Vakataka dynasty and they were emerging as a dominant power in the Deccan. A marriage alliance was concluded between the Guptas and the Vakatakas, Chandra Gupta's daughter marrying the Vakataka king Rudrasena II. Other dynasties of the Deccan also married into the Gupta royal family, the Guptas thus ensuring friendly relations to the south of their domain. Thus Chandra Gupta, although using different means, was achieving the same ends as his father.

The Vakatakas rose to power in the latter half of the third century A.D., basing themselves on what remained of the Satavahana kingdom. Pravarasena I, ruling in the early fourth century A.D., conquered large parts of the western Deccan and central India. The Vakataka kingdom was divided into four parts under the successor of Pravarasena I. This weakened the state, but at the same time prevented the Vakatakas from being humiliated by Samudra Gupta, since he was content to obtain the homage of the Vakataka feudatories in central India and did not harass the main line of the Vakataka kings. Their survival after the Gupta campaigns gave them the opportunity to rearrange their territory to good advantage in dominating the Deccan. In the circumstances the Guptas found a marriage alliance advantageous. As it happened, Rudrasena II died five years after coming to the throne and, his sons being minors, his widow (the daughter of Chandra Gupta II) acted as regent from *c.* 390–410. Thus the Vakataka kingdom became virtually a part of the Gupta empire.

Chandra Gupta II took the title of *Vikramaditya* or Sun of Prowess, yet his reign is remembered for things other than war: for his patronage of literature and the arts – Kalidasa, the Sanskrit poet, being a member of his court – and for the high standard of artistic and cultural life. Fa Hsien, the Chinese Buddhist pilgrim who visited India during the years from 405 to 411 collecting Buddhist manuscripts and texts and studying at Indian monasteries, described the country as a generally happy one.

It was during the reign of Chandra Gupta II's son and successor Kumara Gupta (*c.* A.D. 415–54) that there came the first hints of a new invasion from the north-west, but they were to remain only a distant threat during the first half of the fifth century. A branch of the Huns from central Asia had occupied Bactria in the previous century and were threatening to cross the Hindu Kush mountains, as had so many invaders before them, and attack India. On the whole, Kumara Gupta's reign was peaceful and he succeeded in keeping the empire intact. How-ever, the Hun threat on the Indian frontier continued for the next hundred years and the Guptas were hard put to it to keep them back. Yet they succeeded up to a point, for, when the Huns finally broke through, they had been weakened and India did not meet with the fate of the Roman Empire. It has been plaus-ibly suggested that the resistance offered by the Chinese and In-dians to the central Asian nomads was partially responsible for the fury with which they fell upon Europe.

But the successors of Kumara Gupta could not defend their kingdom as he had done, each repeated wave of the Hun in-vasions making the Guptas weaker. Skanda Gupta battled valiantly but he faced domestic problems as well, such as the breaking away of his feudatories, and there are indications of an economic crisis which would explain the debasing of the coinage. However, by *c.* 460 he had managed to rally the Gupta forces, but 467 is the last known date of Skanda Gupta. After his death, the central authority of the Guptas declined at an increasing pace. The succession of the various kings that followed is uncertain. A number of administrative seals have been discovered with the names of the same kings, but following a varied order of suc-cession, which points to a confused close to the dynasty. A major blow came at the end of the fifth century when the Huns suc-cessfully broke through into northern India. Gupta power was slowly eroded over the next fifty years, after which the empire gave way to a number of smaller kingdoms.

The 'Indian' Huns, or *Hunas* as they are called by Indian writers, were not entirely independent, since they ruled as vice-roys for a Hun overlord. The Hun dominion extended from Persia right across to Khotan, the main capital being Bamiyan in Afghanistan. The first Hun king of any importance was Tora-mana, who ruled northern India as far as Eran in central India. Toramana's son Mihirakula (A.D. 520) appears to have been more of the Hun as pictured by tradition. A Chinese pilgrim travelling in northern India at the time describes him as uncouth in manner and an iconoclast, especially in his hatred for Budd-hism.* Inscriptions from central India suggest that the Guptas

---

* There are local traditions surviving in Kashmir where various places are associated with acts of cruelty and tyranny attributed to Mihirakula.

were still making belated attempts to resist the Huns both by their own efforts and in collaboration with other local rulers. Mihirakula was finally driven out of the plains and into Kashmir where he died in about 542, after which the political impact of the Huns subsided. Gupta power would not in any case have lasted very much longer and the Huns had accelerated the process of decline.

But this was not the sole effect of the Huns. Whatever potential there might have been for the creation of an imperial structure was now demolished, because political energy was directed towards keeping back the Huns. Defence on an all-India scale was unthought of : defence was conceived in local terms with occasional combinations of the smaller kingdoms, which sometimes led to consolidation accentuating the emergence of larger kingdoms under capable protectors, whose military powers rather than concern for their royal antecedents was a deciding factor. To add to the confusion and the atmosphere of insecurity there was a movement of populations and new ethnic combinations of peoples. Together with the Huns came a number of central Asian tribes and peoples, some of whom remained in northern India and others moved further to the south and the west. Among them were the Gurjaras, who rose to eminence a few centuries later. Some of the tribes who lived in Rajasthan fled from their homeland when they were displaced by the new tribes who became the ancestors of some of the Rajput families, and again were to dominate the history of the north in later centuries. The tide of Hun invasions had receded by the end of the sixth century, when the Turks and the Persians attacked them in Bactria, but as elsewhere the Huns had acted as a catalyst in the affairs of north India.

From the decline of the Guptas until the rise of Harsha in the early seventh century the political scene is confused, and there are few records to illuminate it. The large-scale displacement of peoples continued for some time. This was a period when petty kingdoms vied with each other to succeed to the past glory of the Guptas. Northern India was divided into four main kingdoms, those of the Guptas of Magadha, the Maukharis, the Pushyabhutis, and the Maitrakas. The first of these, the Guptas of Magadha, not to be confused with the main Gupta dynasty, were a minor line bearing the same name. The Maukharis at first held the region of western Uttar Pradesh around Kanauj, and gradually they ousted the Magadhan Guptas from their kingdom, after which the Guptas moved to Malwa. The Pushyabhutis ruled in Thanesar, north of Delhi. They had made a marriage alliance with the Maukharis, and, on the death of the last Maukhari king, the Maukhari nobles requested Harsha, the reigning Pushyabhuti king, to unite his kingdom with the Maukhari kingdom and rule from Kanauj. The Maitrakas, it is claimed, were of Iranian origin and ruled in Gujarat (now called Saurashtra), and developed Valabhi, their capital, into an important centre of learning. On the periphery of these four kingdoms were a number of small principalities continually fighting each other and seizing territory. This was particularly the case in Bengal and Assam. Of the four main kingdoms, the Maitrakas survived the longest and continued to rule until the middle of the eighth century, when they succumbed to attacks from the Arabs.

The Pushyabhuti family came to the fore after the Hun invasion and achieved influence on the accession of Prabhakaravardhana, who has been described by Bana, the biographer of Harsha, as:

... a lion to the Huna deer, a burning fever to the king of the Indus land, a troubler of the sleep of Gujarat, a bilious plague to that scent-elephant the Lord of Gandhara, a looter to the lawlessness of the Latas, an axe to the creeper of Malwa's glory.[1]

Prabhakara-vardhana's desire for conquest was eventually carried out by his younger son, Harsha-vardhana, generally known as Harsha.

Harsha began his reign in A.D. 606. Bana has written a colourful biography of his patron, the *Harshacharita* (Life of Harsha). There is also the account of a Chinese visitor, the Buddhist pilgrim Hsuan Tsang, who was in India during Harsha's reign. In the course of the forty-one years that he ruled, Harsha included among his feudatories kings as distant as those of Jalandhar (in the Punjab), Kashmir, Nepal, and Valabhi. Harsha was unable to extend his power into the Deccan or southern India. In fact he suffered his one major defeat at the hands of a Deccan king, Pulakeshin II. Harsha was an energetic ruler who travelled frequently in order to keep himself informed of happenings in his domains and to make himself accessible to his subjects. In the latter half of his reign he spent most of his time in camp, travelling from place to place. He was a man of considerable literary interests and talents and, despite his administrative duties, he managed to write three plays, of which two are comedies in the classical style and the third has a serious religious theme.

Events towards the end of Harsha's reign are described in Chinese sources. His contemporary, the T'ang emperor Tai Tsung, sent an embassy to his court in 643 and again in 647. On the second occasion the Chinese ambassador found that Harsha had recently died and that the throne had been usurped by an undeserving king. The Chinese ambassador rushed to Nepal and Assam and raised a force with which the allies of Harsha defeated the usurper, who was taken to China as a prisoner. His name is recorded on the pedestal of Tai Tsung's tomb. The kingdom of Harsha disintegrated rapidly into small states.

Harsha had realized the weakness of a cluster of small kingdoms and had decided to conquer his neighbours to weld them into an imperial structure. However, this was not possible owing to the particular political and economic conditions of the time. As with the Guptas, Harsha finally found himself ruling a large kingdom in northern India loosely connected by feudal ties, and not a closely connected empire of the Mauryan variety. Why this was so can be seen by an analysis of some of the institutions of this period.

The Gupta kings took exalted imperial titles – 'the Great King of Kings, the Supreme Lord', etc., yet in the case of the later rulers these titles were exaggerated, since their claimants could hardly compare with the emperors of earlier centuries, their political sway being limited. In the Ganges valley, which was under the direct control of the Guptas, the administrative hierarchy was superficially akin to that of the Mauryas. The king was the centre of the administration, helped by the crown prince. The other princes were appointed as viceroys of provinces. Ministers of various kinds and advisers assisted the king. The province (*desha* or *bhukti*) was divided into a number of districts (*pradesha* or *vishaya*), each district having its own administrative offices. But local administration was for all practical purposes independent of the centre. Decisions whether of policy or in relation to individual situations were generally taken locally, unless they had a specific bearing on the policy or orders of the central authority. The officers in charge of the districts (*ayukta*) and a yet higher provincial official (with the title of *kumaramatya*) were the link between local administration and the centre. This was the significant difference between the Mauryan administration and that of the Guptas : whereas Ashoka insisted that he must know of the doings of even the smaller officials in the districts, the Guptas were satisfied with leaving it to the *kumaramatyas* and the *ayuktas*.

Villages came under the control of rural bodies consisting of the headman and the village elders. The tendency was to introduce administration which was representative of local interests rather than an officially inspired system. Similarly, in urban administration each city had a council which consisted of the President of the City corporation, the chief representative of the Guild of Merchants, a representative of the artisans, and the chief Scribe. These may have been duplicated in each ward of the city. Again, the difference between the council and the Committee described by Megasthenes and Kautalya is that the Mauryan government appointed the Committees, whereas in the Gupta system the council consisted of local representatives, on which, interestingly enough, commercial interests predominated.

Harsha maintained contact with public opinion both through his officers and by his own tours, which gave him the opportunity of supervising the administration. By the seventh century a centralized system identical with that of the Mauryas was unworkable in the context of political and economic relations in northern India, and Harsha's extensive tours were an attempt at compromise. He took upon himself, as it were, the duties of a royal inspector and looked into the collection of taxes, listened to complaints, inspected the general working of the administration, and in addition gave charitable donations.

Another significant feature of this period was that salaries were sometimes paid not in cash but in grants of land, as is evident both from the frequency of land-grant inscriptions (in stone and metal) found from this period onwards and also from the specific reference to this practise by Hsuan Tsang in his account of India. Cash salaries were paid for military service alone. Land grants were of two varieties. One was the *agrahara* grant which was restricted to brahmans and was tax free. Although the land was often inherited by the family of the grantee, the king had the power to confiscate it should he be displeased with the behaviour of the grantee. The other variety of land grants was those to secular officials either in lieu of salary or as reward for services. In the early stages this grant was less frequent than the *agrahara*, but in later centuries it became usual. At a time when land grants were tokens of special favour the *agrahara* grant must doubtless have further underlined the privileged position of the brahman. Land grants weakened the authority of the king, although during this period they were not as common as they were to become later. Such grants put the owners far out of reach of the control of the central authority, and they were, moreover, frequently government officials. Although technically a king could terminate a grant, he was unlikely to do so very often, since offended brahmans or officers could well express themselves in political opposition.

Land was of three categories : fallow or waste land owned by the state, which was generally donated by way of salary; cultivated land owned by the state and treated as crown land which could be donated but probably seldom was, because it was already under plough and providing an income; and, finally, privately owned land. When land was given as salary, the donee did not acquire complete rights over the land. He could not, for instance, evict existing tenants. The owner had a right to as much as a third or half of the produce, the remainder being retained by the tenant. Land prices varied according to the nature of the land, cultivated land being rated thirty-three per cent higher than waste. The crops cultivated at this time appear to have remained largely unchanged for many centuries. Hsuan Tsang states that sugar-cane and wheat were grown in the north-west and rice in Magadha and further east. He also mentions a wide variety of fruit and vegetables. Water-wheels used for irrigation had become a familiar part of the rural landscape. The Sudarshana lake made by the Mauryas and repaired by Rudradaman was once again repaired and brought into use.

Land revenue was derived from a variety of taxes – from the land, and from various categories of produce at various stages of production. The maintenance of an imperial façade was a purposeless expense in economic terms and must have resulted in a pressure on the economy. It is not surprising that the later Gupta coinage indicates an economic crisis. The reference to Harsha dividing the national income into a quarter for government expenses, another quarter for the pay of public servants, a third quarter for the reward of intellectual attainments, and the last quarter for gifts, although idealistic in concept, may have been economically impractical.

Revenue came mainly from the land, commercial activities no longer providing as large an income as they had done earlier. Roman trade, which had brought in a vast fortune, declined after the third century A.D., and with the Hun invasion of the Roman empire it came to an end. Indian merchants meanwhile had begun to rely more heavily on the south-east Asian trade. The establishment of Indian trading stations in various parts of southeast Asia meant the diversion of income to this region. The commercial prosperity of the Gupta era was the concluding phase of the economic momentum which began in the preceding period.

Guilds continued as the major institution in the manufacture of goods and in commercial enterprise. They remained almost autonomous in their internal organization, the government respecting their laws. These laws were generally drafted by a larger body, the corporation of guilds, of which each guild was a member. The corporation elected a certain number of advisers and these were its main functionaries. Some of the industrial guilds, such as the silk weavers' guilds, had their own separate corporation which was responsible for large-scale projects, such as endowments for building a temple, etc. The Buddhist church or *Sangha* was by now rich enough to participate in commercial activities. In certain areas the *Sangha* acted as a banker and loaned money on interest. This was in addition to renting land, in areas where land gifts had been made to the *Sangha* and from which it took one sixth of the produce as its legitimate share.

This was the same amount as taken by the state in tax. Privileged brahmans also lived off donations or off grants of land. The Vakataka kings were particularly generous in this matter. The brahmans tended to be a less 'risk-taking' community on the whole, and more rooted to the land than the Buddhist *Sangha*. Evidence of brahmans investing their income from the land in commercial enterprises is rare. The close association of Buddhism with the mercantile community must have encouraged the *Sangha* to invest in commerce.

The rate of interest on loans varied according to the purpose for which money was required. The fantastically high rates demanded during the Mauryan period on loans to be used for overseas trade were no longer demanded, indicating an increased confidence in overseas trade. The average rate was now twenty per cent per annum as against two hundred and forty of the earlier period. Interest could exceed the legal rate provided both parties were agreeable, but it could seldom be permitted to exceed the principal in total amount. The lowering of the rate of interest also indicates the greater availability of goods and the consequent decrease in rates of profit.

The manufacture of textiles of various kinds was among the more important industries of this time. It had a vast domestic market since textiles featured prominently in the north–south trade within the whole of India, and there was considerable demand for Indian textiles in foreign markets. Silk, muslin, calico, linen, wool, and cotton were produced in great quantity. Western India was one of the centres of silk weaving. Towards the later Gupta period there may have been a decline in the production of silk, since many members of an important guild of silk weavers in western India discontinued their traditional vocation and took to other occupations. It is possible that the increasing use of the central Asian route and the sea route to China may have brought such a large amount of Chinese silk as to decrease production in India; or the decline in silk production may have been local to western India and due to the decrease in trade with the West. Ivory work remained at a premium, as did stone cutting and carving, sculpture being very much in favour at this time. Metal-work continued as one of the essential industries, particularly copper and iron and lead.

Bronze was also coming into wider use. Gold and silver were of course always in demand. The pearl fisheries of western India prospered when pearls began to fetch high prices in foreign markets. The cutting, polishing, and preparing of a variety of precious stones – jasper, agate, carnelian, quartz, lapis-lazuli, etc., were also associated with foreign trade. Pottery remained a basic part of industrial production, though the elegant black polished ware was no longer used : instead an ordinary red ware with a brownish slip was produced in large quantities, some of it being made to look more opulent by the addition of mica in the clay which gave the vessels a metallic finish.

The campaigns of Samudra Gupta to the east and the south and the repeated tours of Harsha ensured the continuation of efficient communication, and goods moved easily to all parts of India. On the roads, pack animals and ox-drawn carts were used, and in certain areas elephants were used. The lower reaches of the large rivers such as the Ganges, Yamuna, Narmada, Godavari, Krishna, and Kaveri were the main waterways. The ports of the east coast, Tamralipti, Ghantashala, and Kadura handled the north-Indian trade with south-east Asia, and those of the west coast, Broach, Chaul, Kalyan and Cambray, traded with the Mediterranean and west Asia but the more southerly of these ports were outside Gupta control. The export of spices, pepper, sandalwood, pearls, precious stones, perfumes, indigo, and herbs continued as before but the commodities that were imported differed from those of earlier times. Chinese silk came in greater quantity, as did ivory from Ethiopia. The import of horses, coming from Arabia, Iran, and Bactria, either overland to centres in the north-west or by sea to the west coast, increased during this period. It is strange that India never bred sufficient horses of quality, the best blood having always to be imported;* this was to have disastrous consequences on the cavalry arm of Indian armies, eventually making the cavalry ineffective, particularly in comparison with central Asian horsemen.

Indian ships were by now regularly traversing the Arabian Sea, the Indian Ocean and the China Seas and were seen at every port in these areas. Indian ships going to south-east Asia have

* The only likely explanation for this is that climatic conditions and the particular type of pasture suitable for breeding horses did not exist in India.

been described as 'square-rigged, two masted vessels with raked stem and stern, both sharp without bowsprit and rudder and steered by two quarter paddles'. The 'Island of the black Yavanas' is mentioned and it may have been a reference to the negroid population of either Madagascar or Zanzibar. Indian contacts with the east African coast date to a period in prehistory and by now this contact had developed through trade. Chinese traders were also competing at east African ports. There appears to have been a lively interest in navigation and trade at this time in India. Yet the law-makers were declaring it a great sin for a Hindu to travel by sea, to cross the black waters, and this may have reduced Indian participation in maritime trade. Ritual purity was becoming an obsession with both brahmans and the upper castes. They objected to travelling to distant lands because it meant contamination with the *mlechchha* (impure) and non-caste people. It was also difficult to observe caste rules when abroad. The ban had the additional indirect advantage for the brahman that it curbed the economic power of the trading community.

With the opening of new routes and the rise in the political status of provinces, cities which had had only a local interest now came into prominence. By the time of Harsha, Pataliputra, once the capital of most north Indian dynasties, lost its status, and instead Kanauj (in western Uttar Pradesh) came to dominate the Ganges plain. Mathura became a centre both of the textile trade and temples, as also did Banaras. Thanesar acquired a strategic importance, controlling the upper Ganges plain. Hardwar became a centre for pilgrimage. The plan of most cities was fairly simple, being laid out in squares. Houses had high windows and balconies. Main streets in which the market and shops were located had smaller houses with a balcony giving a view over the street. Wooden buildings had almost totally been replaced by buildings of brick in the richer sections of the city and wattled bamboo in the less prosperous. Houses were orientated to cardinal points, which suggests careful town planning, and this is also borne out by the frequency of drains and wells.

It is evident from excavations, where Gupta levels show a greater frequency of better techniques and quality in the objects found, and from descriptions in contemporary literature, that the standard of living was high. The prosperous urban dwellers lived in comfort and ease with a variety of luxuries in the way of jewels and clothes. The abundance of copper and iron objects in addition to spouted pottery found in houses would suggest that a degree of comfort in the urban centres at any rate was not restricted to the upper classes alone. Yet it was a culture showing a wide variation in living. The comfortably installed town-dweller had on the outskirts of his town the homes of the out-castes, probably much the same as the modern shanty-town. Villages however showed less disparity in the standard of living and, judging from the accounts of foreign travellers, were reasonably prosperous.

The daily life of a comfortably well-off citizen is described in the *Kamasutra* (The book on the Art of Love) as a gentle existence devoted to the refinements of life for those who had both the leisure and the wherewithal for such living : comfortable if not luxurious surroundings were provided to harmonize with moods conducive to poetry and painting, in both of which the young city dilettante was expected to excel. Gatherings were frequently held where poetic recitations and compositions were heard. Painting and sculpture were always on view in the homes of those who executed them. Music was another necessary accomplishment, particularly the playing of the lute (*vina*). The young man had also to be trained in the art of love and for this purpose the *Kamasutra* and other works of its kind were written. The *Kamasutra* is a remarkable document in as much as it analyses and discusses the whole question of the art of love with a precision and a lucidity surprisingly similar to that of modern works on the subject. The courtesan was a normal feature of urban life, neither romanticized nor treated with contempt. Judging by the training given to a courtesan as described in the *Kamasutra*, it was amongst the more demanding professions, for she was often called upon to be a cultured companion like the geisha of Japan or the hetaera of Greece.

Women were idealized in literature and art but in practice they had a distinctly subordinate position. Education of a limited kind was permitted to upper-class women but this was merely to enable them to converse intelligently, not to participate in public life. There are references to women teachers and philosophers, but they tended to be a rarity. Certain features emerged at this period which became characteristic of the status of women in later centuries. Early marriages were advocated, often even pre-puberty marriages. It was also suggested that a widow should not only live in strict celibacy, but preferably should burn herself on the funeral pyre of her husband – in fact become a *sati*.* The burning of widows on a mass scale was known to certain martial tribes of the north when soldier husbands died fighting and their wives were thus saved the humiliation of surrendering to the victors. But widow immolation in such cases was not recommended as a pious, religious action. The earliest evidence of this practice dates from A.D. 510, when it was commemorated in an inscription at Eran. It was largely confined to the upper classes mainly of central and later of eastern India and of Nepal. The only categories of women who had a large measure of freedom were those who deliberately chose to opt out of what were regarded by law books as the 'normal' activities of a woman, and became either Buddhist nuns or joined the theatrical profession or became courtesans and prostitutes.

Theatrical entertainment was popular both in court circles and outside. Dance performances and music concerts were held mainly in the homes of the wealthy and the discerning. Gambling continued to hold the attention of men, as did animal fights, particularly of the ram, the cock, and the quail which were more common in rural areas, but the townspeople also enjoyed these. Athletics and gymnastics were an important part of sporting tournaments, but the Indians never made a fetish of these as did the Greeks and Romans during certain periods. Amusements of various kinds in which the general public participated were essential to the various festivals, whether religious or secular. The Festival of Spring was celebrated with much enthusiasm to the accompaniment of a great deal of eating, drinking, and general conviviality. Contrary to Fa Hsien's statement that vegetarianism was customary in India, meat was commonly eaten. Wine, both the locally produced variety and that

---

*This term is often misused in the phrase 'to commit *sati*'. The literal meaning of the word is 'virtuous woman', therefore *sati* cannot be committed. A woman can only become a *sati*, ie.e a virtuous one – sometimes by the fact of her immolation on the funeral pyre of her husband.

imported from the west, was drunk daily, and the chewing of *pan* or betel-leaf prepared with spices was a regular practice.

The relationship between caste and occupation was maintained, although it did not always adhere strictly to the rules which had been formulated in the social and legal codes. The outcastes remained an excluded category. The status of the *shudra*, however, had improved since Mauryan times. A clear distinction is made between *shudras* and slaves in the legal literature. The Guptas could not assert the same degree of state control as did the Mauryas and this lessened the political pressures on the *shudras*.

The term *dvija* was now beginning to be used increasingly for the brahmans. The greater the emphasis on brahman purity, the greater was the stress laid on the impurity of the outcaste. Fa Hsien refers to the fear of pollution by approach, that is, if an outcaste was even so much as seen at close range by a *dvija*, the latter had to perform a ritual ablution to purify himself. This was in keeping with the regulations laid down in legal codes.

It is evident from the inscriptions of this period that mobility amongst the sub-castes was less rigid than it was to become later. The most interesting example is probably that of the guild of silk-weavers in western India, who, when they could no longer maintain themselves through the production of silk, moved to another part of western India, some of them adopting various other professions, such as those of archers, soldiers, bards, and scholars, professions of a higher status than their original one. Despite the change of profession, loyalty to the original guild seems to have remained, at least for one generation. Being sun worshippers they financed the building of a sun temple and gave the history of the guild in a lengthy inscription located in the temple.

Most of the legal texts took the *Dharmashastra* of Manu as their basis and elaborated upon it. A number of such works were written during this period, the best known being those of Yajnavalkya, Narada, Brihaspati, and Katyayana. The joint family system, which became an essential feature of Hindu caste-society, was prevalent at the time. Fathers and sons had equal ownership in ancestral property and the sons had equal ownership in the property of the father.

Katyayana describes the judicial process at length. The court of justice was attended by the king as the highest court of appeal. He was assisted by the judges, ministers, Chief Priest, brahmans, and assessors, varying in accordance with the needs of the individual cases. On certain occasions representatives of commercial institutions were also invited to assist the king. Recognized judicial bodies were the guild, the folk-assembly or council, a substitute appointed by the king in his own place (generally a brahman), and the king himself. Judgement was based either on the legal texts or social usage or the edict of the king (which could not contradict the first two to any great extent). Evidence was based on any or all of three sources, documents, witnesses, or the possession of incriminating objects. Ordeal as a means of proof was not only permitted but used. Katyayana accepted the theory of caste punishments, though it is doubtful if it was applied in every case.

Formal education was available both in brahmanical institutions and in Buddhist monasteries. Theoretically, the period of studentship at the former was the first thirty to thirty-seven years. It is unlikely that this was so in practice and few even amongst the brahmans spent so many years as students. Buddhist monasteries took students for only ten years, but those wishing to be ordained as monks had to remain for a longer period. Nalanda near Patna grew to be the foremost Buddhist monastery and educational centre in the north. It attracted students from places as distant as China and south-east Asia. The excavations at Nalanda have revealed a large area of well-constructed monasteries and temples. Nalanda was supported by the income from a number of villages which the monastery acquired over the years through donations. These villages and estates covered the expenses of the university, which was thus able to provide free educational facilities and residence for most of its students.

The concentration of formal education was on subjects such as grammar, rhetoric, prose and verse composition, logic, metaphysics, and medicine. The inclusion of medicine in this category was perhaps unfortunate since it led to its becoming more and more theoretical, thus preventing real advance in medical knowledge. The most important medical work of this period is a compilation of earlier texts, with little new knowledge of any significance. An interesting sideline was the first appearance of detailed works on veterinary science, relating mainly to horses and elephants, both important to the army. Indian medical knowledge travelled westwards, and aroused the interest of doctors in western Asia. Among others, a Persian physician came to India in the sixth century to study Indian medicine.

Knowledge of metals had improved tremendously and it is unfortunate that more objects have not survived from this period. The most spectacular survival is the famous iron pillar at Delhi, just over twenty-three feet high, scarcely rusted. There is also a life-size standing Buddha image of copper (now in the Birmingham Museum) cast in two parts. The handling of metal working is seen at its best in the coins and seals of the time. Coins were finely struck and dies carefully engraved. Seals attached to copper-plates are also of fine workmanship.

The more technical and specialized knowledge remained in the hands of the guilds, where the sons of craftsmen were trained in the hereditary trade. These centres had little direct contact with brahmanical institutions and Buddhist monasteries. The study of mathematics was an exception and provided a bridge between the two types of education, and not surprisingly this was an intensely active period in mathematics. Numerals had been in use for some time. They were later introduced to the European world as Arabic numerals, the Arabs having borrowed them from India, and finally they replaced Roman numerals. The decimal system was in regular use among Indian astronomers in the fifth century.

The first major expositions of Indian astronomy in the last few centuries B.C. are recorded in two works, the *Jyotisha-vedanga* and the *Surya-prajñapti*. Contact with the Greek world introduced a variety of new systems, some of which were assimilated and others rejected. Aryabhata was the first astronomer to pose the more fundamental problems of astronomy, in A.D. 499. It was largely through his efforts that astronomy was recognized as a separate discipline from mathematics. He calculated π to 3·1416 and the length of the solar year to 365·3586805 days, both remarkably close to recent estimates. He believed that the earth was a sphere and rotated on its axis, and that the shadow of the earth falling on the moon caused eclipses. His more revolutionary theories were opposed by later astronomers, who tended to compromise with the demands of tradition and religion. Aryabhata was the most scientific of Indian astronomers, and the later objection to his ideas may have been motivated by a wish not to displease the supporters of orthodox ideas. It is significant that in the work of his close contemporary Varahamihira the study of astronomy is divided into three branches each of equal importance – astronomy and mathematics, horoscopy, astrology – a division which Aryabhata would have rejected since Varahamihira's emphasis is on astrology rather than astronomy, an emphasis which was to destroy the scientific study of astronomy. The most interesting work of Varahamihira is the *Panchasiddhantika* (Five Schools of Astronomy), a concise account of the five currently used schools, of which two reflect a close knowledge of Greek astronomy.

Poetry and prose in Sanskrit were encouraged on a lavish scale, through royal patronage. It was the literature of the *élite*, the court, the aristocracy, and those associated with such circles. The name which immediately comes to mind is that of Kalidasa, regarded as the most outstanding writer of classical Sanskrit. His most famous work, the play *Shakuntala*, later came to be known in Europe through the impact it made on Goethe. *Meghaduta* (The Cloud Messenger), his long lyrical poem, was obviously very popular at the time, since inscriptions on occasion carry echoes of it. Plays continued to be romantic comedies in the main, tragic themes being avoided, since the purpose of the theatre was to entertain; a significant exception being *Mrichchha Katika* (The Little Clay Cart) by Shudraka. Of the prose writers Bana was acclaimed, his biography of Harsha being held as an excellent example of the best Sanskrit prose. Bana also wrote prose fiction much quoted in a number of theories on literary criticism. The fables of the *Panchatantra* were elaborated in various versions, and stories from this collection became the nucleus of a number of further anthologies. Literature was judged by the manner in which it depicted emotions (*rasa*), and the test of good literature was that it should provoke an emotional response.

In addition to Sanskrit, literature in Prakrit (a language more closely related to the speech of the times than was classical

Sanskrit) also had its patronage outside the court circle. Prakrit literature written by Jainas tended to be more didactic in style, with a substantial religious content. A notable feature in the Sanskrit plays of this period is that the characters of high social status speak Sanskrit, whereas those of low social status and all the women speak Prakrit, which indicates the standing of Sanskrit and Prakrit in the social context.

The conventional definition of a classical age is one where literature, architecture, and the fine arts reach a high level of excellence to form a standard for later times. Unfortunately, not much has survived of the architectural achievement of the Guptas. It is often said that the iconoclasm of the Muslims five centuries later destroyed the temples of northern India, and this accounts for the lack of Gupta remains. But it is probably nearer the truth to say that Gupta temples were unimpressive shrines which were either absorbed in domestic architecture or else were built over in later centuries. The Buddhists continued to build their monasteries and chapels and these have survived. The Hindu temple in northern India did not really come into its own until the eighth century A.D.

The Hindu temple began with the *garbha-griha* shrine room or (literally) womb-house, in which the image of the god was placed. This was approached through a vestibule, which in turn was entered from a hall which opened out on to a porch. The whole structure was surrounded by an enclosed courtyard which later came to house a further complex of shrines. From the Gupta period onwards, temples were largely built in stone instead of the usual brick or wood. The use of stone introduced the idea of the monumental style and this was given increasing emphasis in Hindu architecture. The free standing temple became necessary with the growth of image worship, since the image had to be appropriately housed and a cave was not adequate for this purpose. Gradually the image came to be surrounded by a host of attendant deities and figures, leading eventually to the rich sculptural ornamentation associated with later styles. Manuals on the construction of stone temples were written giving minute details of construction, and these were faithfully followed.

The highest achievement of classical sculpture is visible in the Buddha images which were found at Sarnath. They reflect a serenity and contentment which have come to be associated with the religious atmosphere of the age. The depiction of the Buddha in human form led to the portrayal of the more important Hindu gods and goddesses in the same manner. The Hindus, however, treated the image as a symbol and not as representational : thus, although the god took a human form, he may well have been given four or eight arms, each arm carrying a symbol of an attribute connected specifically with that particular god. Much of Gupta sculpture emerged from the norms established by the

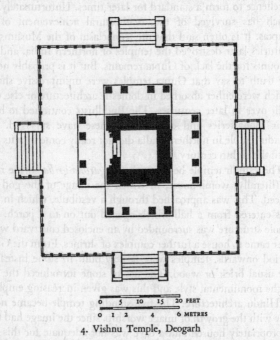

4. Vishnu Temple, Deogarh

Mathura school. The Hindu gods represented during this period in northern India were mainly incarnations of Vishnu. The cult of Shiva was largely confined to phallic worship, and this did not offer much sculptural scope.

Not all the Hindu temples of this time were free standing temples. The Buddhists in the Deccan continued to excavate their shrines in hill-sides as cave-temples, and the Hindus, as in later centuries the Jainas, imitated these, often cutting temples adjacent to those of the Buddhists. Many of these caves had their walls covered with paintings, such as at Ajanta. Literary references to painting are so frequent that it must have been widely appreciated. Terracotta figures are much more typical of north India than elsewhere and have been found in great abundance in the Ganges plain and eastern India. Many of them are mould-made and were therefore mass-produced. Some of the figures were used in religious ritual but most were of a secular nature and used as toys or decorative pieces.

Buddhism and Hinduism were both widely supported during this period : Hinduism acquired characteristics which have remained with it, while Buddhism had assumed a form which was to lead to its decline. Theoretically, Buddhism was a formidable rival to Hinduism, but in the ritual of worship and in practice it had compromised with the brahmanical religion to such an extent that it could almost have been regarded as a sect of the latter. Jainism remained unchanged and continued to be supported by the merchant communities of western India. In certain areas of the Deccan and the south local royalty patronized Jainism, but much of this patronage ceased after the seventh century A.D. In the early part of the sixth century the Second Jaina Council was held at Valabhi and the Jaina canon was defined substantially as it exists today. The use of Sanskrit by all the religions was on the increase, perhaps because Sanskrit was regarded as a prestige language, but it had the same effect on all religions, that of isolating the religious teachers from their following. The Jainas had also by now evolved a series of icons. The straight-standing rather stiff figures of Mahavira and other saints or the cross-legged seated figures became the pattern for Jaina sculpture of their saints. Christianity remained confined to the region of Malabar. Mediterranean writers speak of a Syrian church in the land of Male where the pepper grows (i.e. Malabar), and the port of Calliana (Kalyana near Bombay) is said to have had a bishop appointed from Persia.

Buddhism had by now spread well beyond the frontiers of India, into central Asia, China, and south-east Asia. In India, the *Mahayana* branch had practically driven out the *Hinayana* except in a few restricted areas. The fifth century saw the coming of a new and curious cult which began with the worship of female deities, associated with the fertility cult; they became the nucleus of a number of magical rites which in a later form are called Tantricism. Buddhism was influenced by *Tantric* rites, and in the seventh century A.D. a new branch of Buddhism emerged with its centre in eastern India called *Vajrayana* (Thunderbolt Vehicle) Buddhism. The *Vajrayana* Buddhists gave female counterparts to the existing male figures of the Buddhist pantheon, and these counterparts were termed Taras (or Saviouresses). The cult of Taras remains prevalent in Nepal and Tibet.

Three important aspects of Hinduism became crystallized at this point. The image emerged as the centre of worship and worship superseded sacrifice, although a sacrificial offering to the image remained central to the ritual. This in turn encouraged *bhakti* (devotional) worship, where the priest was not so dominant a figure as in the sacrifice. Worship of a god became much more the concern of the individual, but the ordering of the individual's social behaviour was still the concern of the brahman. Social law based on a man-made tradition had already become Sacred Law and the orthodoxy attempted to maintain its power by rigid rules of exclusion for those who could not conform. Fortunately, there were also many who saw the difficulty of trying to enforce rules which were largely theoretical. They expressed themselves by defining the Four Ends of Man – Religion and the Social Law (*Dharma*), Economic Well-Being (*Artha*), Pleasure (*Kama*), and the Salvation of the Soul (*Moksha*) – the correct balance of the first three leading to the fourth. The description of the balance was left to those who framed the social code, but the demands of earthly life were adequately met in practice.

Practising Hindus were divided into two main sects, *Vaishnavas* and *Shaivas*, each claiming Vishnu or Shiva as the supreme deity. The former, worshippers of Vishnu, were more prevalent in northern India, whereas the worshippers of Shiva were found in great numbers in the south, and still are. *Tantric* beliefs made an impression on Hindu worship as well and in Hinduism there developed the *Shakti* cults, with their basic belief that the male can be activated only by being united with the female. The gods therefore acquired wives and the wives were worshipped in their own right; for example, Lakshmi, the wife of Vishnu, and Parvati, Kali, and Durga, the various manifestations of the wife of Shiva. This cult appears to have been based on the persistent worship of the mother goddess, which has remained an enduring feature of religion in India. Since this could not be suppressed it was given a priestly blessing and incorporated into the regular ritual in the guise of the *Shakti* cult.

Hindu thinkers had evolved a cyclic theory of time. The cycle was called a *kalpa* and was equivalent to 4,320 million earthly years. The *kalpa* is divided into 14 periods and at the end of each of these the universe is recreated and once again Manu (primeval man) gives birth to the human race. At the moment we are in the seventh of these 14 periods of the present *kalpa*. Each of these is divided into 71 Great Intervals and each of these is divided in 4 *yugas* or periods of time. The *yugas* contain respectively 4,800, 3,600, 2,400, and 1,200 god-years (one god-year being 360 human years), and there is a progressive decline in the quality of civilization. We are now in the fourth of these *yugas*, the *kaliyuga* when the world is full of evil and wickedness, and thus the end of the world is by comparison imminent, though there are several millennia yet before the end! The *kaliyuga* is also associated with the coming of Kalkin, the tenth incarnation of Vishnu. There is a curious similarity between these ideas and the idea of the Millennium as it was current in Europe and elsewhere.

A notable feature of intellectual life had been the lively philosophical debates, particularly between the Buddhists and the brahmans. Gradually the debates centred on six different schools of thought which came to be called the Six Systems of Hindu philosophy. Although these systems had their origin in the philosophical thinking of a period considerably earlier than that of the Gupta and continued into a considerably later period, some of their cardinal principles were enunciated at this time. The six systems were:

Nyaya (Analysis) which was based on logic and was predominantly used in the debates with Buddhist teachers who prided themselves on their advanced knowledge and use of logic.

Vaisheshika (Particular Characteristics) which was a type of atomic philosophy. The universe was created from a number of atoms, but these were distinct from the soul, therefore there were separate universes of matter and soul.

Sankhya (Enumeration) which was essentially atheistic and maintained the existence of twenty-five principles which gave rise to creation. The dualism between matter and soul was recognized. Sankhya philosophers supported the theory that the three qualities of virtue, passion, and dullness, correctly balanced, constituted normality. This was perhaps the influence of the theory of humours current in the medical knowledge of the time.

Yoga (Application) which was based on the control of the body physically and implied that a perfect control over the body and the senses led to knowledge of the ultimate reality. A detailed anatomical knowledge of the human body was necessary to the advancement of *yoga* and therefore those practising *yoga* had to keep in touch with medical knowledge.

Mimamsa (Inquiry) which grew out of a feeling that the source of brahmanical strength, the *Vedas*, was being neglected, and its supporters emphasized the ultimate law of the *Vedas* and refuted the challenge of post-Vedic thought. Its main support came from orthodox brahmans.

Vedanta (End of the *Vedas*) which emerged finally as the predominant system and gained wide currency in later times. Vedanta was decisive in refuting the theories of non-brahmanical schools, particularly in later centuries. *Vedanta* also claimed origin in the *Vedas* and posited the existence of the Absolute Soul in all things, the final purpose of existence being the union of the individual and the Absolute Soul after physical death.

It is interesting that, at this stage, only the last two schools were purely metaphysical in character. The first four maintained a strong link with empirical analysis and yet in succeeding centuries it was *Vedanta* which was to come to the fore, to the detriment of the other philosophies. The period of the *Vedas* was now sufficiently remote for them to be cited as the unchallenged authority derived from divine origin and as the arbiters of priestly knowledge and sanction. The *Vedas* were the fountain of all knowledge. *Vedanta* was to remain an undying theme in Indian philosophy, arousing the interest of every newcomer to the country. It was enriched by the impact of other ideas – Islamic, Christian, and European – but the essential core continued as from this period. Even today most Indian philosophers claim either to be Vedantists or to be deeply influenced by *Vedanta*.

The *Puranas* as we know them in their present form were composed during this time. The *Puranas* are the historical tradition as recorded by the brahmans, beginning with the creation of the universe and including detailed genealogies of each dynasty. They were originally composed by bards, but by now, having come into priestly hands, they were re-written in classical Sanskrit, and information on Hindu sects, rites, and customs was added in order to make them into sacrosanct Hindu documents. Curiously enough the succession of dynasties was now recorded in the form of a prophecy, and not surprisingly they were invested in later centuries with a divine origin. Thus, what began as popular memories of the past was revised and re-written in prophetic form and became the brahmanical interpretation of the past.

Religion was to find an ally in commerce to carry the Indian way of life outside India. In this Buddhism took the initiative and introduced Indian culture into various parts of Asia. Buddhism found support in central Asia with monasteries richly endowed by local rulers and merchants in every oasis and trade centre. The Indian script had been adopted and orthodox Buddhist rules were strictly observed. Many Indians had settled in central Asia, among them Kumarajiva, the Buddhist philosopher, who lived at Kuchi where his father had married a Kuchi princess (in the fourth century A.D.). Afghanistan continued to be allied with India culturally, as is confirmed by the evidence from the site of Bamiyan.

Indian Buddhists went in large numbers to China, to preach. In A.D. 379 Buddhism was declared the state religion in China and this swelled the following. However, it had its tribulations, since later centuries saw the severe persecution of Buddhists. Chinese Buddhists were interested in obtaining the original Buddhist scriptures in Sanskrit and Pali and a number of them, such as Fa Hsien, Sung Yun, Hsuan Tsang, and I Tsing, travelled and worked in India between A.D. 400–700. As a result, a number of Indian elements were introduced into Chinese culture. Perhaps the most obvious was the use of Indian techniques in sculpture and painting. Cave temples, widely used in central Asia, became the tradition in China as well, and at first Indian artists were invited to decorate the walls with frescoes and to sculpt Buddhist images. Gradually the work was taken up by Chinese artists, but the Indian impress remained for a considerable time. Music, astronomy, and medical treatises were all enriched by contact with India. The expansion of the south Indian sea trade with China helped to increase Sino-Indian contacts. During the T'ang period (A.D. 618–907) Indian merchants resided at Canton, and T'ang coins have been found in south India. That the Chinese ambassador could so effectively interfere in the political situation after the death of Harsha would point to the relations between the two countries being very close. Buddhism came to Japan via the mainland of China from the seventh century onwards. But in the eighth century an Indian monk visited Japan and was pleasantly surprised at the number of Buddhists he found there and by the knowledge they showed of the Indian alphabet.

The demands of trade with Rome had encouraged Indian enterprise in south-east Asia, since it provided many of the commodities the Romans wanted – gold, spices, scented resins and woods. Siberian gold ceased coming to India when the Romans came to control Parthia, and thus India sought gold elsewhere. Having once discovered the potentialities of southeast Asia, Indian traders developed this trade on a large scale, even after the decline of commerce with Rome. Trade led to settlements, which slowly developed into colonies. Indian influence permeated the local pattern of life, particularly in the regions today known as Thailand, Cambodia, and Java: yet India sent no armies, the process being one of peaceful penetration.

Chinese annals of the time, referring to Indian activities in south-east Asia, mention Funan (the Mekong delta) as the first sphere of activity. Small settlements were also made in the Malay peninsula, since it was connected with nearly all the east-coast maritime centres of India. Ships sailed from Tamralipti and

Amaravati to Burma, Martaban, and Indonesia. The ports of south India sent ships to Tenasserim, Trang, the Straits of Malacca, and Java. The west coast ports also shared in the south-east Asian trade.

The nature of the Indian impact varied according to the region from where it came. Initially, both Buddhists and Hindus visited and settled in these regions. Gradually the tradition of Hinduism became stronger when brahmanical rites and ceremonies and the use of Sanskrit were adopted in court circles. Some of the finest Sanskrit inscriptions come from these areas. Geographical place-names associated with the new religions were adopted : e.g., Ayuthia the ancient capital of Thailand was named after Ayodhya, the capital of the kingdom of Rama, the hero of the *Ramayana*. Indian iconography was repeated in the images which were made in these countries. Yet, with all this, they maintained their indigenous culture as well.

The Indian impact is understandable in terms of a more advanced civilization meeting a less advanced one, with the *élite* of the latter moulding themselves on the pattern of the former, but to refer to south-east Asia during this period as 'Greater India' is certainly a misnomer. The local culture was visible in all aspects of life in these countries, whether it was the Javanese version of the *Ramayana* where only the bare bones of the Indian story have been retained, the rest being the incorporation of traditional Javanese legends, or whether it was the conception of the god-king amongst the Khmer rulers of Cambodia, where the idea of the god-king both had a pre-Indian origin and was also influenced by Indian thought on the subject.

In later centuries Hinduism declined and Buddhism persisted.* In its more orthodox form, that of the *Hinayana* sect, Buddhism in south-east Asia became prevalent in about the seventh and eighth centuries A.D., contemporary with its entry into Tibet. Local modifications in both cases have been so strong that the

* In time the distinction between Hindu and Buddhist in south-east Asian countries became hazy. The Thai court at Bangkok employs, to this day, brahmans from India for all court ceremonies, and the brahmans are maintained in comfort at Bangkok. Yet the state religion of Thailand is Buddhism.

Buddhist from Cambodia would hardly recognize the Tibetan version as being the same religion. In court circles the imitation of things Indian or Chinese (in areas close to the Chinese border) was considerable, but the rest of society in these countries maintained its own identity, despite its assimilation of certain imported customs.

The Gupta period saw the acceptance of the Aryan pattern in northern India, an important aspect of which was that the status of the brahman was firmly established. The fact that a number of texts were re-written with an underlining of the brahman viewpoint indicates that the status was effective and powerful. The granting of land to brahmans, which increased in the post-Gupta period, emphasized the pre-eminence of the brahman in society. The brahmans maintained this position by not only regarding themselves as the essential inheritors of the Aryan tradition but also by monopolizing knowledge through their educational system, and using this monopoly as an additional source of power.

Aryan patriarchal society became the norm and this, as seen for instance in the lowering of the status of women, is indicative of the decline of the indigenous pre-Aryan culture. Yet it was partially due to this continuing conflict between Aryan and non-Aryan cultures that the Aryan pattern did not dominate Indian life in its entirety. If at certain levels, such as those of the political and social *élite*, it was dominant, there were other levels where it had to make concessions. If the patriarchal stamp of Aryan society as typified in the low status of women became evident, so also did the opposing force – in the increasing worship of the mother goddess and the fertility cults. That the imposition of the Aryan patterns on levels of society other than those of the upper castes was uncertain and incomplete is indicated by the development of Hindu worship, particularly in the post-Gupta centuries, where repeated concessions were made to popular cults; or by the fact that Shaivism (prevalent in south India and the northern hill states), in its aspect of *lingam* worship, was in origin non-Aryan. Although the Aryan pattern was well established in the northern plains, the more southerly regions were to make their own contribution to Indian culture, a contribution which was not identical with that of the north.

CONFLICT IN THE
SOUTHERN KINGDOMS

c. A.D. 500–900

WITH the passing of the power and influence of the Guptas and their immediate successors in northern India, the centre of interest shifts southwards again to the western Deccan and even further south to Tamil-nad. The most significant events of the period took place south of the Vindhyas and in spheres other than the purely political. A synthesis of the dominant cultural strains of the time was to emerge – the assimilation of the Aryan pattern with Dravidian culture. The institutions of south India were more firmly established at this time and were to maintain a remarkable continuity. The Pallava period in south India saw the culmination of what had been a gradual process of assimilating Aryan institutions, greater assimilation of Aryan ideas being limited to the upper strata of society. Amongst the rest there was a reaction in which the indigenous culture sought to assert itself. The Pallava period, therefore, also saw the emergence of what might be broadly described as the Tamil personality, which was to contribute substantially to the development of Indian civilization. The process of assimilation and reaction can be seen in various spheres : for instance, the early inscriptions are in Prakrit and Sanskrit, but soon Tamil is introduced until finally the main corpus of inscriptions is in Tamil and Sanskrit. The kingdoms of the western Deccan maintained their historical role of acting as the bridge between north and south and facilitating the transmission of ideas from one area to the other. But this was not a passive role, as is clear from the example of architectural history in this period, where the Deccan style provided new forms both for the Northern and for the Dravidian styles.

The political history of the Deccan and further south evolved a pattern based on the geo-political influences of the region, a pattern which remained unbroken until recent times. It resulted from the conflict of two geographical regions, the western Deccan and Tamil-nad – the vast plateau areas enclosed by mountains along the coasts on the one hand, and the fertile plain south of Madras on the other. Rivers rise in the west and flow into the Bay of Bengal. The division of the peninsula into the plateau kingdoms on the west and the coastal kingdoms on the east increased the desire of each to control the entire waterway, particularly the Godavari and Krishna rivers. Vengi (in modern Andhra Pradesh), lying between the Godavari and Krishna deltas, was frequently the bone of contention. The conflict was thus not so much dynastic as geographic, and consequently it continued through the centuries despite the rise and fall of particular dynasties.

Hsuan Tsang was struck by the fact that the area of cultivated land diminished the further south he travelled. In the absence of vast areas of fertile plains suitable for agriculture, large agrarian-based kingdoms could not develop, and the tendency to form small kingdoms based on local organization was an early and consistent feature in southern India. Not surprisingly the kingdoms of the peninsula were orientated to regional loyalties far earlier than the kingdoms of the north.

For three hundred years after the mid sixth century three major kingdoms were involved in conflict. These were the Chalukyas of Badami, the Pallavas of Kanchipuram, and the Pandyas of Madurai. The Chalukyas built their kingdom on the ruins of the Vakatakas, who in turn had built theirs on the remains of that of the Satavahanas. The Vakatakas, allied to the Guptas, declined when Gupta power was on the wane. The Chalukyas began with a base in northern Mysore at Vatapi or Badami and the adjacent Aihole, from where they moved north-wards and annexed the former kingdom of the Vakatakas, which was centred around Nasik and the Upper Godavari. The eastern part of the Satavahana kingdom, the deltas of the Krishna and the Godavari, had been conquered by the Ikshvaku dynasty in the third century A.D. Ikshvaku rule in this region ended with its conquest by the Pallavas. The latter were also responsible for the overthrow of the Kadamba rulers and the annexation of their kingdom, which lay to the south of the Chalukya kingdom.

The origin of the Pallavas in south India is under debate. Some writers have suggested that Pallava is a variant of Pahlava (Parthian), and that the Pallavas were originally Parthians who moved from western India to the eastern coast of the peninsula, during the wars between the Shakas and the Sata-vahanas in the second century A.D. Others have suggested that they were a tribe from Vengi. Yet another tradition weaves a story round the name. We are told that a young prince fell in love with a Naga princess of the nether world, and, when he finally had to leave her, told her that if she set their child adrift with a young creeper or twig tied to its body he would recognize the child on finding it and would bestow part of the kingdom on the child. This the princess did and the child was duly recognized and installed as the founder of the Pallava (literally meaning a young twig) dynasty. This legend points to a foreign origin of the Pallavas and also suggests that they rose through a judicious marriage, the Naga chiefs being symbolic of local power. This legend is not unique to the Pallavas, for a similar story is told about the Khmer kings of Cambodia, though probably the latter took it from the Pallava legend. The lack of detailed information on the origin of the dynasty probably facilitated the recognition of high caste status for the kings, through a fabricated genealogy.

The earliest records of the Pallavas are inscriptions in Prakrit followed by inscriptions in Sanskrit and subsequently in both Sanskrit and Tamil. The Prakrit inscriptions were made when the Pallavas were still a local dynasty ruling at Kanchipuram. The later inscriptions were carried out by what historians have called the 'Imperial' Pallavas, when the dynasty controlled Tamil-nad and became the first Tamil dynasty of real conse-quence. According to one of the earlier inscriptions the Pallava king performed various Vedic sacrifices, including the *ashva-medha*. It is difficult to determine whether these ceremonies had any real meaning at the time in south India, or for that matter what significance they had for the local population, apart from being symbolic of accepting certain aspects of Aryan culture. Another king is remembered for having bestowed large quanti-ties of gold on his subjects and distributed a thousand ox-ploughs. This clearly suggests that the early Pallavas encouraged the clearing and settling of new land, no doubt having realized the advantages of agriculture, both in tax and produce, as against a largely pastoral economy.

Amongst the later group of Pallava rulers, Mahendra-varman I (600–630) was responsible for the growing political strength of the Pallavas and established the dynasty as the arbiters and patrons of early Tamil culture. He was a contemporary of Harsha of Thanesar and curiously enough was also a dramatist and poet of some standing, being the author of a play, *Matta-vilasa-prahasana* (The Delight of the Drunkards). It was during his reign that some of the finest rock-cut Pallava temples were hewn, including the famous temples at Mahabalipuram. Mahen-dra-varman began life as a Jaina but was converted to Shaivism by the saint Appar, a conversion which was to have disastrous results on the future of Jainism in Tamil-nad. But his reign was not merely one of poetry, music, and temple-building; wars had also to be fought. His northern contemporary Harsha was too far away for there to be any conflict, but nearer home was the recently established Chalukya power, and Mahendra-varman's contemporary was Pulakeshin II, who was determined to confine the ambition of the Pallavas and prevent their control over Vengi. This aim was to start a long series of Chalukya–Pallava wars, which ceased for a while on the termination of the two dynasties but recommenced with the rise of their successors.

Pulakeshin tested the strength of his army by attacking the Kadambas and the Gangas to the south. His success in this campaign led him to make an equally successful attack on Andhra territory, and finally he faced the army of Harsha on the banks of the Narmada, which he defeated, and pressed on to receive the submission of Lata, Malwa, and Gujarat. On returning to Badami he conducted another successful campaign, this time against Mahendra-varman the Pallava, resulting in the Chalukya acquisition of some of the northern Pallava provinces.

The defeat of the Pallava was not to remain unavenged. Mahendra-varman had died but his successor Narasimha-varman I was determined to win back the lost provinces, and this he succeeded in doing with the assistance of the king of Ceylon in 642. Narasimha-varman swept right into the capital of Badami and his occupation of the city justified his claim to the title of *Vatapikonda*, 'the Conqueror of Vatapi'. The next move was now to be made by the Chalukyas. Meanwhile the Pallavas had been involved in naval warfare in support of their ally the king of Ceylon, who was trying to regain his recently lost throne.

A twelve year interregnum in the Chalukya dynasty led to a

respite from war. The Pallavas were busy with Ceylon. The Chalukyas were trying to unite a divided kingdom and curb their feudatories. In 655 one of the sons of Pulakeshin succeeded in bringing about a semblance of unity, and the power of the Chalukyas was gradually restored with the regaining of the territory lost to the Pallavas. The Chalukya provinces north of the Narmada river were ruled by a prince of the main family whose descendants were later referred to as the Lata Chalukyas, named after the region over which they ruled. The Chalukya king was now free to give his attention to the Pallavas, who had been preparing for a renewal of the war. After a long-drawn-out campaign the Pallavas once more swept into Badami. The losses were heavy on both sides, as is clear from a graphic description of the battle contained in a Pallava grant found in the vicinity of Kanchi. Doubtless this was the case in all the campaigns, where the two armies of the Pallavas and the Chalukyas were equally matched and victory was achieved by a narrow margin. The inability of each to hold the other's territory after annexing it would point to a similarity in military strength.

The forty-year reign of Narasimha-varman II was peaceful by comparison with that of other Pallava kings. But this halcyon period ended in 731 with the Chalukyas and the Gangas uniting in an attack on the Pallavas. The reigning king was killed in battle and, there being no direct heir, the council of ministers in consultation with the college of priests appointed a member of the collateral branch of the family, who reigned as Nandi-varman II. The Chalukyas had avenged their earlier defeat in the usual manner by occupying Kanchi. The next move was now with the Pallavas, but at this point there was a change in the situation, with the southern neighbours of the Pallavas joining in the conflict. These were the Pandyas of Madurai, and they were not in sympathy with the Pallava cause, although their enmity was less than that of the Chalukyas. The Pandyas had established their position in the area to the south of Tamil-nad by the sixth century, and they were to remain in control of this region for many centuries. The effectiveness of their control of this region varied according to the effectiveness of their relations with the power in Tamil-nad. Despite the harassment caused to the Tamil dynasties by the Pandyas, the former never could obliterate the latter.

The one exception to this picture of conflict amongst the southern powers was the relationship between the Pallavas and the Cheras, the latter being the people of the Malabar coast (modern Kerala). The Cheras were ruled by the Perumal dynasty. There is evidence of close contact between the Cheras and the Pallavas. Mahendra-varman's play *Mattavilasa* was well-known and frequently performed by the actors of Malabar. Sanskrit works of the period written for the Pallavas show considerable knowledge of Kerala. The Malabar coast at this time (from the eighth century onwards) was acting host to another influx of traders from the west – the Arabs. Unlike the Romans, the Arabs settled permanently in the coastal regions of south India, where they were welcomed as traders and given land for their trading stations. They were free to practise their religion, as had been the Christians in earlier centuries. The present-day Mappillas or Malabar Muslims are descendants of these settlers. The Malabar Muslims, being mainly traders, were not actively concerned with large-scale conversions to Islam, and therefore adjustment with local society was easier.

In the previous century, the Arab armies had overrun Persia and had forcibly converted large numbers of Zoroastrians. Many, however, in the early eighth century fled by sea and by the coastal route from Persia to western India, where they settled after having been given asylum by the Chalukyas, and took to trade and were the founders of a community later known as Parsis, after the land of their origin, Persia.

Meanwhile, the western possessions of the Chalukyas were being threatened by the very people from whom the Parsis had fled. The Arabs had occupied Sind in the eighth century and were advancing towards Chalukya territory. The Lata Chalukyas managed to hold the Arabs back and thus allow time for their southern neighbours to arm themselves. The immediate danger from the Arabs passed, but, as a result, the Chalukyas were faced with an even more formidable threat. One of their feudatories, Dantidurga, claimed independence and by slow stages his family overthrew the Chalukyas and established a new dynasty – the Rashtrakutas. The Pallavas survived the Chalukyas by about a century, but their authority during the ninth century was no longer that of a major power. The last of the Pallavas was assassinated by the son of a feudatory and the 'Imperial' Pallava line came to an end.

The Rashtrakuta kingdom battened on the weakness of the other kingdoms. The Pallavas were in decline, and their successors, the Cholas, had not yet entered the fray. There was no power in northern India strong enough to interfere with the affairs of the northern Deccan. The geographical position of the Rashtrakutas led to their being involved in wars and alliances with both the northern and more frequently with the southern kingdoms. The Rashtrakutas interfered effectively in the politics of Kanauj and this interference cost them many a campaign, though they did gain possession of Kanauj for a brief period in the early tenth century.

Amoghavarsha is probably the best remembered of the Rashtrakuta kings. His long reign (814–80) was militarily not brilliant, but was distinguished for royal patronage of the Jaina religion and of regional literature. Amoghavarsha's main problem was the rebellious feudatories, one which remained a persistent trouble. The Chalukyas, reduced to feudatory status, were once again asserting themselves and were soon to overthrow the Rashtrakutas and install themselves as the rulers, bringing the wheel round full circle. Meanwhile, the rising power of the Cholas in Tamil-nad was another threat to the independence of the Rashtrakuta kingdom. The first half of the tenth century saw the Rashtrakutas still in the ascendant, with one of their kings claiming the title of 'Conqueror of Kanchi'. But this was a short-lived claim; by the end of the tenth century the new rulers of Kanchi and the Chalukyas between them had brought the Rashtrakuta dynasty to an end, and the second line of Chalukyas was ruling the kingdom of the Rashtrakutas.

This see-sawing of dynasties was partly due to the fact that they were all fairly equally balanced in political and military strength. There was an absence of a highly centralized governmental system and corresponding local autonomy at levels of village and district administration without too much interference from the capital. This autonomy was preserved to a far greater degree in Tamil-nad, where the tradition was actively maintained for many centuries, than in western India. The use of the term feudatory in this context applies almost exclusively to political vassalage, the economic contract of feudal tenure and obligations not being identical in every case. The feudal system with feudatories in the usual sense of the term was a later development.

Amongst the Pallavas kingship was held to be of divine origin and hereditary, and they claimed descent from the god Brahma. On one occasion, however, when there was no direct heir, a king was elected, but this was not looked upon as something unheard of. Kings took high-sounding titles, some of which, such as *maharajadhiraja*, were borrowed from northern usage. Others were of local invention, such as *dharma-maharajadhiraja* (great king of kings ruling in accordance with the *dharma*), and the more unusual *aggitoma-vajapey-assamedha-yaji* (he who has performed the *agnishtoma*, *vajapeya*, and *ashvamedha* sacrifices), which sounds rather like a self-conscious declaration of conformity with Vedic ideas. The king was assisted by a group of ministers, and in the later Pallava period this ministerial council played a prominent part in state policy. Some of the ministers bore semi-royal titles and may well have been appointed from among the feudatories.

There was the usual hierarchy of officials in charge of provincial administration in Tamil-nad. The governor of a province was advised and assisted by officers in charge of districts who worked in close collaboration with local autonomous institutions, largely in an advisory capacity. These institutions appear to have been more common in the south than in northern India during this period. They were built on local relationship of caste, profession, and religious adherence. Frequent meetings or assemblies were essential to their functioning. Assemblies were of many varieties and at many levels, including those of merchant guilds, craftsmen, and artisans (such as weavers, oil-mongers, etc.), students, ascetics, and priests. There were assemblies of villagers and also of representatives of districts. General meetings of the members of an assembly were held annually, and more frequent meetings of smaller groups were responsible for implementing policy. The smaller groups were chosen by lot from amongst the eligible persons, and worked in a manner similar to modern committees, each group having its specific function.

In the village the basic assembly was the *sabha*, which was concerned with all matters relating to the village, including endowments, irrigation, cultivated land, punishment of crime, the keeping of a census and other necessary records. Village courts dealt with simple criminal cases. At a higher level, in towns and districts, courts were presided over by government officers, with the king as the supreme arbiter of justice. The *sabha* was a formal institution but it worked closely with the *urar*, an informal gathering of the entire village. Above this was a district council which worked with the *nadu* or district administration. Villages which were populated entirely or largely by brahmans have preserved records of the functioning of assemblies and councils. It is often said that these autonomous bodies were restricted to such villages alone and did not exist in villages with an overwhelmingly non-brahman population, for which records have not survived. But this does not necessarily follow, for it is unlikely that village assemblies, if they were found useful in a particular set of villages, would not become the norm for all villages in that region. The link between the village assembly and the official administration was the headman of the village, who acted both as the leader of the village and the mediator with the government.

Further north in the Deccan there was less autonomy in administrative institutions. In the Chalukya domains, government officers were more involved in routine administration, even at the village level, than in the system prevalent further south. Village assemblies did function but under the paternalistic eye of the official. The role of the headman as the leader of the village was also of a more formal nature. From the eighth century onwards some of the Deccan rulers adopted the decimal system of administrative division, where groups of ten villages or multiples of ten were formed into districts. Grouping in multiples of twelve was also known but was not in frequent use as yet.

Land-ownership rested with the king, who could make revenue grants to his officers and land grants to brahmans, or else continue to have the land cultivated by small-scale cultivators and landlords. The latter was the predominant practice. Crown lands were rented out to tenants-at-will. Private landowners bought land and this gave them the rights of sale and gifting. Grants to officers were largely in lieu of salaries and did not stipulate provision of troops or revenue for the state as was the case in a regular feudal structure.

The status of the village varied according to the tenures prevailing and could be one of three: the most frequent was the village with an inter-caste population paying taxes to the king in the form of land revenue; less frequent were the *brahmadeya* villages where the entire village or the lands of the village were donated to a single brahman or a group of brahmans. These villages tended to be more prosperous than the others because the brahmans did not pay any tax. Associated with the *brahmadeya* grant was the *agrahara* grant, an entire village settlement of brahmans, the land being given as a grant. These were also exempt from tax, but the brahmans could if they so wished provide free education for the local people. Finally, there were the *devadana* (donated to the god) villages, which functioned more or less in the same manner as the first category of villages except that the revenue from these villages was donated to a temple and was consequently received by the temple authorities and not by the state. The temple authorities assisted the village by providing employment for the villagers in the service of the temple wherever possible. This last category of villages gained greater significance when in later centuries the temples became the centres of rural life. During the Pallava period the first two types of villages were predominant.

The term village, as a rural unit, included the homes of the villagers, gardens, irrigation works (mainly tanks or wells), cattle enclosures, waste lands, the village common, forests surrounding the village, streams passing through the village lands, the temple and the temple lands, the cremation ground, and the 'wet' (irrigated) and 'dry' lands under cultivation. Land commonly owned and used for specific purposes, such as that kept for sifting paddy, was also included. Rice was the staple crop and was used both as a unit of barter and as a commercial crop when harvested in surplus. There were extensive coconut palm plantations, the produce of the tree being put to varied use. Both the palmyra and the areca palm were cultivated, the latter largely for export. Orchards of mangoes and plantains were a regular feature of the landscape. Oil extracted from cotton and gingelly seeds was also in great demand.

A special category of land, *eripatti* or tank land, was known only in south India. This was land donated by individuals, the revenue from which was set apart for the maintenance of the village tank, which indicates the dependence of the village on the tank for irrigation. Rain water was stored in the tank so that land could be irrigated during the long, dry spell in each year. The tank, lined with brick or stone, was built through the co-operative effort of the village, and its water was shared by all the cultivators. The maintenance of these tanks was essential to the village. Practically every inscription from the Pallava period pertaining to rural affairs refers to the upkeep of a tank. Wells came next in importance. Water was taken from the tank or the well by canals, and these were fitted with sluices to regulate the water level and prevent overflowing at the source. The distribution of water for irrigation was strictly supervised by a special tank committee appointed by the village. Water taken in excess of the amount permitted to a particular cultivator was taxed.

Information on land tenures and taxation is available from the detailed records in the grants, which have survived mainly on copper-plates. There were two categories of taxes levied in the village : the land revenue paid by the cultivator to the state varied from one sixth to one tenth of the produce of the land, and was collected by the village and paid to the state collector; the second category were local taxes also collected in the village but utilized for services in the village itself and its environs, and included funds for repairing irrigation works, decorating the temple, etc. The state land tax was low and revenue was supplemented by additional taxes on draught cattle, toddy-drawers, marriage-parties, potters, goldsmiths, washermen, textile-manufacturers, weavers, brokers, letter-carriers, and the makers of *ghi* (clarified butter). Unfortunately the percentage of tax is not always indicated and it doubtless varied according to the object taxed. The revenue came almost exclusively from rural sources, mercantile and urban institutions being as yet largely untapped.

An example of a typical land grant engraved and preserved on copper-plate is quoted below. It was found near a village in the vicinity of Pondicherry in 1879. It consists of eleven plates strung on a ring of copper, the two ends of which are soldered and stamped with a royal seal depicting a bull and a *lingam* (the Pallava symbol). It is a record of a grant of a village made in the twenty-second year of the king Nandi-varman (A.D. 753) and it commences with a eulogy of the king in Sanskrit, followed by the details of the grant in Tamil and a concluding verse in Sanskrit. The quotation is from the Tamil section, and it is significant that the most relevant sections of these grants were in Tamil and not in Sanskrit.

The author of the above eulogy was Trivikrama. The above is an order of the king dated in the twenty-second year of his reign. Let the inhabitants of Urrukkattukottam see. Having seen the order which was issued after the king had been pleased to give Kodukalli village of our country – having expropriated the former owners at the request of Brahmayuvaraja, having appointed Ghorasharman as the effector of the grant, having excluded previous grants to temples and grants to brahmans, having excluded the houses of the cultivators to the extent of altogether two *patti* (a measure of land) – as a *brahmadeya* (grant) to Shettiranga-Somayajin (Shettiranga who performs the Soma sacrifice), who belongs to the Bharadvaja *gotra* (a brahman exogamous sept), follows the *Chhandogyasutra* and resides at Puni, we, the inhabitants went to the boundaries which the headman of the *nadu* (district) pointed out, circumambulated the village from right to left, and planted milk-bushes and placed stones around it. The boundaries of this village are – the eastern boundary is to the west of the boundary of Palaiyur, the southern boundary is to the north of the boundary of Palaiyur, the western boundary is to the east of the boundary of Manarpakkam and of the boundary of Kollipakkam, and the northern boundary is to the south of the boundary of Velimanallur.

The donee shall enjoy the wet land and the dry land included within these four boundaries, wherever the iguana runs and the tortoise crawls, and shall be permitted to dig river channels and inundation channels for conducting water from the Seyarau, the Vetla, and the tank of Tiraiyan. . . . Those who take and use the water in these channels by pouring out baskets, by cutting branch channels, or by employing small levers shall pay a fine to be collected by the king. He (the donee) and his descendants shall enjoy the houses, house gardens, and so forth, and shall have the right to build houses and halls of burnt tiles. The land included within these boundaries we have endowed with all exemptions. He himself shall enjoy the exemptions obtaining in this village without paying for the oil-mills and looms, the hire of the well-diggers, the share of the brahmans of the king, the share of *shengodi* (a plant), the share of the *kallal* (a type of fig tree), the share of *kannittu*, the share of corn-ears, the share of the headman, the share of the potter, the sifting of paddy, the price of *ghi*, the price of cloth, the share of cloth, the hunters, messengers, dancing-girls, the grass, the best cow and the best bull, the share of the district, cotton-threads, servants, palmyra molasses, the fines to the accountant and the minister, the tax on planting water-lilies, the share of the water-lilies, the fourth part of the trunks of old trees of various kinds, including areca palms and coconut trees. . . .

The grant was made in the presence of the local authorities, of the ministers, and of the Secretaries.[1]

Since there were no large areas under cultivation on a scale as vast as that in the Ganges plain, the Pallavas and the Chalukyas had a limited income from land. Mercantile activity had not developed sufficiently to make a substantial contribution to the economy. Much of the revenue went to maintain an army. The system of feudal levies was known but was not relied upon to any great extent, the king preferring a standing army under his direct control. The army consisted in the main of foot-soldiers and cavalry with a small body of elephants. Chariots were by now almost out of fashion and in any case were ineffective in the hilly terrain where much of the fighting took place. Cavalry, which was the most effective arm in the circumstances, was also the most expensive, since the availability of horses was limited, and the import of horses from western Asia was costly. Army officers could, if occasion demanded, be used in civil administration, but generally there was a clear distinction between civil and military functions. The Pallavas developed a navy and built dockyards at Mahabalipuram and Negapattinam. However, the Pallava navy was inconsiderable as compared to the naval strength that south India was to acquire under the Cholas.

For the Pallavas their navy had other purposes as well as fighting. It assisted in the maritime trade with south-east Asia, where by now there were three major kingdoms: Kambuja (Cambodia), Champa (Annam), and Shrivijaya (the southern Malay peninsula and Sumatra), which were in close contact with India, with south Indian merchants in particular travelling out in search of trade. On the west coast, the initiative in the trade with the occident was gradually passing into the hands of the foreign traders settled along the coast, mainly the Arabs. Indian traders were becoming suppliers of goods rather than carriers of goods to foreign countries, and communication with the West became indirect, via the Arabs, and limited to trade alone. With southeast Asia, however, the continuity of cultural contacts increased, with Pallava architectural styles and the Tamil script extensively used amongst the local royalty. Tamil-nad was to make a major contribution to the evolution of ideas and forms in this region with the cultural pattern which it exported to south-east Asia.

Perhaps the most obvious sign of the influence of Aryan culture in the south was the pre-eminent position given to brahmans both in status and in gifts of land. Aryanization is also evident in the evolution of educational institutions in the Pallava kingdom. In the early part of this period education was controlled by Jainas and Buddhists, but gradually the brahmans superseded them. The Jainas had brought with them their religious literature in Sanskrit and Prakrit, but they had also begun to use Tamil. Jainism had been extremely popular, but the competition of Hinduism in the succeeding centuries reduced the number of its adherents. In addition, Mahendra-varman I lost interest in Jainism and took up the cause of Shaivism, thus depriving the Jainas of valuable royal patronage. The Jainas had developed a few educational centres near Madurai and Kanchi, and religious centres such as the one at Shravana Belgola, but the majority of the Jaina monks tended to scatter and isolate themselves in small caves tucked away in the hills and forests (the most beautiful amongst them being at Sittannavasal in Pudukkottai, where traces of elegant murals remain).

Monasteries continued to be the nucleus of the Buddhist educational system and were located in the region of Kanchi, the valleys of the Krishna and the Godavari rivers, and the district of Nellore. Buddhist centres were concerned with the study of Buddhism *per se*, particularly as this was a period of intense controversy between Buddhist and Hindu sects, and considerable time was spent in debating the finer points of theology, with Buddhism fighting a losing battle. Royal patronage, which the Buddhists lacked, gave an advantageous position to the protagonists of Hinduism.

Hindu colleges (*ghatikas*) were generally attached to the temples. Entry to these colleges was at first open to any 'twice-born' Hindu. Gradually, however, they became exclusively brahman institutions and consequently confined themselves to advanced study, although in some cases they were endowed by merchants. Extensive royal patronage led to their being politically active, in that they were centres either of loyalty to the monarchy or of political opposition when supported by disaffected members of the royal family. Apart from the university at Kanchi, which acquired fame equal to that of Nalanda, there were a number of other Sanskrit colleges.* In the eighth century, the *matha* became popular. This was a combination of a rest-house, a feeding-centre, and an education centre, which indirectly brought publicity to the particular sect with which it was associated. The *mathas* naturally served a more useful purpose in places where pilgrims gathered and where religious discussions could be more effective.

Sanskrit was the recognized medium in these colleges, and was also the official language at the court, which led to its adoption in literary circles. Two outstanding works in Sanskrit set the standard for Sanskrit literature in the south. These were Bharavi's *Kiratarjuniya* and Dandin's *Dashakumaracharita* (The Tale of the Ten Princes). There was a tendency, however, to conscious literary labouring which was carried to an extreme in another work of Dandin's, a poem, which was written with such skill that it could be read both forwards and in reverse, in the one case narrating the story of the *Ramayana* and in the other the story of the *Mahabharata*. Those who indulged in and acclaimed this degree of artificiality in literature remained unaware of the new languages which were to be the vehicles of new literature – Tamil in the far south and Kannada in the Deccan. References are made to the existence of considerable literature in Kannada at this time, but little has survived. A seventh-century inscription of a Chalukya king at Badami mentions Kannada as

* A residential college for brahman students near Pondi was maintained on the endowment from three villages donated by an official of the king Nripatunga. It specialized in an extremely orthodox training. The Enniyiram temple college provided free education to 340 students and had ten teaching departments.

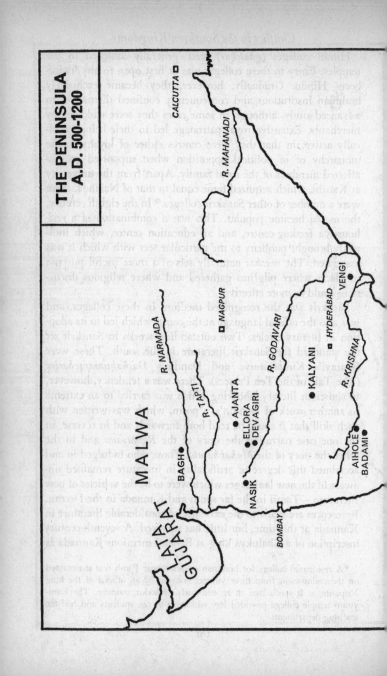

THE PENINSULA
A.D. 500-1200

CALCUTTA

R. MAHANADI

NAGPUR

R. NARMADA

MALWA

R. TAPTI

BAGH

AJANTA

ELLORA

DEVAGIRI

NASIK

BOMBAY

GUJARAT

LATA

R. GODAVARI

HYDERABAD

VENGI

R. KRISHNA

KALYANI

AIHOLE

BADAMI

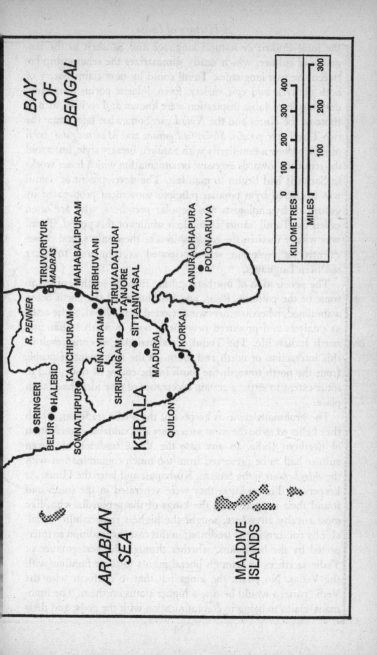

BAY
OF
BENGAL

KILOMETRES

0 100 200 300 400

0 100 200 300

MILES

TIRUVORIYUR
MADRAS
MAHABALIPURAM
KANCHIPURAM
TRIBHUVANI
R. PENNER
TIRUVADATURAI
ENNAYIRAM
TANJORE
SITTANIVASAL
SHRIRANGAM
KORKAI
MADURAI

SRINGERI
BELUR HALEBID
SOMNATHPUR

KERALA

QUILON

ANURADHAPURA
POLONARUVA

ARABIAN
SEA

MALDIVE
ISLANDS

the local Prakrit or natural language and Sanskrit as the language of culture, which neatly summarizes the relationship between the two languages. Tamil could by now claim poetry of both the lyric and epic variety. Even didactic poems frequently deriving from Jaina inspiration were known and recited, such as those of the *Kural* and the *Naladiyar*. Somewhat later came the two Tamil epic poems, *Shilappadigaram* and *Manimegalai*, both of which show a familiarity with Sanskrit literary style, but avoid the tendency towards excessive ornamentation which lesser works in Sanskrit had begun to manifest. The development of Tamil was furthered by a popular religious movement propagated by groups of hymnologists and popular preachers, who are often called the Tamil 'saints' in modern studies of this period. Tamil was widely used in the compositions of these saints, and consequently its evolution was accelerated as compared to other southern languages.

The penetration of northern culture into the south resulted in some of the patterns, ideas, and institutions of the north being assimilated, whereas others were rejected or modified. Some acted as catalysts and produced new forms both in south Indian and north Indian life. The Tamil devotional cult was one result of this interaction of north and south. In the movement of people from the north towards the south in the course of trade, and to some extent to settle, a certain acceptance of new ideas had taken place.

The brahmans came as keepers of the Vedic tradition, which they believed to be the most sacrosanct and valuable contribution of northern India. In any case the Vedic tradition of Aryan culture had to be preserved from too much contamination with the *mlechchhas* – the Shakas, Kushanas, and later the Huns. As keepers of this tradition they were venerated in the south and found their supporters in the kings of the peninsula who, like most royalty anywhere, sought the highest respectability available by conforming to tradition; in this case the tradition as interpreted by the brahmans, whether through the performance of Vedic sacrifices or through liberal grants to those familiar with the Vedas. No doubt the kings felt that to conform with the Vedic pattern would bestow a higher status on them. The brahmans' claim to being in communication with the gods, and their supposed ability to manipulate the unseen powers, was more convincing to the Tamil kings than the claims of the indigenous priests. An additional incentive to accepting the Vedic pattern was the promise of heavenly rewards.

The Vedic tradition was reinforced by other developments. A movement began which sought to cleanse Vedic philosophy of its obscurities and its inconsistencies, and thereby make it both comprehensible and acceptable to people at large. It arose from the attempt of a highly perceptive brahman, Shankaracharya, to face the increasing challenge to organized Brahmanism from the heterodox sects and the popular devotional cult. This brahman, who came from Kerala, achieved fame as the new interpreter of the *Vedanta* school and a propagator of *Advaita* (Monism) philosophy.

Shankara maintained that the world we see around us is an illusion (*maya*), for the reality lies beyond and cannot be perceived through existing human senses. Asceticism alone enables one to control these senses and direct them in a manner which permits of a glimpse of the Reality. He traced his teaching to Upanishadic thought, and for him the *Vedas* were sacred and above question. He was opposed to unnecessary ritual and wished to clear Hindu worship of many meaningless rites to which end he established his own *mathas*, where a simplified worship was practised. The *mathas* were at Badrinath in the Himalayas, Puri in Orissa, Dvarka on the western coast, and Shringeri in the south, all places which collected large numbers of pilgrims. These institutions were richly endowed and soon had branches elsewhere, becoming centres of Shankara's teaching. In addition he encouraged missionary members of his ascetic order to propagate his teaching. The philosophy and organization adopted by Shankara closely resembled those of the Buddhists, who were indignant, as can be well understood, at a movement intended to destroy them by their own methods.

Shankara travelled extensively in the sub-continent, displaying the brilliance of his mind in discussion and debate, and converting others to the cause of *Vedanta* and *Advaita*. His own enthusiasm in debating with the opponents of *Vedanta* spurred the philosophical centres into new speculative thinking, where earlier they had tended to be stagnant. But Shankara's philosophy con-

tained within it the possibilities of a negative reaction as well : if
the world around us is an illusion then there is no incentive to try
to understand its functioning or to derive empirical knowledge
from it. This logical corollary may have been in part the cause
of the rather pedantic intellectualism which became characteristic
of these centres in later centuries.

Vedic culture was not the only type of culture which travelled
south. In the sphere of religion, other groups either anti-Vedic
or non-Vedic in feeling were also present. Apart from Jainism
and Buddhism, there arrived the *Bhagavata* and *Pashupata* cults,
the cults of devotion to Vishnu and Shiva respectively – theism
with an emphasis on personal worship rather than sacrificial
ritual – and these were to strike roots in the populace whilst
royalty was busily concerning itself with Vedic ritual. Eventually, the devotional cult was to prove stronger than any other
religious force in the south, and this was recognized even by
royal patrons.

Jainism and Buddhism had gradually to give way to a new
form of religious worship, the devotional cults of the Tamil
saints, which were among the early expressions of what later
came to be called the *Bhakti* movement. The devotional aspect
was formulated in a relationship between God and man based on
love, a formulation which had not been so strongly stressed in
earlier Hindu thought. The worshipper, recognizing a feeling of
inadequacy, would declare his love for God who, it was believed,
permitted a reciprocal relationship, described poignantly in one
of the Tamil hymns.

> When you see his face praise him with joy,
> worship him with joined palms bow before him,
> so that his feet touch your head,
> Holy and mighty will be his form
> rising to heaven, but his sterner face
> will be hidden, and he will show you
> the form of a young man, fragrant and beautiful
> and his words will be loving and gracious –
> Don't be afraid – I knew you were coming.[2]

Tamil devotionalism achieved a great wave of popularity in the
sixth and seventh centuries A.D. and was continued in the hymns
and sermons of the *Nayanars* (the Shaivite saints) and the

Alvars (the Vaishnavite saints). The hymns dedicated to Shiva and Vishnu have been preserved in two separate collections, the *Tirumurai* and the *Nalayiraprabandham*. Of the Shaivite saints the most popular were Appar (who is said to have converted the king Mahendra-varman), Sambandar, Manikkavasagar, and Sundarar. The Vedic gods were either denied or ignored, the emphasis being not on the object of worship but on the relationship involved in worship, the relationship between man and God.

Manikkavasagar explains it in his hymns:

> Indra or Vishnu or Brahma
> Their divine bliss crave not I
> I seek the love of thy saints
> Though my house perish thereby.
> To the worst hell will I go
> So but thy grace be with me
> Best of all, how could my heart
> Think of a God beside Thee? ...
> I had no virtue, penance, knowledge, self-control
> A doll to turn
> At other's will I danced, whistled, fell. But me
> He filled in every limb
> With love's mad longing, and that I might climb
> There whence there is no return.
> He shewed His beauty, made me His. Ah me, when
> shall I go to Him?[3]

A similar feeling finds expressions in a hymn addressed to Vishnu by Nammalvar:

> Thou has't not yet been gracious enough to extend thy
> sympathy towards thy consort (the singer). Before
> she gives up her ghost in despair owing to thy
> indifference show so much at least of thy mercy as to
> send word to thy consort through thy messenger and
> vehicle Garuda, the store-house of kindness, not to
> pine away but to take courage a little, till
> Thou, Lord and Master, returnest as expected, which
> will assuredly take place soon.*[4]

---

* The author in this case is a man, but feels himself in a feminine relationship towards his God.

Although there were some brahmans among the writers of hymns, the majority belonged to the lower castes, being artisans and cultivators. They came from various parts of the Tamil country and travelled extensively. Perhaps the most revolutionary feature was that there were women saints as well, such as Andal, whose hymns were much revered. Andal saw herself as the beloved of the god Vishnu and sang verses on her love for him which foreshadow the verses of Mirabai, a princess of Rajasthan, who was to become equally famous as a *Bhakti* singer many centuries later.

Although Tamil culture eventually rejected Buddhism and was not particularly loyal to Jainism, the impact of both these religions is evident in the Tamil devotional cult, which in its social approach leaned towards rejecting the established order of society as stratified in the caste structure, and received support from the lower castes. The theism of the *Bhagavata* cult was derived from ideas in the *Upanishads* and the heterodox doctrines, and the theism of the Tamil cult had similar origins. The concept of a compassionate God was due to the influence of Buddhist ideas more specifically in the notion of the compassionate *bodhisattva*, though here the Christians of Malabar may have made a contribution as well. The feeling of human inadequacy and sin which became an important facet of the Tamil cult owes more to Buddhist ancestry than to Vedic. The decline of the heterodox sects coincided with the rise of the Tamil cult and it is probable that the latter deprived the former of much of its potential following.

Although never so recognized by the brahmans, the Tamil devotional cult was in part a resistance to the Aryanization of the region. The brahmans enjoyed royal patronage, but the cult was widely supported by the ordinary people, although, in later centuries, when the established order had arrived at a compromise with it, royal patronage was frequently extended to the cult. The brahmans propagated Hinduism through esoteric theories and the use of Sanskrit; the devotional cult expressed itself in easily understood forms and used only the popular language, Tamil. The brahmans were obsessed with caste regulations and rigidly excluded non-brahmans from participation in religious knowledge; the Tamil saints not only ignored caste but excluded no one for caste reasons alone.

Organized religion under the aegis of the brahmans was well-fortified with finance and patronage, both of which came either from royalty or from the wealthy merchants. The local temple was the nucleus of religious life and here the two levels of religion, the brahmanical and the devotional, met. The temple was maintained from endowments which consisted either of villages and agricultural lands – if the donors were of the royal family – or else came from the investment of capital, if the donors were merchants or guilds. The smaller accessories of the temple, such as subsidiary images, lamps, oil, etc., were generally obtained through the individual donations of lesser members of the community. Temple attendants were of various categories. Brahmans alone could conduct the service in the sanctum sanctorum. Members of the other castes looked after the cleanliness of the temple, played music for the ceremonies in the temple, lighted the lamps and saw to the flowers and garlands necessary for the worship of the images. The unclean *shudras*, such as the potters and the tanners and the outcastes, were not permitted to enter the precincts of the temple, since their presence would pollute it. Whenever the endowments and attendants of the temple increased sizeably, as they were gradually doing, a formal managing committee was appointed to supervise the administration of the endowments and the employees of the temple.

Religious hymns and music were popularized by the Tamil saints, and the singing of these hymns became a regular feature of temple ritual. The *vina* was probably the most frequently used instrument, its origin being the bow-harp familiar to both the Indian sub-continent and the ancient Middle East. Sometime around the fifth century A.D. it was replaced in India by a lute with a pear-shaped body. Some two centuries later it took the form in which it is found today – a small gourd body with a long finger-board. Dancing was also included in the ritual at the temple. Originating with folk dancing, the choreography of temple dancing became the highly sophisticated and complex renderings of religious themes as apparent in its final form, *Bharata natyam* (the dance according to the choreographical rules of Bharata as explained in his text, the *Natya-shastra*). From the

Pallava period onwards trained groups of dancers were maintained by the more prosperous temples.

Pallava temples were usually free-standing buildings, but the vogue set by the Buddhists for cave temples still continued. The brahmans and Buddhists vied with each other in cutting shrines and temples into the Deccan hills, where, by this time, worship at these shrines may have been open to anyone, the rivalry between the two religions not being particularly felt by ordinary people. The most impressive of these cave temples are the Buddhist shrines at Ajanta and the Buddhist and Hindu temples at Ellora. Even the Jainas joined in, and excavated a few temples at the latter site.

The walls of the Buddhist cave shrines were covered with murals illustrating Buddhist narratives. Whilst treating a religious theme, these murals displayed a rich cross-section of contemporary life. To cover the walls of deep-cut caves with murals was an achievement of no mean order, considering the difficulty of adequate lighting and working conditions in these vast caves. The tradition of murals in cave shrines had begun in the early centuries A.D., but the finest examples at Ajanta date to Vakataka and Chalukya patronage in the fifth and sixth centuries A.D. The technique of painting was that of fresco-secco, the actual painting being done on a dry surface. A paste consisting of powdered rock, clay, or cow dung mixed with chaff and molasses was smeared on the wall as a ground. This was carefully smoothed out and whilst still wet was laid over with a coat of fine lime wash. Colour was applied when the ground had dried, and the final work was burnished. The colours were made from minerals and plants and still retain some of their original brilliance.

Murals were common not only in cave temples but in the free-standing temples of the south as well. In the case of the former some of the murals may have been painted by the monks, although artists must have been employed in most cases in order to arrive at the professional excellence of the examples such as those visible today at Ajanta, Sittannavasal, Bagh, and Kanchipuram. Murals were not restricted to religious monuments alone, since, judging by literary descriptions, domestic architecture was also embellished with paintings, but unfortunately these have not survived.

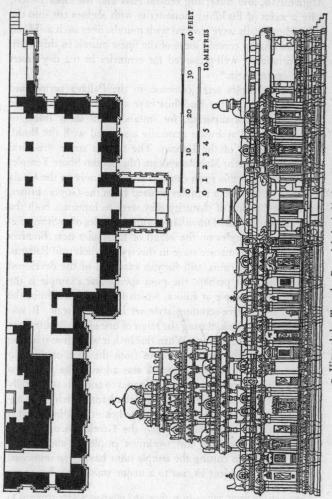

5. Virupaksha Temple, Pattadakal: half-plan and section

40 FEET
30
20
10
0

10 METRES
5
4
3
2
1
0

A more distant region where this tradition of Indian painting was adopted was central Asia. Commencing at Bamiyan in Afghanistan, and traversing central Asia and the Gobi Desert, were a series of Buddhist monasteries with shrines cut into the hills, whose walls were covered with murals. Sites such as Miran and Tun-Huang contain some of the finest murals in this tradition, fortunately well-preserved for centuries in the dry desert sand of central Asia.*

Rock-cut temples were common in the Pallava period and these were akin to the Buddhist cave shrines. The monolithic temples at Mahabalipuram, for instance, still show traces of barrel-vaults and archways generally associated with the Buddhist cave shrines of the Deccan. The earliest stone structural temples were built at Mahabalipuram (the famous Shore Temple) and Kanchi, but this form came to its prime only in the Chola period. The Chalukya temples evolved from the Gupta shrines, but in their period of maturity they were to influence both the Northern Indian and Dravidian (southern) styles of architecture. The rock-cut temples on the island of Elephanta near Bombay are examples of a mature stage in this style. Aihole and Badami, although now in ruins, still furnish examples of the developed Deccan style, but perhaps the most spectacular example is the Kailashanatha temple at Ellora, which is a transition from the rock-cut to the free-standing style on a massive scale. It was built, or rather hewn, during the reign of one of the Rashtrakuta kings in the eighth century. When finished, it was a free-standing temple open to the sky, wholly cut from the rock of the hillside, to which no further material was added. The plan of a free-standing temple is rigorously adhered to and it is stylistically close to the Dravidian temple. The Kailashanatha temple is approximately of the same area as the Parthenon at Athens and is one and a half times higher than the Greek structure. The number of stone-cutters and workmen employed and the expenses involved in cutting the temple must have been immense, perhaps the equivalent in cost to a major war. It has been sug-

---

*Some of the finest murals from these and other sites were removed to museums in Europe in the twentieth century, of which probably the best collection was housed in Berlin, but was severely damaged during the Second World War.

gested that it was nevertheless cheaper to cut the temple from the rock than to build a free-standing structure of the same dimensions. This supposition may in part account for the prolonged popularity of the rock-cut shrine and temple.

The free-standing temples at Aihole and Badami in the Deccan and at Kanchipuram and Mahabalipuram in the Tamil country provide a better background for sculpture than the rock-cut temples. The Deccan style in sculpture shows a close affinity to the Gupta. Pallava sculpture owed more to the Buddhist tradition and remained on the whole both more monumental and more definitely linear in form, avoiding the tendency to ornamentation which occurred quite early in Deccan sculpture. Yet the sculpture and architecture of the Deccan and Tamil-nad were not mere offshoots of the northern tradition. They are distinctly recognizable as different and have a personality of their own; the basic form was taken from the older tradition, but the end result unmistakably reflected its local genius.

These developments were typical of the culture of the peninsula and particularly of south India at this time. With the emergence of the southern personality – an amalgam of Dravidian and Aryan patterns – Indian culture, which had already received enriching infusions, underwent a further change with the impact of yet another influence, this time from south India. It is possible at this stage to think in terms of the entire subcontinent, since there was now far more real contact between the various regions. The rapid diffusion of the ideas of Shankara points to this. The outburst of the *Bhakti* cult in various parts of India, although it was not a contemporary expression, and was inaugurated by the Tamil devotional cult, nevertheless suggests that a minimum of common characteristics was beginning to emerge in the various regions of the sub-continent.

THE SOUTH IN THE ASCENDANT

c. A.D. 900–1300

THE pattern of conflict between warring states persisted for several centuries. Although the Cholas were in the ascendant during the eleventh and twelfth centuries the strains to which they were subjected from other kingdoms continued. The Pallavas succumbed to a combined attack from their southern neighbours, the Pandyas, and their feudatories the Cholas, in the ninth century. For three hundred years the Pallava chiefs remained as minor feudatories of the Cholas until finally they disappeared. During these three hundred years the Cholas fought to assert themselves, finally emerging as the dominant power in the south. Their early conflict was with the declining Rashtrakutas, whose place was then taken by a revived branch of the Chalukyas, known as the Later Chalukyas, rising to power in the western Deccan. The Deccan during this period was divided into a number of smaller kingdoms of similar status with each of whom the Cholas were at war at some stage. Political alignments involved the Later Chalukyas, the Yadavas of Devagiri (northern Deccan in the region of Aurangabad), the Kakatiyas of Warangal (Andhra), and the Hoysalas of Dorasamudra (Mysore). In their last years of power the Cholas were weakened by the continued incursions of the Hoysalas and the Pandyas.

The ascendancy of the south was due not solely to the power of the Cholas but also to the fact that this period saw the crystallization of Tamil culture. In whatever sphere, whether of social institutions, religion, or the fine arts, the standards established during this period were regarded as classical and came to dominate the pattern of living in the south, and to influence and modify at certain levels the patterns existing elsewhere in the peninsula (although in the western Deccan, for instance, this influence did not survive the Cholas). This was also the period which saw the spread of Chola culture to areas in south-east Asia, and the active intervention, both political and economic, of south India in the commerce of this region to a far greater degree than ever before.

The Cholas had ruled as chieftains in Tamil-nad since the first century A.D. Towards the middle of the ninth century, one of them conquered the region of Tanjore (the heart of Tamil-nad), declared himself the ruler of an independent state, and sought to establish his status by claiming descent from the Solar race. In A.D. 907, the first important ruler of the Chola dynasty, Parantaka I, came to power and ruled for almost half a century. He secured the southern frontier of the kingdom by campaigning against the Pandyas and capturing their capital, Madurai. This brought him into contact with Ceylon, with whom the Pandyas had had close relations, and hostilities between Ceylon and Tamil-nad began which were to last through several decades. The later part of Parantaka's reign saw Chola defeat at the hands of the Rashtrakutas, with the latter occupying many of the recently acquired northern districts of the Chola kingdom. There followed a period of thirty years in which a succession of weak kings brought about a decline in the power of the Cholas. Soon the pendulum was to swing the other way, for the Rashtrakutas were being harassed by their one-time feudatories and future overlords, the Chalukyas. In the confusion, Chola territory lost to the Rashtrakutas was gradually recovered and Chola power became solidly established with the accession of Rajaraja I (985–1014) and of his son and successor Rajendra, which allowed of fifty years in which the Chola kingdom could be consolidated and stabilized.

The reigns of both father and son were taken up with extensive campaigns in almost every direction. Rajaraja began by attacking the alliance between Kerala, Ceylon, and the Pandyas, in order to try to break the monopoly of western trade held by these kingdoms. The Arabs were by now well-established as traders on the west coast of India and had the support of the rulers of Kerala. The Cholas were aware of Arab competition in the south-east Asian trade and tried to strike at the root of this competition by bringing Malabar under their control. At a later date, Rajaraja conducted a naval attack on the Maldive Islands, which had assumed importance in the Arab trade. The Cholas, although unable to strike directly at the Arab trade, caused havoc in Ceylon with a devastating campaign when the existing capital, Anuradhapura, was destroyed and the Cholas moved the capital to Pollonnaruva. Campaigns against the rulers of the Deccan states continued apace. The ghost of the old Pallava–Chalukya conflict over the rich province of Vengi reappeared in wars between the Cholas and the Later Chalukyas over the same area.

Rajendra I ruled jointly with his father for two years, succeeding him in 1014. The policy of expansion continued with the annexation of the southern provinces of the Chalukyas (the region of modern Hyderabad). Campaigns against Ceylon and Kerala were also renewed. But Rajendra's ambitions had turned northwards, even as far as the Ganges valley. An expedition set out and, marching through Orissa, reached the banks of the Ganges, from where it is said the water of the sacred river was taken to the Chola capital. Rajendra did not hold the northern regions for long, the position being similar to that of Samudra Gupta's campaign in the south almost seven hundred years earlier.

Even more ambitious was Rajendra's overseas campaign involving both his army and his navy against the kingdom of Shrivijaya in south-east Asia. It has been suggested that this major undertaking arose from a desire for an overseas empire. Had this been so the campaign would have been followed up with Indian colonization of the areas annexed and an attempt to conquer more of the hinterland. Since this did not happen, the cause for the war may be sought in the desire to protect Indian commercial interests from interference. By the tenth century there was a well-developed trade between China and south India. Ships passed through the seas held by the kingdom of Shrivijaya (the southern Malay peninsula and Sumatra), and the latter realized that it would be more lucrative for local traders if the China–India trade could be made to terminate in Shrivijaya with local middle-men taking the goods to their eventual destinations. Indian merchants in Shrivijaya territory were threatened, and this raised the wrath of the Chola, who may well have had his own investment in this trade, and the result was an attack on Shrivijaya. From the point of view of its own mercantile interests, Shrivijaya was justified in wishing to interfere in the China–India trade, but in this case military power decided the issue. The campaign was successful in that a number of strategic places along the Straits of Molucca were captured by the Chola forces, and, for a while at least, Indian shipping and commerce were safe in their passage through Shrivijaya territory.

The successors of Rajendra I turned their attention to conflicts within the peninsula and the struggle with the Chalukyas for the province of Vengi was revived. The old pattern repeated itself – lightning raids into each other's territory. A Chola raid into the heart of Chalukya territory saw the sacking of the capital at Kalyani. This was avenged in 1050 by the Chalukya king. This rivalry became somewhat less intense during the reign of the Chola King Kulottunga I (1070–1118), perhaps because he had Chalukya blood on his mother's side, and this introduced a new element into the relationship. The old enemies of the far south, the Pandyas, Kerala, and Ceylon, remained at war. Shrivijaya, still smarting under defeat by Rajendra, was peaceful, and this permitted a steady improvement in the commerce of south India and better communications with the Chinese, to whom Kulottunga sent an embassy of seventy-two merchants in 1077.

By the third quarter of the twelfth century Chola ascendancy was waning. Provinces on the fringes of the kingdom were being eroded by neighbours. The power of the feudatories in the Deccan had increased when central control weakened. Frequent campaigns had exhausted Chola resources and although they had finally succeeded in establishing their supremacy it was at the cost of their own stability. Furthermore, the eventual breaking of Chalukya power by the Cholas was to recoil on the Cholas themselves since it removed the controlling authority over the Chalukya feudatories, who set up their own kingdoms and prepared to attack the Chola kingdom.

Among these the most powerful were the Yadavas, the Hoysalas, and the Kakatiyas. The Yadavas kept mainly to the northern Deccan, and their contribution to the final disintegration of the Cholas was insignificant. The Hoysalas and the Kakatiyas became active from the twelfth century onwards. The latter, having won their independence from the Chalukyas, retired to enjoy it, except for the periods when they were in action against the Cholas. The main attack on the Cholas from the west came from the Hoysalas, and this the Cholas were able to resist. But their older enemy, the Pandya kingdom of Madurai, saw this as an ideal opportunity to revive hostilities, and the Chola strength had therefore to be diverted to two fronts, the western and the southern.

The rise of the Hoysalas is in many ways representative of several dynasties of the Deccan during this period and in subsequent centuries. The family began as hill chieftains whose main source of revenue was brigandage, an unfailing source in the hilly districts of the Ghats and the higher regions of the plateau. Owing to the political confusion during changes of dynasty, the hill people were eager to gain the protection of a powerful leader. Their support gave enough strength to the early Hoysalas to move down into the plains, from where an even more reliable source of revenue, taxes, was available. The people of the plains bought off the attacks from the hill chieftains by agreeing to pay tribute. The paying of taxes sometimes led to political loyalty as well, and gradually the former hill chieftains found themselves the virtual possessors of small kingdoms on the basis of which they established a dynasty. Not all such dynasties survived, for some were swallowed up by existing kingdoms; those that did became kingdoms in their own right.

It was Vishnuvardhana who established a kingdom for the Hoysala dynasty. He ruled during the first half of the twelfth century when the Hoysalas were still theoretically the feudatories of the Chalukyas. The core of the kingdom was at Dorasamudra, near modern Mysore, and Vishnuvardhana prepared the way for political independence by consolidating his strength around his capital. Vishnuvardhana is also remembered for his interest in the teachings of the Vaishnava philosopher Ramanuja, who persuaded the king to forsake Jainism for Vaishnavism. The consolidation of the Hoysala kingdom was continued by Ballala II, the grandson of Vishnuvardhana, and resulted in the domination of the southern Deccan by the Hoysalas.

To the north, however, the Hoysalas met with opposition from the Yadavas of Devagiri who had also expanded their kingdom at the expense of Chalukya territory, and by the thirteenth century they had laid claim to Gujarat, which, unfortunately for them, they could not hold for long. The Yadavas and the Hoysalas were to last until the fourteenth century, when a totally new force in the politics of northern India, the Turkish sultans of Delhi, intervened in the affairs of the Deccan, an intervention which led to the overthrow of the existing dynasties and the establishment of new kingdoms and political alignments.

By the thirteenth century the Pandyas had superseded the Cholas as the dominant power in the Tamil country and might well have maintained this position in the subsequent century had it not been for the attacks from the Turkish rulers and the threat of interference from the northern Deccan, which was virtually in the hands of the Delhi Sultanate. The Pandyas remained local chiefs and feudatories of the changing rulers of the region. Marco Polo visited the Pandyan kingdom in 1288 and 1293 and has left a vivid description of the richness of the land and the prosperity of its trade.

Political developments on the opposite coast, that of Kerala, were of a quieter nature. The Chera kingdom had been in close contact with the Cholas, whether as a peaceful neighbour or as a warring enemy, but it had little political ambition, except possibly during the reign of Ravivarman Kulashekhara at the end of the thirteenth century, who set out unsuccessfully to acquire a kingdom for himself from the ruins of the existing southern kingdoms. Nor was there any economic pressure to encourage territorial conquest, the Malabar coast being naturally rich in produce and obtaining an adequate income from western trade. In the tenth century, another group of people of Semitic origin came to India. A charter of the king of the Cheras granted land to Joseph Rabban – the earliest evidence of a Jewish community settling in India, although tradition mentions an earlier settlement in Cochin in the first century A.D. The Travancore Jews, as the descendants of Joseph Rabban were called, split into two groups : one preserved its Jewish identity with great rigidity and the second mixed with the local population though continuing to call itself Jewish.

From the number and distribution of dynasties, it would appear that the functioning of a centralized system was not feasible in the Deccan. Whatever ambitions the Chalukyas, Rashtrakutas, Yadavas, and Hoysalas may have had were necessarily restricted by the ambitions of their feudatories. The Cholas alone were able to ignore their feudatories to a significant extent. The

Chola political system was the only one which still maintained contact with the cultivator on a wide scale, and retained characteristics of a centrally organized administration. The political status of Rajaraja I was certainly different from that of Amoghavarsha the Rashtrakuta ruler or Vishnuvardhana the Hoysala. The unobtrusive titles used by the early Chola kings were replaced with high sounding titles, such as *chakravartigal* (emperor, the equivalent of the northern *chakravartin*). The cult of the god-king was encouraged through the worship of images of the deceased rulers and the building of temples which were also monuments to dead kings. The royal household was run on an elaborate scale and royal patronage was lavish. The political role of the *purohita* (priest) as known to northern Indian politics underwent a modification in the Chola system. The *raja-guru* (priest of the royal family) of the Cholas became a confidant and confessor in addition to being the adviser in all matters temporal and sacred. For further advice there was an assembly of officers whom the king could consult, but there is no record of a regular ministerial council.

Administration was carried out by a well-integrated body of officials. The system of recruitment is not described, but presumably it did not differ in essentials from the north Indian system, where selection was based on a judicious balance of birth, caste, connexions, and qualifications. Orders were issued by the king orally in the first instance and were later recorded, and in the case of a contract were attested to by a series of officers. The Chola kingdom was divided into provinces (*mandalam*), there being generally eight or nine of these. Each *mandalam* was divided into *valanadus* or districts. These in turn were subdivided into groups of villages, variously called *kurram*, *nadu*, or *kottam*. Occasionally a very large village would be administered as a single unit, and this was called a *taniyur*.

The administrative unit was the village and to that extent there was little significant difference between Chola administration and that of the Guptas. However, the nature of village administration was certainly of a very different order. The degree of autonomy at village level was something quite remarkable for the times. Chola officials participated in village affairs more as advisers and observers than as administrators. This permitted a certain continuity in local growth and development without too much interference from political changes at the upper level, and may in part account for the general cultural continuity which is among the more noticeable features of the Tamil region as compared with other parts of the sub-continent.

The basic assumption in the type of village autonomy emerging at this period was that each village should be administered by the villagers themselves. To this purpose a village assembly was formed, and authority was vested in this assembly. In the larger villages, where rural organization was more complex, there was a variety of assemblies and a villager could be a member of two or more, depending on the membership requirements. A village could be divided into wards and each ward could call an assembly of its members, some of whom might also be representatives of professional groups, such as the carpenters, smiths, etc., or part of a group supervising other village functions such as the maintenance of the local temple. Relationships between these various groups were basic to the social life of the village. Apart from these smaller groups there would be a general assembly.

The general assemblies included most of the local residents and were of three categories : the *ur* consisted of the tax-paying residents of an ordinary village; the *sabha* was restricted to the brahmans of the village or else was found exclusively in villages gifted to brahmans; and, finally, the *nagaram* was found more commonly in trade centres, since it catered almost entirely for mercantile interests. In some villages the *ur* and the *sabha* are found together. Very large villages had two *urs* if this was more convenient for their functioning.

The working of these assemblies differed according to local conditions. The *ur* was open to all the male adults of the village but in effect the older members took a more prominent part, some of them forming a small executive body for routine matters. The *sabha* had the same system and in addition had the power to constitute smaller committees of any size from amongst its members for specialized work. Election to the *sabha* appears to have been by lot from amongst those who were eligible, though amendments to the working of the *sabha* were made whenever it was thought necessary. An inscription from the temple wall at

Uttaramerur (a village of brahmans) gives details of how the local *sabha* functioned. It dates back to the tenth century and reads :

... There shall be thirty wards.

In these thirty wards those that live in each ward shall assemble and shall select each person possessing the following qualifications for inclusion for selection by lot :

He must own more than one quarter of the tax-paying land.
He must live in a house built on his own site.
His age must be below seventy and above thirty-five.
He must know the *mantras* and *Brahamanas*.

Even if he owns only one-eighth of the land, his name shall be included provided he has learnt one *Veda* and one of the four *Bhashyas*.

Among those possessing these qualifications only such as are well conversant with business and are virtuous shall be taken, and one who possesses honest earnings whose mind is pure and who has not been on any of the committees for the last three years shall also be chosen. One who has been on any of the committees but has not submitted his accounts, and his relations specified below, cannot have their names written on the tickets :

The sons of the younger and elder sisters of his mother.
The sons of his paternal aunt and maternal uncle.
The uterine brother of his mother.
The uterine brother of his father.
His uterine brother.
His father-in-law.
The uterine brother of his wife.
The husband of his uterine sister.
The sons of his uterine sister.
His son-in-law.
His father.
His son.

One against whom incest or the first four of the five great sins are recorded. (The five great sins being killing a brahman, drinking alcohol, theft, adultery, and associating with criminals.) All his relations specified above shall not be eligible to be chosen by lot. One who has been outcaste for association with low people shall not have his name chosen until he performs the expiatory ceremonies.

One who is foolhardy ...
One who has stolen the property of others ...

One who has taken forbidden dishes . . .

One who has committed sins and has had to perform expiatory ceremonies of purification . . .

Excluding all these, names shall be written on tickets for thirty wards and each of the wards in these twelve streets shall prepare a separate covering ticket for thirty wards bundled separately. These packets shall be put into a pot. When the tickets have to be drawn a full meeting of the great assembly including the young and old members shall be convened. All the temple priests who happen to be in the village on that day, shall, without any exception whatever, be caused to be seated in the inner hall where the great assembly meets. In the midst of the temple priests, one of them who happens to be the eldest shall stand up and lift that pot, looking upwards so as to be seen by all people. One ward shall be taken out by any young boy standing close who does not know what is inside and shall be transferred to another empty pot and shaken loose. From this pot one ticket shall be drawn and made the arbitrator. While taking charge of the ticket thus given to him, the arbitrator shall receive it on the palm of his hand with the five fingers open. He shall read out the ticket thus received. The ticket shall be read by all the priests present in the inner hall. The name thus read shall be put down and accepted. Similarly one man shall be chosen for each of the thirty wards.

Of the thirty men thus chosen those who had previously been on the Garden Committee, and on the Tank Committee, those who are advanced in learning and those who are advanced in age shall be chosen for the Annual Committee. Of the rest, twelve shall be taken for the Garden Committee and the remaining six shall form the Tank Committee. The great men of these three committees shall hold office for full 360 days and then retire. Anyone on a Committee found guilty of an offence shall be removed at once. For appointing the committees after these have retired, the members of 'the Committee for Supervision of Justice' in the twelve streets shall convene an assembly with the help of the arbitrator. The Committees shall be appointed by drawing pot-tickets. . . .

For the Five-fold Committee and the Gold Committee, names shall be written for pot-tickets in the thirty wards (and the same procedure followed). One who has ridden an ass (i.e., been punished) or who has committed a forgery shall not be included.

Any arbitrator who possesses honest earnings shall write the accounts of the village. No accountant shall be appointed to that office again before he submits his accounts to the great men of the chief committee and is declared to have been honest. The accounts which he has been writing he shall submit himself, and no other accountant shall be chosen to close his accounts. Thus, from this year onwards as long as the moon and the sun endure, committees shall always be appointed by lot. . . . We, the assembly of Uttaramerur – *chaturvedimangalam* made this settlement for the prosperity of our village in order that wicked men may perish and the rest may prosper. At the order of the great men sitting in the assembly, I, the arbitrator Kadadipottan Shivakkuri Rajamallamangalapriyan, thus wrote the settlement.[1]

Other inscriptions refer to similar procedure, though there are variations in qualifications and requirements and in the sanction of expenditure. The great assembly was summoned by the beat of a drum and generally met in the precincts of the temple. Interchange and cooperation amongst village assemblies was not unknown.

The village assembly was responsible for collecting the assessment for the government. In many cases it was collected as a joint assessment on the entire village. In addition, the assembly could make a levy for a particular purpose : for example, the construction of a water tank. These were kept separate from the taxes collected for the state. The activities of the assembly included the keeping of records, particularly those pertaining to charities and taxes, and the settling of agrarian disputes such as conflicts over tenures and irrigation rights. The larger assemblies kept a small staff of paid officers, but most of the work was done on a voluntary basis in the smaller villages.

The existence of the assembly did not eliminate the need for an intermediary between the village and the king other than the king's officer. The Chola kings had their feudatories such as the Pallava chiefs and other minor rulers, but relationship between the feudatory and the overlord was not the concern of the village assembly. The degree of autonomy at village level was such that shifting relations in the upper levels of the administrative and political structure did not interfere with the routine life of the village. That this was possible is due to the considerable degree of economic and political self-sufficiency of the village and both social institutions and economic activity were organized within this framework. The intermediary or feudatory was chiefly interested in collecting the revenue and passing on the king's share. The actual collection was the concern of the assembly. This system was particular to the Chola country. Elsewhere, in the Deccan and in northern India, the position of the feudatory had by now changed from mere political subservience to one of active political and economic significance; the feudatory did not merely pass on the king's share of the revenue, but had a definite relationship with the ruler which was contracted from a position of comparative power on the part of the feudatory (as will be described in a further chapter).

Tenancy was broadly of two kinds. Land could either be held in communal ownership, where the entire village paid the contracted amount of revenue, or else it could be privately held by peasant proprietors. The latter paid their dues to the king's officer, the assignee, or the temple. The assessment was fixed and whatever remained to the tenant over and above what was due he kept for himself. The system of service tenures was known, where the dues, partially or totally, were remitted in lieu of some service, but these were generally on a very small scale, such as a remittance of tax to the temple in lieu of fetching the water for bathing the deity. In later centuries this tenure came to be used extensively for military service. The recipients of *brahmadeya* grants and *devadeya* grants were treated as secular landowners where any question of tenure was involved.

Brahmadeya donations remained unchanged in pattern from those of Pallava times, as is evident from the Chola grants, such as the Anbil grant of Sundara Chola recording the donations of land to the brahman Anirudha Brahmadhiraja.

. . . we marked the boundaries of the land thus defined by erecting mounds of earth and planting cactus. The several objects included in this land, such as fruit-yielding trees, water, lands, gardens, all upgrowing trees and down-going wells, open spaces, wastes in which calves graze, the village site, ant-hills, platforms built round trees, canals, hollows; rivers and their alluvial deposits, tanks, granaries, fishponds, clefts with bee-hives, deep ponds included; and everything else on which the iguana runs and the tortoise crawls; and taxes such as the income from places of justice, the taxes on betel leaves, the cloths from looms . . . everything that the king could take and enjoy, all these shall be made over to this man. He shall be at liberty to erect halls and upper storeys with burnt bricks; to dig wells, big and small; to plant southernwood and cactus; to dig channels in accordance with watering requirements: not to waste surplus water but to dam it for irrigation; no one shall employ baskets for lifting such water (from his land). In this wise was the old order changed and the old name and old taxes removed, and an *ekabhoga brahmadeya* (land granted to a single brahman) under the name of Karunakaramangalam constituted.[2]

There was a sharp distinction between those who paid land tax, the tenants, and those who did not, the agricultural labourers working for a wage. The distinction was largely that the labourer was not included in the village assembly and could not hold a position of responsibility in local administration. The condition of landless labourers was close to that of serfs, with little hope of improvement. Many were employed on temple estates, yet owing to their being of low caste they were not permitted entry into the temple.

Reclamation of waste land and the clearing of forests was a regular part of the peasant's and labourer's work. This was encouraged by the government, since the increase of land under cultivation meant an increase in revenue. Cattle-raising had by now become a subsidiary occupation except in the upland regions. Two or even three crops of paddy per year were regarded as normal, though the yield varied as also did the value of the land, both being dependent on adequate irrigation. Land tax whether in cash or kind was the largest single source of the income of the Chola state, although other taxes were also collected, such as those on mines, forests, salt, professional taxes, customs dues and tolls, judicial fines and the equivalent in forced labour (*vetti*). Land tax was generally assessed at one third of the produce, which is high by any standards, though in exceptional circumstances remission or commutation was permitted by the king.

Permanent assessment of land for tax purposes was known but was not usual. Assessment required land surveys at frequent intervals. Land-tax in addition to local dues levied by the assembly or the temple must have been a strain on the cultivator, for whom there were few alternatives to paying the tax. He could either appeal to the king for remission or reduction of the tax or else move away to a totally different area. The latter was an extreme step, since mobility amongst the cultivators was restricted. In the case of a village assessed as a unit, the return from the non-taxable land was deducted from the total revenue of the village. Non-taxable land consisted of the residential area, temples, tanks, irrigation channels, areas where the artisans and outcaste population lived, and the cremation ground.

The tendency to hoard wealth was not a characteristic of this period. For most members of a village community there was little wealth to hoard. The average holding yielded enough to feed and clothe a family with little surplus. Food was simple, rice and vegetables in the main; meat was expensive, and a vegetarian diet was customary. Housing was cheap, since the warm climate did not call for elaborate structures. The wealthier members of rural society kept their money employed. There were economic advantages in financing schemes to reclaim land or to improve irrigation. Equally there was much religious merit to be acquired by donations towards the building of a temple or the endowing of a *matha*.

During the early part of this period the village was economically self-sufficient. It provided its own food and clothing and had enough craftsmen to attend to its needs. No large-scale surplus was produced and therefore no exchange of any appreciable amount took place with other areas. This changed with the rapid development of towns from the eleventh century onwards, consequent on the rapid expansion of trade during the Chola period. The existence of towns demanded a surplus production of food and introduced a monetary system to the rural economy. Not surprisingly there is a marked increase in the number of Chola coins as compared to those of earlier dynasties in this region.

Overseas trade was the strength of the Chola merchants. Mahabalipuram, Kaveripattinam, Shaliyur, and Korkai on the east coast and Quilon on the Malabar coast had elaborate establishments controlling the south Indian trade both westwards and eastwards. Persia and Arabia were the destinations of those trading with the west, with Siraf on the Persian Gulf as an entrepôt. Trade with China reached an unprecedented volume during these centuries, which led to its becoming a state monopoly in China, the Chinese government not wishing to lose the income from it. It is believed that there was an Indian settlement on the mainland opposite Formosa. With the Mongols controlling central Asia, merchandise, particularly from southern China, destined for western Asia and Europe was carried almost exclusively by sea. South India exported textiles, spices, drugs, jewels, ivory, horn, ebony, and camphor to China. The same commodities were also exported to the west and, in addition, Siraf received cargoes of aloes wood, perfumes, sandalwood, and condiments.

Marco Polo, as indeed most visitors to this part of India at the time, comments on the vast trade in horses which brought fortunes to the Arabs, and to the merchants of south India, who between them had organized a monopoly of the import of horses. For some strange reason India never took to the breeding of horses and this extremely expensive commodity had always to be imported. Marco Polo writes:

Let me tell you next that this country does not breed horses. Hence all the annual revenue, or the greater part of it, is spent in the purchase of horses; and I will tell you how. You may take it for a fact that the merchants of Hormuz and Kais, of Dhofar and Shihr and Aden, all of which provinces produce large numbers of battle chargers and other horses, buy up the best horses and load them on ships and export them to this king and his four brother kings. Some of them are sold for as much as 500 *saggi* of gold, which are worth more than 100 marks of silver. And I assure you that this king buys 2,000 of them or more every year, and his brothers as many. And, by the end of the year, not a hundred of them survive. They all die through ill-usage, because they have no veterinaries and do not know how to treat them. You may take it from me that the merchants who export them do not send out any veterinaries or allow any to go, because they are only too glad for many of them to die in the king's charge.[3]

Allowing for Marco Polo's usual proneness to exaggeration, there is nevertheless much truth in these remarks.

Foreign trade provided an additional incentive to an already developing local market. Generally production was for local consumption, the manufacture of goods for export being organized on a separate basis. Elephants, horses, spices, perfumes, precious stones, and superior quality textiles were the commodities involved in large-scale trade, with metalware, jewellery, pottery, and salt (produced in salt pans from sea water) being of lesser importance. Trade was controlled by the merchant guilds, the better known of which were the *manigramam* and the *valanjiyar*, and these were a powerful factor in the economic life of the period. They were associations formed by trading merchants to safeguard their trade. Their power was indicated by the fact that they had access to any region of the sub-continent or centres overseas, for political boundaries seemingly were no obstruction to them.

Local merchant guilds, referred to by the general name *nagaram*, existed in most towns and were affiliated with the larger guilds described by more specific names. The merchant guilds bought goods at the place of manufacture and distributed them through an elaborate network. State support was not a condition of their venturing into foreign trade. However, if necessary and where the state felt that it could interfere effectively on their behalf, as in the case of Shrivijaya, it came to their assistance. But even on this occasion the purpose of interference was not to acquire centres of raw material or markets but to remove the obstructions placed by another country on the trade. Doubtless the king and the higher officials of state invested in this trade, or else were provided with exclusive presents by the guilds to ensure support where required.

A merchant guild could be rich enough to buy an entire village and donate it to a temple. The commercial ramifications of the *Nanadeshi* guild were wide enough to cover trade in south India and in Sumatra. It is curious therefore that these merchant guilds did not aspire to greater political power. Possibly the interrelation between guild and monarch was too involved. Many guilds had overseas interests and were therefore dependent in the last resort on the military and naval strength of the Cholas. The brahman element in these guilds, which was not insignificant, was probably averse to challenging the political authority of the king, since they derived their financial capital from the land granted to them by the king. As in the case of guilds many centuries earlier, caste differentiation may well have prevented the necessary amalgamation of the guilds which could have made them politically significant. It is also possible that by now the concept of monarchy as the legitimate form of political power was too strongly rooted. The bestowers of political legitimacy – the ministers and the college of priests – would certainly have used every effort to curb the political power of the guilds. However, in the small maritime kingdoms, these merchant guilds were more powerful, since the kingdoms were largely dependent on the financial success of the merchants.

Unfortunately, detailed records of trade transactions have not survived. One of the advantages of the merchant guilds having bases in various parts of the country was that the system of promissory notes was in regular use. The use of coins was, however, equally extensive. The circulation of gold coin was unrestricted, although they appear to have been debased from the eleventh century onwards. This is, however, a debatable point since the gold content of coins varied from region to region. Differences in weights and standards compelled the Gold Committee in the villages to value gold and gold currency. Copper coins in local circulation became more frequent in the latter part of the Chola period. In the rural areas commonplace articles were acquired through barter, a unit of paddy being the basis of exchange. In these areas money was reserved for long distance trade and for articles of a very high value where barter would be cumbersome.

The centre of social and economic life at the time, particularly in the rural areas, was the temple. The temple would either be donated by the king, in which case it would generally be in the capital and intimately associated with the court, as was the case with the Rajarajeshvaram temple at Tanjore : or else it was built and maintained through the donations of guilds and merchants in a city and would therefore be associated with a dominant section of the city's population; or a smaller temple would be built by the village. In villages the temple came naturally to be the centre of activity and interest, since the assembly was held there, as was the school, and since the temple was maintained by the village people. Even the process of building a large temple, often involving many years, provided employment to artisans and altered economic relationships within certain areas which provided the building materials.

The maintenance of the temple compares with that of any large-scale institution of modern times. The temple at Tanjore, possibly the richest during this period, had an income of 500 lb. troy of gold, 250 lb. troy of precious stones, and 600 lb. troy of silver, which was acquired through donations and contributions and in addition to the revenue from hundreds of villages. As temple staff, it maintained in considerable comfort 400 women associated with entertainment (the *devadasis*), 212 attendants, 57 musicians and readers of the texts, quite apart of course from the many hundreds of priests who also lived off the temple. It became imperative for the temple authorities to keep the income flowing in and this was done in part through the temple financing various commercial enterprises and acting as banker and money-lender to village assemblies and similar bodies, loaning money at the generally accepted usurer's rate of twelve per cent per annum. In this matter the temples were now following the tradition of the wealthier monasteries.

Devadasis (female slaves of the gods) were commonly found in most temples in Chola times. They were in origin a special and venerated group of women attendants some of whom, like the Vestal Virgins of Rome, were dedicated to the temple at birth or when quite young. The more talented among them were selected for the extremely difficult training of becoming a *Bharata Natyam* dancer (some of the best dancers to this day are descendants of *devadasi* families). But the system was abused, and eventually in many temples the *devadasis* degenerated into shamefully exploited prostitutes, their earnings being collected by the temple authorities. In contrast, the city courtesans, who were frequently highly accomplished women, were treated with deference. Courtesans and upper-class women had a certain freedom of movement in that they could defy social conventions to a greater degree than most other women. The vast majority of women had to work, either in their homes or in the fields.

Caste-consciousness had become a marked feature in social relationships. The brahmans stood out distinct from the rest of society, confident of their privileged position. For the south Indian brahman, prestige as a religious leader and economic power came almost simultaneously. They were frequently exempt from tax, many of them owned land, and in addition they had royal support. They were the symbols of what was in origin an alien culture, but their very security and status brought them added respect. Unlike the north Indian brahman landowners, the southern brahmans were more adventurous and invested their surplus income in commerce. In certain areas their commercial enterprises were such that the brahmans came to be associated with the trading castes. Some even journeyed out to south-east Asia, where they settled down in spite of the ban on crossing the ocean.

The main stress in the ordering of castes appears to have been the division of society into brahmans and non-brahmans. Among the non-brahmans there is, as compared to north India, little mention of *kshatriyas* and *vaishyas* but the *shudras* are prominent. The *shudras* were divided into the clean *shudras* – whose touch was not polluting – and the unclean *shudras*, who were debarred from entry into the temple. The picture which emerges suggests that the brahmans were in control of the powerful positions and that the non-brahmans were more or less working for them. The brahmans naturally emphasized caste-loyalties and caste-assemblies, since this would prevent a wider basis of unity developing amongst the non-brahmans.

Slavery was frequent, with men and women either selling themselves or else being sold by a third party. Many such persons were sold to the temple, particularly in cases of poverty or during a famine. But slaves were limited in number, since they were largely domestic slaves or attached to temples. The use of slave labour for large-scale production was not known.

Amongst the intermediary castes (other than brahman and *shudra*) the distinctions were perhaps not so rigid. Caste status was often modified by economic status. For instance those who worked for the court were on occasion given special privileges required by other caste groups. Those who engraved the copper-plate charters of king Rajendra, or the weavers of Kanchipuram who wove the textiles for the royal family, or the stone-masons working on the royal temple or palace were exempt from paying certain dues and although some of them, such as the weavers, were of low caste status they were regarded with greater respect than other members of their castes. References are occasionally made without rancour, to mixed castes, and this would suggest that the rigidity of caste rules was stressed by the brahmans but in practice lapses were known and excused.

The temple was also the centre of formal education in Sanskrit, a system which had continued from an earlier period. Pupils were either taught by the temple priests as in the smaller village temples or else attended the colleges attached to the larger temples. In the case of brahmans those that were thus educated were absorbed either into the temple as priests or in the administration of the region. Education was also available in the Jaina and Buddhist monasteries, but since these were few in number their impact was slight. Courses in the colleges were organized in a systematic manner demanding regular attendance and instruction. The better known of these colleges were those at Ennayiram, Tribhuvani, Tiruvaduturai, and Tiruvorriyur. As the medium of instruction was Sanskrit almost to the exclusion of the vernacular language, Tamil, formal education, and the life of most students attending the colleges, became cut off from everyday life. Professional education continued to be maintained through the training given to apprentices in guilds and among groups of artisans. At a more popular level oral instruction much simpler than the Sanskrit learning of the colleges was imparted through the medium of the Shaivite and Vaishnavite hymns composed by the Tamil saints, hymns which were sung, taught and explained to illiterate audiences.

Literary works in Sanskrit continued to be written within the framework of grammars, lexicons, manuals, or rhetoric, commentaries on the older texts, prose fiction and poetry. The latter of these adhered to the classical conventions of composition, rarely experimenting with new forms, and tended with a few exceptions to become increasingly artificial. Some of these works had their counterparts in Tamil, where the models of literary composition were now taken largely from Sanskrit literature. But Tamil literature of this period shows great liveliness and vigour as in Kamban's version of the *Ramayana* or the works of Kuttan, Pugalendi, Jayangondur and Kalladanar. Many of the inscriptions contain long passages in Tamil which indicate that it was a well-developed language, having enriched its vocabulary by association with Sanskrit. Had Tamil been encouraged to a greater extent in the centres of higher education it would have assisted in producing a far more vigorous intellectual tradition than was actually in existence in these centres.

The branching off of regional languages from Sanskrit took place throughout the peninsula. The new languages were not totally divorced from Sanskrit, since some, such as Marathi, had evolved from the local Prakrits, and others stemming from a Dravidian root, such as Tamil, Telugu, and Kannada, had a vocabulary which owed much to Sanskrit. But the memory of this derivation was becoming more and more vague as the new languages evolved and came into current use. Telugu took shape and form in the Andhra region during the ninth century. A number of Sanskrit works were adapted to Teluga during the next couple of centuries, such as those of Kalidasa and the *Mahabharata* and *Ramayana*, and these were written largely for popular audiences. Lack of royal patronage militated against the literary use of Telugu.

In this respect Kannada, the language of the region around Mysore, began at an advantage, what with having royal patronage, and receiving support from the Jainas who were then an influential body in the region, and eventually becoming the language of the *Virashaiva* or *Lingayata* movement (which was to be, and still is, an important religious force in Mysore). In the early part of this period, Kannada was a serious rival to Telugu, but gradually Telugu managed to establish its hold in Andhra. The first writings in Kannada were also largely adaptations from Sanskrit works.

The same holds true of early writing in Marathi, the language current in the western Deccan and which received particular encouragement under the patronage of the Yadava rulers. Even more significant was the adoption of Marathi by the local supporters of the devotional cult, which had by now travelled from the Tamil country and was well-entrenched in the northern and western Deccan. This involved not only the composition of popular hymns in Marathi but also the exposition of older religious texts such as the *Gita*, which helped to establish Marathi as the language of intellectual communication.

The parting of the ways of Sanskrit and the regional languages is reflected also in religion. Sanskrit remained the language of Hindu theology and of the brahmans. Curiously enough it was also more widely used now by the Buddhists and Jainas, whose numbers were on the decrease. Buddhism practically disappeared by the end of this period, the Buddha being commonly accepted as an incarnation of Vishnu, but Jainism managed to survive with a following in Mysore. The decline of these two religions is partially linked with the rise in popularity of the devotional cult, which was no longer restricted to the Tamil country, and of a number of other sects, of both *Shaiva* and *Vaishnava* following. The hymns of the earlier saints were collated at this time. The theism of these hymns, which was their greatest appeal, was given further expression in regional literature and in more philosophical treatises which traced the origin of theism to Upanishad sources and in a sense assisted in the compromise between Vedic brahmanism and the devotional cult which had begun to take place in the Tamil country. The Vaishnava *acharyas* who took over, as it were, from the saints, the *Alvars*, contributed to this aspect of religious development. Shaivism was more popular in the south and its followers not only continued the tradition of the saints, but supported the new sects.

When compared with some of the more extreme sects the devotional cult was conformist. The former were a variety of esoteric and mystical groups such as the Tantric and *Shakta* cults and those of the *Kapalikas*, *Kalamukhas*, and *Pashupatas*, which by now had gathered supporters in various parts of the sub-continent. Some of these sects indulged in strange rites involving blood sacrifices and sexual orgies and were evidently designed for those with whom non-conformity was almost an obsession and the disregard of even a minimum of social obligations became a necessity on certain ritual occasions. Yet, as it has been suggested, most followers of these sects led a normal life, indulging in the cult rites only at certain periods, and for them these rites were probably a sort of catharsis. Some members of these sects were dissident groups who deliberately indulged in anti-social acts as a form of protest, their extreme non-conformity giving them the publicity they desired; but these acts were disguised as asceticism or some religious ritual which it was claimed possessed magical qualities. The *Kalamukha* sect ate food out of a human skull, smeared their bodies with the ashes of a corpse (which ashes they also ate on occasion), were generally seen carrying a pot of wine and a club, and are believed to have indulged in human sacrifice, although there is no proof of this. In some cases these rites may have been practices going back to an early period which were revived. For some, non-conformity was also a genuine protest against the limitations placed on thought and knowledge by the orthodoxy. The interest in magic, for instance, was not merely sensationalism, but could as well result from a curiosity to experiment with objects and to inquire further than was permitted by the custodians of knowledge.

Not all protests were expressed in the form of social aberrations. Shaivism itself produced other sects at this time which were of far more positive consequence to the evolution of social institutions. Amongst these was the *Lingayata* or *Virashaiva* sect which emerged in the twelfth century with characteristics of a reform movement, probably influenced both by Buddhist and Jaina and Islamic thinking in addition to the Tamil devotional cult. The founder Basavaraja, an apostate Jaina, had a certain cynical strain which lent sharpness to the point he wished to make.

The lamb brought to the slaughter-house eats the leaf garland with which it is decorated . . . the frog caught in the mouth of the snake desires to swallow the fly flying near its mouth. So is our life. The man condemned to die drinks milk and *ghi*. . . .When they see a serpent carved in stone they pour milk on it: if a real serpent comes they say, Kill. Kill. To the servant of God who could eat if served they say, Go away. Go away; but to the image of God which cannot eat they offer dishes of food.[4]

The *Lingayatas* differed from the devotional cult in that they did not rest content with preaching devotion to a theistic God, but actively attacked religious hypocrisy. The authority of the *Vedas* was questioned, as was the theory of re-birth. Shiva was worshipped in the form of the *Lingam* or phallic emblem. The *Lingayatas* had a strong element of social conscience and encouraged certain social practices disapproved of by the brahmans, such as late post-puberty marriages and the remarriage of widows. Not surprisingly the *Lingayatas* themselves came under attack from the brahmans. Their more liberal social attitudes brought them the support of the lower castes.

Those who were excluded from worshipping at the temple had to find their own forms of worship. On occasion these were incorporated into the ritual of the various sects and the devotional cults. Sometimes this resulted in the worship of local anthropomorphic deities. One of these was the cult of Panduranga or Shri

Vitthala at Pandharapur in western India, which came into prominence in the thirteenth century and was connected with a mother goddess cult. The god was identified with Vishnu at an early stage. It became one of the centres of the devotional movement in the Deccan attracting preachers and hymn writers such as Namadeva, Janabai, Sena, and Narahari (by profession tailor, maid-servant, barber, and goldsmith), who composed their hymns in Marathi and gathered around them the local people. These cult centres also became the foci of local trade.

The philosophical aspect of Hindu thought was almost exclusively the prerogative of the brahmans. Debates were held in the various *mathas* and colleges throughout the sub-continent, the link between them being the common language, Sanskrit. But their intellectual sphere of influence was restricted. Shankaracharya's ideas continued to be developed and improved upon, and the theories of other teachers were also discussed, some of which were opposed to the ideas of Shankara. Foremost from among the latter was the *Vaishnava* philosopher, Ramanuja (whose dates traditionally are 1017–1137). He was a Tamil brahman born at Tirupati who spent a considerable part of his life teaching at the famous temple at Shrirangam.

Ramanuja disagreed with Shankara's theory that knowledge was the primary means of salvation. According to Ramanuja it was merely one of the means and was not nearly as effective or reliable as pure devotion, giving oneself up entirely to God. As in the devotional cult Ramanuja's God was a being full of love and forgiveness, and although the relationship was posed in philosophical terms it was essentially a personal relationship based on Love. The emphasis on the individual in this relationship carried almost a protestant flavour. Ramanuja was an effective bridge between the devotional cult and Hindu theology, attempting as he did to weave together what appeared to be two divergent strands.

Ramanuja's ideas were carried to the various centres of Hindu theology and teaching in the sub-continent. His stress on God's forgiveness led to a dichotomy in his teaching, where one group known as the Northern group maintained that man must strive for this forgiveness and eventual salvation; but the other group, the Southern group, maintained the theory that God himself arbitrarily selects those that are to be saved, an idea curiously close to that of the Calvinists.

Madhva, a thirteenth-century theologian teaching in Kannada, made further attempts to synthesize the ideas of the devotional cult with Hindu theology. Madhva was also a *Vaishnava* and his concept of Vishnu as the one and true God was influenced by the southern school of Ramanuja's followers, since he held that God granted his grace to save the souls only of the pure, which implies selection, although the selection was not quite as arbitrary as the Southern School believed. Some of Madhva's ideas suggest that he was familiar with, and possibly influenced by, the Christian church of Malabar. Vishnu bestows his grace on a devotee through his son Vayu, the Wind-god. This is an idea quite alien to orthodox Hindu theology but resembles the concept of the Holy Ghost in Christianity.

Ramanuja, whilst accepting special privileges for the higher castes, was nevertheless opposed to the excluding of *shudras* from worship in the temple. He pleaded for the throwing open of temples to *shudras*, but without much success. The growing strength of the devotional cult and the attempts at syntheses by theologians such as Ramanuja and Madhva did, however, force the orthodox to recognize the need for compromise. Although the temple was not opened to the *shudras*, the deities and rituals of a vast number of subsidiary cults crept into the temple. This was an inevitable process if the temple was to retain its vitality as the centre of social and religious life, at least in upper caste society. This in turn led to some physical changes in the temple. Subsidiary shrines had to be accommodated, pavilions built for the recitation of sacred literature before large audiences, and images of the saints in addition to the gods had to be housed within the temple precincts. The area of the temple was considerably enlarged. The economic prosperity of the temple during the Chola period permitted of greater embellishment with larger and more ornate structures. The lesser dynasties of the Deccan, such as the Hoysalas, sought to impress their subjects by building impressive religious monuments.

Chola architects abandoned the temple cut from the rock and concentrated on free-standing stone structures. Unfortunately, domestic buildings have not survived from this period; only temples have remained. Chola temples laid stress on the central chamber of the shrine, which was approached through one or more halls, depending on the size of the temple, and which was surmounted on the outside by a tall *shikhara* or corbelled tower broadly pyramidal in shape, proportionate in size to the temple itself. The temple was surrounded by an enclosed courtyard, the actual enclosing wall often having a colonnade of pillars on the inside, as at Tanjore and Gangai-konda-chola-puram. The entrances had elaborate gateways reflecting the style of the *shikhara*, and these were gradually given more and more emphasis until they rivalled the *shikhara*, as in the case of the Minakshi temple at Madurai and Shrirangam near Trichinopoly.

Stone sculpture was largely an adjunct to architecture and had the same monumental qualities as the building. It was frequently used as a decorative motif in friezes and the ornamentation of pillars and balustrades. It was however in bronze sculptures that the Chola craftsman excelled, producing images rivalling those produced anywhere in the world. They were mainly images of deities, donors, and saints, made by the *cire perdu* process, and were kept in the inner shrine of the temple. These images, more than anything else, indicate the sculptural genius of the southern craftsman.

The temples of the Deccan preserved the earlier tradition of the Chalukya style, although they gradually became more ornate, a tendency which was accentuated by the extensive use of soapstone – a softer stone than the sandstone in earlier use. The temples built by the later Chalukyas and Hoysalas broke away in ground plan and elevation from both the Northern and Dravidian styles. The finest examples of these are the Hoysala temples at Halebid – the old Dorasamudra – Belur, and Somnathapur. The ground plan was no longer rectangular, but was star-shaped or polygonal, within which was accommodated the entire temple consisting of shrine-room, ante-chamber, and halls with aisles and porch, the whole complex being built on a raised platform. This elevation gave it a flattened effect, the larger temples having dispensed with towers. This effect was emphasized by the exterior surface decoration which consisted of a series of narrow panels running horizontally right around the temple walls, carrying frieze decorations of animal and floral motifs, musicians, dancers, battle scenes, and the depiction of well-known events from religious literature. The star-shaped plan provided more wall space for sculpture and low-relief than would a rectangular plan. Perhaps the most curious feature of these Hoysala temples are the wide, squat pillars which give the impression of being lathe-turned, and obviously considerable skill must have gone into their making.

The temples had their secular symbolism in that they were monuments to royal grandeur. The Chola temples certainly could claim to be such symbols. The political ascendancy of the Cholas, although resented by the powers of the western and northern Deccan, served to force home the fact that the centre of power in the sub-continent was not confined to one region and could and did shift from area to area. During these centuries the initiative in progress was with the southern part of the sub-continent. Northern India had become timid and conservative and it was the peninsula which saw the birth of new ideas and experiments – whether in the evolution of local civic responsibility or in the philosophy of Shankaracharya and Ramanuja, or in the socio-religious experiment of the devotional cult led by Tamil and Maharashtrian artisans, or even at the more basic level of welcoming Arab traders on the one hand, and, on the other hand, venturing out into the south-east Asian and Chinese trade. Whilst the north remained static, the peninsula advanced.

THE BEGINNINGS OF REGIONAL STATES IN NORTHERN INDIA

c. A.D. 700–1200

KINGDOMS rising in the western and northern Deccan were 'bridge' kingdoms between the north and the south of the sub-continent, and this was in some ways a handicap, since it involved them in the politics of both parts. The Satavahanas arose at a time when the contacts between the north and the south were still of a limited nature, and the Satavahana kingdom thus be-came the initial transmitter of goods and ideas from one part to the other. The Vakatakas, however, had to make a choice and they opted for alliance with the north, which was at the time the more powerful of the two. The Chalukyas managed fairly well to maintain their independence. Had the Rashtrakutas restricted their ambition to the same end, they could have built a powerful kingdom in the Deccan. But the Rashtrakutas tried to exploit their position as a bridge to dominate both banks, the northern and the southern. By the time that the Rashtrakutas came to power, communication between the north and the south was well established, and therefore the political pull on the Rashtrakutas was equally strong in both directions. This to a large extent pre-vented their establishing themselves as a dominant power as they might well have done.

The participation of the Rashtrakutas in the politics of the Peninsula has already been described. In the onrth, the object of political ambition at this time was to conquer and hold the city of Kanauj, which had become a symbol of imperial power, per-haps owing to its connexion with Harsha and with Yashovar-man, who maintained this status for the city. Kanauj became a bone of contention between three powers, the Rashtrakutas, the Pratiharas, and the Palas, and much of the military activity of these powers was directed towards its conquest. This was to exhaust all three of them, leaving the field open to their feuda-tories, which resulted in the founding of small regional kingdoms all over northern India.

Amongst these were the Pratiharas, who are said to be descended from the Gurjara people of Rajasthan in western India. Their social origin is uncertain and the Rashtrakutas claimed they were door-keepers (*pratihara*), in order to suggest an insultingly low origin for their enemies. The Pratiharas may have been palace officials who rose to power, a pattern which was to become increasingly familiar during this period. The first important Pratihara king is said to have been a fierce enemy of the *mlechchhas* or barbarians, though who these *mlechchhas* were is not indicated. Possibly this was a reference to the Arabs in Sind. Sind, conquered in A.D. 712, was the eastern extremity of the general Arab expansion through Asia and Africa. The Arabs did not meet with any sizeable resistance, since the area was by now largely desert. But attempts at further conquests were resisted both by the Pratiharas and the Rashtrakutas, although this resistance was not organized as an effort to exclude the Arabs altogether from the sub-continent. There was no comprehension at that stage of the significance of the Arabs as an emerging power, and the weight of Arab power was remote. Having successfully resisted the Arabs, the Pratiharas looked eastwards, and by the end of the eighth century were not only ruling over a large part of Rajasthan and Ujjain but had captured Kanauj.

The third power involved in the three-sided conflict over Kanauj was the Pala dynasty, which was to control most of Bengal and Bihar. This in itself was a rich area, but in addition the Palas derived an income from their substantial commercial interests in south-east Asia. Little is known of the early Palas until the reign of Gopala in the eighth century. Gopala attained renown from the fact that he was not the hereditary king but was elected. The details of the election are unfortunately not known, it being merely said that Gopala was chosen king to avoid a state of anarchy in the land. The Buddhist monk Taranatha, writing a history of Tibet in the sixteenth century, has referred to this event. He states that Bengal was without a king and suffered accordingly. The local leaders gathered together and elected a king, but on each occasion a demoness killed him on the night following his election. Finally, Gopala was elected and he was given a club by the goddess Chandi (one of the names of the consort of Shiva) with which to protect himself, and he killed the demoness with this club and survived. The story suggests that Gopala was elected because of his ability as a leader and protector, and in all likelihood he was a follower of a Chandi cult.

Gopala established the Pala dynasty but it was his son Dharmapala who made it a force in north Indian politics. Despite the fact that he began with a severe reverse – a defeat at the hands of the Rashtrakutas – by the end of his reign Pala power was dominant in eastern India. Towards the end of the eighth century Dharmapala led a successful campaign against Kanauj, resulting in the removal of the reigning king, a protégé of the Pratiharas, with Dharmapala claiming overlordship in his place. This affronted the Rashtrakutas and the Pratiharas, but Dharmapala stood his ground. Friendly relations with Tibet ensured the safety of his northern borders. Relations between the Palas and the countries of south-east Asia were close. It is on record that a king of Sumatra requested the Pala king's permission to endow a monastery at Nalanda. The ties between the Buddhists in eastern India and south-east Asia were strengthened at this time and were to be of considerable consequence in later centuries when the Buddhists, harried by the Turks and Afghans, fled and sought refuge in the monasteries of south-east Asia.

Meanwhile the Pratiharas had consolidated their position and the initiative was now with them. The first step was obvious. Kanauj, which had been taken by the Rashtrakutas from the Palas, was now captured by the Pratiharas and the other two powers were driven back behind their own borders. The Arab menace in the west was firmly tackled by king Bhoja, probably the most renowned of the Pratiharas. But his efforts to hold back the Arabs to the west and the Palas in the east made it impossible for him to invade the Deccan as was his intention.

The Rashtrakutas waited for their opportunity and in 916 they struck for the last time, but struck effectively by attacking Kanauj, and in so doing ended all cohesion in the north. The rivalry between the Pratiharas and the Rashtrakutas was self-destroying. The Arab traveller, al Masudi, visited Kanauj in the early tenth century and wrote that the king of Kanauj was the natural enemy of the king of the Deccan : that he kept a large army and was surrounded by smaller kings always ready to go to war. A hundred years later the Pratiharas were no longer a power in northern India. A Turkish army sacked Kanauj in 1018 and this virtually ended Pratihara rule. In the western Deccan, the Rashtrakutas had been supplanted by the Later Chalukyas.

The decline of the Pratiharas in the tenth century gave the Palas an opportunity to participate more fully in north-Indian affairs. Turkish raids into north-western India in the early eleventh century kept the local kings occupied and soon the Palas had come as far as Banaras. This expansion was, however, checked by the advance of the Chola king Rajendra, whose successful northern campaign was a threat to the independence of Bengal. The western campaign of the Palas was therefore abandoned and the king, Mahipala, hastily returned to defend Bengal against the Chola armies. The Pala dynasty declined soon after the death of Mahipala and gave way to the Sena line.

The almost simultaneous decline of the three rival powers, the Pratiharas, Palas, and Rashtrakutas, is not surprising. Their strength was closely matched and was dependent on large well-organized armies. Sources of revenue to maintain these armies were similar and excessive pressure on these sources was bound to produce the same result. The continued conflict over the possession of Kanauj diverted attention from their feudatories, who succeeded in making themselves independent. The insubordination of the feudatories and invasions from the north-west and the south destroyed what little had remained of the political unity of northern India.

On the periphery of what had been the three major kingdoms there had arisen a number of small states. These were kingdoms such as Nepal, Kamarupa (Assam), Kashmir, Utkala (Orissa), the kingdoms of the eastern Chalukyas and the Gangas along the east coast and that of the Chaulukyas (also known as the Solankis) of Gujarat in western India. The emergence of these kingdoms coincided with the general tendency at the time for small local rulers to declare their independence and set themselves up as fully-fledged monarchs. This tendency was also reflected in the cultural life of the period, when there was an increased attention to local culture; histories of the region and of local dynasties were written, local cults and literature were encouraged, and the courts vied with each other in attracting the best writers and poets and in using local craftsmen to build monumental temples.

The foothills of the Himalayas lent themselves admirably to such small kingdoms, owing to the nature of the country. The ninth century saw the rise of a number of hill states, some of which maintained their identity if not their independence until recent years, despite their wars with each other and the frequent raids from the men of the plains. States such as Champaka (Chamba), Durgara (Jammu), Trigarta (Jalandhar), Kuluta (Kulu), Kumaon, and Garhwal managed to remain outside the main areas of conflict in the northern plains.

Kashmir had come into prominence in the seventh century, and through gradual expansion and conquest it controlled a major part of northern Punjab. Meanwhile the Arabs were advancing up the Indus valley, and in the eighth century a king of Kashmir asked for assistance from the Chinese to repel Arab attacks on the Punjab. The reign of Lalitaditya in the same century took the armies of Kashmir into the Ganges valley, and in the Punjab they pushed back the Arab forces. In subsequent centuries the kings of Kashmir consolidated their position in the mountainous areas and the upper Jehlum valley, leaving the Punjab to fend for itself. Many irrigation works were undertaken : embankments and dams were built on the main rivers – a difficult engineering task since the rivers of Kashmir are the fast-flowing, unruly upper reaches of the Punjab rivers – and these brought a large area of the valley under cultivation, which was in effect a stabilizing factor in Kashmir politics since the need to move out into the fertile regions of the plains became less pressing.

The tenth century saw the regency of two famous queens, who, in spite of much opposition, were determined to direct the affairs of state. In this they had to contend with a new phenomenon which was to dominate Kashmiri politics for a hundred years – the existence of bodies of troops with fixed and unswerving political loyalties. There were two rival groups, the Tantrins and the Ekangas, who between them made and unmade kings in turn. Queen Sugandha used the Ekangas against the Tantrins effectively, but was unable to control them and was deposed in 914. Her defeat meant almost unlimited power for the Tantrins, and none of the succeeding rulers was able to assert his position. Finally, the *damaras* or feudal landowners had to be called in to destroy the power of the Tantrins, which they did with such success that the rulers of Kashmir were faced with the new problems of curbing the power of the landowners as is evident from political events during the rule of Queen Didda. The twelfth century in Kashmir is associated with the writing of the famous history of the kingdom, the *Rajatarangini* by Kalhana, generally counted amongst the best of the Indian historians. The work is of a quality which is rare as it displays a remarkable clarity and maturity in historical analysis.

Another hill state which came into prominence during this period was Nepal, having revolted against the hegemony of Tibet in 878, from which year a new era was started to commemorate the independence of Nepal. This not only meant political freedom but also resulted in substantial economic progress. Nepal being on the highway from India to Tibet, both the Chinese and the Tibetan trade with India passed through the new state. The reign of Gunakamadeva in the eleventh century saw the building of new towns such as Kathmandu, Patan, and Shanku, mainly from the income brought in by trade. But the kings of Nepal were also to suffer from the presence of powerful landowners, the Ranas. The power of the Kashmiri landowners was crushed when Kashmir was conquered by the Turks, and a new dynasty was established. But Nepal was not conquered by any foreign power, which might have reduced the strength of the Ranas, and the precarious balance between the position of the king and that of the Ranas was a constant feature of Nepali politics.

Kamarupa (Assam) was yet another mountainous region which developed into an independent kingdom based on trade, it being the link between eastern India and eastern Tibet and China. Much of Kamarupa was conquered in 1253 by the Ahoms, a Shan people who came from the mountains to the south-east of Assam. It was they who finally gave the place its name, Assam being derived from Ahom.

In the ninth century, a Turkish family – the Shahiyas – ruled over the Kabul valley and Gandhara. The king had a brahman minister who usurped the throne and founded what has been called the Hindu Shahiya dynasty. He was pushed eastwards by pressure from other Afghan principalities and finally established his power in the region of Attock, thus becoming a buffer state between northern India and Afghanistan. His descendant Jayapala consolidated the kingdom and made himself master of the entire Punjab plain. It was Jayapala who had to face the armies of the ruler of Ghazni when the latter invaded northern India in the eleventh century.

It is during this period that the now well-known Rajputs enter the scene of Indian history. Where and how the Rajputs originated remains in doubt. That they were of foreign origin is suggested by the efforts that were made by the brahmans to give them royal lineage and accord them *kshatriya* status, which status the Rajputs have always insisted upon with almost undue vehemence. They were provided with genealogies which connected them with either the solar or the lunar race, thereby conferring upon them the utmost royal respectability in keeping with the tradition of the *Puranas*. The Rajputs rose to political importance in the ninth and tenth centuries A.D. when they were divided into a number of clans of which four claimed a special status. These four – the Pratiharas or Pariharas (not to be confused with the main Pratiharas with whom this clan had connexions), Chahamanas, more commonly called Chauhans, Chaulukyas (distinct from the Deccan Chalukyas) or Solankis, and Paramaras or Pawars – claimed descent from a mythical figure who arose out of a vast sacrificial fire pit near Mt Abu in Rajasthan. Consequently these four clans were described as the *Agnikula* or Fire Family. This was probably the first occasion when deliberate and conscious attempts were made by rulers to insist on their *kshatriya* status. Previous dynasties had ruled irrespective of their caste status and were, by virtue of being rulers, accepted as members of high castes.

Most authorities accept the view that the Rajput clans were either descended from the Huns settled in northern and western India or from those tribes and peoples who had entered India together with the Hun invaders. Judging from Gupta inscriptions the tradition of small republics appears to have survived in the area of Rajasthan until the coming of the Huns. It must have been easier for the tribes to be assimilated in republican states, which were probably less tradition-bound than the kingdoms. The unsettled conditions in north-western India must have helped in this assimilation.

The four clans which claimed *Agnikula* origin dominated early Rajput activities. The kingdoms which they founded arose from the ruins of the older Pratihara kingdom. The Pariharas based themselves in southern Rajasthan. The Chauhans ruled an area in eastern Rajasthan, south-east of Delhi. They began as feudatories of the main Pratihara kings and assisted them in holding back the Arab advance. Later they declared their independence, and took imperial titles, such as *maharajadhiraja*, by now the symbol of a feudatory having become independent. As was the case with all Rajput clans, branches of the main family ruled in neighbouring areas, and these remained as feudatories of the Pratiharas.

Solanki power was concentrated in the region of Kathiawar with branches of the family scattered in Malwa, Chedi, Patan, and Broach. By the second half of the tenth century, the Solankis were at war with practically all their neighbours. The Pawars established their control in Malwa with their capital at Dhar near Indore. They began as feudatories of the Rashtrakutas but revolted against their overlords at the end of the tenth century. Although the earlier tradition of the Pawars relates them with the Rashtrakutas, later tradition tells an interesting story as to how they acquired their name, a story which recalls the Chauhan version of the fire sacrifice. The sage Vasishtha had a *kamadhenu* (a cow which grants all one's wishes) and this was stolen by another sage, Vishvamitra. Vasishtha therefore made an offering to the sacrificial fire at Mt Abu, whereupon a hero sprang out of the fire, brought the cow back, and returned it to Vasishtha, who bestowed the name Paramara (slayer of the enemy) on the hero, from whom the Paramara clan was descended. This was obviously an attempt to adjust the origin of the clan to the story of the *Agnikula*, which story was a later development. The fire-rite traditionally had a purificatory symbolism and the insistence on the *Agnikula* story is significant in view of the uncertain origin of the Rajputs.

Other Rajput clans claiming descent from the solar and lunar races established themselves as local kings in various parts of western and central India. Among them were the Chandellas, prominent in the tenth century in the region of Khajuraho. The Guhilas of Mewar to the south of the Chauhans participated in the campaigns against the Arabs. The Arab threat had spotlighted the weakness of the Rashtrakutas and Pratiharas as suzerain powers and encouraged their vassals in western India to break away and claim independent status. The north-eastern neighbours of the Chauhans were the Tomaras, who were also the feudatories of the Pratiharas, and ruled in the Hariyana region surrounding Delhi, including Thanesar, the home of Harsha. The city of Dhillika (Delhi) was founded by the Tomaras in 736. The Tomaras were overthrown by the Chauhans in the twelfth century. There was yet another family which began as feudatories of the Pratiharas but soon acquired independence. These were the Kalachuris of Tripuri (near Jabalpur).

Northern India had had a long period of respite from foreign aggression. The impact of the Huns had been forgotten and the thrusts of the Arabs were easily countered. For over four centuries the campaigns and battles were internal. Minor bickerings were magnified into major causes for endless campaigns which devoured the funds and energy of each dynasty. Breaking away from a suzerain power also necessitated the maintaining of independence by military campaigns on all sides. Contact with the world outside became more and more limited as the obsession with local affairs increased. Trade with the west diminished and the need for India to interest herself in that part of the world became less. There was a mood of self-satisfaction in the subcontinent. The image of politics was created and chiselled by local happenings. This image received its first shattering blow in the eleventh century. Rajendra Chola campaigned successfully along the east coast and the region of Orissa, and his armies came as far north as the Ganges. From the north-west of the subcontinent began the raids of Mahmud of Ghazni.

Ghazni, a principality in Afghanistan, came into prominence in 977 when a Turkish nobleman annexed adjoining parts of central Asia and the Trans-Indus regions of the Shahiya kingdom. Twenty-one years later his son Mahmud decided to make Ghazni a formidable power in the politics of central Asia. Mahmud's interest in India was based on the proverbial wealth of

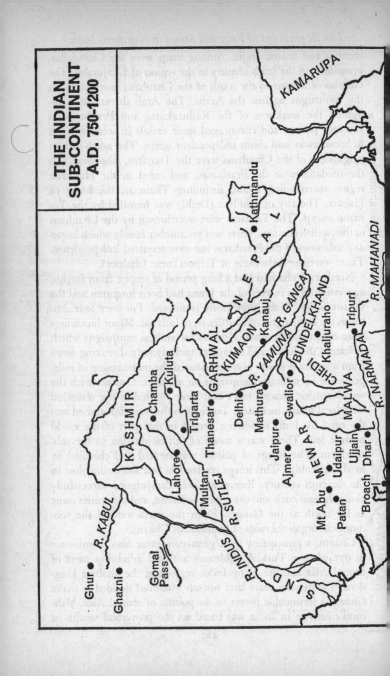

THE INDIAN
SUB-CONTINENT
A.D. 750–1200

KAMARUPA

Kathmandu

NEPAL

KASHMIR

Chamba
Kuluta
Trigarta
Thanesar
Lahore
Multan
GARHWAL
KUMAON
Delhi
Mathura
Kanauj
R. YAMUNA
R. GANGA
BUNDELKHAND
Khaljuraho
Gwalior
Jaipur
CHEDI
Tripuri
Ajmer
MEWAR
MALWA
Udaipur
Ujjain
Mt Abu
Patan
Dhar
R. NARMADA
Broach
R. MAHANADI

R. KABUL

Ghur
Ghazni

Gomal
Pass

R. INDUS

R. SUTLEJ

SIND

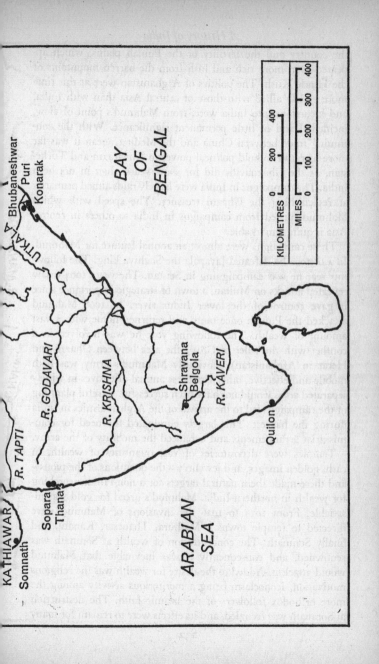

the country and the fertility of the Punjab plains, which appeared even more rich and lush from the barren mountains of the Hindu Kush. The politics of Afghanistan were at this time more closely allied with those of central Asia than with India, and incursions into India were, from Mahmud's point of view, incidental and of little permanent significance. With the continuing trade between China and the Mediterranean it was far more lucrative to hold political power in Khvarazm and Turkestan, as the Ghaznavids did for some years, than in northern India. The campaigns in India were largely raids aimed primarily at replenishing the Ghazni treasury. The speed with which Mahmud turned from campaigns in India to others in central Asia is quite remarkable.

These campaigns were almost an annual feature for Mahmud. In A.D. 1000 he defeated Jayapala the Shahiya king. The following year he was campaigning in Seistan. The years 1004–6 saw repeated attacks on Multan, a town of strategic importance since it gave control of the lower Indus river. In 1008 Mahmud attacked the Punjab once more and returned home with a vast amount of wealth. The following year he was involved in a conflict with the ruler of Ghur (the area between Ghazni and Herat in Afghanistan). Obviously Mahmud's army was both mobile and effective, otherwise these annual offensives in widely separated areas would not have been successful. Careful planning of the campaigns led to the arrival of the Afghan armies in India during the harvest. This largely eliminated the need for commissariat arrangements and enhanced the mobility of the army.

Temples were depositories of vast quantities of wealth, in cash, golden images, and jewellery – the donations of the pious – and these made them natural targets for a non-Hindu searching for wealth in northern India. Mahmud's greed for gold was insatiable. From 1010 to 1026 the invasions of Mahmud were directed to temple towns – Mathura, Thanesar, Kanauj, and finally Somnath. The concentration of wealth at Somnath was renowned, and consequently it was inevitable that Mahmud would attack it. Added to the desire for wealth was the religious motivation, iconoclasm being a meritorious activity among the more orthodox followers of the Islamic faith. The destruction at Somnath was frenzied, and its effects were to remain for many centuries in the Hindu mind and to colour its assessment of the character of Mahmud, and on occasion of Muslim rulers in general. A thirteenth-century account from an Arab source refers to this event.

Somnat – a celebrated city of India situated on the shore of the sea and washed by its waves. Among the wonders of that place was the temple in which was placed the idol called Somnat. This idol was in the middle of the temple without anything to support it from below, or to suspend it from above. It was held in the highest honour among the Hindus, and whoever beheld it floating in the air was struck with amazement, whether he was a Musulman or an infidel. The Hindus used to go on pilgrimage to it whenever there was an eclipse of the moon and would then assemble there to the number of more than a hundred thousand. They believed that the souls of men used to meet there after separation from the body and that the idol used to incorporate them at its pleasure in other bodies in accordance with their doctrine of transmigration. The ebb and flow of the tide was considered to be the worship paid to the idol by the sea. Everything of the most precious was brought there as offerings, and the temple was endowed with more than ten thousand villages. There is a river (the Ganges) which is held sacred, between which and Somnat the distance is two hundred *parasangs*. They used to bring the water of this river to Somnat every day and wash the temple with it. A thousand brahmans were employed in worshipping the idol and attending on the visitors, and five hundred damsels sung and danced at the door – all these were maintained upon the endowments of the temple. The edifice was built upon fifty-six pillars of teak covered with lead. The shrine of the idol was dark but was lighted by jewelled chandeliers of great value. Near it was a chain of gold weighing two hundred *mans*. When a portion (watch) of the night closed, this chain used to be shaken like bells to rouse a fresh lot of brahmans to perform worship. When the Sultan went to wage religious war against India, he made great efforts to capture and destroy Somnat, in the hope that the Hindus would become Muhammadans. He arrived there in the middle of . . . December A.D. 1025. The Indians made a desperate resistance. They would go weeping and crying for help into the temple and then issue forth to battle and fight till all were killed. The number of slain exceeded 50,000. The king looked upon the idol with wonder and gave orders for the seizing of the spoil and the appropriation of the treasures. There were many idols of gold and silver and vessels set with jewels, all of which had been sent there by the greatest personages in India. The value of the things found in the temple and of the idols exceeded twenty thousand dinars. When the king asked his companions what they had to say about the marvel of the idol, and of its staying in the air without prop or support, several maintained that it was upheld by some hidden support. The king directed a person to go and feel all around and above and below it with a spear, which he did but met with no obstacle. One of the attendants then stated his opinion that the canopy was made of loadstone, and the idol of iron, and that the ingenious builder had skilfully contrived that the magnet should not exercise a greater force on any one side – hence the idol was suspended in the middle. Some coincided others differed. Permission was obtained from the Sultan to remove some stones from the top of the canopy to settle the point. When two stones were removed from the summit the idol swerved on one side, when more were taken away it inclined still further, until at last it rested on the ground.[1]

Mahmud died in 1030 to the relief of the people of northern India, who had come to associate his name with annual raids and idol breaking. Yet he used the loot from India to give expression to the other side of his character – the cultivated aristocrat. A library and a museum were founded, and a mosque was built at Ghazni incorporating all that was finest in contemporary Islamic architecture. From his campaign in Khvarazm Mahmud brought back with him a scholar by the name of Alberuni, perhaps the finest intellect of central Asia, and who spent ten years in India at the order of Mahmud. Alberuni's work on India *Tahqiq-i-Hind* contains observations on Indian civilization which are remarkably incisive and acute.

The raids of Mahmud did not make India aware of the world to her north-west or of the events taking place there. Confederacies had been formed, but not with a view to organizing defence on a national scale, utilizing resources from various parts of the sub-continent or even northern India. Defence was linked to the immediate purpose of assisting kings to maintain their kingdoms. The significance of Mahmud's raids as paving the way in northern India for further attacks from the north-west was not fully grasped. Mahmud was just another *mlechchha* as had been the Shakas and the Huns. They had been absorbed and forgotten and so too presumably would Mahmud and his armies. The death of Mahmud in any case removed the need for vigilance on the north-west, especially as his successors were less interested in the plains of northern India. The Indian rulers returned to their internal squabbles. When the second attack came from the north-west under the leadership of Muhammad Ghuri at the end of the twelfth century India was, for all practical purposes, as unprepared as she had been for meeting the invasions of Mahmud of Ghazni.

The eastern Ganges plain did not experience the disruption of the Punjab, despite Mahmud's attack on Kanauj. Kanauj was soon restored and became once more the prize and on account of this suffered continual attacks from various states – the Chalukyas, and later the Gahadavalas who claimed Rajput status. Bihar came under the domination of the Karnataka dynasty, the name suggesting a southern origin. A number of officers from various parts of the peninsula had found employment in eastern India, as is evident from the inscriptions of the time, and some of them acquired kingdoms. The Kalachuris continued to rule uneventfully at Tripuri near Jabalpur. Bengal experienced a brief efflorescence under the Senas, but eventually fell prey to the Turkish general Muhammad Khalji who attacked it in the beginning of the thirteenth century and brought about the virtual collapse of the Sena dynasty.

The Rajput clans fought each other unceasingly in the eleventh and twelfth centuries. The possession of kingdoms was a precarious business and the competition for territory a perpetual activity. War became a part of the general chivalric code. The Paramaras concentrated their strength in Malwa. The Solankis remained in Gujarat centred round Kathiawar. The Chandellas busied themselves in campaigns against the Paramaras and the Kalachuris. They were attacked by the Chauhans in the twelfth century. The Guhilas were dominant in Mewar and the region around modern Udaipur. The Kachchhapaghatas, yet another clan, ruled over Gwalior and the surrounding districts.

The power of the Chauhans, who had occupied the Tomara kingdoms in the region of Delhi, remained constant despite severe reverses on occasion. The last of the Chauhan kings, Prithviraja III, has become a romantic hero owing to the manner in which he wooed and won the daughter of the king of Kanauj. A long epic poem, *Prithvirajaraso*, composed by the bard Chand Bardai, narrates the incidents of this Lochinvar story. The daughter of the king of Kanauj was to marry and as was customary among princesses a *svayamvara* was held, where the eligible suitors were assembled at her father's court and she was expected to choose her husband from amongst them. But she had set her heart on the gallant Prithviraja, who unfortunately was the enemy of her father. The king of Kanauj, in order to insult Prithviraja, had not only failed to invite him to the *svayamvara* but had placed a statue of Prithviraja in the position of a doorkeeper in his court. To the bewilderment of those present, the princess of Kanauj rejected the princes assembled and instead placed a garland, indicating her choice, around the statue's neck. Before the courtiers realized what had happened, Prithviraja, who had been hiding in the vicinity, rode away with the princess and took her to his kingdom, where they were married. But they did not live happily ever after. Their happiness was marred by the second invasion from the north-west – that of Muhammad Ghuri – for Prithviraja was defeated in battle and killed.

Muhammad, the ruling Ghuri prince, had planned and carried out a campaign in India. He entered the Indus plain from the Gomal Pass, and not from the more commonly used Khyber Pass further north, and by 1182 the rulers of Sind were acknowledging his suzerainty. But Muhammad was thinking in terms of establishing a kingdom and not merely of indulging in looting raids. He realized that the richer regions were in the Upper Indus valley and in the Punjab, which he therefore planned to conquer.

This campaign was conducted through the northern route and 1185 saw Muhammad as the conqueror of Lahore. This led to visions of further conquests in India and an attack was commenced on the Rajput kingdoms controlling the Ganges plain. The Rajputs gathered together as best they could, not forgetting internal rivalries and jealousies. Prithviraja led them against Muhammad Ghuri at the first battle at Tarain in 1191 and the Rajputs were successful. Muhammad sent for reinforcements and a few months later, in 1192, a second battle was fought at the same place. Prithviraja was defeated and the kingdom of Delhi fell to Muhammad, who passed on and conquered both Delhi and Ajmer. But in 1206 Muhammad was assassinated. Unlike the previous occasion this did not mean the temporary withdrawal of Turkish-Afghan interests in India. Muhammad had been determined to retain his Indian possessions and this policy was adhered to by his successors.

The question remains as to why the Afghan* armies were so successful in their Indian campaigns. The earlier nibbling raids of the Afghans tended to act as irritants rather than to reveal the political threat of what lay beyond the frontier. The Afghan conquest of the far north went by slow stages, the implications of this conquest remaining vague for some time. The Afghan armies were in constant contact with troops and horse reinforcements across the border, but the strength of the Indian armies remained largely static. The Afghan soldiers were eager to fight, with the attraction of plunder to keep them going, whereas the Indian soldiers were by now weary of fighting and were exhausted from the many internal campaigns.

Reinforcements of good central Asian horses provided a better livestock for the Afghan cavalry, which was used to excellent effect in pitched battles. The Indian army had always suffered from the inferior breed of horse and consequently was chary of exploiting the cavalry. Indian commanders put more faith in elephants, which when pitted against swift central Asian horses fought an unequal fight. The Afghans used central Asian military tactics, emphasizing swiftness and light equipment which allowed greater ability to manoeuvre. The Indian army tended to fight in solid phalanxes relying on force to carry them through, and were handicapped in trying to match the shock tactics of the Afghans. The latter tended increasingly to concentrate on capturing forts which had a strategic advantage, and the Indian army was therefore forced into defensive positions in hill country, which did not add to its comfort. Guerrilla warfare may have been one means of harassing the Afghan armies, particularly

* The earlier rulers of what came to be called the Delhi Sultanate and a major part of their followers, both aristocratic and others, were Turks – mainly from central Asia – who had settled in Afghanistan and also some Afghan nobles. The armies with which they invaded India consisted of Turkish, Persian, and Afghan mercenaries, but for convenience' sake have here been referred to as Afghan armies, on the assumption that the majority of soldiers must have been Afghan.

when they were on the march, but this does not appear to have been used very effectively.

The psychological approach to war was also rather different. The Afghans regarded war as a matter of life and death, but, for the Indian princes in particular, it was almost a form of sport with its own rules of play. To apply the chivalric code in minor campaigns may have relieved the tedium of war, but the campaigns against the Afghans were of an entirely different nature, and this fact may not have been fully realized to begin with. The organization of Indian armies added to their weakness. Each army had as its permanent core the standing army, but the majority of soldiers were feudal levies which had not always previously fought as a single consolidated army.

The biggest puzzle is why a conjoint effort of the various Indian rulers was not made, through the centuries, to defend the north-west passes. Time and again various invaders had poured in through these passes, yet little attempt was made to prevent this, the defence of the region lying arbitrarily in the hands of local rulers. Even if the building of a Great Wall was not feasible, the construction of fortifications along the passes was always a possibility. Perhaps there was a basic lack of consciousness of the need for defence.

The Ghuri kingdom in Afghanistan did not long survive Muhammad's death, but the Indian part of the kingdom became the nucleus of a new political entity in India – the Delhi Sultanate or the rule of the Turkish and Afghan Sultans. Muhammad had left his Indian possessions in the care of a General, Qutb-ud-din Aibak, who, on the death of his master, ruled the Indian provinces and founded what came to be called the Slave Dynasty, the founder having once been a slave. Qutb-ud-din established himself at Delhi by clearing the area of Chauhan control and consolidating his position in Gwalior and the northern *doab* (the fertile region between the two rivers, Yamuna and Ganges). He made frequent attempts to gain control over Rajasthan, the importance of which was evident to him, but he was foiled by the easy mobility of the Rajput clans.

In the uncertain years between 1193 and 1206 when both Muhammad Ghuri and Qutb-ud-din were insecure in their Indian possessions, it would have been possible to organize resistance against them and dislodge them from northern India. Surprisingly, this opportunity was also allowed to slip by. Had the implications of the invasions from Afghanistan been fully understood in terms of both domestic and foreign politics, the resistance might have come about. This comprehension was in a sense thwarted by the fact that the region of the Punjab, i.e. the land to the north of the Sutlej river, throughout the centuries had been involved in the politics of Afghanistan and central Asia. This closeness prevented a properly focused perspective by the Punjab kingdoms on central Asia. The Turks were seen in the same light as the Shakas, Kushanas and the Huns, as central Asians seeking to extend their control over the Punjab. That they would carry their power into the very heart of India was not fully recognized even in the kingdoms of northern India south of the Sutlej.

Another obstacle was the general attitude and organization of life in northern India in regions other than the Punjab at the time, which hindered a correct assessment of the new factor entering the life of the sub-continent.

Perhaps the best summing up of this attitude is available in Alberuni's opening chapter where he writes :

. . . The Indians believe that there is no country but theirs, no nation like theirs, no king like theirs, no religion like theirs, no science like theirs. . . . They are by nature niggardly in communicating what they know, and they take the greatest possible care to withhold it from men of another caste from among their own people, still more of course from any foreigner.[2]

When speaking of the ordering of knowledge among Indians he states :

They are in a state of utter confusion, devoid of any logical order, and in the last instance always mixed up with silly notions of the crowd. I can only compare their mathematical and astronomical knowledge to a mixture of pearls and sour dates, or of pearls and dung, or of costly crystals and common pebbles. Both kinds of things are equal in their eyes since they cannot raise themselves to the methods of a strictly scientific deduction. . . .

It is indeed unfortunate that Alberuni visited India at a time when knowledge was at a low ebb. Had he come four centuries earlier, a mind such as his would have eagerly participated in the vigorous discussions of the time. Insularity at every level was characteristic of northern India in the eleventh century and the price of this insularity was the shaking up of the country by the coming of the Turks and Afghans. Fortunately, this did not result in total disruption. It introduced new vitality into the pattern of life.

11

FEUDALISM IN THE REGIONAL STATES
c. A.D. 800–1200

THE political fragmentation of northern India and the Deccan which occurred in this period in the form of regional kingdoms was due to a number of developments, which led to the crystallization of regional loyalty based on a common culture and history. With the passing of the earlier larger and highly centralized states there was no longer the compulsion of a central authority and the economic pull of a metropolis to lessen the strength of local feeling, which could now be concentrated upon more immediately local interests and resources. This whole area became preoccupied with local rather than with countrywide matters.

One result of this new outlook was the increase in historical writings. There appeared many histories of comparatively small geographical regions such as Kashmir and family histories of still lesser dynasties, such as that of Nepal. A king did not have to be of the status of Samudra Gupta to become the subject of eulogy, minor kings being described with the same enthusiasm as important monarchs. The process of providing impressive genealogies led to associating fairly insignificant dynasties with historical personalities of the past or, even, with the very gods themselves. Local pride found an outlet in the ballads and epics concerning local rulers, such as the *Prithviraja-raso*, probably the most popular of its type (although the version now current is a later composition).

This significant change from a centralized viewpoint was due largely to the emergence of a new politico-economic structure, which dominated north and, later, south India, which can broadly be termed feudalism. The use of this term has been contested, since the type of feudalism in India during these centuries was not identical with the feudal system in other parts of the world. Consequently, some historians have preferred to qualify the description by using terms such as quasi-feudalism, feudalistic, etc. This is perhaps being unnecessarily cautious once it has been stated that Indian feudalism, though similar in the main, differed in some aspects from other types of feudalism. For instance, Indian feudalism did not emphasize the economic contract to the same degree as certain types of European feudalism, but the difference is not so significant as to preclude the use of the term feudalism for conditions prevailing in India during this period.

The basic requisites of a feudal system were present in India. The king granted the revenue from varying proportions of land to his officers or selected holders, who were the equivalent of vassals elsewhere. The tendency from the seventh century onwards of granting land in lieu of cash salaries intensified the feudal process. The work of cultivation was carried out by peasants, generally *shudras*, who in effect were almost tied to the land and who handed over a fixed share of their produce to the landowner. The feudatories could hire out their assigned land to cultivators, from whom they collected the revenue agreed upon. Part of the revenue from the land they sent to the king. Out of the revenue retained by the vassal he was expected to maintain the feudal levies which, underlying his oath of loyalty to his king, he was in duty bound to furnish for the king's service. To break his oath was regarded as a heinous offence. He might also be called upon to give his daughter in marriage to the king; he used the currency of his feudal lord, whose name he dutifully mentioned in such monuments, inscriptions, and the like, which he caused to be made.

The relationship of the vassal to the king was thus close but subordinate, and its precise terms depended largely on how the relationship originated. Feudatories conquered in war were allowed little scope for independent action. On the other hand, some of the more powerful feudatories were permitted to grant land in their turn, without first obtaining permission from the king. Such feudatories often had their own sub-feudatories, thus building up a hierarchy. An inscription from the latter part of the Gupta period refers to this and is one of the earliest evidences of the beginnings of a feudal hierarchy : the Gupta monarch had Surashmichandra as his feudatory who in turn had Matrivishnu as his sub-feudatory. This hierarchy is frequently described in the inscriptions of the Later Chalukyas.

Apart from paying a portion of his dues regularly and maintaining a specified number of troops for the king, the feudatory had other obligations as well. Attendance at court on certain occasions, such as the king's birthday, was obligatory. The occasions varied from court to court. The smaller feudatories had to obtain permission from the king for any changes in the administration of their property. In return, the feudatory was permitted the use of a title and various symbols of feudal dignity, such as a throne, a fly-whisk, a specially designed palanquin, the riding of an elephant in state processions, and being heralded by the sound of five special musical instruments. Titles varied according to the rank of the feudatories. The more important called themselves *mahasamanta, mahamandaleshvara*, and so on. The lesser feudatories took the titles of *raja, samanta, ranaka, thakura, bhogta*, etc. Some of these usages date back to the Gupta period, although their sanction became more precise in later centuries.

The military aspect of the feudal relationship – the obligation on the part of the feudatory to supply men at arms when required by the king – became increasingly important as wars between the various states became more frequent. In certain cases an annual tribute to the king was accepted in lieu of supplying soldiers, but this was not a common practice. On a declaration of war by the king, the feudatory was expected of his own accord to send soldiers and equipment. During peacetime the king held periodic reviews both to inspect the feudal levies and indirectly to re-affirm his overlordship. Forts and garrison towns were kept well-manned so that centres of defence were always available.

These obligations tended to strengthen the martial aspect of the system which lent itself admirably to the rise of the Rajput clans. Military obligations came to be more significant after *c.* A.D. 1000, when the smaller land grants were made with greater frequency in favour of officials than in previous centuries. In the earlier period, the majority of the feudal tenants appear to have been persons associated with religion, either brahmans or Buddhist establishments, and these were exempt from both tax and military requirements.

Theoretically only the revenue from the land was granted to the feudatory and not the land itself, and if he failed to fulfil the terms of the grant his land could be confiscated by the king. The grant was only for the life of the tenant and was subject to re-assignment on his death. In practice, however, the land held by a feudatory tended to become hereditary, particularly in periods when the control of the king weakened. There is evidence of one brahman ministerial family holding a benefice through five generations, the head of the family performing the same office as the original beneficiary. From regarding a benefice as hereditary it was a simple step to assume the right to dispose both of the revenue and the land itself, although this was not legally permissible.

In order to assess the income of a particular area, villages were grouped together in units of ten in the Deccan kingdoms and in units of twelve or sixteen or multiples of these in areas further north, particularly in some of the Rajput kingdoms. Pala grants refer to assignees receiving the revenue of ten villages (*dashagramika*). The Pratihara administration divided villages into groups of eighty-four and later such a group became the standard size of the estate of a clan chief in Rajasthan, making it possible to trace the origin of some later clan kingdoms to these administrative units of the tenth century. Groups of twelve villages were common in other areas, and these could easily be formed into the larger eighty-four unit.

Villages were based on a self-sufficient economy where production approximated to local requirements, with little attempt at producing a surplus to be used specifically for trade or exchange. Surplus production would hardly have benefited the peasant, since it would have led to a demand from the landowner for a larger share. The existing system led to accepting the standard of minimum production, since the incentive to improve production was absent. As the pressure on the peasantry increased, production at subsistence level became useful. Lack of incentive in this case had nothing to do with the fatalistic beliefs of the Indian peasant, as some writers have urged; it arose from the practical economics of the situation. Limited production and lack of trade led to a decrease in the use of coins, and trade was further hampered by the emergence of a wide range of local weights and measures, making long distance trade more difficult. The surplus wealth of the feudatories and the king was not invested in craft production or trade, but was used for conspicuous consumption. The palatial homes of the feudatories were richly ornamented, and much of the income was spent in building magnificent temples, richly endowed, and on occasion as pretentious as the exalted titles taken by their donors. No wonder these temples attracted invaders whose desire to achieve religious merit by destroying idols was less than their greed for plunder.

The possibilities of multiplying sub-feudatories at various stages in the feudal structure led to a wider diffusion of the income from the land. This weakened the position of those at both ends of the scale – the cultivator and the king – who suffered from the diversion of income into the hands of the intermediaries. Loss of revenue placed the king politically in a vulnerable position *vis à vis* his feudatories, since he was in any case dependent on their honouring their obligations. It also led to the economic depression of the peasantry. With an increase in the number of intermediaries the peasant was forced to pay taxes additional to the basic land tax. Whereas in previous centuries the revenue paid to the central authority was in part used to maintain public works such as roads, irrigation, etc., under the feudal system, separate taxes distinct from the land tax were levied by the feudal tenants for such purposes. The temple authorities also levied additional dues. Land grants to the brahmans were tax free, so the loss of revenue from these lands had to be made good from other sources. Goods produced by the craftsmen were also taxed and were liable to a series of taxes. Inscriptions relating to Chauhan history mention a great variety of taxes, and the position was similar in most feudal kingdoms. The land tax was in any case high; some peasants paid as much as the value of one third of the produce to the landowner although the more usual assessment was one sixth. These taxes, together with the obligation to provide free labour, and the fact that as the power of the feudal intermediaries grew they began to appropriate even the common lands of the villages such as the pastures, reduced the cultivators to a condition of hopelessness.

From the administrative point of view, the feudal system had the advantage of obviating the need for a centrally administered bureaucracy. Revenue was collected by vassals who could also carry out judicial functions, as they were sufficiently powerful to assert their authority in cases of dispute. The feudatories, therefore, had both a political and administrative function, whilst brahman grantees, who were often given land in newly settled areas, could be relied upon to disseminate Sanskrit culture.

The whole of a kingdom was not granted to feudal holders. The king retained a sizeable area as crown land which he directly administered. For administrative purposes the kingdom was divided into provinces, and these in turn were sub-divided into units consisting of a specified number of villages. A province might contain both crown land and land held in fief. The powers and duties of the king's administrative officers *vis à vis* the feudatories were clearly defined and observed. Village autonomy in administrative matters was naturally hampered by the privileges and powers of the landowner. The relationship between the landowner and the village authorities varied. There is a reference to the *Thakura* of a Chauhan village having to obtain the sanction of the village assembly for raising new dues for the local temple. But this need not necessarily have applied in the case of other dues, or other villages.

The village assemblies continued in some areas, but had lost much of their powers. In villages held by feudatories they gradually died out and were ineffective as representative political institutions. In directly administered villages they assisted in administration. In one specific case the village assembly consisted of elected persons from each ward of the village, but the nominees for election had to be approved of by the ruler, so that they were in essence merely tools of the administration. A smaller group from amongst the assembly, known as the *panchakula* committee, collected the state revenue, recorded religious and secular grants, supervised the sale of goods and trade, and acted as arbiters in disputes. This committee may well have been the prototype of the *panchayat*, a similar institution in later centuries.

The aristocracy consisted of the feudatories, including the brahmans. Grants to the brahmans were obviously based on the desire to acquire religious merit and were a category apart. The brahmans performed sacrifices for the king, who by accepted theory acquired one sixth of the merit from such religious activities; the king accordingly was careful to patronize the brahmans, who in turn, to show their gratitude, composed fictitious genealogies for the king.

The secular feudatories generally came from families which had risen by military power. The Rajput obsession with *kshatriya* status was largely to acquire military bonafides and emphasize the fact of belonging to a warrior caste. Frequent campaigns were essential to perpetuate this image and also to establish the reputation of military prowess. Where the desire for plunder was alone not a sufficient excuse for war, an elaborate code of etiquette was worked out by which a noble was justified in going to war should the merest disparaging remark be made about him. The literal application of certain political theories may also explain partially the eagerness for war – such as for instance that inter-state politics should be based on the system of *mandala*, which assumes that one of the neighbours is a natural enemy. War became a grand pageant, and death on the battlefield the highest possible honour. In the Chandella kingdom villages were donated to maintain the families of soldiers who had died in war. This was also a means of encouraging the continuing flow of soldiers which the system required. Heroic virtues were instilled into the child from birth and a man who shirked fighting was held in contempt. Women, too, were taught to admire men who fought well. A woman had to be ready to die should her husband be killed and the becoming of *sati* whether voluntary or forced became fashionable.

The possession of land was essential to the legitimacy of the leadership claimed by the nobility, since land and caste differentiated them from the rest of society. Feuds over land often led to family vendettas which continued for generations. The existence of clans among the Rajputs together with caste relationships stressed the idea of kinship through blood and this feeling was more dominant amongst the Rajputs than among the other feudal chiefs.

The nobility loved to use exalted titles. The least important of rulers thought it appropriate to use what was once an imperial title, *maharajadhiraja*, and this was generally embedded in a mass of eulogistic and bombastic phraseology. More important kings surpassed themselves in inventing titles. Prithviraja III, who aspired to rule the whole of northern India, called himself *bharateshvara*, 'the lord of Bharat' i.e. India. A twelfth-century ruler of Kanauj described himself as 'The most exalted – the great king of kings – the supreme lord – the king over horses, elephants, and men – the sovereign of the three worlds. . .'. This was incongruous, considering the actual political position of the rulers, who obviously lived in a world of make-believe. Minor deeds were exaggerated to become major acts of heroism, and flattery even of the most abject kind was regarded as normal to courtly behaviour, though admittedly the more intelligent of rulers preferred subtler forms.

The aristocracy lived on the revenue from the land without participating in the cultivation of it themselves. Many of the brahman holders employed cultivators, since they were forbidden by caste laws to cultivate land. Buddhist monasteries also farmed out their land. The actual work of cultivation was done entirely by the peasant who was generally of *shudra* caste. Thus the peasantry was subservient to the feudal chiefs, and the consequent concentration of political and economic power in the hands of the comparatively few was a new feature. Previously the distribution of power had been wider, since both the bureaucracy and the leaders of the commercial and urban groups, such as the merchant and artisan guilds, had also shared in it. This power of the few was accentuated by the increasing self-sufficiency of the villages which discouraged communication and association with other villages. It also facilitated a strict supervision of the division of labour and reduced the mobility of the peasant population, both of which factors were instrumental in increasing the feudal chief's control over the peasantry.

The balance of power between the king and the feudatories could fluctuate, since it was based on the king's control over the feudatories, despite his dependence on them for revenue and soldiers. Fortunately for the king the balance usually inclined in his direction, as he had the support of the political thinkers, generally brahmans, whose interest it was to support the authority of the institution which safeguarded their well-being. Even more fortunately for the king the sanction obtained from the older texts supported his claim in broad terms. Thus the principle of hereditary kingship was heavily stressed. The automatic succession of kings was an effective means of preventing interference from vassals, because in its absence the feudatories could interfere in the selection of the next king, and confer upon themselves greater power. It was therefore natural that the election of a king, as in the case of Gopala the Pala king, would cause a stir. The divine origin of kingship was much emphasized during this period, as was also the king's obligation to protect the *kshatriya* caste, which obligation assigns to the feudatories a subordinate position. Since the king no longer had direct communication with his subjects they had tended to transfer their loyalty to their immediate protector the feudal lord – thus increasing the latter's power. To counteract this trend the age-old obligation of the king to protect his subjects was continually reiterated.

Much of the political theory of this time consisted of underlining passages from the older texts, relevant to contemporary affairs, in the form of a commentary. There was one striking exception to this in the works of Hemachandra (1089–1173), a Jaina by religion who lived and worked in western India. The puritan strain of Jaina thought permeated his political ideas, which remained largely unaffected by the general tendency to compromise with the established order of things. One of his theses was a direct challenge to the orthodox position, in that he maintained that society could be changed for the better by proper legislation, with the logical corollary that there was nothing sacrosanct about the existing order.

Legal writing reflected the tendency of seeking the sanction of older sources for contemporary usage. This resulted in detailed commentaries on earlier works accorded high authority, such as Manu's *Dharmashastra*. The commentary of Medhatithi in the tenth century and that of Kulluka in the thirteenth were the most widely used. To refer to the authority of an older text meant the re-editing of the text in certain cases, with an emphasis on those aspects which related to contemporary problems. The discussion of legal institutions is probably the most valuable contribution of the period to technical literature.

Problems concerning the division of land and inheritance (since land was now the chief economic asset in most wealthy families) came in for special attention. The two systems of family law, *Dayabhaga* and *Mitakshara*,* became the basis of civil law and were to remain so until very recent years. They deal with property rights in a Hindu joint-family system, the latter having become usual in most landowning families.

Ownership of land did not exclude other forms of economic activity, although income from land was highly regarded, because it was both secure and regular. The economic self-sufficiency of the villages led to a decline in trade, which in turn affected the growth of towns. Those that had already attained a certain economic momentum continued, but the founding of new towns was less frequent than before. Arab geographers writing of this period have commented on the paucity of towns in India as compared with China. Continual wars were also detrimental to trade. In the coastal areas maritime trade still supported prosperous port towns, particularly in regions such as Gujarat, Malabar, and the Tamil coast, which still had a large overseas trade.

The prosperity of coastal towns was due partly to the settlements of foreign merchants who controlled most of the trade between India and western Asia and were also encroaching on the eastern trade. Arab merchants strove to eliminate the Indian middlemen in the trade between India and China, by going directly to China and to south-east Asia. The ports along the west coast of India referred to in Arab geographies – Debal (in the Indus delta), Cambay, Thana, Sopara, and Kaulam (Quilon) – were frequented mainly by Arab ships, which carried to the West cargoes of goods either produced in India or brought by Indian merchants from places in the East. The north Indian overland trade with China via central Asia gradually declined with the opening up of central Asia to Persian and west Asian traders. This trade virtually came to an end in the thirteenth century when the Mongol invasions cut India off from central Asia.

* Both systems refer among other things to property held jointly by the male members of a family. According to the *Dayabhaga* school it is only on the death of the father that the sons can claim rights to the property, whereas in the *Mitakshara* school the sons can claim this right during the lifetime of the father. In either case the father does not have absolute rights over the property.

Internal trade had not disappeared entirely, since there remained an irreducible minimum. Artisans worked both in the villages and the towns, the concentration being greater in the towns, where professional associations were recognized. But the guilds and associations had lost their earlier dominant position in urban centres. Power had now shifted to the landowning community, which tended to be somewhat suspicious of the craft associations in the towns, since these bodies were more independent than their village counterparts. The really powerful guilds were now confined to south India.

In eastern India a decline in the prosperity of the towns was prevented by two factors: trade with south-east Asia during the twelfth and thirteenth centuries resulted in the maintenance of sufficient business to keep the towns busy; this trade also helped to keep money in circulation, and gradually a cash assessment on the land was introduced under the Senas. The re-introduction of a money economy together with better possibilities of surplus production (although of a limited kind) enabled the towns to act as centres of trade and distribution once more. But this was not a consistent and stable return of a mercantile economy, for the coinage of this period frequently shows a debasement of the metal as compared with Gupta coins. This is particularly so in gold and silver coins, where, in the case of the former, the depreciation is sometimes as much as fifty per cent.

The only category of commercial professionals whose prosperity increased were the money-lenders. Interest on money lent was normally fifteen per cent, but there are records in Chauhan sources of higher interest such as thirty per cent, and twenty-five per cent in those of the Rashtrakutas. Higher rates were due perhaps to the decline in trade and the unavailability of money. Caste considerations in the matter of money-lending appear by now to have been regularized, the brahman being charged two per cent and the *shudra* five per cent or more on the same capital. This was an additional factor limiting the mobility of the peasant as he was unable to free himself from debt.

The specialization of labour in the working of the rural economy led to the proliferation of sub-castes in the villages. Thus it became difficult for the village to develop as an organic whole, the tendency being for various castes and sub-castes to pursue their own separate organization. Thus caste association further diluted political loyalties. In later centuries caste exclusiveness was to become absolute and to reach its peak in caste *panchayats*, separate tribunals for each caste in the village, each regarded as the supreme authority for the particular caste.

Brahmanical sources refer to the modification of the caste structure and, in the process of seeking support from the older texts, the brahmans became even more aloof and the caste structure was made theoretically more watertight. In the contest for primacy between the brahman and mercantile communities, the brahmans, having acquired political power by becoming landowners, were emerging as victors. The decline of the mercantile community led to a lowering of the status of Buddhism, since the Buddhists were largely dependent on it for financial support. The only region where Buddhism held its own was eastern India, where it had royal patronage. Thus the main religious competitors of the brahmans had become unimportant. The desire for exclusiveness on the part of the brahmans led to an obsession with keeping aloof from the lower castes in particular. Not only was the touch of the *chandala* (outcaste) polluting but even for his shadow to cross the path of the brahman called for ritual ablution. Such social observances reduced still further the status of the *shudra* and the outcastes. Gradually untouchability was extended to even the heretical sects of quite high caste but who were opposed to the brahmans.

There are, however, indications that the intermediate castes – *kshatriyas* and *vaishyas* – were not so strict in their adherence to caste rules as the brahmans would have wished. There are references to the emergence of a number of sub-castes which were later provided with a mixed-caste origin. Among these were the *kayasthas*, the scribes of the administration, responsible for writing documents and maintaining records. When they came to be regarded as a sub-caste, in about the eleventh century, there was some confusion as to their original caste. Some described them as *kshatriyas*, others ascribed their origin to a brahman–shudra combination. The mixed-caste origin ascribed to them may well have been a later invention of those who had to fit them into a caste hierarchy. Contact with royalty gave them social status : in some cases they also received land grants and became prosperous landowners.

A number of the new sub-castes were associated with technical professions, as for instance those requiring surgical, medical, or mathematical knowledge. The brahmanical writings of this period attack professions where technical knowledge was essential. Medhatithi regards handicrafts as low occupations. According to contemporary commentaries on Manu, mechanical work was a minor sin, and this category of work included the construction of bridges and embankments to control the flow of water. Perhaps those in authority were conscious of the power inherent in technical knowledge.

Some sub-castes claim origin from highly respected ancestors who through economic necessity had to change their profession. The *khatris*, an important sub-caste in northern India to this day, claimed that they were of *kshatriya* origin, but took to commerce, which brought them the contempt of their caste fellows; thus they had to accept *vaishya* status. The Gurjaras, Jats, and Ahirs all claimed *kshatriya* origin but had lost caste status. The emergence of new sub-castes had been a feature of the caste system since its inception. But in the early agrarian communities the development of sub-castes had been slower. The period of mercantile activity and the movement of populations had accelerated this process. The four major castes still constituted an umbrella beneath which sub-castes kept emerging and finding their own inter-caste relationships which, though broadly in keeping with the theoretical structure, were nevertheless modified by local requirements and expediency.*

The caste structure was closely linked to the educational system of the society. Formal education of the type given in brahmanical centres and described in Sanskrit works was becoming increasingly theological in spirit. Theoretically, such schools and centres, which were now receiving considerable royal patronage,

---

*It is curious that foreign accounts, when mentioning the castes of Indian society, often refer to seven and not the usual four. The seven are generally made up of the theoretical four plus three sub-castes. The Arab writer, Al Idrisi, writing in the twelfth century, lists seven – the nobility, the brahmans, the soldiers, the cultivators, the artisans, the singers, and the entertainers – an even more confused assortment than that of Megasthenes.

were open to the three upper castes, but in fact they were used almost exclusively by brahmans, who had converted them into theological seminaries.

Most large villages had schools attached to the local temple. Colleges for advanced learning received special endowments as also did the *mathas* associated with the *Shaiva* and *Vaishnava* religion, which were located in almost all places of pilgrimage in northern India. With the strengthening of the brahmanical tradition and the emphasis on older texts, formal education tended to become a repetition of statements rather than a questioning of facts in an attempt to obtain further elucidation. Such exceptions as there were to this pattern were unfortunately too weak to change significantly the mould of intellectual activity. Contempt for technical knowledge was an almost inevitable outcome of this attitude.

For non-brahmans the older system of being trained in guilds or as apprentices to artisans continued, the education being limited to professional training. Buddhist monasteries had included some non-theological education and the presence of many non-Indian scholars had encouraged a more catholic outlook, but even these were being changed into centres of Buddhist teaching alone. Such monasteries survived mainly in eastern India, Nalanda remaining the best known. The destruction of Nalanda by the Turks virtually brought Buddhist education in India to a close. Jaina centres of education were closer in spirit to the Buddhist than the brahmanical, and these were concentrated in western India, in Saurashtra, Gujarat, Rajasthan, and at Shravana Belgola in Mysore where Jainism still had a sizeable following, particularly amongst the mercantile class.

The theological content of brahmanical education, although admirably suited to brahmanical purposes, had a restrictive effect on the intellectual tradition, heightened by the fact that the medium of instruction was Sanskrit, which by the end of this period had become a language spoken and read only by the brahmans and the privileged few who had received a formal education. The result was intellectual inbreeding, which both isolated and weakened the brahmanical tradition. The emerging regional languages were to become the media of popular expression. The denigration of technical knowledge is an instance of the split in the educational tradition of this period, which was to impoverish both formal and technical education. The scientific works of the period were largely commentaries on earlier works, e.g. the medical texts of Charaka and Sushruta; or else of theoretical analyses with rare attempts at referring to empirical knowledge. Where experiments were made practical results ensued, as with the introduction of the use of iron and quicksilver in medical practice. Astronomy had come to be regarded almost as a sub-section of astrology. Algebra remained the sole major contribution to mathematics during this period.

Literature of various kinds continued to be written in Sanskrit. Much of it was pedantic and imitative of earlier works, characterized by verbal embellishments and linguistic virtuosity. Lyric poetry and prose romances, the most common forms, usually had as themes familiar stories from the epics and the *Puranas*, so that the narrative aspect could safely be subordinated to the linguistic. Prosody and the technicalities of poetic composition came in for detailed study. Sanskrit writers and poets were welcome at the courts of the various kings, who felt that they would thus be reviving the glories of earlier courts, although on a smaller scale.

Prose stories tended to be less contrived and artificial. The themes were familiar stories from traditional sources and were treated in the highly romantic style of the time. An exception was Somadeva's anthology, *Kathasaritsagara* (The Ocean of the Stream of Stories), which, although written in poetic form in the eleventh century, is popular even to this day.

Related to the prose romances and resulting from the growing feeling of regional loyalty were the historical narratives, which assumed a new importance. These were either in verse or prose, though the latter was more common. Most of them were historical biographies such as Padmagupta's life of a king of Malwa or Bilhana's biography of the Chalukya king Vikramaditya VI – the *Vikramanka-deva-charita*. Others were narratives of the history of a region, such as Kalhana's *Rajatarangini*, or else were works of a more general nature with references to historical persons and to institutions, as in the *Parishishtaparvan* of Hemachandra.

Drama, despite the fact that it was still an adjunct of the

court, managed to retain something of the earlier plays. Vishak-hadatta's *Mudrarakshasa* (The Signet Ring of Rakshasa) which has political intrigue during the Mauryan period as its theme, had, at an earlier period, made a departure from the romantic comedy. The plays which followed, those of Bhavabhuti, have a tender-ness and subdued dramatic quality with a minimum of comic effects. Later playwrights – Murari, Hastimalla, Rajashekhara, and Kshemeshvara – wrote plays which appear to have been more successful when read rather than performed.

Lyric poetry of a different quality, less sophisticated and more personal than the works mentioned, was also written. Perhaps the most spontaneous was the great outburst of erotic poetry which is characteristic of this period, such as the single stanza poems of Bhartrihari. Some of the erotic poetry probably evolved from the symbolism of certain sections of the devotional cult where the depiction of the love of Radha and Krishna provided the excuse. Jayadeva's *Gita Govinda* (Song of Krishna), written in the twelfth century, describes with sensuous abandon the love of Krishna, the incarnation of Vishnu, for Radha, the lyrical quality of the verse being unsurpassed. Others such as Govard-hana, or Bilhana in the *Chaurapanchashika*, introduced erotic descriptions into their verses with a directness and candour which did not require the disguise of a religious theme.

The cult of the erotic had come into its own, not only in poetry but also in temple sculpture and in Tantric ritual. Much has been said and written on the depravity of taste, the pandering to the sensuous, and the degradation of morals in India during this period. Yet there is considerable sensitivity and beauty even within the erotic themes in, for instance, the *Gita Govinda* or the sculpture at Khajuraho. It is held that the period of decline in every culture exhibits an unhealthy interest in sexual be-haviour, yet the objective analysis of any culture reveals that the description and portrayal of such behaviour is evident at many levels and periods, although the form and symbolism may vary. This was an age of abandon, with the lifting of the puritan impress of Buddhism which associated guilt with pleasure, which led to a more uninhibited reference to sexual behaviour in both literature and the arts. The seclusion of women introduced through feudal chivalry in upper-class society cast a romantic aura around the simplest of relationships between men and women. In some other cultures the desires evoked by this were sublimated but in India they were permitted uninhibited expression, which was one way of registering a protest against an unnatural social convention. The 'spiritual' interpretations which some writers seek to associate with erotic symbols in Indian culture have little relevance to the poetry and art of this period.

Despite the limitations of Sanskrit, it was in this language that court literature still flourished, since none of the new vernacular tongues of the north were as yet sufficiently developed to be suitable literary vehicles of sophisticated thought. Pali had little to show except for a few local chronicles, commentaries, grammars, and legal texts with a limited – generally Buddhist – readership. The fate of Prakrit was similar, having been caught between Sanskrit and the newly emerging languages. Even the Jainas, much of whose canonical writings was in Prakrit, turned to Sanskrit, and the ornate Sanskrit style had begun to influence Prakrit literature. Vakpati's *Gauḍavadha*, a biography of Yashovarman of Kanauj, was the last major work in the older tradition of Prakrit literature.

However, unlike Pali and Sanskrit, Prakrit is of linguistic interest as illustrative of the linguistic evolution from Prakrit to Apabhramsha and finally to a new regional language. Apabhramsha (literally 'falling down'), a corrupt form of Prakrit dialect, is believed to have originated in the north-west and travelled from that region with the migrations of people who scattered and settled in central and western India after the Hun invasions. The Prakrit of the Jainas was heavily influenced by Apabhramsha and it is here that the link between the older and the newer languages is evident – and even more so in the Jaina Maharashtri and Gujarati.

Marathi developed rapidly after it had been adopted by the Maharashtrian saints of the devotional cult. Gujarati, spoken in modern Saurashtra, was encouraged both by Jaina monks and by the popular poems composed to accompany the famous *Rasa-lila* dance – depicting the young Krishna and the milkmaids – which poems became the literary nucleus of early Gujarati. Bengali, Assamese, Oriya (spoken in Orissa), and the dialects of Bihar (Bhojpuri, Maithili, and Magadhi) evolved from the

Prakrit earlier spoken in Magadha. The new religious sects played an important part in accelerating the growth of the vernacular languages, as they wished to communicate with the ordinary people in the popular tongue.

Regional interest and variation was beginning to express itself in many forms, including those of architecture and sculpture, where the breaking away from classical models is evident in the temples of this period. There are three regions in the north where large but elegant temples have survived; Rajasthan and Gujarat in western India, Bundelkhand in central India, and Orissa in the east. The overall architectural style is similar, conforming to the *nagara* or north Indian style, but this did not exclude local variation. The *nagara* temple was square in plan but gave the impression of having a cruciform shape owing to graduated projections in the middle of each of the four sides. The central tower was tall, inclining gradually inwards in a convex curve. The Jaina temples at Mt Abu, built in white marble, are representative of the western Indian group. They are richly adorned with sculpture which, though profuse, is subsidiary to the architecture.

The temples at Khajuraho are the best example of the Bundelkhand group and these are again richly decorated with sculpture. The temples display a balance of size and form which makes of each an impressive structure. The erotic sculpture at Khajuraho (as at Konarak) has led to these temples being regarded as exhibitions of pornographic art, and the eagerness of visitors to see the erotic often diverts attention from the aesthetic qualities of both the architecture and the sculpture. The temples of Orissa at Bhubaneshwar, Puri, and Konarak are more monumental: the towers rise higher and the curve in their elevation is more pronounced and elegant.

The area included in the temple precincts of the northern temples was far less than that of the Dravida temples. The northern Indian temples were not centres of civic and corporate life to the same degree as their southern counterparts. Temples such as those at Khajuraho were used largely by the upper classes. The worship of popular cult images was kept apart from the main temple, although sometimes included within its precincts. Temple architecture in northern India virtually ceased to evolve subsequent to these temples, since later temples were largely imitations of the older ones.

Eastern India produced a distinctive school of sculpture in stone and metal. The stone, dark grey or black, when polished shone with a metallic lustre. Buddhist icons at Nalanda set the standard and Pala patronage extended to Hindu icons as well. From the little that has survived of the painting of this period it would appear that its quality was nowhere as high as that of sculpture. In the field of fine arts the Indian contribution was primarily in sculpture. Had it preserved an independent form it might have continued to evolve its own style in subsequent centuries, but application solely as a part of architecture caused it to decay aesthetically together with the temples of later centuries.

The upper classes of the north were reluctant to admit popular deities into their religious system. The distinction between the religion of the *élite* and the religion of the masses becomes more evident during this period. Yet the popular deities could not be totally excluded. In the upper levels of society the more sophisticated forms of Hinduism held sway. The use of the term Hinduism to cover both *Vaishnava* and *Shaiva* following became current after the arrival of the Arabs and Turks, who used the word Hindu primarily to mean the inhabitants of the Indian sub-continent* and by extension to distinguish them with their non-Islamic religion, from themselves, the followers of Islam. The term persisted and is now associated only with the brahmanical religion of the sub-continent. The Arabs and the Turks did differentiate between the Hindus and the Buddhists, Jainas, etc., but the distinction was vague and with the gradual decline of the latter the term was applied only to *Vaishnavas* and *Shaivas*, the two major sects of the brahmanical religion.

By the end of the period these two sects were dominant in northern India. Jainism was restricted to the west, which has the largest Jaina communities in modern times. Buddhism, which had been almost confined to eastern India, was fast losing support. Buddha had been incorporated into the Hindu pantheon as an incarnation of Vishnu. But the popular mind never quite

* The Arabic name for the sub-continent, al-Hind, was derived from the Greek 'Indus' and the Persian 'Sindhu'.

accepted this : the worship of Buddha by non-Buddhists remained a formal and deferential relationship with the god. The militaristic values of the feudal system doubtless found the Buddhist and Jaina emphasis on *ahimsa* (non-violence) unpalatable. The Hindu gods did not preach non-violence, neither Shiva nor the two major incarnations of Vishnu – Krishna and Rama. Where the idea of non-violence survived was amongst the leaders of the devotional cults who opposed violence for the same reasons as did the Buddha.

Many of the changes introduced into Hinduism at this time were the result of a compromise between orthodox belief and popular demand for a more personal religion. Image worship increased substantially and a multitude of new forms were introduced which necessitated the building of shrines and temples to house them. The incarnations of Vishnu became more popular and interest in the *Puranas* and epic literature, particularly through the versions in regional languages, provided the tradition in which to incorporate the legends of the incarnations.

Perhaps the most popular of the incarnations was Krishna. Earlier tradition had treated Krishna as the hero-god, the philosopher of the *Bhagavad-Gita*. Now it was the pastoral and erotic aspect which appealed to his worshippers. Krishna, meaning 'dark', has led to his being associated with the flute-playing Tamil god Mayon, 'the dark one', the herdsman who spent many hours in the company of the milkmaids, which is what the cowherd of Mathura is associated with in the northern tradition. It is believed that the Abhiras, a pastoral tribe of the peninsula, brought this god with them when they travelled north and settled in central and western India. The cult became popular in the region of Mathura, from where it spread rapidly to other parts of northern India. At the popular level Krishna and his favourite, the milkmaid Radha, were worshipped as part of a fertility cult. More sophisticated symbolism was attached to this cult when the love of Radha for Krishna was interpreted as the longing and attachment of the human soul for the Universal Soul.

Philosophical debate had moved northwards from the peninsula, though perhaps the liveliest controversy was still in the southern centres. The six schools of philosophy continued their debates from earlier times, but there was a noticeable tendency towards theistic interpretations. The orthodox brahmanical schools united in opposing Buddhist philosophy, as, for instance, in the later works of Vachaspatimishra and Udayana. Of the six schools, *Vedanta* was gradually coming to the forefront. Some of the philosophical debate expressed itself in the rivalry between the *Vaishnavas* and the *Shaivas*, taking as their starting-point the teaching of Shankara and Ramanuja.

The devotional cult moved northwards from where it originated in south India and the Deccan. In some areas the followers of the older heterodox sects now directed their loyalty to the devotional cult, which was in any case in sympathy with the social attitudes of the earlier sects. Drawing support from both *Vaishnavas* and *Shaivas*, it acted as a bridge not only between the two major sects of Hinduism but also between the esoteric and the popular levels of the religion. The devotional cult represented the more puritanical protest of the professional classes. The popular cults and sects sometimes demonstrated their protest in a more startling manner such as the rites of the *Kalamukhas* and *Kapalikas*. Some of their rituals, however, were rooted in the primitive, unbroken ritual of the outcaste sections of society who had hardly known Hinduism as formulated by the brahmans, and who were therefore not protesting but merely worshipping according to their own beliefs. Brahman orthodoxy had to adjust itself to this formidable range of religious expression in order to maintain its position. This it did most successfully and the adjustment was to prove its salvation. When a cult or sect became popular, it was gradually made respectable by being included at some level in the orthodox hierarchy. Complications arose only when the new movement came into political or economic opposition to brahmanism.

The *Shaivas* were particularly given to a variety of cults, which ranged from the austere practices of Shankara's followers to magical Tantric rites. Perhaps the Tantric cult, named after its scriptures, the *Tantras*, was the most curious of these and influenced both *Shaiva* and Buddhist practices.

Tantricism had originated in the sixth century but became current from the eighth century onwards. It was strongest in north-eastern India and had close ties with Tibet, some of its ritual doubtlessly coming from Tibetan practices. It claimed to be a simplification of the Vedic cults and was open to all castes as well as to women which identified it with the anti-orthodox movements. Tantric practice centred on prayer, mystical formulae, magical diagrams and symbols, and the worship of a particular deity. The mother image was accorded great veneration, since life was created in the mother's womb. In this connexion it was also linked with the *Shakta-Shakti* cult, which regarded female creative energy – *shakti* – as essential to any action.*

Those desirous of becoming members of a Tantric sect had to be initiated by a guru. Tantric ritual culminated in the partaking of the five M's – *madya* (wine), *matsya* (fish), *mamsa* (flesh), *mudra* (grain), and *maithuna* (coition). In the final state of purification everyone and everything was equal. The ritual being what it was, secret meetings became necessary, and the sect was denounced by others for depravity. Although the Tantric cult has often been condemned for this reason it originated in a conscious and deliberate opposition to the orthodox Hindu ritual and the brahmanical ordering of society, which it expressed by incorporating non-orthodox cults, such as the worship of *shakti*, and by protesting against what were regarded as the established standards of social behaviour. Incidentally, the Tantric interest in magic led to some discoveries of a semi-scientific nature owing to experiments with chemicals and metals in particular. The Tantrics claimed that the taking of mercury in combination with certain chemicals prolonged life. Doubtless they must also have taken part in the experiments in alchemy, which, judging by the thirteenth-century works on the subject, were very popular at this time.

The influence of Tantric ideas on Buddhism is evident in *Vajrayana* Buddhism (the Vehicle of the Thunderbolt.) The Taras or Saviouresses, spouses of the male *bodhisattvas*, received a veneration similar to that of Shakti. Among the many magical formulae which *Vajrayana* Buddhism has popularized is the oft-repeated Tibetan prayer *om mani padme hum*, (Behold, the Jewel

*The emphasis on *shakti* and the mother-goddess would suggest that Tantricism was rooted in pre-Aryan culture, which is not unlikely considering that it originated in essentially non-Aryan areas.

is in the Lotus), which is the symbolic representation of divine coitus.

The minor sects and cults were not totally rejected by brahman orthodoxy. Some were tolerated, others were encouraged by priests who participated in the ritual as a means of securing a livelihood. The local priest always tends to be more sympathetic to popular religion than the distant theologians. The worship of the sun-god returned to popularity about this time perhaps under the influence of Zoroastrianism which the Parsis had brought into western India. Existing deities took on fresh significance and new gods emerged. Ganesha or Ganapati, the elephant-headed god, worshipped in village shrines as he is to this day, rose to popularity. In origin a god who could take on the shape of a beast, (and perhaps a totem-god), a respectable parentage was attributed to him by the brahmans who now described him as the son of Shiva and Parvati. The worship of the mother-goddess associated with the fertility cult remained unabated.

Of the older heterodox sects, Jainism was ousted from Mysore when the *Lingayatas* won the support of those who would otherwise have been Jainas. In western India Jaina followers came mainly from the trading community. The Jainas remained on the whole a small but prosperous community. Since they were forbidden agriculture as a profession, whatever profits they made in commerce were re-invested in commercial activities. A further stabilizing factor was that the Jainas often had the favour of the royal court at Gujarat. In 1230, two hundred years after the destruction of the temple at Somnath, a magnificent Jaina temple was built at Mt Abu. But by now Jainism had become a minor religion, regarded almost as a Hindu sect.

Buddhism, however, was not to retain the status of even a minor religion. Its decline was gradual but certain and towards the thirteenth century became rapid. The association of Buddhism with magical cults was a confusing development, since much of its original ethical teaching was now further submerged in ritual. The support of the Pala kings sustained it in eastern India and royal patronage kept it going in Orissa, Kashmir, and parts of north-western India, but this survival was firmly founded upon the support of the laity. The coming of Islam was the final blow. Buddhism and Islam, both being institutionalized, proselytizing religions, attracted the same potential following. This led to a strong antagonism between the two and the attacks on the monasteries resulted in an exodus of Buddhists from eastern India to south-east Asia. Islam found its largest following in previously Buddhist areas of India, the north-west and the east. From the fourteenth century onwards the *Bhakti* movement became a dynamic force in north Indian society and, up to a point, filled the vacuum created by the retreating Buddhists, since it attracted the professional castes.

The coming of the Arabs, Turks, and Afghans brought a totally new religion to India – Islam. Apart from the Muslim theologians, the initial impact of Islam in the religious sphere was the arrival of Muslim mystics from Persia. The *Sufis*, as they were called, first settled in Sind and Punjab from where their teaching trickled into Gujarat, the Deccan, and Bengal. At first the *Sufis* in India were an extension of the Persian schools of mystics, but later the amalgamation of Indian and Islamic ideas produced an Indian school. The *Sufis* lived an isolated life, devoting themselves to the means of perceiving God. They were generally disapproved of by the Muslim theologians, who often found *Sufi* methods and beliefs too unorthodox. But *Sufi* ideas attracted sympathy and interest in India, particularly among those who were in any case inclined to mysticism and asceticism. In the centuries immediately following, the impact of the *Sufis* on the devotional cult was considerable.

The period from the eighth to the thirteenth centuries is sometimes referred to as 'the dark age', when classical Hindu culture declined and political disintegration facilitated the conquest of the sub-continent by a totally foreign power. But, far from being a dark period, it is a formative period which rewards detailed study, since many institutions of present-day India began to take enduring shape during this period.

Feudalism as the basis of the politico-economic structure survived in a broad sense until recent times and influenced the development of society accordingly. Many of the sub-castes which evolved during this period continue to function in the social hierarchy. The languages spoken in the various states of India today derive from the regional languages spoken in thirteenth-century India. Religious cults, as distinct from established religion, which dominate the lives of the rural population today (the majority of the Indian people) also emerged at this time. Furthermore, the fullness of historical evidence from this period allows of the reconstruction of a more complete picture of the time.

12

THE RE-ALIGNMENT OF
REGIONAL KINGDOMS

c. A.D. 1200–1526

THE successful campaigns of Mahmud of Ghazni and Muhammad Ghuri introduced a new political factor into the Indian sub-continent – for they initiated the rule of the Turks and the Afghans. There was an awareness that an entirely new force had arrived on the Indian scene, but there was hardly any curiosity about it. That the conquerors would supersede the indigenous rulers in the political sphere was acknowledged; but the wider implications – such as the likelihood that the newcomers would alter and modify the pattern of Indian culture – was not at first clearly realized.

The Turks and Afghans concentrated on establishing themselves in the region of Delhi, from where they ruled. Delhi had a strategic position allowing access both to the Ganges valley and to central and western India. Chauhan resistance to the Turks came from this region, and Delhi was associated in their minds with the core of resistance. In addition, Delhi was a convenient point on the route from Afghanistan. The Turkish rule from Delhi is referred to as the Delhi Sultanate, and this phrase is often applied to the history of northern India in general from the thirteenth to the sixteenth centuries. It is convenient, though not strictly applicable, since it conveys the impression of a unified kingdom stretching right across northern India, which was not the case, although the Sultanate was certainly the dominant political factor there at the time.

The initial impact of Turkish and Afghan rule came in other parts of northern India – Gujarat, Malwa, Jaunpur, Bengal, and the northern Deccan – where the influence of Islamic culture on existing Indian culture found a freer field. The court at Delhi in the early stages kept aloof from indigenous life in an attempt to preserve its dignity. It was kept in being by transfusions not of indigenous blood, but of immigrants from various parts of central and western Asia – Mongols, Afghans, Turks, Persians, and Arabs, and even by Abyssinians – adventurers and fortune-seekers who either established themselves in the upper administrative ranks of the Sultanate, and on occasion usurped the throne, or who, after making their fortunes, returned home. In the latter part of this period the Sultanate was reduced to the status almost of a provincial kingdom.

In the early stages the Delhi Sultans certainly envisaged establishing an empire embracing all of India. Expeditions were constantly organized and campaigns launched in all directions. The Deccan proved to be the biggest obstacle, and it was the Sultanate's failure to hold the Deccan that led to their reluctantly abandoning the idea of empire. It was only when this aim was finally abandoned that the provincial monarchies could assert their political independence. But the idea was never forgotten by the Delhi Sultans and was revived on the coming of the Mughuls in the sixteenth century, when empire became a reality.

In the general rivalry for power, the Sultanate emerged as a decisive factor, attempting as it did to prevent the rise of regional powers. With its pre-eminent position the court at Delhi attracted many political thinkers and writers. Consequently, there is enough literature on the working of the Sultanate to provide useful information about the political institutions and practices; these as they evolved under the Sultanate were not merely lifted from the classical Muslim traditions in Arab and Persian writings: much was based on practical expediency and was a response to Indian conditions. Political and administrative patterns evolved under the Sultanate therefore closely resembled those existing in regional monarchies ruled by Turks and Afghans.

The works of chroniclers and poets attached to the court at Delhi provide the main source of information on the history of the Sultanate, but their concern was mainly with the court and particularly with the Sultan, and little is said about life outside this narrow circle. Many writers were dependent on the patronage of the ruler and cannot be regarded as disinterested commentators on Sultanate politics. They had as models the historical writings of scholars from the Islamic world, and, although they regarded historical events as subordinate to religion, not all of them explained these events purely in terms of the will of Allah, which, judging by the works of the chronicler Barani, appears to have been the most usual interpretation. Barani, however, belonged to an age when it was thought that God had forsaken the Sultanate owing to the eccentricities of some of the Sultans. Other historians, such as Amir Khusrav, Isami, and Afif were less severe in their judgements.

Fortunately, the chroniclers of the time are not the only source of information. Incidental references to this period in other literary works, including those of the post-Sultanate period, such as the works of Firishta and Badauni, and also Sufi literature, supplement their chronicles. The accounts of the travellers who visited India during these centuries are more objective : of these the best known is Ibn Batutah, a north African Arab who was in India from 1333 to 1346. For a while he worked as a judge for the Sultan, after which he was sent on a mission to China. He returned to North Africa in 1348 and set out to explore the river Niger, which also took him to Timbuctu. He kept a detailed account of all he did, including his years in India, which makes fascinating reading, since he was an adventurer in both personal and public matters. Life came to him in exciting instalments involving bandits, shipwrecks, high office, and innumerable wives.

Some of the Arab geographers and merchants collected information on the countries which interested them and with which they traded, without actually visiting them, and India was one of these. Later, various European travellers, for example Marco Polo and Athanasius Nikitin, also visited India in search of gold and adventure, but they tended to confine themselves to the coastal areas of the peninsular kingdoms and recorded little of any significance on the northern states, as was also the case with the writings of Abdur Razzaq, the ambassador from Samarqand at the Bahmani court.

On the death of Muhammad Ghuri in 1206, his general, Qutb-ud-din-Aibak, declared himself Sultan over Muhammad's Indian possessions. The significance of this was that the Sultanate came to be regarded as an Indian state and not as an extension of an Afghan kingdom. But the Turks in India felt themselves insecure, since they feared the possibility of a Rajput confederation against them, which strangely never materialized. Nor did their own divided loyalty make for security. The ruler of Ghazni made no secret of his wish to annex the Punjab, a move which Qutb-ud-

din tried to thwart by moving his capital to Lahore, closer to
Afghanistan than was Delhi. But the Turkish nobles at Delhi –
the Delhi faction – proved stronger than any other group, and on
the death of Qutb-ud-din they selected his son-in-law Iltutmish
as Sultan and the government moved to Delhi.

Iltutmish realized that, if anything was to be saved of the
Turkish possessions in India, he would have to strengthen the
Sultanate and prevent the Turkish nobles from breaking away
and founding independent principalities. By 1220 he had established the northern frontier of the Sultanate along the Indus
river and had imposed his authority on the nobles. But by now
the Rajputs had bestirred themselves and recovered the famous
fort at Ranthambhor, which they had earlier lost to the Turks.
Iltutmish began a campaign against the Rajputs, the first of
many inconclusive campaigns which the Turks and the Rajputs
were to fight.

The northern frontier may have been secure against the Ghaznavids, but it was not respected by the Mongols, who had by
now moved far afield from their homeland in central Asia.
Through a series of raids between 1229 and 1241 they gained
control of western Punjab, and Iltutmish was powerless to stop
them. On the death of Iltutmish intrigue amongst the Turks increased, although there was a stable but brief interlude when his
daughter Raziyya was on the throne. A contemporary historian,
Siraj, wrote :

> Sultana Raziyya was a great monarch. She was wise, just, and
> generous, a benefactor to her kingdom, a dispenser of justice, the
> protector of her subjects, and the leader of her armies. She was en-
> dowed with all the qualities befitting a king, but she was not born of
> the right sex, and so, in the estimation of men, all these virtues were
> worthless.[1]

She was resented both for being a woman and for keeping the
control of the realm to herself, and was finally murdered. Court
intrigue continued unabated until the emergence of Balban, who
rose from minister to become Sultan in 1265.

The necessity of the moment was an iron-willed king if the
Sultanate was to survive as a political entity. The nobles were
only too eager to break away, particularly those in the outlying
parts of the Sultanate. The smaller Rajput chiefs and local lead-

ers had discovered the effectiveness of guerrilla tactics to harass the Sultan's armies. This necessitated punitive expeditions, which were costly and often disastrous when the armies were required to go into unfamiliar territory. The presence of the Mongols, who remained in the Punjab until about 1270, meant that access to Afghanistan was cut off. It was now imperative that Turkish power in India be consolidated, and this was to be Balban's achievement. He put down rebellions with determination and severity and in potentially troublesome areas settled groups of soldier–farmers, who were both informers and checks on local administration. Administrative procedures were made uniform and systematic. The pre-eminent position of the Turk racially and politically was stressed even to the point of excluding Indian Muslims from positions of political authority. Turkish solidarity was emphasized in an attempt to end intrigue and to direct loyalty to the symbol of Turkish power, the office of the Sultan.

The Delhi Sultanate survived, although Balban did not found a dynasty. Another group of Turks – the Khaljis – came to power in 1290. The Khaljis used their Afghan descent to win the loyalties of the discontented Afghan nobles, who felt that they had been neglected by the earlier Sultans. The Khaljis were also in favour of giving high office to Indian Muslims and to this extent reversed the policy of Balban. The new dynasty had its vicissitudes in the way of rebellions and campaigns against the Rajputs and Mongols, but the foundation of the Sultanate had been soundly laid by Balban and the Khaljis had merely to strengthen it by entrenching themselves more firmly.

The aged Khalji Sultan had an ambitious nephew, Ala-ud-din, who had campaigned successfully in eastern India and the Deccan. In 1296 he attacked the city of Devagiri, still in the hands of the Yadavas. The Yadava king capitulated and paid a vast amount of gold to Ala-ud-din as part of the treaty. Ala-ud-din returned to the north, had the Sultan assassinated, and was proclaimed Sultan, having bought the loyalty of the nobles with Yadava gold. The reign of Ala-ud-din marks the highest point of the Sultanate's political power, both in terms of the area of the kingdom and the power of the Sultan; with regard to the latter, his policy displayed an independence of opinion which was almost unique amongst the rulers of the Sultanate.

Iltutmish had received a robe of honour from the Caliph at Baghdad. This was no mere gesture, for, although the Caliph had little or nothing to do with the Sultanate, he was nevertheless the temporal head of Islam and all other kings were his vassals. The Delhi Sultan was therefore technically a viceroy of the Caliph. In practice the Sultan's sovereignty was absolute. He was the supreme judicial authority, subject only to the tenets of the *Sharia*, the Holy Law of Islam. The *Sharia*, drawn up for a different country and a different era, was not always the most suitable law for Indian conditions, so minor modifications were permitted by the theologians, provided they received their sanction. Thus, if the Sultan had the support of the theologians, there was theoretically no one to challenge his position; but he was in fact challenged from another quarter, by his nobles and the vassals.

With the establishment of the Sultanate the question of land revenue had to be examined, this being the basis of the income of the state. Revenue from the land and the availability of troops were recognized as being interrelated and indispensable to the Sultanate. Land tenure under the Sultanate was not significantly different from what had existed before, although it was a combination of the ideas current in the Islamic system and the actual institutions as functioning in India.

The *Sharia* permits rulers an income from four different sources : the tax on agricultural produce, the tax on non-Muslims, one fifth of the booty captured in battles against infidels, and finally an additional tax paid by the Muslims to be used for the benefit of the Muslim community, particularly in religious charity. The tax on agricultural produce was a regular income for the Sultanate, usually being one fifth of the produce, though it was sometimes raised to a half. This was by far the largest source of income.

The levying of *jaziyah*, the tax on non-Muslims, varied according to the whim of the Sultan and was not counted as a major source of income. Theoretically, many categories of persons were exempt, although exemptions were variable. Often the tax was used as a legitimate means of increasing the revenue and not necessarily with the intention of persecuting the non-Muslim population. A *jaziyah*-paying citizen would cease to pay the tax on conversion to Islam; thus, increasing conversions could lead to a loss of revenue! The Sultans, therefore, may not have been too eager to encourage large-scale conversions. The *jaziyah* was levied theoretically mainly on urban professions and the artisans, whereas obtaining the same amount by increasing the land tax would have resulted in a further depression of the peasantry.

The special tax from the Muslims was similarly dependent on the Sultan's will. The share of the spoils of war was usually exceeded, and the Sultan often took as much as four fifths for himself. A further source of income was customs and import dues on articles of trade, ranging from two and a half per cent to ten per cent of the value of the articles.

The Sultanate was divided into provinces, each under a governor, generally termed *muqti*, who was responsible for the administration of the province and the collection of revenue from those peasants who paid their tax directly to the state. The appointment of the *muqti* was not permanent, and he was liable to be transferred to any part of the kingdom if the Sultan so wished. A fixed share of the revenue constituted his salary, the rest being remitted to the Sultan. From the share which he received, the *muqti* was required to maintain a quota of horse and foot soldiers, to be at the Sultan's disposal. The *muqti* was assisted by officials mainly concerned with the assessment and collection of revenue. In addition to the revenue raised by the *muqtis*, the Sultan was entitled to the income from the *Khalsah* or crown lands. These were reserved for the needs of the Sultan and were administered directly by the revenue department.

The bulk of the land was still available to the Sultan to grant or assign to his officers as reward for services rendered or in lieu of cash salaries. This was known as the *iqta* or land-grant system, and was in many respects similar to the agrarian system prevalent in northern India in the pre-Sultanate period. The *iqta* could vary in extent from a village to a province, and there were many categories, the most common being those given in lieu of cash salaries. As in the previous system, land itself was not granted, but only the revenue from it. Continuance of the assignment depended on the will of the Sultan, since none of the *iqtas* could be treated as hereditary property. There was some farming out of land, where an officer administering an area undertook to pay a fixed annual sum to the Sultanate, irrespective of the amount he might have collected in revenue. This system was open to abuse if the officer was unscrupulous. Existing grants of land made by the Sultanate rulers were not generally tampered with unless the holder offended the Sultan, as for instance by inciting rebellion, which was not infrequent. The *iqta* system was sufficiently elastic to permit the incorporation of the existing smaller chieftains and holders into the new administration.

The *muqtis* and *iqta*-holders had to provide soldiers for the Sultan, that is to say they had to recruit them from the peasants. The army of the Sultanate was composed of a variety of troops. The Sultan's standing army consisted of his bodyguard, often selected from his personal slaves, and several other regiments, some in the capital and others posted to forts and garrisons along the frontier. Soldiers in the standing army were either paid cash salaries or given small *iqtas*. The levies maintained by the *muqtis* and *iqta*-holders outnumbered the standing army. These were theoretically loyal to the Sultan, but tended to be independent and sometimes loyal to the *muqti*.

Such was the framework of the state which Ala-ud-din inherited. That he was confident of his authority is clear from the changes which he made in the agrarian system, designed to strengthen the position of the Sultan at the expense of the *iqta*-holders. He took the bold step of revoking all grants made by previous Sultans, whether of gifts, proprietary rights, pensions, or religious endowments. Land was re-assessed (which was in any case necessary at intervals to ascertain any increase or decrease in produce) and fresh grants were made. The revoking of earlier grants underlined the fact that an *iqta* was not a permanent right. The State share of the revenue was increased to one half of the produce and no concessions were permitted. In addition, a grazing tax was imposed in areas where the village supplemented its income by keeping animals. Assessment was calculated on the basis of average yields from a particular area, which was reasonable in years when the harvest was good; but a poor harvest brought great hardship upon the cultivator.

Ala-ud-din's aim was to ensure that surplus income went to the treasury, not to the *iqta*-holders, who were not permitted to levy any additional cesses as a source of income. In an effort to diminish the possibility of the nobles becoming active forces of opposition he banned the drinking of intoxicants, since convivial gatherings could become foci of rebellion. The Sultan's permission was necessary before a marriage could be arranged among members of the nobility, presumably to prevent marriage alliances of a political nature. Not unnaturally, efficient espionage was essential to make this policy effective.

The increased income was necessary to build up military strength. To meet the threat of invasion by the Mongols and the Rajputs, and the strain of the campaigns in the Deccan, required a large standing army, which could only be maintained if there was enough surplus revenue. Fearing that his agrarian tax policy would create problems, Alu-ud-din tried to introduce price controls covering almost the entire market. Grain was rationed and the price fixed. A restriction was placed on the sale and purchase of high quality cloth. But this control was effective only in the areas in and around Delhi, where the transport, supply, and price of goods could be checked and defaulters punished.

The Mongols continually threatened northern India, harassing the Sultanate, until 1306, when domestic troubles in Transoxiana caused their return to central Asia. Meanwhile, Ala-ud-din had campaigned in Gujarat and Malwa, had captured the two important Rajput forts of Ranthambhor and Chitor, and had mounted an expedition to the south, though this had been unsuccessful. He still dreamed of bringing the peninsula under the Sultanate. Another expedition was sent under one of his officers, Malik Kafur, a handsome Hindu convert from Gujarat, and this was extremely successful. The peninsula awoke to the existence of a new power in northern India. Malik Kafur attacked in every direction, and concluded his expedition with a series of peace treaties. He had even attacked the city of Madurai, the seat of the Pandyas, and this was more than any other northern ruler could claim. It seemed that Ala-ud-din was in the process of building a stable empire, when his plans were wrecked by intrigues in the northern kingdoms. The dream of empire began to fade as Gujarat, Chitor, and Devagiri broke away from the Sultanate. Ala-ud-din died, a disappointed man, in 1316.

Kings followed in quick succession in the next four years, the last of whom was a low-caste Hindu convert who had risen to be the favourite of the Sultan, whom he eventually killed to usurp his throne. The chroniclers make much of his low-caste origin, which theoretically should not have been of any consequence in the allegedly egalitarian Islamic society. Both his Indian origin and his low-caste status were exploited by a Turkish family in successfully organizing a revolt against him. Ghiyas-ud-din Tughluq, the warden of the marches in the north, led the revolt, and in 1320 he proclaimed himself Sultan at Delhi and founded the Tughluq line.

The new Sultan had similar political ambitions to those of Ala-ud-din, and his campaigns in Warangal, Orissa, and Bengal revived the dream of empire, but his economic policy was not consistent with his political ambition. The measures taken by Ala-ud-din were either rescinded or relaxed. Price controls were removed, the land tax was lowered, and the *iqta*-holders were permitted their earlier perquisites in the form of a variety of taxes. The only check on the *iqta*-holders was a dubious one – the provincial governors, who may well have connived with them. Gradually power slipped back into the hands of the nobles.

The successor of Ghiyas-ud-din was Muhammad bin Tughluq; a rather controversial figure, some historians considering him mad owing to the unconventional nature of his actions. Yet, although his policies did on occasion border on the fantastic, there was some logic behind them.

Muhammad, perhaps inspired by the ideas of Ala-ud-din, also thought in terms of an India-wide empire. Added to this was his desire to lead an expedition to Khurasan in central Asia. His economic policy was therefore based on these ambitions. His first step was to increase the revenue imposed on the Doab (the fertile region between the Yamuna and Ganges rivers). But this time the peasants refused to acquiesce as they had done when Ala-ud-din had raised the tax, and showed their resentment by widespread rebellion, which had to be suppressed, and the taxation policy was revised. Unhappily for Muhammad, this coincided with a famine in the Doab.

Muhammad's next step, and it seemed a fairly rational one, since the northern Deccan was under the Sultanate, was to establish a new capital further south, closer to the southern provinces and to the southern kingdoms which the Sultanate wished to annex. Consequently the court was ordered to move to Daulatabad, the old Devagiri of the Yadavas, which it did during the years 1327–30. Had the transfer involved merely the court it would have been feasible, but Muhammad is said to have tried to move the entire population of Delhi. In this he was unsuccessful, luckily, since Daulatabad was found to be unsuitable and eventually the court returned to Delhi.

Meanwhile, other troubles accumulated. The fort at Chitor was re-taken by the Rajputs, the governor of Bengal revolted, and the Mongols plundered Sind and had to be bought off. Having tackled these problems, Muhammad returned to the idea of an expedition to central Asia. But for this yet more money was needed. It was then that the Sultan thought of issuing token currency in brass and copper; perhaps he had heard of the monetary system prevalent in Persia and China, where token currency was in use. This new idea might have solved some of his financial problems, but unfortunately he failed to maintain a check on the minting of tokens. The result was financial chaos, with traders producing faked tokens in abundance. Sadly, the Khurasan expedition had to be abandoned. Instead, Muhammad contented himself with a small campaign in the hills of Kangra, in the Himalayan region. This was not totally purposeless, for the hill chiefs often harboured rebels from the plains and the Kangra expedition served as a warning to them.

The transfer of the capital back to Delhi from Daulatabad was in a sense symbolic. Ala-ud-din had realized that the Sultanate could never hope to conquer the whole peninsula, and that therefore the best possible arrangement was that the kingdoms of the south, although outside the boundaries of the Sultanate, should be made to pay tribute, thus becoming an economic asset without being a political liability. But such an arrangement could at best be temporary. Muhammad was aware of this and decided on a more effective control over the peninsula, in part by moving the capital to the Deccan and thus establishing a base for the Sultanate in the peninsula itself. Muhammad returned to Delhi; but the base in the Deccan was not altogether without consequence, since it provided a footing for the Bahmani dynasty which emerged soon after in the northern Deccan. In 1334, the Pandyan kingdom

(Madurai) rejected the authority of the Sultanate, and this was followed by similar moves further north by Warangal. The coastal regions of the south were thus independent. In 1336 the kingdom of Vijayanagara was founded, and for the next two centuries it became the dominant power in the south. The dream of empire had come to an end.

The cracks in the Sultanate, so well cemented by Ala-ud-din, appeared once more. There were revolts in the provincial capitals, and a famine in and around Delhi led to a rising of the Jat and Rajput cultivators and landowners. The theologians at the court – the keepers of religious and political authority – began to denounce Muhammad's policies. The Sultan died of fever in 1357 while pursuing rebels in Sind – his ambitions had consistently been beyond the means at his disposal.

The nobles and theologians at the court selected his cousin Firuz Shah as the next Sultan. His immediate concern was to quell the rebellions, but many of his campaigns ended with his having to concede virtual independence to the provinces, as in the case of Bengal. Having become Sultan with the support of the nobles and the theologians, he had to ensure their satisfaction by restoring to them a considerable amount of political power, based on a fairly lax policy in agrarian matters. Religious endowments which had reverted to the state under previous rulers were returned to the earlier holders or their descendants – an indirect concession to the hereditary principle. Firuz was generous in granting land to civil and military officers and in farming out land. This required the revaluation of the land to ascertain the most recent assessments. It took six years to complete this, and the total assessment was valued at almost seven crore *tankas*.*

Some of the Delhi Sultans gained notoriety as temple-breakers and idol-smashers. These activities have been written about at length by the chroniclers, presumably to prove the devotion of their patrons to Islam. In fact there may have been more than piety involved. Firuz is also described on occasion as being as

*One crore is ten million. The silver *tanka* was valued at 172 grains of silver and was roughly equivalent to a rupee (1s. 4d.), but the *tanka* had a far higher purchase value since it could buy about seventy-five kilograms of wheat. Gold *tankas* were also minted but were used only for presentation purposes. The *tanka* was sub-divided into forty-eight *jitals*.

iconoclast. A campaign in Orissa was given its finale with the destruction of the Jagannatha temple at Puri.

The chroniclers had to show that the Sultan was making life difficult for the infidels, in order to earn him the respect of the orthodox in his community. Purely religious iconoclasm may be understandable in the raids of Mahmud, though even here the treasure was probably more attractive than the religious motive. But for a reigning king to decree the destruction of temples to earn religious merit would appear foolish in the extreme.

A document relating to the Arabs in Sind points to one obvious motive for iconoclasm. Muhammad bin Qasim, the Arab conqueror of Sind, wrote to his superior and received the following reply.

... The letter of my dear nephew Muhammad bin Qasim has been received and the facts understood. It appears that the chief inhabitants of Brahmanabad had petitioned to be allowed to repair the temple of Budh and pursue their religion. As they have made submission and agreed to pay taxes to the Caliph, nothing more can be properly required from them. They have been taken under our protection, and we cannot in any way stretch out our hands upon their lives or property. Permission is given them to worship their gods. Nobody must be forbidden or prevented from following his own religion. They may live in their houses in whatever manner they like. . . .[2]

Allowing for the fact that the Arabs were more civilized and humane than the Turks, nevertheless inconoclasm served the purpose of impressing the superiority of the foreign rulers on the indigenous population.*

The Muslim population was still only a fraction of the total, and the Muslim *élite* could not have felt entirely secure. Those converted to Islam in the early days were usually low-caste Hindus who chose to leave the Hindu social fold for that of Islam, believing that under Islam they would have better opportunities than if they remained low-caste Hindus. Such converts could provide little support for the ruling Muslim *élite*.

---

* Or for that matter of impressing the authority of one state on another, as in the case of a later Sultan, Sikandar Lodi, who wished to destroy the mosques of the ruler of Jaunpur in order to demonstrate his power. In this case the question of antagonistic religions was not involved, since both rulers were Muslims.

Converts from higher Hindu social strata to Islam rarely made the change out of religious sympathy with Islam but out of opportunism, realizing that conversion was a necessary step before they could hope for economic and social advancement or political power. Ostensibly they were made much of, but actually, and quite naturally, they were regarded with suspicion by the Turkish and Afghan nobles.

Orthodox Hindus and Muslims alike resisted any influence from the other in the sphere of religion. Although the Muslims ruled the infidels, the infidels called them barbarians. To the Muslims the Hindu temple was not only a symbol of a pagan religion and its false gods, but a constant reminder that despite their political power there were spheres of life in the country over which they ruled to which they were strictly denied access. And these were not merely religious rituals, because the temple had long been the centre of Hindu social life in the village. The temple was a place where Hindus congregated, and congregations are feared by those in power, as they can become centres of revolt. (It was for the same reason that the Sultanate was suspicious from time to time of the centres of Sufi teaching.) The temple was the bank, the landowner, the employer of innumerable artisans and servants, the school, the discussion centre, the administrative centre for the village, and the place for major entertainments in the form of festivals. The ruling (Muslim) *élite* was excluded from all this, and the sight of a temple served to remind them of this exclusion. Exclusion, in turn, was the only weapon which orthodox Hinduism could use to prevent assimilation, having lost its political ascendancy.

Firuz's iconoclasm is somewhat incongrous, in view of his tremendous interest in the historical and cultural past of India. A visit to a library in Kangra led him to order the translation – from Sanskrit into Persian and Arabic – of various manuscripts on the subject of Hinduism. He saw the pillars of Ashoka at Meerut and Topra, and was so fascinated by them that he had them transported to Delhi, difficult as this was, and one of them was placed in a commanding position on the roof of his citadel. He was curious to know what the inscription said, but no one could read it, the script having changed since the time of Ashoka. He was told that it was a magical charm and that it was associated with religious ritual. If objects of infidel worship had indeed been so abhorrent to Firuz, he would have had the pillars destroyed : instead they were placed in positions of prominence.

The worst of the Mongol raids took place in 1398 under the leadership of the notorious Timur (Tamerlane), a central Asian Turk, who maintained that the Tughluqs were not good Muslims and therefore had to be punished. The provinces of Gujarat, Malwa, and Jaunpur took the opportunity to proclaim their independence. Timur, having sacked Delhi, returned to central Asia, leaving a nominee to rule in the Punjab. The Tughluq line ended soon after, but not so the Sultanate, which continued, though a shadow of its former self. Timur's nominee captured Delhi and was proclaimed the new Sultan, the first of the Sayyid dynasty which was to rule during the earlier half of the fifteenth century. The Sultanate had survived, but only just.

The Sayyids kept the machinery going until a more capable dynasty could take over. A governor of a northern province, Buhlul Lodi, saw the opportunity of ousting the Sayyids and made himself Sultan of Delhi in 1451, to become yet another inheritor of the Sultanate. The Lodis were of pure Afghan origin, which meant the eclipse of the Turkic nobility.

The Afghan nobles, as compared to the Turks, were less amenable to authority and jealously guarded their tribal independence. Yet they were the main prop of the Lodi kings. Attempts were made to pacify them by granting them large *iqtas*. The first two Lodi kings modified the autocracy of the Sultanate and thus made an appeal to Afghan loyalty, but the last Lodi, Ibrahim, asserted the absolute power of the Sultan and did not consider tribal feelings. This led to his making enemies amongst them. Some grumbled quietly, others more openly. Tribal and clan rivalries were forgotten as the opposition to Ibrahim grew, culminating in the nobles inviting foreign assistance to overthrow him, which they hoped would re-establish their equality and independence within the Sultanate. The governors of the Punjab and Sind appealed for help to Babur, a descendant of Tamerlane and Genghis Khan, seeking his fortune in Afghanistan. Babur was only too willing to bring his armies to northern India, since he had wished to annex the Punjab. The Afghans were not alone in supporting Babur. One of the Rajput kings had also dreamed of ruling from Delhi and had made an alliance with Babur. In 1526 Babur faced Ibrahim on the plain at Panipat. The victory was Babur's. Ibrahim was killed, and with him died the rule of the Lodis, for Babur was to found his own dynasty in India, and his descendants, the Mughuls, achieved the dream of the Delhi Sultans, to rule an Indian empire.

The overthrow of the Sultanate led inevitably to attempts on the part of provincial states to establish their independence. Some of these successfully exploited the disorder which prevailed prior to the establishment of the Mughul power. Others discovered that their fortunes had been too closely tied to those of the Sultanate and they succumbed to the Mughuls. On the periphery of the Sultanate had emerged a number of kingdoms, large and small, with ambitions as great as those of the Sultans themselves. Some of them, for example Gujarat, Malwa, Mewar, Marwar, Jaunpur, and Bengal, had maintained their independence almost throughout the latter period of the Sultanate, despite the attempts of the Delhi Sultans to prevent this. These attempts did not lead to a sense of unified opposition amongst the kingdoms, and if they were not at war with the Sultanate they were at war with each other. Nor were the alliances and wars based on differences of religion. A Hindu ruler saw nothing unusual in allying with and obtaining aid from a Muslim ruler in order to fight another Hindu ruler, and the same held true of Muslim dynasties. Religion did not count unless it could serve a definite political purpose. Where it could, however, it was exploited to the full.

The smaller kingdoms rose and fell with greater rapidity, many being land grants in origin. This was a period of complete opportunism, and the making and breaking of alliances went on continually. But culturally it was in these areas that the assimilation of Islamic institutions into Indian culture took place. In these areas the need to preserve the separateness of the Turkish or Afghan nobility was not as great as in Delhi; in fact it was wiser for those in power to mingle with those whom they governed, since this made for greater loyalty.

The kingdom of Gujarat originated with the revolt of the governor against the Sultanate, and it became powerful under Ahmad Shah. Malwa had been founded in 1401 by a member of

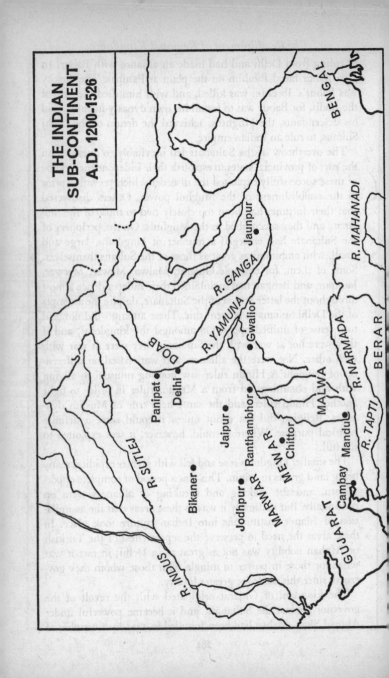

THE INDIAN SUB-CONTINENT
A.D. 1200-1526

BENGAL

R. MAHANADI

Jaunpur

R. GANGA

R. YAMUNA

Gwalior

DOAB

BERAR

R. NARMADA

R. SUTLEJ

Panipat

Delhi

Jaipur

Ranthambhor

MEWAR

Chittor

MALWA

Mandu

R. TAPTI

Bikaner

MARWAR

Jodhpur

GUJARAT

Cambay

R. INDUS

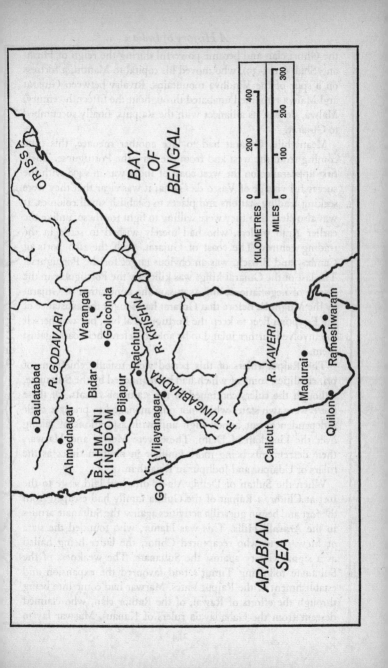

the Ghuri clan and became powerful during the reign of Hush-
ang Shah (1405–35), who moved his capital to Mandu, a fortress
on a spur of the Vindhya mountains. Rivalry between Gujarat
and Malwa remained unabated throughout the fifteenth century.
Malwa, despite its alliances with the Rajputs, finally succumbed
to Gujarat.

Meanwhile, Gujarat had to face another menace, this time
coming from the west and from the sea – the Portuguese. Their
first appearance on the west coast of India was in 1498 with the
successful voyage of Vasco da Gama; it was clear that they were
seeking trading stations and places to establish small colonies. It
was also clear that they were willing to fight for these, unlike the
earlier Arab traders, who had merely wished to settle in the
trading centres. The coast of Gujarat, with the rich ports of
Cambay and Broach, was an obvious target for the Portuguese.
The last of the Gujarat kings was killed by the Portuguese in the
course of negotiations, and 1537 saw the annexation of Gujarat
by the Mughuls. Before that Gujarat had sought the assistance of
the Egyptian fleet to keep the Portuguese at bay, but was herself
too involved further inland to be able to defend her coast against
them.

The Rajput rulers of this period were usually chieftains of
principalities, some of which had been annexed by the Sultanate,
although the rulers continued in the status of vassals. Of these
there were two states which not only managed to preserve their
independence, but aimed high and with aspirations of taking
over the kingdom of Delhi. These were Mewar and Marwar,
their descendants being more familiar in modern times as the
rulers of Udaipur and Jodhpur in Rajasthan.

When the Sultan of Delhi, Ala-ud-din, had laid siege to the
fort at Chitor, a Rajput of the Guhila family had escaped from
the fort and begun guerrilla activities against the Sultanate armies
in the Aravalli Hills. This was Hamir, who founded the state
of Mewar and who recaptured Chitor, the latter being hailed
as a signal victory against the Sultanate. The weakness of the
Sultanate following Timur's raid favoured the expansion and
establishment of the Rajput states. Marwar had come into being
through the efforts of Rawal, of the Rathor clan, who claimed
descent from the Gahadavala rulers of Kanauj. Marwar lay to

the west of Mewar in the region of the city of Jodhpur built by Jodha, the great-grandson of Rawal. The discovery of silver and lead mines in Mewar brought new prosperity to the state, and it seemed as if the Rajputs were again going to assert themselves as a major power in northern India. In an effort to strengthen the bonds between the two states, a marriage was arranged between the two royal families, but this was to lead soon to a bitter feud over a complicated succession issue.

Mewar survived the conflict partly because it was ruled at the time by the powerful Rana Kumbha, almost a legendary figure: he was a playwright, a literary critic who wrote one of the finest commentaries of Jayadeva's *Gita Govinda*, and a lover of music, and a keen student of the art of fortification. His life ended in tragedy; he went insane and was killed by his son. But this was not the end of Mewar, which was again to see a brief period of glory when hopes of Rajput domination in the north were rekindled.

In 1509, Rana Sanga became king of Mewar and began to defy the power of Delhi. The Lodi kings were too involved in their own internal problems to bother much about Mewar, and Sanga contemplated an attack on Delhi. Sanga allied himself with Babur against Ibrahim Lodi, and agreed to attack Delhi from the south and west whilst Babur attacked from the north. This he believed would enable him to take the capital, and having done so he would dispense with Babur and inherit the Sultanate. Trouble from Gujarat, however, prevented Sanga from keeping his part of the agreement, and the battle at Panipat ended in victory for Babur. What was worse for Sanga was the realization that Babur intended to stay in India and rule from Delhi. The alliance broke on this, and in 1527 Sanga was in action against Babur: he was defeated, and after his death Mewar gradually sank to a minor state.

Marwar had begun to disintegrate a few years earlier. Many of the princes at the court migrated to neighbouring areas, where they founded small principalities such as Satalmer, Bikaner, and so on, some of which survived into the twentieth century. Clan consciousness was extremely strong in the Rajput states, and as long as a single clan constituted the ruling house loyalty was unswerving. But the introduction of personalities from a different clan invariably led to dissension. Clan rivalries were uncontrollable and were probably the fastest means of creating dissension. But this period was only a temporary eclipse of the Rajputs, for they were to rise again in later centuries.

Towards the end of the fourteenth century, the kingdom of Jaunpur was established under the first of the Sharqi kings, an ex-officer of the Sultanate. Jaunpur was in the unhappy position of having the Sultanate on its west and Bengal on its east, with both of which its relations were uncertain. The Sharqis frequently planned the capture of Delhi during some period when the power of the Sultanate was at an ebb, but the plans never materialized. The Lodis were being constantly provoked by the Sharqis, but finally the ruler of Jaunpur was defeated and fled to Bengal, where he died in obscurity.

Bengal owed its independence to its remoteness from Delhi and to the fact that communication between the two lay through areas which were not always hospitable to the Sultanate officials. It became an independent state as early as the thirteenth century, when one of the local governors revolted. The Sultanate tried repeatedly to reassert its control over Bengal or at least to prevent Bengal from extending its frontiers, but it was rarely successful. There was a break in the dynasty of the Bengal Sultans when a landowner from north Bengal, Raja Ganesha, became a powerful minister at the court, and so manipulated things that his son, a convert to Islam, was made Sultan in 1419 and ruled for sixteen years. That he was permitted to rule for so many years suggests that he enjoyed the confidence of the Muslim nobility. It is interesting that he appointed brahmans as ministers and even had a *purohita* at the court. Obviously there was no strong feeling among the brahmans about his being a Muslim, or they would not have accepted any honours, least of all from a Hindu apostate.

The prosperity of Bengal during this period is described in the annals of the Ming emperors of China, who sent traders and missions to various parts of the Indian sub-continent. The annals refer to the visit of Cheng-ho to Bengal in 1421 and 1431. In the latter part of the fifteenth century Bengal was destined to witness a strange series of rulers. The Abyssinian palace guards revolted and their commander usurped the throne. Later, the Abyssinian had to give way to an adventurer of Arab descent, who annexed parts of Assam and Orissa. The defeat at Panipat of the Afghans supporting Ibrahim Lodi sent them fleeing eastwards, and in 1538 Sher Khan Sur, an Afghan nobleman, overthrew the reigning Sultan and became the ruler of Bengal.

The kingdom of Kashmir remained independent of the Sultanate and had few connexions with Delhi until it was annexed by the Mughuls. Sind retained some degree of independence, the desert of Thar being a fairly effective barrier to frequent communications with Rajasthan and Delhi. The Arabs who conquered Sind in the eighth century, after the reverses they met with, appear to have lost interest in enlarging their Indian possessions. During the period of the Sultanate Sind was ruled by obscure tribes, until it came under Mughul control in the sixteenth century.

By this time the major part of the sub-continent was being ruled by dynasties of Turkic and Afghan descent. The comparative ease with which they took over from existing dynasties appears at first sight rather surprising, but in fact what happened was little more than a transfer of suzerainty from one set of rulers to another. There was a period of two hundred years between the raids of Mahmud of Ghazni and the establishment of the Sultanate, and this was time enough for northern India to become acquainted with the Turkic tribes and the Afghans, so that when they eventually settled in India they were not total strangers.

The insularity of the kingdoms of the north was such that even the Sultanate could not claim to be an empire. The ambitions of the nobles were perpetually turning towards the acquisition of independent kingdoms, with visions of majesty and power for themselves. There was no consistent policy at the centre to keep them under control, and the frequent changes of dynasty destroyed all political continuity.

The impact of such dynastic changes was felt most strongly in the highest circles, where resentment was often pronounced. On the other hand the rest of society accepted the new rulers. There were few major changes in political and administrative matters. In many cases local rulers and chiefs continued as before, though possibly with smaller incomes. The land system also remained basically unchanged – the peasants continued to cultivate the land and to pay their taxes either to the king's officers or to the local landowner. They were little concerned with a change of Sultan. Nor was there any displacement of population comparable to that which followed the invasion of the Huns. Owing to the small number of Turks and Afghans, the minor administrative officials remained unaltered. Yet it was at the lower levels that the new culture of Islam was to enter the pattern of Indian civilization and make its strongest impact.

13

ASSIMILATION ON TRIAL

c. A.D. 1200–1526

As we have seen, northern India was not spared foreign invasion. The Greeks, the Scythians, the Parthians, and the Huns held power for considerable periods. They came as aliens and they came to rule, yet they were assimilated. And as long as the *mlechchhas* could be assimilated into existing institutions, the fact of their being *mlechchhas* could be overlooked. It is true that these earlier invaders established themselves in areas which were not the strongholds of Hindu orthodoxy. Entry into the various levels of social institutions was easier, and consequently the tendency on the part of the Indian religious hierarchy to exclude and reject the newcomers was less pronounced. The Buddhists hastened to make converts and were successful.

It is also true that the Greeks, Scythians, and Huns did not bring their own theologians with them, nor did their coming necessitate a confrontation of two strongly established religions such as Islam and Hinduism. Islam brought a new pattern of life. The modifications in Hinduism and Buddhism which resulted from contact with the earlier invaders were acceptable to the orthodoxy of both these religions, or at least they were willing to make a compromise. Not so with Islam. Nevertheless, assimilation did take place, not merely in superficial ways such as the Turks adopting local habits of eating and dressing, but in more fundamental fields, as with the introduction of new social ideas, which became an integral part of Indian life.

In an indirect way, the Mongols contributed to this assimilation by cutting off the possibility of large-scale immigration from Afghanistan and western Asia. Each year the sea brought a mere handful of traders, who settled in the west-coast ports. Islam therefore had to rely increasingly on Hindu converts. The existing Indian population was slow in being converted. The fact that the Muslims have always been a minority community in India would suggest, as has been pointed out elsewhere, that the vast majority of Hindus were not in so desperate a plight as to seek conversion. Perhaps at the lower levels of society the advantages to be gained by conversion were not spectacular. The Muslim community consisted mainly of converted Hindus, and obviously their pattern of living would not differ radically from that of the larger community in the midst of which they lived.

This made assimilation easier. Two groups of artisans, having worked together for generations as part of the same sub-caste or guild, would continue, on the conversion of one group, to maintain certain ties. But the cultural fusion of the two ideologies was less predictable amongst the ruling classes and their separateness was insisted upon by the theologians of both religions and on occasion by politically ambitious sections of the aristocracy. The call to Muslim loyalty or Hindu loyalty could always be used for purposes other than religious, and this sentiment could be exploited when convenient.

Hindu theorists paid little attention to the lack of conscious assimilation at the level of political functioning : this was in part due to the insistence on maintaining the social order, which was given preference over political activities, and in part because the nature of political institutions as developed under the Sultanate resembled those of an earlier period. These institutions were not always in conformity with those described by the political theorists of Islam. For example, the association of divinity and kingship is not to be found in the *Quran*. The Turks were familiar with the idea, having known of it through the Sassanian kings of Persia. On arriving in India they discovered that this was already an accepted notion in the office of kingship. It merely required the sanction of the theologians to incorporate it into the political framework of the Sultanate.

The *Ulema* – Muslim theologians – were agreeable to providing and interpreting passages from the *Quran* which would authorize these innovations on condition that the Sultan would allow the *Ulema* to be the religious and legal arbiters in state matters. This compact between church and state was concluded and the *Ulema* became a political voice which could not be disregarded. It came to be believed that the Sultan was necessary for the very existence and security of the state, for without him there would be anarchy : a belief not dissimilar to earlier Hindu ideas on the relationship between the king and the state. The Sultan had now to show respect, at least ostensibly, for Islamic institutions, and pre-eminently to the *Ulema*. This involved the granting of endowments to religious causes and offices to the *Ulema*, the building of mosques, and the occasional display of anti-infidel activities such as iconoclasm.

Not every Sultan was willing to make these concessions, and in such cases the *Ulema* had to move very tactfully, since it would have been impolitic in a country of non-believers to show any internal dissensions publicly. The Sultans generally were not concerned with the niceties of political and religious thought. They were primarily military adventurers, bent upon prolonging their rule as long as possible and enjoying every luxury. Political thinkers and writers were welcome at the court provided they did not take their duties too seriously. Barani complained that the Sultans were not giving due attention to their office, which was an exalted one, since it was in fact the exercise of God's power. Barani was exiled. It is significant that the *Ulema*, who might have been expected to make such complaints, remained quiet.

The court of the Sultan displayed vast wealth, and each day was a procession of elaborate ceremonial, much of which was deliberately exaggerated in order to emphasize the distance between the ruler and the ruled. Revenue from the crown lands was used to maintain palaces, harems, slaves, and a huge retinue of court officials. The Sultan's household required an extensive staff, not least amongst them being the personal bodyguard, whose support was essential to any group which hoped to overthrow the Sultan. The officer in charge of the royal 'workshops' (*karkhanah*) was also a person of some eminence. Articles required by the Sultan's household, both for personal use and for giving away as gifts, were produced in these workshops, and their output was large; for example, the robe of honour which the Sultan bestowed on his officers as a special mark of appreciation was manufactured to the number of several hundred thousand each year.

The Sultanate followed the basic law of Islam, the *Sharia*, as interpreted by the *Ulema*. The Sultan, advised by the chief *Qazi* (judge), was the highest arbiter, and all cases of capital punishment had to be brought before the Sultan. To begin with the new law was put into effect only at the court and in the towns where there was some considerable Muslim population. In the villages the old law continued. Non-Muslims were free to maintain their own legal institutions, which naturally led to many complications. Finally it was conceded that a non-Muslim code could apply to a non-Muslim provided it did not endanger the state. The interpretation of the code was kept amorphous, and this enabled decisions to be taken on the basis of expediency rather than by following the letter of the law. There was some discussion, for instance, on the question of women becoming *satis*. According to the *Sharia* suicide is illegal and becoming a *sati* was an act of suicide, but it was permitted to Hindu women.

Legally the Sultan was a representative of the Caliph, though in fact he was virtually independent. Yet the absolute authority of the Sultan was subject to certain checks, the most obvious being that in the final analysis he had to rely for support on the call to Islam. Thus he had to conform publicly to the *Sharia* and the Islamic tradition. That Akbar in the sixteenth century was able to disregard this in proclaiming his own ideology – the *Din-i-Illahi* – suggests that by then the relationship between political policy and religion had changed considerably. The *Ulema*, the nobles, and the soldiers of the standing army had all to be kept satisfied. The quick replacements of Sultans in certain periods underlines the fact that the Sultans were not supreme and absolute.

Nationalities were mixed in the army, with Turks, Afghans, Mongols, Persians, and Indians fighting under the same banner. The fact that every *iqta*-holder had to provide troops suggests that the Indian percentage must have been fairly high, since provincial levies would be largely Indian. There was no ban on the recruitment of Hindu soldiers in the army or in the levies. The fighting units were organized in units of 50, 100, 500, and 1,000, a system used by the Mongols.

Civil administration was headed by the *wazir* – chief minister – who supervised the collection of revenue, the checking of accounts, and the regulation of expenditure. His importance as an adviser to the Sultan on matters other than revenue depended on the personal relationship between the two. The *wazir* and three other ministers were looked upon as the four pillars of the state. The other three were the head of the military department, which kept a record of soldiers and equipment in the Sultan's army and of the feudal levies; the minister in charge of inter-state relations, and finally the Chancellor, who dealt with state correspondence and relations between the Court and provincial officials. The latter had his agents, stationed in various parts of the kingdom, who kept him informed on all matters of interest to the state.

The power of provincial governors was limited by two factors – proximity to the capital and the presence of the agents of the court. But there were often theoretical limitations, since power depended on personal relationships. Provincial administration had counterparts of the various administrative departments at the court. A smaller administrative unit was the *parganah*, which was perhaps the most important, being the level at which the officials came into direct contact with the cultivators. Each *parganah* had its own group of officials – the executive officer, in general charge, the officer recording assessments and produce, the treasurer, and two registrars, of whom one kept a record in Persian and the other in Hindi. A specially appointed officer was the *munsif*, who was the chief revenue collector and assessment officer and also was empowered to settle agrarian disputes : the resemblance to the *rajuka* of the Mauryas is striking. The village was the smallest unit of administration, with three main officials, the headman, the accountant (*patwari*), and the registrar (*chaudhuri*). Cities were divided into sectors, the administration of each being in the charge of two officials responsible to the chief city administrator.

The civil administration of the Sultanate was thus a continuation of existing forms, with little attempt at a fundamental change. The designations were certainly changed, with Persian names, more familiar to the new rulers, coming into common use. At the village level and to a large extent in the *parganah*, many of the officers doubtless were still Hindus, belonging to families associated with administration. Some features of the Sultanate pattern continued until recent times, the names and designations being familiar even at the present day.

The efficiency of the administration depended in part on communications. Ibn Batutah is enthusiastic in his praise of the transport system and postal service of the Tughluqs, and he had cause to use the roads frequently. They had stone surfaces, on which the most commonly used vehicle was the ox-drawn cart. The nobility used horse carriages. Those travelling at a more leisurely pace were carried in palanquins. Regular stops along the route provided *serais* (rest-houses), shops, and relays of porters and horses. The journey from Delhi to Daulatabad took forty days. The fastest postal service was the horse post, although the foot post was more generally used. Relays of both were available at almost every village. The postal service was used by the state and by any who could afford it. The runners of the foot post carried a baton with bells attached to it, the sound of which was intended to scare away the animals from the forest paths and to announce the arrival of the runner in the village. The postal runner was a familiar feature of rural India until the last century.

The incoming Turks and Afghans tended to settle in the towns, and this gave rise to a vigorous urban culture. The villages and rural areas maintained much of their local autonomy but were nevertheless required to provide revenue. The village remained the basic economic unit and production was largely for local consumption. Each village had its own craftsmen, who spun and wove cloth, made ploughs, yokes, wooden carts with large wooden wheels, leather buckets for carrying water, household pottery, ropes, mats, baskets, metal utensils, horse shoes, knives, daggers, swords, and all the various articles used in the village. The techniques used by the artisans were primitive but adequate for their limited production. Artisans were organized in craft castes, and the distinction between castes continued even among those converted to Islam. To begin with, upper-caste Hindus probably regarded the Muslims as a new sub-caste, rather low in the scale. But as the pre-eminence of the Muslims in the administration became clear the Hindus began to treat them with greater tolerance. Craft labour, because of its association with caste, tended to be hereditary among both Hindu and Muslim craftsmen.

But gradually there was a change, and towns began to flourish once more, as the demand for goods increased. The Turkish–Afghan raids had opened up northern India to trade. The Mongols brought central Asia into closer contact. Traders and merchants re-established links which soldiers and Sultans had lost.

Within the country the pattern of aristocratic living encouraged the exchange of goods. Rural production became linked in certain areas to nearby towns. Maritime areas had in any case been producing for export. The rise in production for exchange was by no means sudden and sharp, but it was appreciably more than in the previous period.

The requirements of town-dwellers were met by artisans who worked in towns. Certain areas specialized in production for export, and here the techniques were more advanced. The towns of Gujarat and Bengal produced a variety of textiles, white cotton, silk, velvet, satin, quilts, etc. The Cambay cottons were renowned in the textile trade for their quality, abundance, and cheapness. Towns became centres of both internal and external trade. Internal consumption of luxury articles was increased by the growing demands of the court, which was emulated by the aristocracy in the provincial capitals and the border kingdoms.

Every town had a market-place where traders and merchants congregated, and fairs were held regularly. Certain communities came to be associated with trade, for example the Gujarati *baniyas*, who were found as far south as Malabar, the Multanis from Multan, and the Marwaris from Rajasthan, who were beginning to establish a reputation as merchants. The *banjaras* were roving traders with large caravans, which were often used for transportation by other traders. In lean years they were accused of pilfering and came to be regarded as the gypsies were in Europe. Pedlars with pack animals sold their goods from house to house; or, if they travelled further than their own locality, they used the inn of the town as a temporary shop. The coming and going of merchants made the inn almost as important a place for commerce as the market.

Provincial capitals, as centres of local administration, attracted large markets. The market of Delhi was said to be particularly prosperous, receiving goods through both inland and foreign trade. Ibn Batutah describes Delhi as the most magnificent city in the Muslim world – a magnificence which was due not only to the presence of the Sultan and his court but also to the wealthy commercial community. Many of the state workshops were also situated in Delhi and these contributed substantially to internal production, in which, for example, a silk-weaving workshop employed as many as four thousand weavers.

But the greatest interest was in foreign trade, and this was centred on the coastal regions, where colonies of foreign merchants gave a cosmopolitan air to the cities. Many found this trade so profitable that they married local women and settled permanently in these towns. The coastal cities had large business houses with branches overseas. Wealthy bankers gave loans and took promissory notes, and many lived entirely on lending money to traders. Conditions having been somewhat unsettled, one would have expected cheating and fraud to be common, yet traders and travellers alike testify to the high level of integrity in India.

Overseas trade involved India in contact with Europe and Asia. This was also the age when China competed for profits from both the Indian and East African trade and Europe sought openings for direct trade with Asia in order to by-pass the Arabs. India was slowly losing its monopoly both of eastern and western trade. The process was gradual but seemingly inevitable. Indian traders brought spices from south-east Asia; where previously Indian ships had carried these to the ports of western Asia, the monopoly in the carrying trade between western India and western Asia passed to the Arabs, with a consequent loss to Indian trade. However, this was compensated to some extent by an increase in the export of Indian-made goods. Indian traders were gradually being confined to inland ventures, largely controlled by Hindu traders, since the Turks and Afghans were too busy soldiering and governing to undertake commercial activities. However, there was at least a common sentiment between those in political power and the major commercial interest in foreign trade. The fact that some Arab merchants settled in India meant that some at least of the profits from overseas trade remained in the country.

Trade routes by sea changed little. The old lines were still followed : from the west coast of India via the Persian Gulf and Iraq to the Mediterranean, or via the Red Sea and Egypt to the Mediterranean. The only additional route was due to the opening up of ports along the east coast of Africa at places such as Malinde, Mombasa, and Kilwa. Ships from Indian ports unloaded at Ormuz, Aden, and Jiddah, then the most important emporia of western Asia, though some travelled further to east Africa, where Cambay cloth was exchanged for gold.

Horses remained the most expensive single item of import into India. Turkestan still bred the finest stock, equal in quality to Arab thoroughbreds, and some of these trickled through the north-western land routes during intervals between the Mongol raids. But the sea was the more regular channel for the import of horses. Apart from horses, ships from Aden brought perfumes, coral, quicksilver, vermilion, lead, gold, silver, alum, madder dye, and saffron. Indian exports from Gujarat consisted mainly of rice, cloth, precious stones, and indigo.

Bengal continued its trade with south-east Asia. Malacca had by now become the largest port and market centre of south-east Asia with settlements of merchants from all parts of Asia. Indian ships were frequently in its harbour, bringing pepper, incense, textiles, saffron, and quicksilver. Some of these were then shipped to Java, Sumatra, Timor, Borneo, and the Moluccas. In return the ships brought back to India gold, cloves, white sandalwood, nutmeg, mace, camphor, and aloes. Much of this merchandise was shipped to the west coast of India, but some of it found its way to Bengal.

The Chinese continued with their attempts at trade with India. This had become more feasible and regular with the enlarging of Chinese trade with east Africa, since India was on the way there. Chinese ships visited the ports of both Bengal and Malabar, though the latter saw them more frequently. Cheng-ho led seven expeditions to south Asia and east Africa, and on two of these he stopped for a brief period in Bengal. Chinese ships carried silk, taffeta, satin, cloves, blue and white porcelain, gold, and silver, all of which were sought after by Indian merchants.

Trade had encouraged the use of money, which circulated in the towns throughout northern India. Coins issued in the region of Delhi were adapted from the previous issues of the Chauhans and Gahadavalas, which was a sensible method of creating confidence in the new currency amongst the local people. Even the bull, traditionally associated with Shaivism, was retained, together with the name of the Sultan in *Devanagari* script. The *jital* and the *tanka* are most frequently referred to.

The former was a copper coin, and the latter was of silver (172·8 gr.) and was started by Iltutmish. The *tanka* was to become the standard monetary unit of the Sultans, and was the ancestor of the modern Indian rupee.

Gold coins called *mohurs* were used largely for commercial purposes or on special occasions. The Sultanate had a number of mints in various parts of the kingdom. The provincial kingdoms issued their own currency, with coins having either a different name or a different weight content from those of the Sultanate. The weights, as standardized at Delhi (*man, seer, chattaka*), lent their names to weights current in northern India prior to the recent introduction of the metric system. The circulation of money was stimulated by the vast expenditure involved in aristocratic living and the growth of urban centres. The Turks and Afghans had found riches in India and were determined to make the most of them. It was an era of conspicuous consumption, both for the court and for the aristocracy in the provinces.

Muslim society as it evolved in India fell into three broad divisions – the nobility both secular and religious, the artisans, and the cultivators. The nobility was made up of diverse strands, Turks, Afghans, Persians, and Arabs, with the first two predominant, since they held political power. To begin with, clan affiliations kept them divided, but once they were forced to accept India as their permanent home they began to coalesce into a fairly homogeneous group. The fact of their being a minority in the country assisted this process.

Elevation to the nobility was open to all, and many of the most exalted nobles had begun as retainers of the Sultan. Titles and offices were not hereditary and were dependent on the goodwill of the Sultan. In later years, when they came to be looked upon as hereditary, the nobility acquired elaborate genealogies to prove their aristocratic origins, and Indian converts began to assert a foreign ancestry. This was considered essential, since superiority lay in having Turkish or Afghan blood, and the racial qualification was important. Intermarriage with Indian Muslims on an increasing scale did, however, gradually reduce this characteristic in the nobility.

The nobles derived their income from the revenue of their *iqtas*, and those attached to the court from their office at the court. Despite the obligation to maintain troops, the revenue from the *iqta* was sufficient to allow of luxurious living. The Sultan may have suspected that excessive income was accruing to the nobility, but there was little he could do to prevent this. State inspectors were unreliable, since they could be bribed. Ala-ud-din had made a serious attempt at curtailing the incomes of the nobles, but this policy did not survive him. The relationship between the Sultan and his nobles depended on their relative strength. This was also the case with the Rajput chiefs and other local rulers, who step by step were accepted as a part of the nobility when the Sultanate found that it had to come to terms with them.

Functionally, the nobility was divided into two categories, described as 'men of the sword' (*ahl-i-saif*) and 'men of the pen' (*ahl-i-qalam*). The former were either the military commanders or those whose power was based on military strength. The latter were the religious leaders and the administrators, of whom the former were certainly the more powerful. These were chiefly the *Ulema* or theologians, of whom some were advisers to the Sultanate and others occupied judicial offices. They were the followers of the more rigid *Sunni* doctrine of Islam, and were opposed to the *Shia* sect, which was the generally more liberal-minded group.

Theoretically, the religious category included the mystics or saints, who could play a significant political role in spite of abandoning temporal attachments. Nizam-ud-din Aulia, for instance, who lived in the vicinity of Delhi, was a powerful voice, and his opinion could not be disregarded by the Sultan, in spite of the fact that he showed his contempt for the Sultan by refusing to associate with him. Sidi Maula started a hospice near Delhi which became the centre of a Turkish revolt against the Khaljis; though in this case there is some doubt as to whether Sidi Maula was a genuine saint or merely a charlatan, exploiting the readiness of the people to place their faith in a charismatic leader. Even if he was a charlatan, the fact that he could use the guise of a mystic for political ends is significant.

The pre-Islamic tradition in India of the *gurus* and *sannyasis* (religious teachers and ascetics) prepared the ground for the acceptance of their Muslim equivalents, the *pirs* and *shaikhs*.

They lived in comparative isolation, and were believed to be endowed with tremendous religious power, which gave them an assured leadership amongst the people whenever they chose to use it, of which the state was not oblivious. Deference to the 'saint' on the part of the Sultan may well have carried with it the unspoken request that he should direct popular loyalty towards the Sultan. The 'saints' in some cases received endowments which made life for them and their descendants both secure and comfortable.

The Muslim population of the towns consisted mainly of artisans, with a smaller floating population of traders. The latter were generally of Arab or Persian origin and were independent merchants. In addition to the artisans, the royal slaves working either at the court or in the royal workshops were large enough in number to form a considerable part of the urban Muslim population, both in the capital of the Sultanate and other capital cities. The Muslim element in the peasant population grew in numbers towards the latter part of this period. The pattern of living of the cultivators, whether Hindu or Muslim, was almost identical in essentials.

The fusion of Islamic culture with existing Indian culture achieved its most positive expression in the activities of the artisan classes of the towns and amongst the cultivators, as is evident from the socio-religious ideas of the time, and also in primarily artisan activities such as building monuments, the fusion being evident in the architecture of the period. The pattern of living in both these classes came to be interrelated to a far greater degree than amongst the nobility. Domestic ceremonies and rituals such as those connected with birth, marriage, and death became mingled. The converted Muslims were also heirs to long-standing rituals practised by the Hindus. New ceremonies which had come with Islam, and which were regarded as auspicious, crept into Hindu ritual.

Although, theoretically, caste was not accepted by Islamic society, it was by no means ignored in Muslim social life. The development of Muslim castes began with an ethnic distinction. Families of foreign extraction, such as the descendants of Arabs, Turks, Afghans, and Persians, formed the highest caste and were later called *Ashraf* (*Ashraf* in Arabic means 'honourable').

Next in order of status came the upper-caste Hindu converts, such as the Muslim Rajputs. Occupational castes formed the two final castes and were divided into 'clean' and 'unclean' castes. The former included the artisans and other professional people and the latter were the scavengers and those associated with unclean work.* As in the case of Hindu sub-castes the status of the person could improve only if the entire *zat* (= *jati*/sub-caste) moved up the social scale. Restrictions on inter-dining were less severe, though commensality extended only to clean castes. In the arranging of marriages, however, caste was of fundamental importance. The grafting of caste on to profession was so firm and strong by now that no minority community could hope to dislodge it, and this was at the very root of social relationships. However, the observance of caste was more rigid and automatic amongst the Hindus than amongst the Muslims, Jainas, Syrian Christians, and heterodox sects, the latter not being avowedly caste-conscious.

Owing to the largely foreign origin of the nobility, their fusion was more superficial, with Turks and Afghans deliberately trying to preserve their separate identity. The adoption of seemingly innocuous indigenous habits, such as those of dress and food, gradually led to the submerging of this identity. The need to marry into local families accelerated the process. A number of concessions were made and indulgences introduced which were not in keeping with orthodox Islam. Many of the characteristic forms in north Indian classical music trace their ancestry to innovations made by the Muslim nobility of this period. Polo, horse-racing, gambling, and hunting, their favourite pastimes, sometimes offended against fundamental tenets of Islam, but in such instances the *Ulema* found compromise by subtle interpretations of the holy law.

Among all classes, whether Hindu or Muslim, the preference for a son underlined the inferior position of women. Upper-class women like Mirabai and Raziyya had more freedom to use their talent, but the former could do so only by becoming a religious mendicant and the latter only my imitating male rulers.

---

*This, broadly, was the framework of Muslim castes in Uttar Pradesh, until recent years. The roots of this system doubtless go back to the period of the Sultanate.

Romances were written on the love of Deval Rani, a Hindu princess, for a prince of the Sultanate, Khizr Khan, or of Rupamati for Baz Bahadar; both romantic sentiment and women were extolled in poems and ballads. But these sentiments were restricted to literature. In fact women were kept secluded in *pardah* (literally, curtain) in a separate section of the house known as the *zenana* or women's apartments, outside which they were not permitted to appear unless veiled.

What was originally an attempt by the Hindu and Muslim aristocracy to shield their womenfolk from the unpleasant and often primitive aspects of life resulted in an extreme seclusion and consequent emptiness, in which amorous, and sometimes political, intrigue became a frequent if banal diversion. Peasant women and those belonging to the artisan classes still had relative freedom within society, and this was doubtless due to economic necessity. Marriage was regarded almost entirely as a social obligation, based on caste rules, the auspicious matching of two horoscopes, or, increasingly, on property considerations. First-cousin marriages among Muslims were often encouraged in order to keep the property within the family.

There was one section of the Muslim nobility which kept strictly aloof from any attempt at fusion, and this was the *Ulema*; this was matched by an equal aloofness on the part of the brahmans. Apart from its impact upon religion, Muslim rule had reduced the political and economic pre-eminence of the brahmans. Grants of land to the brahmans had been reduced, since Muslim rulers had to cater for the needs of their own theologians. Brahmans were now required to pay taxes, from which they had generally been previously exempt. Nor did they enjoy the same political power at the courts as earlier. The *Ulema* for their part were conscious that only by maintaining a clear identity could they retain political power and ensure their economic security. Religious observances at mosques and temples remained quite distinct, with not the slightest intermingling of ritual. This separateness was rigorously maintained by the priests of both communities.

The greatest damage done by this exclusiveness was to the educational system. Formal education was given at schools attached to temples and mosques, which emphasized religious training. Centres of higher education concentrated on theology and linguistics to the almost complete exclusion of other subjects. The majority of the Muslim schools, or *madrasahs*, were financed by the state. It is clear that the Sultans were generous in their patronage of education, for it is estimated that during the Tughluq period there were up to a thousand educational institutions in Delhi itself. It is unfortunate that this patronage was in fact buttressing theological education alone.

Nevertheless, there was an interest in Indian and Arab learning, on both sides, in non-religious circles, and some intellectual exchange was inevitable. In medicine the interchange was particularly fruitful. Indian medical systems gained popularity in western Asia, and in reverse medical practices derived from these parts, called *yunani* medicine, were widely used in India, together with the earlier *Ayurvedic* system, as they are even to this day. Technical knowledge was in any case a thing apart and was not included in the syllabus of formal education. Vocational training remained in the hands of the artisans or in the state workshops. Intellectual exchange was confined to limited sections of society and did not influence the core of the educational tradition. In a sense, Timur's raid on Delhi resulted in a dissemination of learning, since many scholars fled from the capital and went to the provinces.*

By the sixteenth century a pattern of living had evolved in which an appreciable degree of assimilation had taken place. Nevertheless, amongst the upper classes certain resentments remained. However free the Hindus may have been in their daily life, theoretically they were not equal citizens with the Muslims. What rankled most was that socially the Indian Muslims may have been of a lower origin, and yet they were now in a superior position. Had the Muslims remained a foreign community there

---

*It would be interesting to speculate on the possibilities of intellectual development in India had the Arabs acquired political power in place of the Turks. The intellectual exchange might have been of a far more positive kind, leading to a genuine progress of knowledge. The contemporary Arab sense of inquiry and eagerness for empirical knowledge might have inspired the centres of conventional scholarship in India and saved them from a state of near stagnation.

would have been a readier acceptance of their ideology by high-caste Hindus.*

In the process of preserving their exclusiveness, the brahmans concentrated upon their own internal resources and traditional literature. This led to a revival of the study of older texts, with detailed commentaries and digests. When the new rulers asked to see the legal basis and interpretation of Hinduism the brahmans provided the material based on early texts, which dealt with a theoretically ideal state which envisaged no conflicting divisions within society. There was little or no attempt to recognize, let alone come to terms with, a powerful group which did not fit into a caste hierarchy.

The two dominant sects of Hinduism, the *Vaishnavas* and the *Shaivas*, were the main props of Hindu orthodoxy, though within these sects there were smaller groups with their own variations in belief. Vaishnavism remained more popular in the north, although many of its leaders, such as Ramanuja and Vallabha, had been teachers from south India. Their impact on the reformers of the *Vaishnava* movement in the north was considerable. Some of these reformers have been associated with the *Bhakti* movement. But a distinction can be made between those whose teaching was influenced by Islamic ideas as well. The orientations of these two broad groups were significantly different, although the overall sentiment of their religious expression may have been similar. Some confined themselves to introducing a more personal element into Hindu religious activity, particularly the *Vaishnavas*. Ramananda expresses it best.

I had an inclination to go with sandal and other perfumes to offer my worship to Brahman [the god]. But the *guru* revealed that Brahman was in my own heart. Wherever I go I see only water and stones worshipped; but it is Thou who has filled them all with Thy presence. They all seek Thee in vain amongst the Vedas. My own true *guru*, Thou hast put an end to all my failures and illusions. Blessed art Thou. Ramananda is lost in his Master, Brahman, it is the word of *guru* that destroys all the million bonds of action.[1]

*The Jesuits were after all wise in seeking to convert the emperors of Asia rather than the submerged tenth, which would only have won them the disdain of the upper-class Asians, as in fact happened with later Christian missions in Asia.

A Bengal school-teacher, Chaitanya (1486–1533), became a devotee of Krishna after experiencing a strange hysterical trance. He held devotional meetings where hymns were sung and the meaning of *Vaishnava* belief was expounded. He travelled through the country inspiring people with *Vaishnava* teaching through the cult of Radha and Krishna. Chaitanya was concerned almost solely with bringing *Vaishnava* teaching to as many people as possible, and he was motivated by purely religious feelings.

Another group sought a retreat in their devotion, and to them all that mattered was self-abnegation in an attempt to discover God. Everything was to be subordinated to this single aim. Such was the message of the songs of Mirabai, the sixteenth-century Rajput princess who became a wandering mendicant composing verses on her love for Krishna; or of Surdas, the blind poet of Agra; and in the mystical verses of Lalla, who lived in Kashmir and dedicated her songs to the god Shiva.

The leaders of the *Bhakti* movement, who were to make a deeper impact on social rather than purely religious ideas, were those who had been influenced by Islam, and more particularly by the teachings of the *Sufis*.

The united front which Islam had attempted to present in a predominantly non-Muslim country could not be maintained for long. Whilst the Sultanate was in the process of establishing its power, sectarian conflicts occurred, one of which seriously threatened the Sultanate itself. This took place during the reign of the queen Raziyya. The two dominant sects of Islam were the *Sunnis* and the *Shias*,* and the Sultans, being *Sunnis* supported by *Sunni* theologians, disapproved of the *Shias*. The latter had entered India with the Arab conquest of Sind and were therefore powerful in Sind and Multan. Mahmud of Ghazni had attempted to destroy *Shia* power in Multan, but had failed. The ascendancy of Turkish power had diminished the possibilities of *Shia* influence in India. The *Shias*, together with other schis-

---

* The main schism in Islam occurred in its very early days over the rule of succession to the Caliphate. The *Shias* wanted it to be hereditary, through Ali, and the *Sunnis* elective. From then various differences developed. It was from the *Shias* that the more divergent sects such as *Sufis* and dervishes derived. The *Sunnis* are considered more orthodox.

matics, revolted unsuccessfully against the Sultanate during the reign of Raziyya, after which the *Shias* ceased to be a challenge to *Sunni* domination during the Sultanate.

There was, however, another challenge to the *Sunnis* from a group of Muslims whose influence, though indirect, was nevertheless a force to be contended with. These were the *Sufis*, the saints and mystics who had also come to India with the establishment of Turkish power. They isolated themselves from society, and this disassociation had a historical explanation which is partially pertinent to the Indian situation. The *Sufis* came into prominence in about the tenth century in Persia, with their mystical doctrines of union with God achieved through the love of God.

Such doctrines were attacked by orthodox Islam and the *Sufis* were regarded as heretics. This led to their becoming secretive and aloof and living in seclusion. Their language became highly symbolic and esoteric. Sometimes they formed an order under a *pir* or *shaikh*, the equivalent of the Hindu *guru*, and the members of the order were called *faqirs* (mendicants) or dervishes. Some of the orders evolved a special ritual, often hypnotic in character, such as dancing until a state of trance is experienced. India, with its earlier experience of asceticism, the philosophy of the *Upanishads*, and the devotional cults, provided a sympathetic atmosphere for the *Sufis*. There were three chief orders of *Sufis* in India; that of *Chishti*, which included the historian Barani and the poet Amir Khusrav among its followers and was popular in and around Delhi and the Doab, that of Suhrawardi, whose following was mainly in Sind, and that of Firdausi, whose order was popular in Bihar.

The *Sufis* in India dissociated themselves from the established centres of orthodoxy often as a protest against what they believed to be a misinterpretation of the *Quran* by the *Ulema*. They believed that the latter, by combining religious with political policy and cooperating with the Sultanate, were deviating from the original democratic and egalitarian principles of the *Quran*. The *Ulema* denounced the *Sufis* for their liberal ideas and the *Sufis* accused the *Ulema* of having succumbed to temporal temptations. Those *Sufis* who were still in contact with society were often suspected of being disaffected, but the *Sufis* were never deeply committed to the idea of rebellion since they were both in theory and practice isolated from those conditions which they opposed. At this time also began the *Sufi* belief that the millennium was approaching and that the *mahdi* (the redeemer) would come to restore the pristine faith of Islam. The existence of recluses living apart from their fellows was familiar in India and the *Sufis* were thus a part of an established tradition. It is not surprising, therefore, that the *Sufi pirs* were as much revered by the Hindus as were the Hindu *gurus* and ascetics, all of them being regarded by the Hindus in general as being of the same mould.*

The Islamic stress on equality was respected by the *Sufis* far more than by the *Ulema*, and this brought the mystic orders into contact with the artisans and cultivators. Thus the *Sufis* became more effective religious leaders than the distant *Ulema* for the peasants. The *Sufis* often reflected the non-conformist elements in society, and on occasion even the rationalist forces, since their mysticism was not in every case religious escapism. Some opted out of society in order to pursue knowledge based on empirical observation, when they felt that the more established tradition of rational thought had become entangled with the rigid doctrines of the orthodox. Nizam-ud-din Aulia, for instance, followed an inquiry on the laws of movement which displays a remarkable degree of empirical thought. In the popular mind mystics were also frequently associated with magic. Sidi Maula had no visible source of income, yet he was lavish in his donations to the poor, which gave rise to the suspicion that he was an alchemist; in fact his funds may well have come from the disaffected nobles who were using his hospice as a base to organize opposition to the Sultanate. In all this the *Sufis* had had their precursors in Indian society in the previous centuries.

It is unfortunate that the *Sufis*, who in the early crucial years were the most effective original thinkers in the spheres of both

---

*To this day an annual fair is held at the tomb of a comparatively obscure *pir* in one of the most hallowed sites of Hinduism, Kurukshetra, where thousands of Hindu villagers from the countryside around gather to worship at the tomb. The same villagers will point to a site barely half a mile away, where on an island in the midst of the sacred tank are the visible remains of a Hindu temple believed to have been destroyed by an irate Muslim governor.

politics and religion, should have detached themselves from the social framework. Had they contributed from within society, their impact would have been more direct and they could have mobilized support of a less purely religious nature. This might in turn have been of considerable help to the leaders of the new socio-religious development within the *Bhakti* movement. Although this was a continuation of the earlier devotional cult, *Sufi* ideas influenced its doctrines, as did also certain typically Muslim concepts, particularly those about social justice.

Sufi and *Bhakti* thought and practice coalesced at various points. The essential belief in the need to unite with God was common to both, as was the stress on love as the basis of the relationship with God. Both believed also that the acceptance of a *guru* or a *pir*, at least in the initial stages, was necessary. But the mysticism of the *Sufis* was not encouraged by all the *Bhakti* saints,* since the purpose of the latter was not to remain aloof and isolated from the people, but rather to make their teaching comprehensible even to simple minds.

The *Bhakti* saints, like those of the devotional cults, came from a diversity of backgrounds. Many were artisans by origin or belonged to the class of less prosperous cultivators. The occasional brahman also joined the *Bhakti* movement, but by and large its adherents were from the lower castes. Institutionalized religion and objects of worship were attacked, caste disregarded, women were encouraged to join in the gatherings, and the teaching was entirely in the local vernacular language.

From the historical point of view the most significant contribution of the *Bhakti* movement during this period came from Kabir and Nanak, who expressed the sentiments of the urban class in towns and of the artisans in the villages who were in contact with the towns. The ideas of Kabir and Nanak were drawn from both the existing and the Islamic traditions, and the inclusion of the latter makes them very different from the other leaders of the *Bhakti* movement. That this aspect of the movement was essentially urban-based becomes evident on a compari-

---

* The leaders of the *Bhakti* movement were called *santas* – the worthy and virtuous ones – but modern usage in English has come to describe them as 'saints', as also happened in the case of those associated with the earlier Tamil devotional cult.

son with the earlier period, when the devotional cult was very much in the background, not having the support of a large urban class. The mystical sects were not essentially of urban origin.

Kabir (1440–1518) is said to have been the illegitimate son of a brahman widow. His foster-father was a weaver, and consequently Kabir was trained in the same lower-caste profession. His experience as a weaver was to provide him with many similes drawn from the weaver's craft when he came to compose his verses. He became a disciple of Ramananda, the *Vaishnava* reformer, but eventually left him and began to preach his own ideas. Kabir was concerned with much more than mere religious reform. He wished to change society. He expressed his ideas in single couplets which were easy to memorize and contained imagery which was commonly understood. His verses gathered into two collections on his death incorporate his ideas.

Nanak (1469–1539) came of a rural background, being the son of a village accountant. He was educated through the generosity of a Muslim friend, and later was employed as a store-keeper in the Afghan administration. In spite of his having a wife and three children, he left them and joined the *Sufis*. But after a while he left the *Sufis* and travelled throughout the sub-continent; he is also believed to have visited Mecca. Finally, he rejoined his family and settled in a village in the Punjab, where he preached, gathered his disciples, and eventually died. His teachings are contained in the *Adi Granth*.

With Kabir and Nanak the *Bhakti* movement took a new turn. Theirs was neither an attempt to reform institutionalized Hinduism by attacking the system of worship, nor a means of escape through submerging consciousness in devotion. The new attitude can perhaps best be understood in the idea of God as described by Kabir and Nanak. Kabir either denied the Hindu and Muslim ideas of God or else equated them by stating that they were identical.

O servant, where dost thou seek Me:
Lo, I am beside thee.
I am neither in temple nor in mosque: I am neither in Kaaba*
    nor in Kailash:*

* The Kaaba is the sanctuary in Mecca containing the sacred Black Stone of the Muslims. Kailash is the mountain revered as the abode of Shiva.

Neither am I in rites and ceremonies, nor in Yoga and renunciation.

If thou art a true seeker, thou shalt at once see Me: thou shalt
meet Me in a moment of time.

Kabir says, 'O Sadhu, God is the breath of all breath.'

*

If God be within the mosque, then to whom does this world
belong?

If Ram* be within the image which you find upon your pilgrimage,
then who is there to know what happens without?

Hari is in the East; Allah is in the West. Look within your
heart, for there you will find both Karim† and Ram;

All the men and women in the world are His living forms.

Kabir is the child of Allah and of Ram: He is my Guru,
He is my Pir.[2]

Nanak went a step further and described God without reference
to either Hindu or Muslim conceptions.

The True One was in the beginning, the True One was in the
primal age,

The True One is now also, O Nanak; the True One also shall be.

By His order bodies are produced; His order cannot be described.

By His order souls are infused into them; by His order greatness
is obtained.

By His order men are high or low; by His order they obtain
pre-ordained pain or pleasure.

By His order some obtain their reward; by His order others must
ever wander in transmigration.

All are subject to His order; none is exempt from it.

He who understands God's order, O Nanak, is never guilty of
egoism.[3]

Kabir and Nanak were not trying to bridge the gulf between
Hindus and Muslims by means of an eclectic ideology which
deliberately combined facets of both faiths. Such an idea was yet
to come in the *Din-i-Illahi* of the emperor Akbar. Kabir and
Nanak were leading a new religious group in which God was
not merely a remodelled version of the concept of Rama or of

* Ram, the hero of the *Ramayana*, was worshipped as an incarnation of
Vishnu.

† Karim is a title of Allah in Islam.

Allah, but a new concept. This concept was derived from the two existing religious forces, but neither of them consciously tried to combine and reconcile them. This would explain the sharp antagonism of the brahmans and *Ulema* against these two *Bhakti* leaders in particular, since they saw them as the propagators of new religions.

The followers of Kabir and Nanak founded independent religious communities – the Kabirpanthis and the Sikhs. Both won large followings from amongst the artisans and the cultivators to whom the emphasis on simple living and an absence of incomprehensible ritual made a strong appeal. There was also much honest common sense and practicality in the writings of both men, extreme patterns of living being rejected in favour of a normal balanced life as a part of the society in which one is born. For instance, the *yogi* who enjoys demonstrating his excessive detachment from life is ridiculed by Kabir.

The popularity of these new orders was not due to religious reasons alone. Kabir and Nanak were concerned with the conditions of Indian society, where both caste and the distinctions between Hindu and Muslim, as expressed in organized religion, kept men apart. Their stress was on a reordering of society on egalitarian lines and not the mere coexistence of differing ideologies. The call to social equality was a powerful magnet, and expressed itself in the firm denunciation of caste by both Kabir and Nanak. One of the methods of escaping caste was by joining a non-caste group in which one's caste would be eliminated, as had happened in the past with certain sects and cults. What Kabir and Nanak had to say about caste must have met with an instantaneous response from the artisans, who suffered the contempt of both high-caste Hindus and upper-class Muslims.

That the Sikhs survived as an independent religious community more successfully than the Kabirpanthis resulted largely from the differences between their teaching. Kabir may have been indifferent to the Hindu and Muslim God, but the repeated reference to God by names familiar to these two religions tended to associate him with the less orthodox members of both religions. In time, the Kabirpanthis came to be regarded as a Hindu sect, although the name Kabir itself remains a common Muslim name today. To become a follower of Nanak demanded a greater rejection of the outward manifestations of Hinduism or Islam. This tended to create a stronger feeling of community among the Sikhs. Nanak insisted that the new community must be actively involved in society and not become another isolated sect. After the death of Nanak the Sikhs emerged with a separate religion. The later adoption of visible distinguishing symbols by the Sikhs further accentuated their separateness.*

A feature common to all the *Bhakti* saints was that they composed their verses in the language best understood by the people whom they taught. This led to an interest not only in *Bhakti* literature but also in translations of some of the earlier scriptures, previously available only in Sanskrit and as such inaccessible to the majority of people. The most widely loved of these texts, largely owing to their narrative character, were the epics and the *Puranas*. Commentaries on sacred literature such as the *Bhagavad Gita* were also written, and in these an attempt was made to explain the philosophical nuances in simple terms. Literature in the regional languages was strikingly different from Sanskrit literature in one main respect; it was as spontaneous and imbued with genuine sentiment as the latter had become artificial and forced. The themes of the new literature were often of common interest to more than one region, and literary innovations travelled quickly and widely in northern India.

Amongst the eastern group of languages, Bengali was used by Chaitanya and by the poet Chandidasa, who wrote extensively on the theme of the love of Radha and Krishna. Ballads on events of contemporary interest composed by wandering minstrels were equally popular. The Turkish rulers of Bengal, being even more distant from their homeland than the Delhi Sultans, had early identified themselves with the life of the region. And they had a genuine interest in Bengali literature, a considerable encouragement to those writing in Bengali, since it assured them of a measure of royal support.

It was also a *Bhakti* leader, Shankaradeva, who popularized the use of Assamese in the Brahmaputra valley in the fifteenth century. He used an entirely new medium to spread his ideas –

* Such as the carrying of the five K's – *Kesha* (the ban on cutting hair), *Kanga* (a small comb), *Kara* (an iron bangle), *Kirpan* (a small dagger), and *Kachha* (underwear).

he wrote a number of short one-act plays, of the nature of morality plays, incorporating themes from the *Puranas*. The Jagannatha Temple at Puri in Orissa has a collection of manuscripts which date from the twelfth century, and the language of these contains elements of what was later to develop as Oriya, the language of the region. Chaitanya spent his last years at Puri and doubtless encouraged his followers to use Oriya in preference to Sanskrit. The development of Maithili, spoken in the region of modern Bihar, was also associated with *Vaishnava* and *Bhakti* literature.

In western India, Gujarati was used by the Jaina teachers, who assiduously collected all the Jaina literature written in Old Gujarati. A close relationship existed between Gujarati and Rajasthani. The language of Marwar, called Dingal, was commonly spoken in most parts of Rajasthan and was almost an immediate ancestor of modern Gujarati. Mirabai wrote her songs in Rajasthani, but she was influenced by other *Bhakti* poets who wrote in Hindi.

Hindi was the language spoken in the region around Delhi, and modern Uttar Pradesh, there being a slight difference between eastern and western Hindi. It first developed with the historical epics composed by local bards at the courts of the Rajput kings, poems such as the *Prithviraja-raso*, *Vishaladeva-raso*, etc. The *Sufis*, when they settled in this region, used Hindawi, as they called early Hindi when they wished to address a wider audience, and this increased its popularity. Later it was used by the *Bhakti* movement, in particular by Kabir, Nanak, Surdas, and Mirabai, which gave it an improved status. Earlier, it had been used by writers such as Amir Khusrav, a poet of the Sultanate, who normally wrote in Persian. What gave it greater importance was that it was a co-parent of Urdu. Urdu, literally the camp-language, was becoming the *lingua franca* of the Sultanate, since it had evolved through a combination of Hindi syntax and Persian–Arabic vocabulary. Inevitably those who used Urdu were also familiar with Hindi.

The rule of a Persian-speaking *élite* brought Persian to India, both as the official language and as a new literary influence. The supplanting of Sanskrit by Persian as the official language, in many north Indian kingdoms, encouraged the use of regional languages, since Persian was an unfamiliar language. Arabic was less frequently used. The early Persian literature written in India tended to be largely derivative, using forms and imagery more familiar to Persia. Gradually the Indian element asserted itself, through a growing acquaintance with Indian literature either in the original or through translations. In this respect the works of Amir Khusrav are significant, since he represents the beginnings of Indian-based Persian and Islamic literature.

Amir Khusrav was of Turkish origin, though Indian-born. He studied under Nizam-ud-din Aulia, the *Sufi* saint who lived near Delhi, and eventually settled in Delhi, which was then an exciting city for a young man of his talents. He made his way in the court, and his poems commemorating personalities and events won him both recognition and status. His sensitivity was not blunted by the pleasures of court life and the impact of Nizam-ud-din's teaching remained with him throughout his life. Most of his poetry, which included a great variety of forms – lyric, ode, epic, and elegy – and his historical writing were in Persian. In technique his poetry followed Persian models, but in sentiment it was Indian. Amir Khusrav's imagery was based on what he saw around him and he did not seek the prestige often associated with those who used foreign models. However, the praise bestowed on his works in the highest literary circles in Persia greatly encouraged those writing in Persian in India.

The use of regional languages for all purposes did not result in the discontinuance of writing in Sanskrit. There were still many kings who preferred to patronize Sanskrit poets, regarding them as more distinguished than the poets writing in the new languages. This was particularly so amongst those who desired their family histories to be written in the classical form of a Sanskrit eulogy. In an age of rapidly rising and falling dynasties, these eulogies could be produced to what was almost a set formula. Yet this trend resulted in the writing of innumerable histories, some of local personalities and some of regions. A Jaina scholar, Nayachandra Suri, wrote a verse composition on the life of Hamira, the last of the Chauhan kings. Historical poems in Sanskrit were not restricted to Hindu kings alone. Pride in regional history and local personalities was legitimate, and was certainly of a more manageable and comprehensible compass than the history of a larger area. Udayaraja was the court poet of Sultan Mahmud Begarha of Gujarat, and his poem *Raja-vinoda* is a biography of the Sultan.* Related to the historical literature were the semi-historical texts called *prabandhas*, written in large numbers at this time. The quality is mixed, some being over-full of legend and fanciful invention, but others, such as Merutunga's *Prabandha chintamani* and Rajashekhara's *Prabandhakosha*, contain useful historical material.

A centre of Sanskrit learning developed at Mithila (in northern Bihar), which had remained untouched by Turkish invasions for a longer period than most other places and had thereby acquired a large number of brahmans, who preserved the tradition of Sanskrit literature in their writing. Brahman scholars in Bengal and Jaina scholars in Gujarat also maintained an interest in Sanskrit, though as a language of lively intellectual value it was restricted mainly to places in south India. Sanskrit was preserved by the brahmans where they could find patrons (and some could still be found) to finance them. But in the main the intellectual currents of the age had by-passed Sanskrit.

The Jainas, writing their manuscripts on palm-leaves in Gujarat, illustrated them with small miniature paintings. The paintings are highly stylized, with the human figures predominant, the background and the action being subordinate. Faces, drawn in profile, have a sameness of type which is repeated in all the paintings. The lines are angular and drawn in black against a background of strong colours. The protrusion of the further eye is another characteristic, and also gives a folk quality to the paintings.

The Jaina miniature illustrations appear to have an ancestry in the temple murals of the Deccan and south India, painted from the ninth century onwards. Unfortunately the range of such surviving murals is not sufficiently large for the ancestry to be clearly followed, but there is little doubt of a connexion. Perhaps the dwindling of Jaina influence in the south led to the arrival of Jaina monks, with a taste for painting in western Indian centres of Jainism. In place of murals, manuscript illustrations

---

*The tradition of writing the biographies of reigning kings continued into recent times, as in the case of the life of Queen Victoria appropriately called *Viktoriya-charita* (The Life of Victoria).

became the vogue. From the ninth to the twelfth centuries, in Bengal and Bihar, Buddhist manuscripts were also illustrated with miniatures, but these were of a different style, more akin to the Deccan murals than those of southern India. The library at Nalanda was destroyed during the Turkish attack, so the few such manuscripts which survived were preserved in Nepal. Stylistically they have little in common with the Jaina miniatures of western India. The introduction of illustrations in manuscripts may also be ascribed to the relaxing of the more severe puritanical habits generally associated with Jainism, a step in keeping with the mood of the times.

The need to preserve the Jaina scriptures led to a vast amount of transcribing from older texts and the writing of fresh ones based on the old. The palm-leaf was long and narrow, and consequently the paintings were fitted into a small square, which accentuated the squat appearance of the figures. By the fifteenth century two major changes had occurred in the Jaina miniature paintings. Arab traders had introduced the use of paper to western India, and the Jaina manuscripts were now being written on paper. The shape of the page changed from being long and narrow to a wide rectangle, which allowed a higher format for the painting. The figures did not have to be squat, and the background could be more fully depicted. The copyists were not the illustrators, the paintings probably being done by trained artisans.

The second innovation came via the Turks, who in the process of introducing Persian culture to northern India brought with them books illustrated with exquisite miniatures by Persian artists who, among other things, excelled in the juxtaposition of colours. This was noticed by the Indian illustrators. The flat large spaces of brick-red or blue, so common to the early Jaina miniatures, now gave way to a greater range of more subtle colours, recalling the colours of the early murals at Ajanta. This new type of Jaina miniature was to influence in turn the Rajasthani miniature paintings of the sixteenth century and later.

The most visible change in the Indian landscape brought about by the Turks was the introduction of a new architectural style, of which the mosque and the mausoleum were typical. The plan of the mosque served the requirements of the ritual of prayer in Islam, and was at first an enclosed area where Muslims could congregate for prayer. It could be square or rectangular, open to the sky, with cloisters on three sides interrupted only for entrances. The west wall, faced by those at prayer, was elaborate and contained the prayer niches, from which the *imam* led the prayer, which were often covered with a series of small domes. A single minaret, or in later mosques one at each corner, was used by the *muezzin* to call the faithful to prayer five times a day. The only parts of the mosque not directly related to the ritual were the domes. These gave elegance to the building, of which the finest examples are undoubtedly to be found in Persia. The mausoleum at this date was equally simple, the tomb being enclosed in an octagonal or square-shaped room with a dome.

The Turks brought with them the traditions of Arab and Persian architecture, particularly the latter. Persian features included the pointed arch, the transverse vault, the dome, and the octagonal form of the building under the dome. These were all new to Indian architecture, where the arch was topped by a lintel, or was rounded, and the towers of temples were corbelled. The combination of the arch and the dome gave to Islamic buildings a distinctive character quite different from Hindu and Buddhist architecture. The increased use of concrete also allowed the covering of wider spaces than before. These two totally distinct styles gradually merged, though by no means completely, and this merging was due to the employment of Indian craftsmen. The latter were trained to use the Persian forms, which they modified gradually, and the ornamentation of buildings was dependent on the techniques existing in India. Indian motifs, such as the lotus in various forms, found their way into the new buildings. These motifs were introduced together with the classic Islamic decorative motifs – the geometrical patterns, arabesques, and calligraphic forms.

The earliest and most interesting example of Islamic architecture in India was the literal grafting of a mosque on to a temple at the site of the Quwwat-ul-Islam mosque at Delhi. There was a tenth-century Chauhan temple at the site. The central sanctuary of the temple was removed, leaving the cloisters along the four sides. The prayer niche was built into the western wing of the temple, and the temple was now ready for use as a mosque, as was to be the case with many other temples. However, the essentially Hindu treatment of the sculpture on the columns of the cloisters was unpalatable to the Turks who came to pray at the mosque. In order to hide this a screen of five arches was built across the façade of the western wing. The Indian origin of these arches is evident in the use of corbelling instead of radiation voussoirs, and in the decorative motifs, which are a mixture of the lotus scroll and Arabic calligraphic designs. This mosque was being constantly enlarged during the early period of the Sultanate, and initiated the Pathan style of architecture, as this Indo-Islamic style is called.

Sultanate architecture underwent a change during the reign of the Tughluqs. The simplicity of the lines, the reduction of ornamentation to a minimum, and the use of large stone blocks all combined to produce an effect of strength and austerity. The tomb of Ghiyas-ud-din displays curious features resulting from the fusion of Indian and Islamic styles. The arches are pointed and true, but there is a lintel, functionally unnecessary, across the base of the arch, presumably a relic of the Hindu arch.

The Lodis reverted to a more elegant style. In fact their architects were so concerned with the aesthetics of proportion that the double dome was used. The walls of their buildings being extremely thick, it was difficult to decide where the balance of the dome should lie – in proportion to the outer elevation and size or to the interior. The double dome solved this problem, since the outer dome conformed to the exterior proportions. A new type of decoration was introduced, again borrowed from Persia – enamelled tiles; these on the grey sandstone monuments were remarkably effective.

Provincial architecture developed along lines similar to that of Delhi, with local modifications often conditioned by the availability of building material. This was especially so in Bengal, where stone was not readily available and brick was more frequently used, although this led to lower buildings. Terracotta decorative work, which had been used to great effect in Buddhist buildings, continued to be used on mosques and palaces. Architecture in Gujarat and Malwa achieved a high aesthetic standard, since the indigenous tradition was more alive here than in other areas and patrons were more willing to experiment with architectural forms. The impact of the new architecture was also felt in Rajasthan, where domestic architecture shows less sculptural confusion on the outside, and certain ornamental features such as the use of enamelled tiles, which would point to borrowing from the new Pathan style.

The combination of Muslim and native techniques in architecture, particularly in mosques and mausoleums, was a considerable departure from the orthodox on both sides. The inclusion of what might have been regarded as essentially Hindu motifs, such as the lotus, escaped notice. This amalgamation symbolizes in many ways the nature of the Hindu–Muslim fusion. Despite the utterances of the *Ulema* and the brahmans and the court chroniclers, who sought to preserve the separate identity of each, the graft took, and it grew in a quiet, unostentatious manner.

In the last fifty years many attempts have been made to prove that the Hindu and Islamic cultures at no time approached any kind of fusion, and that over the many centuries when they lived side by side Hindus and Muslims existed as two separate communities. This is a clear example of a case of historical 'back-projection', where sanction is sought from the past to justify contemporary attitudes. The concept that there was a separate community or 'nationality' of Hindus and Muslim did not exist during this period. Had the Turks and Afghans preserved their foreign identity and had they, as foreigners, constituted the majority of Muslims, the persistence of such a separate nationality might have been possible: but in fact the vast majority of Muslims were Hindu converts.

The argument for the reality of a separate nationality is drawn from the writings of the theologians and court chroniclers, who consciously emphasized the distinctions between Hindus and Muslims because it was in their interests to do so. Sources such as these cannot be accepted uncritically, since their own prejudices are writ large in their attitudes. The fusion of cultures in any case cannot be judged by the writings of a prejudiced minority determined to hold aloof: it can only be judged by the cultural pattern of the society as a whole. From the pattern of society in the Sultanate period it is evident that a synthesis of the two cultures took place, although this synthesis did not occur at every level and with the same intensity. Furthermore, the pattern which emerged was to mature in the period subsequent to that of the Sultanate.

The coming of Islam did not introduce major changes in political institutions, but, as is evident from the development of the *Bhakti* movement, the challenge to the social pattern was intensified. Since caste loyalty was stronger than political loyalty the really significant impact of Islam was upon social structure, and was seen in the creation of new sub-castes and of new sects within those castes most permeated with Islamic ideas. To this extent, the earlier pattern of the assimilation of foreigners was repeated. In spite of its egalitarian philosophy, the influence of Islam did not lead to the disappearance of caste. The fact that Islam in India succumbed to and accepted caste society reduced the social dynamism of Islam. Where the *Shaikhs* and the *Sayyids* (members of the high *Ashraf* caste) had a caste status analogous to that of the *dvijas*, the threat to the caste system was slight. Authority and social prestige remained with the castes traditionally associated with power. The lack of vertical mobility in caste society isolated the castes and by the same token isolated thinking within the castes. This made the *Bhakti* movement politically ineffective during this period. In subsequent centuries, however, the followers of Nanak, for instance, developed into an effective political community. But the traditional pattern of opposition to orthodoxy was to continue until the late nineteenth century, when, with the emergence of the Indian middle class as a result of various factors, a new social and political pattern began to evolve.

THE SOUTH CONFORMS
c. A.D. 1300–1526

THE Delhi Sultanate failed to establish an all-Indian empire, but its efforts to conquer the south had repercussions throughout the whole Indian peninsula. The kingdoms which emerged in the Deccan and in south India in the fourteenth century were the result of both the attempt and the failure of the Sultanate to control the southern regions. What happened in the North now had repercussions on events in south India, and vice versa, to a far greater degree than ever before, and this was not limited to political events alone. The development of parallel institutions in many spheres was to make the similarities between north and south close.

The ambitions of the Sultanate to control southern India during the thirteenth century, resulting at times in military campaigns, created an atmosphere of uncertainty, and the innumerable small kingdoms of the peninsula continually wondered if it would be their fate that the Turks would conquer them. But this atmosphere changed in the fourteenth century, for the Sultanate had revealed its weaknesses. The Turkish governor of the Deccan revolted and established the dynasty of the Bahmanis, which was to rule the northern Deccan for two centuries. A decade earlier, the independent kingdom of Vijayanagara had been established further south, where once the Hoysala kings had ruled. The founding of the kingdom of Vijayanagara was also indirectly related to the failure of the Sultanate to master the peninsula.

The dividing line between the Bahmani kingdom and Vijayanagara was the Krishna river. The conflict between the Deccan kingdoms and those of the south, which had by now become almost traditional, was renewed in the fourteenth century, the conflict arising over the possession of the Raichur doab, the fertile area between the Krishna and its tributary the Tungabhadra, which was also rich in mineral resources. Added to this was the lure of the diamond mines in Golconda which each wished to possess. The political history of south India during the fourteenth, fifteenth, and early sixteenth centuries was dominated by this conflict and the changing loyalties of the border kingdoms of the peninsula.

It was during these centuries that a new element was introduced into India – the Europeans who came in search of trade. The Arabs had come to control not only the trade which passed through the posts they had established in western Asia but also that which they conducted further to the east, and this monopoly was a source of disquiet to European traders. The adventurers and the occasional merchant who travelled to Asia (and these included men such as Marco Polo, Nicolo Conti, Athanasius Nikitin, and Duarte Barbosa) brought back stories which were very tempting to European traders, who realized that if they had direct access to Asia without using Arab intermediaries they would reap much higher profits. Thus a steadily increasing stream of traders was attracted and with them came missionaries, the majority of whom were Roman Catholics. Amongst the pioneers there was one country above all – Portugal – which showed great zeal both for trade and for making converts, following upon the discovery by Portuguese mariners of a new route to Asia via the Cape of Good Hope. It was in the closing years of the fifteenth century that the Portuguese arrived on the Malabar coast, and the colonies which they established they hung on to with great tenacity till the very last. Within a few years of their arrival they established themselves as serious rivals to the Arabs for the trade of Asia.

At the opening of this period south India was already well acquainted with Islam. Arab merchants, settled on the west coast since the eighth century, had moved inland in search of trade. The concentration, however, was still greatest along the coast, where they were welcomed and respected and lived in communities such as those of the Mappillas or Malabar Muslims. They had a monopoly of the import of horses and this rapidly brought them prosperity. A single horse fetched 220 dinars, and importation at the rate of 10,000 per year led to affluence. Ibn Batutah, visiting Malabar in the fourteenth century, mentions the existence of innumerable mosques along the coast, each the nucleus of a flourishing Muslim community. The assimilation of Islam in south India was a smoother process than in the north, since the Arabs were traders and not contestants for political power, and consequently were not concerned with maintaining a separate identity.

The campaigns of the Turkish rulers under Malik Kafur in 1311 took the army of the Sultanate as far as Madurai, and this resulted in a state of confusion in south India. On the evacuation of Madurai by the army of the Sultanate, the ruler of Quilon (Malabar) took his armies across to the east coast, annexing the territory as far as Kanchipuram, and so enabled the south to organize itself against further attacks from the Sultanate. These alliances were not, as has been suggested in the past, directed primarily against the Muslims. The ruler of Quilon was too dependent on Arab trade to consider such a possibility. Rather it was an anti-Turkish stand, since the Turks were foreigners in south India and were seen as a threat to the established coastal trade, without which the maritime kingdoms of the south would have been at a grave disadvantage. North of Kanchi the retreating armies of the Sultanate left the field open for the rise of new kingdoms, an opportunity which was seized by the founders of both the Bahmani and Vijayanagara dynasties.

The founding of the Bahmani dynasty followed the familiar pattern of a governor revolting and declaring his independence of the Sultanate. Zafar Khan, appointed by the Sultanate at Daulatabad to govern the Deccan, proclaimed himself king of northern Deccan, with the title of Bahman Shah. But Bahman Shah's ambition to extend his kingdom south to Madurai was thwarted by the emergence of two new kingdoms – Warangal in Andhra and Vijayanagara south of the Tungabhadra.

An expedition against Warangal led to the latter agreeing to pay an annual tribute, which was in later years to become the cause of continual conflict, with the Bahmanis sending expeditions against Warangal to exact tribute whenever it refused to pay. Attempts at subduing Vijayanagara also resulted in a series of wars between the Bahmanis and Vijayanagara, also involving the surrounding kingdoms, which switched their alliances from one to the other as seemed most expedient. The Bahmani kingdom was more involved with the peninsula than with the Sultanate.

In the course of its campaigns in Warangal, the army of the Sultanate took prisoner two local princes, Harihara and Bukka, and brought them back to Delhi, where they were converted to Islam and later sent back to the south to restore the authority of the Sultanate. In this the two princes succeeded, but the temptation to found their own kingdom proved irresistible. In 1336, Harihara was crowned king of Hastinavati (modern Hampi), the nucleus of what was to become the Vijayanagara kingdom. In addition, the two brothers took the most unusual step of reverting to Hinduism. This might have been even more difficult than acquiring a kingdom, for their conversion to Islam had made them out-castes, and by existing caste laws readmission to caste status was impossible. But Vidyaranya, a locally respected religious leader, not only re-admitted the brothers to caste status but removed all tabus by explaining that Harihara was in fact the vice-regent of the local deity Virupaksha, and therefore that which had divine sanction could hardly be questioned. In effect, Harihara was as much a Hindu ruler as any other, his position being unchallenged owing to his political power.

The Vijayanagara kings were conscious of this initial handicap with which the dynasty began, and much of their patronage of religious institutions may have been motivated by a desire to appease religious authority, lest the apostacy of the founder be used against the dynasty. It has often been asserted that the rise of Vijayanagara represents a Hindu revival in the south, but there is little evidence for this. Royal patronage was responsible largely for embellishing older temples and building new ones, and was not concerned with stirring up anti-Muslim sentiments, as might have been expected of Hindu revivalism at that period. The Hindu kingdoms did not form an alliance against the Muslims, and the kings of Vijayanagara did not hesitate to attack Hindu kings wherever they felt them to be an obstacle, as often happened with the smaller southern kingdoms, as for instance in the war against Hoysala in 1346, when success made Vijayanagara pre-eminent in the south.

Harihara planned and built the city of Vijayanagara (the City of Victory) near Hampi, and in 1343 it became the capital and gave its name to the kingdom. But Harihara's kingdom was surrounded by enemies – the kings of Andhra, the coastal kingdoms, and later the Bahmanis, who were to become recurrently a northern enemy of Vijayanagara. A permanent enemy necessitates elaborate defence preparations, and these in turn require a large reserve of wealth. Revenue had to be increased, and in order to do this forests were cleared and new land settled, while the existing land-tax system and the collection of revenue were made more efficient. Large irrigation tanks were built, and dams across rivers, involving considerable hydraulic engineering, were constructed. Income was thus increased for the additional expenditure on expanded armies. Cavalry was improved by importing horses in large numbers and encouraging Turkish mercenaries to join the Vijayanagara forces. The standing army was increased and a stricter check was kept on feudal levies.

Conflict between Vijayanagara and the Bahmanis was unavoidable and hostilities began in 1358, with both kingdoms claiming the Raichur Doab. The boundary kept shifting according to the outcome of each campaign. Vijayanagara secured its southern frontiers by conquering Madurai in 1370, but the east coast kingdoms, Orissa and Warangal, proved to be more difficult. The capture of Goa by Vijayanagara was strategically important, apart from the revenue it brought in from trade. Had the east coast also fallen to Vijayanagara it would have been possible to maintain a coast-to-coast control, with only the northern frontiers to defend. This would also have prevented any active interference by the Bahmanis in southern affairs.

In the latter half of the fifteenth century the Bahmanis developed a more positive policy both in domestic affairs and in inter-state relations. This was largely due to the efforts of the minister Mahmud Gavan. The threat of attacks from Malwa was reduced by its expulsion from the northern borders of the Bahmani kingdom with the aid of Gujarat. Soon after this, Gavan recaptured Goa from Vijayanagara and trade was diverted back to the Bahmani kingdom. Vijayanagara also suffered reverses along the eastern coast with the kingdom of Orissa, which for a brief period extended its power as far south as the Kaveri delta. Dynastic complications added to the confusion, until in 1485 a change of dynasty led to the Saluva family occupying the throne.

The administration of the Bahmani kingdom was ruined by an internal crisis, which Gavan had tried to prevent but to which he eventually fell victim. The Muslim nobles of the Bahmani kingdom were split into two factions – the *Deccanis* who were domiciled immigrants and local converts, and the *Pardesis* (literally the foreigners) who were in temporary service or were recently arrived foreigners. The latter, more enterprising and successful, were resented by the former, and there occurred an uncalled for massacre of the *Pardesis* by the *Deccanis*. Gavan, however, was regarded as a *Pardesi*, and, as assassination was the only way in which his power could be curbed, the *Deccanis* assassinated him in 1481 and assumed complete control, a control which was made all the more effective with the death of the king in the following year and the accession of a minor.

The rivalry between the *Deccanis* and *Pardesis* was more than just a local political faction fight, as it precipitated a serious internal crisis which caused the power of the Bahmani kingdom to dwindle. Provincial governors increased their strength until the suzerainty of the Bahmanis was nominal, and the latter's power was further undermined by repeated attacks from the armies of Vijayanagara. In 1538, the old Bahmani kingdom gave way to five new kingdoms – Bijapur, Golconda, Ahmednagar, Bidar, and Berar.

The Bahmani kingdom was in many respects similar to the Sultanate. Its income came overwhelmingly from the land, and the administration revolved around the assessment and collection of land revenue. The kingdom was divided into four provinces each under a governor who collected the revenue and raised a fixed number of troops for the king, and who in addition had the power of making civil and military appointments, which often led to the governors regarding the province as their own domain. Continual wars called for an unceasing supply of troops, which prevented the king from interfering too frequently in provincial administration. Normal checks such as transfers and inspections had to be dispensed with in wartime, and the eventual fragmentation of the Bahmani kingdom was virtually inevitable.

The death of Gavan ushered in the decline of the Bahmani kingdom, but for Vijayanagara this was the period of its greatest power in south India, particularly during the reign of Krishna Deva Raya (1509–30). The Bahmanis made a final attempt to annex the Raichur doab in 1509, but Krishna Deva Raya drove them back and advanced to the heart of their kingdom. This in itself might have ended Bahmani rule, but Krishna Deva reinstated the Sultan, realizing that the retention of a Bahmani king would prevent the provincial governors from declaring their autonomy, and that one weak Bahmani king was better for Vijayanagara than four smaller but strong kingdoms. The Bahmani ruler, knowing that his chief prop was the Vijayanagara king, did not attack the latter. Thus the status quo was maintained during the reign of Krishna Deva. This policy was to have fateful repercussions later, for it led to an alliance of the five kingdoms which succeeded the Bahmanis against Vijayanagara.

Krishna Deva conquered the east coast in a brilliant campaign against Orissa. On the west coast he maintained friendly relations with the Portuguese on a basis of mutual assistance. Krishna Deva was dependent on Portuguese traders for horses – the horse trade having come into Portuguese hands – and the Portuguese trade with south India was generally dependent on the prosperity of Vijayanagara. The Portuguese tried repeatedly to draw Krishna Deva into political alliance against Gujarat and the Bahmanis, but he refused to commit himself. For him the Portuguese were primarily the suppliers of horses, and he wished not to be involved with them politically.

The five kingdoms of the northern Deccan were biding their time, waiting for an opportunity to attack Vijayanagara. Opportunity came in 1564 when four of them united to attack and destroy the southern power. But they unintentionally cleared the way for their own destruction. The south lay exhausted and in the north of India new power had established itself – the Mughuls who were in turn preparing for further conquests.

The peripheral kingdoms continued their uncertain existence. The Malabar coast was dotted with small principalities, ruled by both Hindu and Muslim rulers, surviving on the western trade. Of these the Zamorin of Calicut, claiming descent from the old Perumal rulers of Kerala, was the most powerful; their strength was based largely on the fact that Calicut attracted trade from both west and east Asia – from Yemen, Persia, the Maldive islands, Ceylon, Java, and China. The coming of the Portuguese, however, altered the relationships between these principalities. The Pandya kingdom on the opposite coast was very unstable, was repeatedly conquered only to re-establish itself again. A portion of the older Pandya kingdom – the area of Madurai – was declared the independent kingdom of Ma'bar in 1334 by a local Muslim governor, but by 1364 it had been incorporated into the Vijayanagara kingdom.

While the maritime kingdoms were dependent largely on trade, the larger kingdoms inland derived the major part of their revenue from the land. The economy of the Vijayanagara kingdom continued the Chola pattern, obtaining its income from agriculture and trade. The administrative structure had become more stratified and more closely connected with the pattern of the economy, a tendency which had begun to emerge in the Chola period. The pattern was now broadly similar to that of northern India, except that the larger volume of trade in the south maintained a proportionately larger number of towns, mainly concentrated in the coastal areas.

Commenting on the economic structure of Vijayanagara, Fernão Nuniz writes :

... This king Chitrao has foot-soldiers paid by his nobles, and they are obliged to maintain six lakhs of soldiers, that is 600,000 men and 24,000 horses which the same nobles are obliged to have. These nobles are like renters who hold all the land from the king, and besides keeping all these people they have to pay their cost; they have to pay to him every year 60 lakhs of rents as royal dues. The lands they say yield 120 lakhs of which they must pay 60 to the king, and the rest they retain for the pay of soldiers and the expenses of the elephants which they are obliged to maintain. ... During his feasts and the alms-giving to his temples all these captains, who are thus like renters, must always attend this court, and of those whom this king always has about him and by whom he is accompanied in his court there are more than 200. They are obliged always to be present with the king, and must always maintain the full number of soldiers according to their obligations, for if he finds that they have a less number they are severely punished and their estates confiscated. These nobles are never allowed to settle in cities or towns because they would there be beyond reach of his hand; they only go thither sometimes. But a concession is granted to the kings that are subject to him, namely they do not go to court unless they are summoned and from their own cities they send to him their rents and tributes. ... When he wishes to please his captains or persons from whom he has received or wishes to receive good service, he gives them scarves of honour for their personal use, which is a great honour; and this he does each year to the captains at the time they pay him their land rents. This takes place in the month of September when for nine days they make great feasts. . . . Within these nine days the king is paid all the rents that he receives from his kingdom; for, as already said, all the land belongs to the king and from his hand the captains hold it. They make it over to the husbandmen, who pay nine tenths to their lord, and they have no land of their own for the kingdom belongs entirely to the king; only the captains are put to charges on account of the troops for whom the king makes them responsible and whom they are obliged to provide in the way of service. . . .[1]

The system of farming revenue to the highest bidder was also known. This was not restricted to agricultural land alone but was applied to places of commercial value as well, as for example the vicinity of the city gate at Vijayanagara where the merchants would congregate. Of this Nuniz writes:

. . . For through this gate all things must enter that come into the two cities, since in order to enter the city of Bisnagar there is no other road but this, all other roads meeting there. This gate is rented out for 12,000 *pardaos* each year, and no man can enter it without paying just what the renters ask, country folk as well as strangers. In both these cities there is no provision or merchandise whatever, for all comes from outside on pack-oxen, since in this country they always use beasts for burdens; and every day there enter by these gates 2,000 oxen and every one of these pays 3 *vintees*, except certain polled oxen without horns which never pay anything in any part of the realm. . . .[2]

There was a large variety of taxes which went into the making of the national revenue; despite the revenue from commerce, land tax remained the most substantial single source. A detailed land survey and assessment was conducted during the reign of Krishna Deva, and the tax rate was fixed between one third and one sixth, depending on the quality of the land. Commercial taxes consisted of levies, duties, and customs on manufactured articles of trade, and this added up to a substantial amount, as also did the tax on property. Those engaged in non-agricultural professions had to pay a professional tax. Private owners of workshops paid an industries tax. Special dues on marriages, and others raised for temple requirements, were listed under a social taxation scheme. A periodic military contribution was used for maintaining forts and garrisons. Judicial fines were an additional source of revenue for the state. Finally, free labour could be exacted for specific projects, such as the building of an irrigation tank. The villages continued to be largely isolated and self-sufficient, a parochialism intensified by the practice of processing local produce on the spot. For instance, sugarcane grown in a certain village could only be pressed in a mill located in that village or certain specified nearby villages. To take it elsewhere was not only illegal but almost tabu. However, there was one rural institution which tended to break the isolation of the village and this was the local fair. Fairs were held frequently, and were not merely occasions for disposing of surplus produce but were a means of bringing villagers and townspeople into contact.

The tradition of village councils familiar to the Tamil country was still maintained in the *brahmadeya* villages. In the other villages, the councils were slowly disintegrating under the changing system, where the effective power was falling into the hands of the grantees. As in the case of northern India there was a tendency for caste loyalty to assume more significance than political loyalty in a given area. This resulted from the diminishing strength of the cultivator class and the increasing importance of the landowner. The temple, the *matha*, and the secular grantees were the owners of land, in effect, and this land was worked by hired labourers and tenant farmers. The former were paid a seasonal wage and they could in principle move from village to village, though in practice this was hardly feasible owing to the closely knit structure of each village. The tenant farmers paid a fixed rate of one half to three quarters of the value of the crops to the landowner. Their mobility was also restricted.

Rural credit was still largely in the hands of the temple authorities who gave loans to individuals or villages. Interest on loans ranged from twelve to thirty per cent. Where a debtor could not pay back the loan, the temple took over his land. The temple continued to play an important role in rural life. It was the largest employer in the village, finding work for a variety of persons. It was often the biggest single landowner and consumer in an area. It encouraged rural development through projects such as buying waste land and settling a community of weavers on it, or supervising irrigation schemes. All this added to the wealth of the temple. That it could command both money and power naturally led to its becoming the focus of influence in the area, and this further strengthened the ties between monarch and religious authority.

The status of the artisan whether in the towns or villages remained largely unchanged from Chola times. The smiths and carpenters were high in the social scale, whilst the weavers and the potters – although equally essential to community life – occupied a lower position, as also did the oil-pressers, toddy-drawers (toddy being the fermented juice of the coconut), and the leather workers. The artisans were organized in guilds, but the artisan guilds worked for the powerful merchant guilds, who had effective control over goods produced for exchange and as such were virtually regarded as employers by the artisan guilds. Merchant guilds continued to have a wider sphere of operations than the artisan guilds, as they had had in the Chola period. They were also the financiers and the distributors of the articles of trade. These were limiting factors on the independence of the artisan guilds. Inland trade tended to remain local, although its area was being gradually enlarged. The Arabs in overseas trade served alike all the various parts of the sub-continent and the increased mobility of Indian traders was beginning to be felt towards the end of this period, though this mobility was still confined mainly to the coastal areas.

Economic power gave the merchant guilds a position of political importance in the country, which was manifested in their influence at the court. Innovations in taxation policy and related matters, for instance, were discussed with the guild leaders, and they gradually came to represent public opinion. The power of the merchant guilds counter-balanced that of the landowners and officials at the court. The Chettis were amongst the better known merchants and middlemen who operated in the Mysore, Andhra, and Madras region, and maintained the traditions set by their forefathers during the Chola period, as do their descendants to the present day. Some migrated to south-east Asia and continued the family business overseas.

The state was fully aware of the potential wealth to be had from overseas trade. Krishna Deva refers to this in his Telugu poem, *Amuktamalyada*.

A king should improve the harbours of his country and so encourage its commerce that horses, elephants, precious gems, sandalwood, pearls, and other articles are freely imported into his country. He should arrange that the foreign sailors who land in his country on account of storm, illness, and exhaustion are looked after in a manner suitable to their nationality. ... Make the merchants of distant foreign countries who import elephants and good horses be attached to yourself by providing them with daily audience and presents and by allowing decent profits. Then those articles will never go to your enemies. ...[3]

The fear that trade might be diverted to the enemy was an important consideration with Vijayanagara. Friendly relations with the Portuguese were maintained precisely for this reason. Foreign traders were given facilities and concessions, few goods being subject to dues which were not heavy. Customs duty varied from two and a half to five per cent of the sale price of the goods. The duty on imported cloth and oil was higher (ten and fifteen per cent) in order to discourage their import, both being locally produced. The maritime principalities along the Malabar coast undermined the income which would normally have gone to Vijayanagara, since the former were the first to receive the consignments and charge taxes. In periods of prosperity this was probably only a marginal loss to Vijayanagara, but in periods of depression it could be a grievous burden.

Imports into Vijayanagara included gold and silver bullion, elephants from Ceylon and Pegu (the Bahmanis having cut off access to the north Indian elephant trade), and horses, which had originally been supplied by the Arabs but the supply of which the Portuguese controlled in the sixteenth century, when they captured the Arab ports from where the horses were shipped. Spices came from south-east Asia; heavy textiles such as velvets, damasks, and satins were imported from Jiddah, Aden, and China. Exported goods went chiefly to Persia, Africa, China, and Ceylon and included rice, sugar, coconut, millet, dyes (cinnabar, henna, indigo, myrobalan), sandalwood, and teak, pepper, cloves, ginger and cinnamon, cotton cloth and printed textiles.

Although the carrying trade in Indian ships had declined, the shipyards in the Maldive islands still built a few large ships for long sea voyages. Indian ships, according to Conti, were larger than the Italian ships but smaller than the Chinese. Chinese vessels were the finest of all the shipping visiting Indian ports, as they were built for long voyages through dangerous seas. Travelling by ship was tedious since the average daily run was some forty miles and there were frequent stops at ports along the coast. The journey by sea from Calicut to Ceylon took fifteen days. Eli, Calicut, and Quilon were the most frequently visited ports with ships coming from the trading centres of both the east and the west.

Foreign trade demanded a greater use of currency in preference to barter. There were many mints in the Vijayanagara kingdom, each provincial capital having its own. Coins were elegantly designed and were minted in a mould with legends in the Kannada and Nagari script. In addition to local issues, foreign coins such as the Portuguese *cruzado*, the Persian *dinar*, and the Italian *florin* and *ducat* were also in circulation in the coastal areas.

The material prosperity of the upper classes did not result in the cultural sphere in innovations and experiments in form and idea: on the contrary, they conservatively held to existing patterns. This led to a staleness in conception and a concentration on unimportant details, as typified in the architecture of the time. An entire city was built in Vajayanagara, with lavish temples, but what remains shows that it was characterized by sumptuous and rich ornamentation. Stone construction gave way to brick and plaster buildings, which lent themselves more easily to elaborate ornamentation. Pillars became blocks of statuary. Temple worship involved a variety of rituals requiring a cluster of shrines. The *gopurams* or gateways became the dominant feature of the temple. The major temples acquired an open pavilion – the *kalyana-mandapam* – where the wedding of the god and goddess was ostentatiously celebrated. At the same time, further north, the great dome of the Gol Gumbaz at Golconda was built and was acclaimed as an outstanding engineering achievement, yet it made no impact on Vijayanagara architecture.

The kings of Vijayanagara were said to rule on behalf of a Shaivite deity, Virupaksha, and thus royal patronage strengthened the existing popularity of Shaivism in the peninsula. By now the devotional cult was a recognized part of Hinduism. Its centre of activity had shifted from the Tamil country to Mysore and further north and west to Maharashtra. Jñandeva was amongst the early Maharashtrian saints who recited the *Gita* in Marathi. He was followed in the fourteenth century by Namadeva who uncompromisingly attacked the worship of images and whose following included a wider cross-section of people than that of earlier Maharashtrian preachers. His teaching was more radical and closer in spirit to that of Kabir and Nanak. A significant concession to the growing strength of the *Bhakti* cult was made by Krishna Deva, who extended his worship to Vithoba, a popular deity associated with the early *Bhakti* teachers in Maharashtra.

The regional languages – Tamil, Telugu, Kannada, and Marathi – were fully accepted and mature. Although most of the literature in these languages, excluding Tamil, consisted of adaptations from Sanskrit originals, particularly the Epics and the *Puranas*, they were becoming the media of cultural transmission, for which the *Bhakti* movement was largely responsible. In the northern Deccan the Bahmanis had introduced Persian and Arabic, which made this region closer linguistically to the Sultanate. In Malabar, another language had acquired an independent status – Malayalam – spoken in the state of Kerala today. Originating as a dialect of Tamil, the political isolation of Malabar from Tamil-nad and the infusion of linguistic forms brought by foreigners led to its developing independently of Tamil.

As was the case in northern India, Sanskrit remained the language of learning in certain sections of society. Court circles encouraged the writing of historical narratives and biographies of the Hoysala and Vijayanagara kings. Commentaries such as that of Sayana on the Vedas attracted the attention of scholars. Hemadri spent a major part of his life writing commentaries on the *Dharmashastras*, with interpretations, which tally closely with those of his northern contemporaries. The contribution of such writings to the advancement of social institutions was, however, small.

Culturally and intellectually Vijayanagara marked a static period in south India. Riches flowed in from trade and from the land, and life for the upper class was comfortable if not luxurious. The assimilation of Islam took place unobtrusively, and the so-called Hindu 'revival' did not lead to any dramatic conflicts intellectually or otherwise. That there was a conscious Hindu revival is extremely debatable. It would be more valid to attribute the patronage of Hindu institutions under the kings of Vijayanagara to the fact that this was the only substantial kingdom ruled by Hindu kings who were rich enough to endow Hindu institutions. Something similar but on a smaller scale occurred in the Rajput kingdoms of Mewar and Marwar. But if there had been a real Hindu revival there would certainly have been indisputable signs of this at least in the sphere of religion; and these are conspicuously lacking in the culture of Vijayanagara.

The importance of Vijayanagara in the history of the peninsula lies in the fact that it encouraged the evolution of a pattern which, although of independent origin, was nevertheless broadly in alignment with the pattern of northern India. This did not come about through deliberate design, nor was it purely accidental. Such a development occurred because a similar feudal pattern emerged both in the north and in the south.

The emergence of regional cultures within a common framework of similar institutions resulted in the growth of local loyalties and divisions; nevertheless, there was a common unifying bond in the general similarity of the various cultures. Those who spoke Bengali could not understand those whose language was Kannada, but the underlying circumstances which had led to these separate vernacular languages were everywhere quite similar. Moreover, on the religious side the *Bhakti* cult had released the same sorts of forces in both the north and the south, even though in its aspect of social protest the *Bhakti* movement was earlier exhausted in the south. The teachings of reformers such as Shankara and Ramanuja had in one sense unified the whole of India through the general diffusion of common beliefs. To the pious Hindu the seven sacred sites of pilgrimage included Badrinath in the Himalayas and Rameshvaram in the far south. Coastal trade encouraged the mobility of traders, so that Gujarati merchants were not debarred from entering into competition with those of Malabar. Despite local diversity there was now a certain sense of similarity throughout the sub-continent, an atmosphere ripe for the establishment of an all-inclusive state.

The sixteenth century brought two new factors into Indian history – the Mughuls who came by land and began by establishing themselves in the north, and the Portuguese who came by sea to establish themselves in the south and the west. Both these new factors were to shape the course of Indian history – the Portuguese by striving to win a monopoly of the overseas trade of India, the Mughuls by founding an empire. Though the Portuguese failed the Mughuls succeeded, and between them they carried India into a new age.

CHRONOLOGICAL TABLE

ONE of the problems in ascertaining the chronology of events in ancient India is the uncertainty of accurately dating the various eras which were in use. Most of the important dynasties of the early period used their own system of reckoning, which resulted in a number of unconnected eras. Among these perhaps the most familiar are the Vikrama Ere (58–7 B.C.), the Shaka Era (A.D. 78), and the Gupta Era (A.D. 319–20). Knowledge of these eras is based on epigraphical and literary evidence. Buddhist sources generally reckon from the year of the death of the Buddha, but unfortunately there are three alternative dates for this event – 544 B.C., 486 B.C., and 483 B.C. Although it is more usual to use either of the two latter dates there is nevertheless a discrepancy of three years. The accounts of foreign travellers are sometimes of assistance in calculating eras, as they provide a means of cross-evidence in dating. The confusion of eras became worse after the tenth century A.D., when the various regional kingdoms adopted their own eras. However, the Turks and their successors from the thirteenth century onwards uniformly used the Islamic system of dating in the Hijri Era of A.D. 622.

B.C.

c. 2500	The Harappan Culture
c. 1500	The Migration of the 'Aryans' to India
c. 800	The use of iron. The spread of Aryan culture
c. 600	The rise of Magadha
c. 519	Cyrus, the Achaemenid emperor of Persia conquers parts of north-western India
493	Accession of Ajatashatru, king of Magadha
486	Death of the Buddha
c. 468	Death of Mahavira, the founder of Jainism
413	Shishunaga Dynasty
362–21	Nanda Dynasty
327–5	Alexander of Macedon in India
321	Accession of Chandragupta, the founder of the Mauryan dynasty
c. 315	Visit of Megasthenes to India

268–31	Reign of Ashoka
c. 250	Third Buddhist Council held at Pataliputra
185	Decline of the Mauryas. Accession of a Shunga king in Magadha
180–65	Demetrius II, Indo-Greek king of the north-west
155–30	Menander, Indo-Greek king of the north-west
128–10	Rise of Satavahana power under Satakarni
c. 80	Maues, first Shaka king in western India
c. 50	Kharavela, king of Kalinga

A.D.

c. 50 B.C.– A.D. 100	Roman trade with south India
c. 50	Mission of St Thomas to India?
c. 78	Accession of Kanishka, Kushana king of the north-west
150	Rudradaman, the Shaka king ruling in western India
86–114	Gautamiputra ruling the Satavahana kingdom
114–21	Vasishthiputra ruling the Satavahana kingdom
319–20	Accession of Chandra Gupta I, and establishment of the Gupta dynasty
335	Accession of Samudra Gupta
375–415	Chandra Gupta II
405–11	Visit of Fa-Hsien
476	Birth of Aryabhata, the astronomer
505	Birth of Varahamihira, the astronomer
c. 500	Hun control over north-western India
606–47	Harsha-vardhana, king of Kanauj
630–44	Hsuan Tsang in India
600–30	Establishment of Pallava power under Mahendra-varman I
608–42	Establishment of Chalukya power under Pulakeshin II
c. 620	Defeat of Harsha by Pulakeshin II
642	Defeat of Pulakeshin II by Narasimha-varman the Pallava king
712	Arab conquest of Sind
736	Founding of Dhillika (the first city of Delhi)
740	Defeat of the Pallavas by the Chalukyas

c. 750	Pala dynasty founded by Gopala in eastern India
c. 757	Defeat of Chalukyas by Rashtrakutas
c. 800	Shankaracharya, the philosopher
814–80	Reign of Amoghavarsha the Rastrakuta king
c. 840	Rise of the Pratiharas under king Bhoja
c. 907	Parantaka I establishes Chola power in south India
985–1014	Rajaraja I extends Chola power
997–1030	Raids of Mahmud of Ghazni in north-western India
1023	Northern campaign of Rajendra Chola
1030	Alberuni in India
c. 1050	Ramanuja, the philosopher
1077	Embassy of Chola merchants to China
1110	Rise of Vishnu-vardhana and Hoysala power
1192	Prithviraja Chauhan defeated by Muhammad Ghuri at the battle of Tarain
1206	Establishment of the Slave Dynasty under Qutb-ud-din Aibak
1211–27	Reign of Iltutmish
1265	Reign of Balban
1288, 93	Marco Polo's visits to south India
1296–1316	Reign of Ala-ud-din Khalji
1302–11	Malik Kafur's campaigns in south India
1325–51	Reign of Muhammad bin Tughluq
	Ibn Batutah in India
1336	Founding of the kingdom of Vijayanagara
1345	Founding of the Bahmani kingdom
1357	Firuz Shah Tughluq in power
1414–50	Rule of the Sayyids at Delhi
1411–41	Ahmad Shah ruling in Gujarat
1421, 31	Cheng-ho's visits to Bengal
1451	Accession of Buhlul Lodi at Delhi
1440–1518	Kabir, a leader of the *Bhakti* movement
1469–1539	Nanak, a leader of the *Bhakti* movement
1485–1533	Chaitanya, a leader of the *Bhakti* movement
1481	Assassination of Mahmud Gavan
1498	Arrival of the Portuguese in India
1509	Rana Sanga of Mewar in power
1509–30	Krishna Deva Raya, king of Vijayanagar
1526	The First Battle of Panipat

GLOSSARY

Spelling. Diacritical marks in the transliteration of Indian words have not been used in this book. For those who are unfamiliar with these marks it is difficult to become accustomed quickly to their use. Furthermore, the Indian words referred to derive from Sanskrit, Tamil, Arabic, or Persian roots. Each of these languages has its own system of transliteration and to use each of these systems would create unnecessary complications for the reader. Consequently, the standard form of transliteration has been adopted.

Pronunciation. The pronunciation of the words listed below is comparatively simple if each word is split into its syllables and then pronounced.

acharya teacher

Advaita ('without a second') a philosophical system of monism

agrahara royal donation of land or village to brahmans

Agnikula the family of Agni (fire) from which certain Rajput clans claim descent

ahimsa non-violence

Ajivika a heterodox sect of the Buddha's time

Alvar Vaishnavite hymnodists of the Tamil devotional cult

amatya official designation for civil governor frequently used in the Gupta period

Aranyakas Vedic texts, traditionally composed by forest hermits

artha prosperity and well-being, one of the four aims of Hindu life

Arthashastra the theory of political economy; also the title of a book on this subject by Kautalya

ashrama refuge, also the four stages of life

ashvamedha horse-sacrifice

ayukta official designation, frequently used in the Mauryan period

banjaras tribe of caravan-traders

banya a trading community

Bhagavata a cult of devotion to Vishnu

bhakti devotion

Bharata Natyam a classical dance form named after Bharata, the author of a treatise on dance, the *Natya-shastra*

bharateshvara lord of Bharat

bhogta one who enjoys, and therefore a term used for those who enjoyed revenue rights over certain lands

bhukti an administrative unit of a kingdom

bodhisattva one who works for the welfare of the world and voluntarily postpones release from rebirth; also regarded as an incarnation of the Buddha, prior to his own birth in the world

Brahman the first in rank among the four castes of Hindu society

brahmacharin celibate studentship, the first of the four stages of life

brahmadeya revenue from a villager or land donated to a brahman

Brahmanas Vedic texts dealing with ritual and sacrifice

Brahmi the earliest known and deciphered script of India

chaitya a sacred enclosure. The term was later used for Buddhist places of worship

chakravartigal ⎫
chakravartin ⎭ emperor or universal monarch

chandala a group from amongst the out-caste section of society

Chandravamshi belonging to the Lunar race of royalty

Charvaka a heterodox sect of the Buddha's time, following a materialist philosophy

chattaka a unit of weight

chaudhuri a village officer

chetti ⎫
chettiyar ⎭ merchants

Daivaputra son of Heaven, or of the gods

danda the force of punishment

dasa slave

desha territory, or administrative unit

devadana revenue donated to a temple

devadasi slave-girl of the gods, used with reference to the women dedicated to a temple

devanagari 'city of the gods', the script in which modern Sanskrit and certain other Indian languages are written

Digambara a Jaina sect

Dharma Piety, Morality, or the religious and social order

Glossary

Dharmashastras texts on laws relating to society and religious observances of the Hindus

doab the area between two rivers

dvija the twice-born; referring to the three upper castes of Hindu society – brahman, *kshatriya*, and *vaishya* – where the first birth is the physical birth and the second the initiation into caste status

eripatti special land, the revenue of which is kept aside for maintaining irrigation tanks in south India

faqir a religious mendicant

garbha-griha 'womb-house', the *sanctum sanctorum* of the Hindu temple

gayatri the holiest of the verses of the *Rig-Veda*

ghatika a college for higher studies, generally in Sanskrit

ghi clarified butter

grama village

guru a teacher or spiritual guide

Hinayana one of the two major Buddhist sects

imam the person who leads the prayer in the mosque

iqta the grant of revenue from land or from a village

Jana people, subjects

jati sub-caste

jaziyah a tax paid by non-Muslim subjects of a Muslim ruler

jital a unit of measure

kahapana (*karshapana*) a coin either in gold, silver, or copper. The silver coin of 57·8 grains was commonly used

kakini copper coin of 2·25 grains

kalpa a day of Brahma equivalent to 4,320 million earth years

kaliyuga the fourth and final age of the aeon

Kalamukha a Shaivite sect

kama desire

Kapalika a Shaivite sect

karkhanah workshop

karma action or deed, and also the theory of conditioning one's future births by the deeds of the present or previous lives

kayastha a sub-caste of medieval origin

khalsah ('pure') in revenue terms it refers to crown lands

kharoshthi a script used in north-western India, deriving from Aramaic *khatri* a sub-caste of medieval origin

kottom an administrative unit

kula family

kumaramatya an official designation

kurram an administrative unit

kshatriya the second in rank among the four castes of Hindu society

lingam the phallic symbol worshipped largely by Shaivites

madhu ('sweet'), also the name of a type of mead

madrasah school attached to a mosque

Mahabharata one of the two major epic poems of ancient India

mahakshatrapa 'great governor', a title taken by rulers of the north-west in the early centuries A.D.

maharajadhiraja 'great king of kings', an imperial title

mahasammata 'the great elect', referring to the person elected as ruler on the basis of the Buddhist theory of social contract as the origin of government

mahasamanta the great vassal

mahasenapati commander-in-chief

Mahayana one of the two major sects of Buddhism

man a unit of weight

mandala theory of inter-state alliances where one neighbour is a natural enemy and the other a natural friend

mandalam an administrative unit

manigramam a guild of merchants

mantra charm or spell or a verse with religious connotations

matha a centre of education and hospice attached to a temple

matsyanyaya a political theory where in a state of anarchy the strong devour the weak

maya illusion

Mimamsa one of the six major philosophical schools of ancient Indian philosophy

mlechchha 'impure' or sullied

mohurs coins current at the time of the Sultanate

moksha salvation, one of the four aims of Hindu life

muezzin the person who calls the Muslims to prayer five times a day from the mosque

munsif an official designation of the Sultanate

muqti the recipient of a grant of revenue or a provincial governor *nadu* an administrative unit

nataka dance or drama

nagara style in architecture developed in central and northern India

nagaram local councils in urban areas

Nanadeshi a powerful merchant guild

Nayanars Shaivite hymnodists of the Tamil devotional cult

Nirvana release from rebirth

nishka a unit of value in the early period, later the term was used for a coin

Nyaya one of the six major philosophical schools of ancient India

Pali a Sanskrit-based language in which the Buddhist scriptures were recorded in Ceylon

pan betel-leaf

pana a coin sometimes identified with the *karshapana*

panchayat a council of five

panchkula the representative of five families

pardah ('curtain') used by extension to mean the seclusion of women

parganah an administrative unit

Pashupata a Shaivite sect

patwari a village official

pipal the ficus-religiosa tree

pir a person imbued with religious powers of a certain kind and associated with thinking similar to that of the *sufis*

pradesha an administrative unit

Puranas texts sacred to Hinduism composed in the first millennium A.D. and containing traditional material referring back to an earlier period

purohita chief priest

qazi Muslim legal expert

Quran the sacred book of the Muslims

raja-guru royal priest

rajasuya special sacrifice performed by the king

rajuka an official designation used in the Mauryan period

Ramayana one of the two major epic poems of ancient India

ranaka a feudal lord

rasa emotion

rashtra country, or an administrative unit

ratnin 'jewel', one of the twelve persons given a special place at a particular royal ceremony

sabha an assembly

samanta vassal

samiti an assembly

Sangha the Buddhist Order

Sankhya one of the six major schools of philosophy in ancient India

sanyasi ascetic

sati a virtuous woman; one who has immolated herself on the funeral pyre of her husband

seer a unit of weight and quantity

senapati commander of the forces

serai inn

seth merchant or trader

shaikh a Muslim of high social status or a religious guide

shakti power

Shangam the literature of the early Tamils

Sharia the legal code of Islam

shatamana a coin series, the silver issue of which weighed 180 grains

shikhara tower surmounting the temple

shreni guild

shudra the last of the four main caste divisions

shunyata non-reality; void

Shvetambara a Jaina sect

soma the plant from which the intoxicant *soma* juice was prepared, to be used in Vedic ritual

stupa a tumulus-like structure containing relics of the Buddha or others revered by Buddhists

Suryavamshi kings of the solar dynasty

suvarna ('of an excellent colour') gold

svayamavara ('self-choosing') the ceremony by which a princess would choose her husband from among an assembly of suitors

tanka a coin used in the Sultanate period

taniyur an administrative unit

Tantric a religious cult

thakura a feudal lord

Theravada a Buddhist sect

ulema Muslim theologians

Upanishads philosophical and mystical texts included in Vedic literature

ur village assembly

vaishya the third of the four castes of Hindu society

valanadu administrative unit

varna ('colour') used more commonly for caste

Vedanta one of the six major philosophical schools in ancient India

vihara Buddhist monastery

vina stringed instrument

wazir minister

Yavana used in Indian sources for the people of western Asia

Yoga one of the six major schools of philosophy in ancient India

yuga an age of the world

zenana section of the house reserved for women

REFERENCES TO QUOTATIONS

CHAPTER 1

1. V. Smith, *Early History of India* (1924), p. 442.

CHAPTER 2

1. *Rig-Veda*, x, 90, transl. A. L. Basham, *The Wonder That Was India*, pp. 240–41.
2. *Rig-Veda*, x, 129, transl. A. L. Basham, *The Wonder That Was India*, pp. 247–8.
3. *Chhandogya Upanishad,* vi, 13, transl. A. L. Basham, *The Wonder That Was India*, pp. 250–51.

CHAPTER 3

1. Ktesias, quoted in Pausanius, ix, 21, transl. J. W. McCrindle, *Ancient India as Described in Classical Literature*, Westminster, 1901.
2. Nearchus, quoted in Arrian, *Indica,* xvi, transl. J. W. McCrindle, *Ancient India as Described by Megasthenes and Arrian*, London, 1877.
3. Strabo, *Geography*, transl. H. L. Jones, *The Geography of Strabo*, Harvard.
4. *Dighanikaya*, i, 55, transl. A. L. Basham, *The Wonder That Was India*, p. 296.

CHAPTER 4

1. Rock Edict xiii, transl. R. Thapar, *Aśoka and the Decline of the Mauryas*, p. 255. Ibid.
2. Naqshi-i-Rustam Inscription, transl. R. Ghirshman, *Iran*, p. 153.
3. Rock Edict iii, transl. R. Thapar, *Aśoka and the Decline of the Mauryas*, p. 251.
4. Quoted – Diodorus, ii, 41, transl. J. W. McCrindle, *Ancient India as described in Classical Literature*. Westminster, 1901.
5. Rock Edict xii, transl. R. Thapar, *Aśoka and the Decline of the Mauryas*, p. 255.

6. Pillar Edict VII, transl. R. Thapar, *Aśoka and the Decline of the Mauryas*, p. 265.

CHAPTER 5

1. Junagadh Rock Inscription of Rudradaman, *Epigraphia Indica*, VIII, pp. 36 ff.

CHAPTER 6

1. Nasik Cave Inscription No. 10, *Epigraphia Indica*, VIII, pp. 78 ff.

CHAPTER 7

1. Bana, *Harshacharita*, transl. *Cowell*, p. 101.

CHAPTER 8

1. Kasakudi Plate of Nandivarman, *South Indian Inscriptions*, II, 3, p. 360.
2. Pattuppattu, Tirumunganarrupadai, 285–90, transl. A. L. Basham, *The Wonder That Was India*, p. 330.
3. Kingsbury and Phillips, *Hymns of the Tamil Saints*, pp. 89, 127.
4. Ibid., p. 54.

CHAPTER 9

1. Uttaramerur Inscription, *Archaeological Survey of India Report* (1904–5), pp. 138 ff.
2. K. A. Nilakantha Sastri, *The Colas*, p. 577.
3. Marco Polo, *Travels*, p. 237 (Pelican Edition).
4. Basavaraja, transl. *Sources of Indian Tradition* (ed. Th. de Bary), p. 357.

CHAPTER 10

1. Al Kazwini, transl. Eliot and Dowson, *The History of India as Told by its Own Historians*, Vol. I, p. 97.
2. Alberuni, *Tahqiq-i-Hind*, transl. Sachau, *Alberuni*.

CHAPTER 12

1. Eliot and Dowson, *The History of India as Told by its Own Historians*, Vol. I, p. 332.
2. Ibid, p. 185.

CHAPTER 13

1. *Cultural Heritage of India,* vol. II, p. 249.
2. R. Tagore (transl.), *Songs of Kabir*, pp. 45, 112.
3. M. A. Macauliffe, *The Sikh Religion*, I, pp. 195–6.

CHAPTER 14

1. *Fernão Nuniz*, transl. Sewell, *A Forgotten Empire*, pp. 373–4
2. Ibid.
3. *Amuktamalyada*, IV, V, 245–58.

References & Quotations

CHAPTER 13
1. Cultural Heritage of India—vol. II, p. 290.
2. R. Tagore (transl.) Song of Kabir, pp. ...
3. M. A. Macauliffe, The Sikh Religion, II, pp. 105 ff.

CHAPTER 14
1. Fernão Nunes, transl. Sewell, A Forgotten Empire, pp. ...
2. Dorasampudi, IV, v. 24–25.

GENERAL BIBLIOGRAPHY

V. Smith, *Oxford History of India* (Oxford, 1958).

A. L. Basham, *The Wonder That Was India* (London, 1954).

D. D. Kosambi, *The Culture and Civilisation of Ancient India in Historical Outline* (London, 1965).

Th. de Bary ed., *Sources of Indian Tradition* (New York, 1958).

A. B. M. Habibullah, *Foundation of Muslim Rule in India* (Lahore, 1945).

P. V. Kane, *History of the Dharmashastra* (Poona, 1930–46).

K. M. Ashraf, *Life and Condition of the People of Hindustan* (Delhi).

J. N. Farquhar, *Outline of the Religious Literature of India* (Oxford, 1920).

Tarachand, *Influence of Islam on Indian Culture* (1954).

J. E. Charpentier, *Theism in Medieval India* (1919).

A. Bose, *Social and Rural Economy of Northern India* (Calcutta, 1961).

U. N. Ghoshal, *The Agrarian System in Ancient India* (Calcutta, 1930).

T. Moreland, *Agrarian System of Muslim India* (Cambridge, 1929).

K. A. Nilakantha Sastri, *A History of South India* (London, 1958).

A. Cunningham, *The Ancient Geography of India* (Calcutta, 1924).

J. Filliozat, *La Doctrine Classique de la Médicine Indienne* (Paris, 1949).

A. Cunningham, *A Book of Indian Eras* (Calcutta, 1883).

A. K. Coomaraswami, *History of Indian and Indonesian Art* (London, 1927).

B. Rowland, *The Art and Architecture of India* (London, 1953).

G. T. Garratt ed., *The Legacy of India* (Oxford, 1937).

K. M. Pannikar, *Geographical Factors in Indian History* (Bombay, 1959).

BIBLIOGRAPHICAL NOTE ON SOURCES

THE sources mentioned in this section refer to works revelant to the ideas discussed in the various chapters of this book. Where possible, English translations of source material are referred to. A list of the more important journals and periodicals is added at the end of this section.

CHAPTER I

James Mill, *The History of British India* (London, 1826), reflects the attitudes of those Europeans who measured India by standards they were familiar with, and found it lacking. Max Müller, *Collected Works* (1903), presents the other viewpoint of enthusiastic support for things Indian. V. Smith, *The Oxford History of India* (1st ed., 1919), and *Early History of India* (1924), are administrator's histories. K. P. Jayaswal, *Hindu Polity* (Calcutta, 1924), is a consciously nationalistic interpretation of the past. The Hindu–Muslim–British periodization of Indian history is followed in most standard textbooks such as that of Smith mentioned above, or the more frequently used work of R. C. Majumdar, H. C. Raychaudhuri, and K. K. Datta, *An Advanced History of India* (London, 1961).

An example of the application of the principles of sociological analysis to Indian sources can be seen in Max Weber, *The Religion of India* (Glencoe, 1958). Not all of Weber's analyses are acceptable in their entirety, but at least an attempt is made at relating religion to society and to the people who practised it. This in itself raises a number of fundamental and worthwhile questions.

A useful book on the discovery of India's ancient past through a variety of sources is J. Cumming (ed.), *Revealing India's Past* (London, 1939). Much of it deals with early archaeological work. A number of books have been written in recent years on the pre-history and proto-history of the Indian sub-continent. Among them may be mentioned B. Subbarao, *The Personality of India* (Baroda, 1958), R. E. M. Wheeler, *Early India and Pakistan* (London, 1958), S. Piggott, *Prehistoric India* (Harmondsworth,

1962), and H. D. Sankalia, *The Prehistory and Protohistory of India and Pakistan* (Bombay, 1963). The most up-to-date information on excavations is available in two periodicals published by the Archaeological Survey of India – *Ancient India* and *Indian Archaeology, a Review*; and also in monographs published by various University Departments of History and Archaeology and by the Deccan College, Poona. On the Harappa culture, Sir John Marshall's report on the earlier excavations, *Mohenjo-daro and the Indus Civilisation* (London, 1931), provides factual and detailed information, but a more recent report is that of R. E. M. Wheeler, *The Indus Civilisation* (Cambridge, 1953). B. S. Guha, *An Outline of the Racial Ethnology of India* (Calcutta, 1937), is a standard study of the subject.

CHAPTER 2

Among the early researchers of comparative philology was Sir William Jones, who worked in the last quarter of the eighteenth century. His own work and that of others is incorporated in *Asiatic Researches*, the journal of the Asiatic Society of Bengal which Jones founded in 1784.

Evidence on Aryan culture comes from a variety of literatures included under the general title of Vedic Literature. Of these the ones most relevant as historical source material are, *The Hymns of the Rig-Veda*, transl. R. T. H. Griffiths (Banaras, 1896–7), *Aitareya Brahmana*, transl. A. B. Keith (HOS xxv, Cambridge, Mass., 1920), *Shatapatha Brahmana*, transl. J. Eggeling (Oxford, 1882–1900), *Taittiriya Brahmana*, ed. R. Mitra (Calcutta, 1855–70), *Thirteen Principal Upanishads*, transl. F. Max Müller (Oxford, 1921). *The Griha-sutras*, transl. H. Oldenberg (Oxford), *The Dharma-sutras*, transl. G. Buehler (Oxford).

Gordon Childe has worked on the archaeological material pertaining to the Indo-European homeland and the diffusion of the tribes associated with Aryan culture in *The Aryans* (London, 1926) and *New Light on the Most Ancient East* (London, 1952). Relevant chapters in the *Cambridge History of India*, Vol. I (1922), are useful descriptions of Aryan culture. Attempts at reconstructing the political history of this period are made in H. C. Raychaudhuri, *The Political History of Ancient India*

Bibliography

(Calcutta, 1953), and *History and Culture of the Indian People*, Vol. I *The Vedic Age* (Bombay, 1951). A. A. Macdonnell, *Vedic Mythology* (Strassbourg, 1897) and A. B. Keith, *Religion and Philosophy of the Vedas and Upanishads* (Cambridge, Mass., 1925), are detailed studies on Aryan mythology and religion. C. Drekmeier, *Kingship and Community in Early India* (Stanford, 1962), has interesting chapters on the political and social role of the sacrifice. The religious aspect is analysed in greater detail in M. Mauss and H. Hubert, *Mélange d'histoire des religions* (Paris, 1929). J. H. Hutton, *Caste in India* (Cambridge, 1946), remains a useful survey of the evolution of caste. I. Karve, *Hindu Society, an Interpretation* (Poona, 1961), incorporates more recent sociological research on the subject of caste.

CHAPTER 3

Sources relating to events which took place during this period range widely in scope. Buddhist and Jaina texts add to the brahmanical sources, and there is further evidence from Greek accounts and from the excavations of various town sites.

Amongst the Buddhist sources are the *Anguttara Nikaya* (London, 1932–6), *Dhammapada*, transl. Max Müller (Oxford, 1898), *Digha Nikaya*, transl. T. W. Rhys Davids (London, 1899), *Jataka*, ed. E. B. Cowell (Cambridge, 1893–1913), and *Vinaya Pitaka*, transl. H. Oldenberg and T. W. Rhys Davids (Oxford, 1881–5). Jaina texts include *Parishishtaparavan*, *Uvasagadasao*, *Kalpasutra*, and *Acharanga*, relevant sections of which have been translated by H. Jacobi in *Jaina Sutras* (Oxford, 1884–95).

Some of the *Puranas*, although written later, refer back to this period. Of these the *Vishnu Purana*, transl. H. H. Wilson (London, 1864–70) and the *Bhagavata Purana*, transl. E. Bournouf (Paris, 1840–98), are useful. The grammatical work of Panini, *Ashtadhyayi*, provides incidental references. Greek accounts both of visitors and others have been collated and translated by J. W. McCrindle in a series of books – *Ancient India as Described by Ktesias the Knidian* (Calcutta, 1882), *Ancient India as Described in Classical Literature* (Westminster, 1901), and *The Invasion of India by Alexander the Great* (Westminster,

1896). In addition, Herodotus's *History* (Oxford, 1913–14) has references to north-western India.

Excavation reports include J. Marshall, *Taxila* (Cambridge, 1951), A. Ghosh, *Rajagriha*, G. R. Sharma, *Kaushambi* (Allahabad, 1960). B. C. Law, *Geography of Early Buddhism* (London, 1932), is useful in this connexion.

B. C. Law, *Some Kshatriya Tribes in Ancient India* (Calcutta, 1924), describes the republican states. H. C. Raychaudhuri, *Political History of Ancient India* (Calcutta, 1953), discusses the political history of the period. Y. Mishra, *An Early History of Vaishali* (Delhi, 1962), is a more detailed work on one region. T. W. Rhys Davids, *Buddhist India* (London, 1903) and R. Fick, *Social Organisation of North-eastern India in the Buddha's Time* (Calcutta, 1920), contain data on society and economics of this time. D. Chanana, *Slavery in Ancient India* (Delhi, 1960) and R. S. Sharma, *Shudras in Ancient India* (Delhi, 1958), are both more recent contributions to social history in ancient India and refer to this period as well. E. Conze, *Buddhism, its Essence and Development*, is a good introduction to Buddhism, and E. J. Thomas, *Early Buddhist Scriptures* (London, 1935), provides a selection of translated Buddhist texts. One of the best summaries of Jaina teaching is contained in S. Stevenson, *The Heart of Jainism* (Oxford, 1915).

Alexander's campaign is narrated at length in V. Smith, *Early History of India* (Oxford, 1924). A standard biography is that of W. W. Tarn, *Alexander the Great* (Cambridge, 1950).

CHAPTER 4

Moving into the historical period it is possible to compare the traditional sources with other types of historical source material, e.g. inscriptional material. The former are collated in F. E. Pargiter, *Dynasties of the Kali Age . . .* (London, 1913). The major epigraphical evidence is the corpus of Ashokan inscriptions which has been edited and translated by E. Hultzsch in *Corpus Inscriptionum Indicarum*, Vol. I (London, 1925). Recently discovered inscriptions both in Brahmi and Greek have been published in various learned journals.

Kautalya's *Arthashastra* has been edited by T. Ganapati Sastri and translated by R. Shamasastri (Mysore, 1958). Vishakhadatta's play, *Mudrarakshasa*, has been edited by K. H. Dhruva (Poona, 1923).

Buddhist sources on the Mauryan period are contained in the *Dipavamsa*, ed. Oldenberg (London, 1879), *Mahavamsa*, ed. Geiger (London, 1908), *Divyavadana*, ed. Cowell and Neil (Cambridge, 1886), and J. Przyluski, *La Légende de l'Empereur Açoka* (Paris, 1923), which is a collation of the stories on Ashoka from the Northern Buddhist tradition and Chinese sources.

Megasthenes' *Indica* has been translated by J. W. McCrindle in *Ancient India as Described by Megasthenes and Arrian* (Calcutta, 1877).

Excavations of urban centres at Mauryan levels are described in reports on these sites in *Ancient India*, e.g. reports on Hastinapur and Shishupalgarh, etc. For monographs on the Mauryas see V. Smith, *Asoka* (Oxford, 1903), K. A. Nilakantha Sastri, *The Age of the Nandas and Mauryas* (Banaras, 1952), R. Thapar, *Aśoka and the Decline of the Mauryas* (Oxford, 1961), and the *History and Culture of the Indian People*, Vol. II, *The Age of Imperial Unity* (Bombay, 1951).

CHAPTER 5

Information on the Shungas is available from the Puranic king-lists compiled by Pargiter in *Dynasties of the Kali Age* and in Kalidasa's play *Malvikagnimitram*. A summary is available in Raychaudhuri's *Political History of Ancient India* (Calcutta, 1953). The Hathigumpha inscription of Kharavela has been published in R. Mitra, *Antiquities of Orissa*, Vol. II (1880).

The history of the Indo-Greeks is based largely on numismatic and epigraphical evidence. For the former see A. Cunningham, *Coins of Alexander's Successors in the East. . .* , R. B. White-head, *Catalogue of Coins in the Punjab Museum*, Lahore, Vol. I. (Oxford, 1914), V. Smith, *Catalogue of Coins in the Indian Museum Calcutta*, Part I (Oxford, 1906), J. Allan, *Catalogue of Coins in the British Museum, Ancient India* (London, 1936), P. Gardner, *Catalogue of Coins in the British Museum, Greek and Scythic Kings* (London, 1886). The most up-to-date study of this material is that of A. K. Narain, *The Indo-Greeks* (London, 1957), though there is an earlier study by W. W. Tarn, *The Greeks in Bactria and India* (Cambridge, 1951). Inscriptional evidence referring to this period is available in S. Konow, *Corpus Inscriptionum Indicarum*, Vol. II (Oxford, 1929). The *Milinda-panho* has been translated as *The Questions of King Malinda* (Oxford, 1890–94). Sources relating to the Scythians are discussed in J. E. van Lohuizen de Leeuw, *The 'Scythian' Period* . . . (Leiden, 1949). R. Ghirshman, *Bégram* (Cairo, 1946), is useful on the Kushanas.

The more important inscriptions of the Satavahana period have been published in *Epigraphia Indica*, particularly Vols. VII and VIII. There is an index to these and other relevant inscriptions in *Epigraphia Indica*, Vol. X. E. J. Rapson has collected the numismatic evidence in *Catalogue of Coins in the British Museum, Andhras and Western Kshatraps* (London, 1908). The chapter on the Satavahanas in G. Yazdani ed., *The Early History of the Deccan*, and D. Barratt, *Sculpture from Amaravati in the British Museum* (London, 1954), contain recent material on Satavahana history and chronology.

The standard English rendering of the Tamil *Shangam* litera-ture is that of J. V. Chelliah, *Ten Tamil Idylls* (Colombo, 1947). Studies on the south during this period include those of P. T. S. Aiyangar, *History of the Tamils to 600 A.D.* (Madras, 1929) and K. N. Shivaraja Pillai, *Chronology of the Early Tamils* (Madras, 1932).

References to routes can be gathered from a variety of sources such as the *Jatakas*, Pliny's *Natural History*, and Ptolemy's *Geo-graphy*, and these are discussed by W. W. Tarn in *Hellenistic Civilisation* (London, 1930). Indian contacts with central Asia and China have been discussed by P. C. Bagchi, *India and China* (Calcutta, 1944), and N. P. Chakravarti, *India and Central Asia* (Calcutta, 1927), as also in Aurel Stein, *Ancient Khotan* (Oxford, 1907) and *Serindia* (Oxford, 1921).

CHAPTER 6

Information on the guilds during this period has to be collated from a number of sources. Among them are the Buddhist and Jaina sources mentioned earlier, which provide incidental refer-ences and descriptions, inscriptions referring to guilds such as the Satavahana Nasik inscriptions, and references to guilds and their functioning in *Dharmashastras* or Law Books. Of the latter the best known are the *Manusmriti*, translated by G. Buehler, *The Laws of Manu* (Oxford, 1886), and that of Vishnu, translated by J. Jolly, *The Institutes of Vishnu* (Oxford, 1880).

The excavation report on Arikamedu written by Wheeler, Krishna Deva, and Ghosh has been published in *Ancient India*, 2, 1946. Kaverippattinam has also been excavated but the report has yet to be published. The Roman trade has been discussed by R. E. M. Wheeler in *Rome Beyond the Imperial Frontier* and by E. H. Warmington in *Commerce between the Roman Empire and India* (Cambridge, 1928). J. W. McCrindle has translated sections of Ptolemy's work referring to India in *Ancient India as Described by Ptolemy* (Calcutta, 1927), and W. H. Schoff has a translation of the *Periplus of the Erythreaen Sea* (London, 1912). R. K. Mookerjee, *History of Indian Shipping* (London, 1912), is the sole monograph on the subject but lacks technical accuracy.

J. Marshall, *Gandhara Art*, is an adequate survey of this school of art. The development of Buddhist architectural styles is discussed in P. Brown, *Indian Architecture* (Buddhist and Hindu) (Bombay, 1949). Selections and translation of Mahayana Buddhist texts are available in *Buddhist Mahayana Sutras* (Oxford, 1894). Apart from Conze's book on Buddhism, a useful companion is T. W. Rhys Davids, *Buddhism, its History and Literature* (London, 1923). The history of the Jaina sect is described in the chapter on Jainism in the *Cambridge History of India*, Vol. I. H. C. Raychaudhuri, *Early History of the Vaishnava Sect* (Calcutta, 1926) and S. Radhakrishnan transl. *Bhagavat Gita* (London), indicate changes in Vaishnavism. The legend of Thomas's mission in India is discussed in A. E. Medlycott, *India and the Apostle Thomas* (London, 1905).

CHAPTER 7

The inscriptions pertaining to the Gupta period have been edited and translated by J. Fleet in *Corpus Inscriptionum Indicarum*, Vol. III (Calcutta, 1888). Evidence from coins can be studied in J. Allan, *Catalogue of the Coins of the Gupta Dynasty in the British Museum* (London, 1914); and A. S. Altekar, *Catalogue of the Gupta Gold Coins in the Bayana Hoard* (Bombay, 1954). Fa Hsien's account of his travels in India has been translated by H. A. Giles, *The Travels of Fa-hien* (Cambridge, 1923).

Bibliography

Literary works include Vishakhadatta's *Devichandraguptam*, the works of Kalidasa – *Abhijnyan Shakuntalam*, transl. W. Jones (London, 1790), *Kumarasambhava*, transl. R. T. H. Griffiths (London, 1789), *Meghadutam*, transl. C. King (London, 1930) – and others which have been discussed in A. B. Keith, *History of Sanskrit Literature* (Oxford, 1920). Vatsyayana's *Kamasutra*, transl. B. N. Basu (Calcutta, 1944), is an additional source. Other literature includes *Kamandaka Nitisara*, ed. T. Ganapati Shastri (Trivandrum, 1912), *Vishnu Purana*, transl. H. H. Wilson (London, 1864–70), and a series of *Dharmashastras* or Law Books available mainly in two translations – G. Buehler, *Sacred Laws of the Aryas* (Oxford, 1879–82), and J. Jolly, *The Minor Law Books* (Oxford, 1889).

The reign of Harsha is documented by Bana, *Harshacharita* (London, 1897), Hsuan Tsang's description of his visit to India, *On Yuan Chwang's Travels in India*, ed. Watters (London, 1904–5), S. Beal, *Life of Hiuen Tsiang by the Shaman Hwui Li* (London, 1911), and S. Beal, *Si Yu Ki, Buddhist Records of the Western World* (London, 1883). R. K. Mookerji's *Harsha* (London, 1926), though somewhat out-of-date, is the only monograph so far on the subject.

The political history of the post-Gupta dynasties can be reconstructed on the basis of epigraphical and numismatic sources (apart from literary evidence listed above), which have not however been collated into a single monograph. A list of such sources can be consulted in *History and Culture of the Indian People*, Vol. III, *The Classical Age* (Bombay, 1954), pp. 678–84. Two standard monographs on this period are R. C. Majumdar, *The Gupta-Vakataka Age* (Lahore, 1946), and B. P. Sinha, *The Decline of the Kingdom of Magadha* (Patna, 1954). F. A. von Schiefer has translated a history of Buddhism in India written by a Tibetan monk Taranatha, *Geschichte des Buddhismus in Indien* (St Petersburg, 1869), which throws light on certain events of Indian history. Excavation reports of Gupta levels at various sites are available in *Ancient India*.

Information on administration and the agrarian system can be collected from the inscriptions and the law books. U. N. Ghoshal, *The Agrarian System in Ancient India* (Calcutta, 1930), has attempted to systematize the material. A useful summary of early

Indian political thought is available in J. Spellman, *Political Theory of Ancient India* (Oxford, 1964). B. Brown, *Indian Architecture – Hindu and Buddhist* (Bombay, 1944), discusses the evolution of temple architecture. R. G. Bhandarkar, *Vaishnavism, Shaivism and the Minor Religious Sects* (Strassbourg, 1913), A. Avalon, *Shakti and Shakta* (Madras, 1929), H. M. Eliot, *Hinduism and Buddhism* (London, 1922), and T. D. Suzuki's translation of the *Lankavatara-sutra* (London, 1932) are all relevant to studying changes in religious belief at this time. S. Radhakrishnan, *Indian Philosophy* (Lohdon, 1923–7), and S. N. Das Gupta, *History of Indian Philosophy* (Cambridge, 1923–49), are both standard works on interpreting Indian philosophy. R. le May, *The Culture of South-east Asia* (London, 1954), C. Coedes, *L'État Hindouisé d'Indochine d'Indonesie* (Paris, 1948), R. C. Majumdar, *Hindu Colonies in the Far East* (Dacca, 1927), and H. G. Quaritch Wales, *The Making of Greater India* (London, 1951), are concerned with the spread of Indian culture in south-east Asia. G. Thibaut, *Indische Astronomie und Mathematik* (Strassbourg, 1899), is a good introduction to the scientific development of this period.

CHAPTER 8

For political and adminstrative history there is a large amount of epigraphical evidence. The more important inscriptions have been edited in a series entitled *South Indian Inscriptions*, and are also referred to in the *Annual Report of Indian Epigraphy*. Of the former relevant editions are those by K. V. S. Aiyer (Madras, 1928, 1933), E. Hultzsch (Madras, 1890–1929), H. K. Shastri (Madras, 1924–6), V. V. Ayyar (Madras, 1943). In addition, R. Sewell and S. K. Aiyangar have edited *Historical Inscriptions of South India* (Madras, 1932).

G. Yazdani ed., *The Early History of the Deccan* (London, 1960), and D. C. Sircar, *Successors of the Satavahanas* (Calcutta, 1939), cover the post-Satavahana period in the Deccan. G. M. Moraes, *The Kadamba Kula* (Bombay, 1931), is the history of a lesser dynasty in the south.

Detailed studies of the history of the Pallavas include R. Gopalan, *History of the Pallavas of Kanchi* (Madras, 1928), A. Jouveau-Dubreuil, *The Pallavas* (Pondicherry, 1917) and *Pallava*

Antiquities (London, 1916), and C. Minakshi, *Administrative and Social Life under the Pallavas* (Madras, 1938).

The hymns of the Tamil saints have been translated by F. Kingsbury and G. E. Philips, *Hymns of the Tamil Shaivite Saints* (Calcutta, 1921), and J. S. M. Hooper, *Hymns of the Alvars* (Calcutta, 1929). Literature of the period after the *Shangam* anthologies but prior to the classical Tamil literature has been translated by G. U. Pope in *Naladiyar* (Oxford, 1893) and *The Sacred Kural* (London, 1888).

The two classics are available in translation, *Manimegalai*, transl. K. A. Aiyangar (London, 1928) and *Shilappadigaram*, transl. V. R. R. Dikshitar, *The Lay of the Anklet* (Oxford, 1939), as also Dandin's *Dashakumaracharita*, transl. A. W. Ryder (Chicago, 1927).

G. Yazdani, *Ajanta* (London, 1930, 33, 46), is an illustrated study of the Ajanta murals. A. H. Longhurst, *Pallava Architecture* (Memoirs of the Archaeological Survey of India, Nos. 17 and 33, 1924, 28), contains useful studies of Pallava architecture, as also the two detailed works on architecture, P. Brown, *Indian Architecture*, and J. Fergussen, *History of Indian and Eastern Architecture* (London, 1910).

CHAPTER 9

Inscriptional material of this period is again scattered in various publications. A representative selection of Chola inscriptions is listed in *History and Culture of the Indian People*, Vol. IV, *The Age of Imperial Kanauj*, pp. 486 ff., and in Vol. V, *The Struggle for Empire,* pp. 819 ff. (Bombay, 1955, 1957). *South Indian Inscriptions, Epigraphia Carnatica* and *Epigraphia Indica* may also be referred to. R. S. Panchmukhi, *Karnataka Inscriptions* (Dharwar, 1941, 51), L. Rice, *Mysore and Coorg from the Inscriptions* (London, 1909), V. Rangacharaya, *Inscriptions of the Madras Presidency* (Madras, 1919), are further selections of relevant material. Inscriptions relating to the Rashtrakutas have been listed in *History and Culture of the Indian People*, Vol. IV, *The Age of Imperial Kanauj*, p. 470.

W. Elliot, *Coins of Southern India* (Strassbourg, 1897), has indicated the more important coins of the south.

Secondary works on this period include A. S. Altekar, *The*

Rashtrakutas and their Times (Poona, 1934), D. Derrett, *The Hoysalas* (Oxford, 1957), T. V. Mahalingam, *South Indian Polity* (Madras, 1955), a comprehensive work on the Chola period by K. A. Nilakantha Shastri, *The Cholas* (Madras, 1955), and, by the same author, *The Pandyan Kingdom* (London, 1928), and *A History of South India* (London, 1958). For the development of Tamil literature in the context of other south Indian languages see M. S. Purnalingam Pillai, *Tamil Literature* (Tinevelly, 1929) and V. R. R. Dikshitar, *Studies in Tamil Literature and History* (London, 1930). On religious movements there are various works such as S. K. Aiyangar, *Some Contributions of South India to Indian Culture* (Calcutta, 1942), C. V. N. Ayyar, *Origin and early History of Shaivism in South India* (Madras, 1936), and K. R. Subramaniam, *Origin of Shaivism and its History in the Tamil Land* (Madras, 1941). *The Travels of Marco Polo*, edited and translated by R. E. Latham (Harmondsworth, 1958), relates to this period.

CHAPTERS 10 AND 11

Inscriptional evidence has again to be collated from a variety of publications. Those relating to Pala history are listed in N. G. Majumdar, *Inscriptions of Bengal*, Vols. I–III, and *History and Culture of the Indian People*, Vol. IV, p. 473, and those relating to Orissa on p. 476 of the same volume, and the Pratihara inscriptions on p. 472 of the same volume. The basic source on Kashmir is Kalhana, *Rajatarangini*, transl. M. Stein (London, 1900). The biography of king Yashovarman of Kanauj, *Guadavadha*, written by Vakpati, has been edited by S. P. Pandit (Bombay, 1887). Other literary sources on the period include Somadeva's *Kathasaritasagara*, transl. C. H. Tawney (Calcutta, 1880–87), Somadeva Suri, *Nitivyakamritam*, ed. R. Soni (Bombay, 1929), Medhatithi, *Manubhashya*, transl. G. Jha (Calcutta, 1922–29), Bilhana, *Vikramankadevacharita*, ed. G. Buehler (Bombay, 1875), Rajashekhara, *Karpuramanjari*, transl. C. R. Lanman (Cambridge, Mass., 1901), Merutunga, *Prabandhachintamani*, transl. C. H. Tawney (Calcutta, 1901), and Chandbardai, *Prithvirajaraso*, ed. S. S. Das (Banaras, 1904). J. Tod, *Annals and Antiquities of Rajasthan*, has occasional references to early traditions of Rajput history

(London, 1960). A. Cunningham has edited a volume on *The Coins of Medieval India* (London, 1894).

It is during this period that works begin to be written in Arabic and Persian on India or else references to India can be collected in the writings of scholars in both these languages. The most outstanding of such sources is Alberuni's *Tahqiq-i-hind*, which is available in an English translation by E. C. Sachau, *Alberuni's India* (London, 1914). Other sources referring to the Arab conquest of Sind and the invasions from the north-west have been collected by H. M. Eliot and J. Dowson in *The History of India as Told by its Own Historians*, Vol. I. This volume also contains incidental references to India from a variety of Arabic and Persian writings. Among monograph studies on Mahmud of Ghazni may be mentioned that of M. Habib, *Sultan Mahmud of Ghazni* (Bombay, 1927), and M. Nazim, *Life and Times of Sultan Mahmud of Ghazni*. G. F. Hourani, *Arab Seafaring in the Indian Ocean in Ancient and early Medieval Times* (Princeton University Press, 1951), places Arab maritime activities in India in the context of the broader picture of the Arab world at the time.

Secondary works on this period include *History and culture of the Indian People*, Vols. IV and V – *The Age of Imperial Kanauj* and *The Struggle for Empire* (Bombay, 1954, 1955). Monographs of a more detailed nature are R. S. Tripathi, *History of Kanauj* (Banaras, 1937), H. C. Ray, *Dynastic History of Northern India* (Calcutta, 1931), R. C. Majumdar, *History of Bengal* (Dacca, 1943), E. Pires, *The Maukharis* (Madras, 1934), C. V. Vaidya, *History of Medieval Hindu India* (Poona, 1921–26), R. D. Banerji, *History of Orissa* (Calcutta, 1931), A. C. Banerji, *Rajput Studies* (Calcutta, 1944), D. Sharma, *Early Chauhan Dynasties* (Delhi, 1959), D. C. Ganguli, *History of the Paramara Dynasty* (Dacca, 1943), A. K. Majumdar, *The Chalukyas of Gujerat* (Bombay, 1956), S. K. Mitra, *The Early Rulers of Khajuraho* (Calcutta, 1958), and B. P. Mazumdar, *Socio-Economic History of Northern India* (Calcutta, 1960). R. S. Sharma has suggested a new interpretation of the land system at this period which he discusses in *Indian Feudalism c. 300–1200 A.D.* (Calcutta, 1965). Another recent work is that of L. Gopal, *The Economic Life of Northern India* (Varanasi, 1965).

CHAPTERS 12 AND 13

Important sources of this period have been selected, translated, and edited by H. M. Eliot and J. Dowson in *The History of India as Told by its Own Historians*, Vols. II, III, and IV (Cambridge, 1931). These contain selections from the major chroniclers of the time and some later writers on this period. (The complete works of these authors have been separately edited.) References to India in the works of certain Arab geographers have also been included in these volumes. M. Hussain has translated relevant sections of the *Rehla* of Ibn Batutah (GOS, cxxii, 1953). The *Futuhat-i-Firuz Shahi* on the reign of Firuz Shah is available in *Islamic Culture*, Vol. XV. Ferishta's history has been translated by J. Briggs (Calcutta, 1908), and that of Minhaj-u-Siraj, *Tabaqat-i-Nasiri*, by H. G. Raverty (1881). O. Spies, *An Arab Account of India in the Fourteenth Century* (Stuttgart, 1936), is a translation of a work by al Qalqashandi. An anonymous work on geography completed in A.D. 982, the *Hudud-ul-Alam*, has been translated by V. Minorsky (London, 1937). A. S. Beveridge has translated the memoirs of the Mughul emperor Babur, the *Babar-nama* (London, 1922). The traditions recorded by J. Tod in *Annals and Antiquities of Rajasthan* (London, 1960) are of interest in the emergence of the Rajput states at this time. Merutunga, *Prabandhachintamani*, transl. C. H. Tawney (Calcutta, 1901), and Rajashekhara, *Prabandhakosha*, ed. J. Muni (Shantiniketan, 1935), are additional literary sources relevant to this period. More detailed information on scattered literary sources pertaining to north Indian kingdoms contemporary with the Sultanate is available in *History and Culture of the Indian People*, Vol. VI, *The Delhi Sultanate*, pp. 763–76. C. J. Rodgers, *Catalogue of Coins in the Indian Museum*, Part I (Calcutta, 1894), and S. Lane-Poole, *The Coins of the Sultans of Delhi* (London, 1884), refer to the numismatic material of the time, and H. N. Wright, *The Sultans of Delhi, their Coinage and Metrology* (Delhi, 1936), is an interesting supplementary study.

Translations of Chinese material referring to India have been published in *Toung Pao*, XVI, 1915, transl. W. W. Rockhill; and in *Vishvabharati Annals*, I, 117–27, transl. P. C. Bagchi;

and in J. Duyvendak, *Ma-Huan Re-examined* (Amsterdam, 1933).

A translation of Sufi writing has been edited by J. Arberry, *Doctrine of the Sufis* (Cambridge, 1935). Kabir's verses are pre-served in three anthologies entitled *Bijaka, Banis,* and *Sakhi.* Some of these have been translated by R. Tagore, *One Hundred Poems of Kabir* (London, 1914). Nanak's teaching was collected by Guru Arjun in the *Adigranth.*

For the architecture of the period P. Brown, *Indian Architec-ture – Islamic,* is the standard work. There is a good summary by J. H. Marshall in the form of a chapter in the *Cambridge History of India,* Vol. III, entitled 'Monuments of Muslim India'.

Secondary works on this period consist of A. B. M. Habibullah, *Foundation of Muslim Rule in India* (Lahore, 1945), A. S. Tripathi, *Some Aspects of Muslim Rule in India* (Allahabad, 1956), K. S. Lal, *History of the Khaljis* (Allahabad, 1950), and, by the same author, *The Twilight of the Sultanate* (1963), M. Hussain, *Life and Times of Muhammad bin Tughluq* (London, 1938), T. Moreland, *Agrarian System of Muslim India* (Cam-bridge, 1929), I. H. Qureshi, *The Administration of the Sultan-ate of Delhi* (Lahore, 1945), K. M. Ashraf, *Life and Condition of the People of Hindustan* (Delhi), M. Hasan, *Kashmir under the Sultanate* (Calcutta, 1959), K. A. Nizami, *Some Aspects of Religion and Politics in India during the Thirteenth Century* (Aligarh, 1961), M. Habib, *Hazrat Amir Khusrau of Delhi* (Bombay, 1927), Tarachand, *Influence of Islam on Indian Cul-ture* (1954), Y. Hussain, *Glimpses of Medieval Indian Culture* (Bombay, 1957), K. M. Sen, *Medieval Mysticism in India* (Lon-don, 1936), J. E. Charpentier, *Theism in Medieval India* (1919), G. H. Westcott, *Kabir and the Kabirpanth* (Calcutta, 1953), M. A. Macauliffe, *The Sikh Religion* (Oxford, 1909), and Kushwant Singh, *A History of the Sikhs,* Vol. I (Princeton, 1963).

CHAPTER 14

The major sources for the history of the Bahmani and Vijay-anagar kingdoms are inscriptions and the accounts of foreign travellers. Inscriptions relevant to Vijayanagar history are to be found in *Epigraphia Carnatica,* Vols. III–XII, and in *South Indian Inscriptions,* Vols. IV–VI, XII part ii. R. Sewell in *A Forgotten Empire* (London, 1900) has included the writings of Domingo Paez and Fernão Nuniz on Vijayanagara and extracts from the account of Nicolo Conti. H. Yule and H. Cordier include various accounts in *Cathay and the Way Thither* (London, 1915–16). R. H. Major, *India in the Fifteenth Century*, has translated the impression of the Russian visitor Athanasius Nikitin. M. L. Dames has translated Duarte Barbosa's account in *The Book of Duarte Barbosa* (London, 1918, 1921). Marco Polo, *The Travels*, transl. R. E. Latham (Penguin Books, 1958), completes the list. S. Krishnaswami Aiyyangar, *Sources of Vijayanagara History* (Madras, 1946), is a useful survey of sources on this period. Unfortunately, a good translation of Krishna Deva Raya's *Amuktamalyada* does not exist. T. V. Mahalingam draws extensively on these sources in his studies, *Administrative and Social Life under Vijayanagara*, and *Economic Life in the Vijayanagara Empire* (Madras, 1951). B. A. Saletore, *Social and Political Life in the Vijayanagara Empire* (Madras, 1934), may also be referred to. Studies of the maritime areas have been made by K. V. Krishna Ayyar, *The Zamorins of Calicut* (Calcutta, 1938), and K. M. Pannikar, *Malabar and the Portuguese* (Bombay, 1929).

References are made to events concerning Bahmani history in the writings of Ferishta, Nizam-ud-din, and Rafi-ud-din Shirazi. The account of the ambassador Abdur Razzaq is available in H. M. Eliot and J. Dowson, *History of India as Told by its Own Historians*, Vol. IV. Incidental references also occur in the accounts of European travellers mentioned above. H. K. Sherwani has published studies on the Bahmani kingdom among which are *The Great Bahmani Wazir Mahmud Gavan* (Bombay, 1942) and *The Bahmani Kingdom* (Bombay, 1947). S. K. Aiyangar relates the invasion of the south to politics of the Sultanate in *South India and her Muhammadan Invaders* (Madras, 1921).

JOURNALS

Annals of the Bhandarkar Oriental Research Institute
Acta Orientalia
Ancient India
Indian Archaeology, a Review
Bulletin of the School of Oriental and African Studies
Ceylon Historical Quarterly
East and West
Indian Antiquary
Indian Culture
Indian Economic and Social History Review
Indian Historical Quarterly
Islamic Culture
Journal Asiatique
Journal of the Asiatic Society of Bengal
Journal of Asian Studies
Journal of the American Oriental Society
Journal of the Economic and Social History of the Orient
Journal of the Numismatic Society of India
Journal of the Royal Asiatic Society
Journal of the Bombay Branch of the Royal Asiatic Society
Journal of the Bihar Research Society
Man in India

INDEX

Index

374

Index

Index

Index

Index

MORE ABOUT PENGUINS, PELICANS,
PEREGRINES AND PUFFINS

For further information about books available from Penguins please write to Dept EP, Penguin Books Ltd, Harmondsworth, Middlesex UB7 0DA.

In the U.S.A.: For a complete list of books available from Penguins in the United States write to Dept DG, Penguin Books, 299 Murray Hill Parkway, East Rutherford, New Jersey 07073.

In Canada: For a complete list of books available from Penguins in Canada write to Penguin Books Canada Ltd, 2801 John Street, Markham, Ontario L3R 1B4.

In Australia: For a complete list of books available from Penguins in Australia write to the Marketing Department, Penguin Books Australia Ltd, P.O. Box 257, Ringwood, Victoria 3134.

In New Zealand: For a complete list of books available from Penguins in New Zealand write to the Marketing Department, Penguin Books (N.Z.) Ltd, Private Bag, Takapuna, Auckland 9.

In India: For a complete list of books available from Penguins in India write to Penguin Overseas Ltd, 706 Eros Apartments, 56 Nehru Place, New Delhi 110019.

A HISTORY OF INDIA

VOLUME TWO

Percival Spear

From the coming of the Mughals to the Post-Nehru era.

It is the aim of this book to relate the history of the Indian people as a whole, and to make plain the unity of texture in the development of Indian society in the period covered by this concise and very readable Pelican.

Dr Spear, a specialist in Indian history, makes the unusual and illuminating approach of dealing with the Mughal and British periods together in one volume, on the principle of continuity. He views the Mughal rule as a preparation and precondition for the modern age ushered in by the British and British Raj as a harbinger to India of western civilization, which precipitated the transformation of India that is still in progress.